Greatness Is In The Heart:
A Tribute to Inspiration That Empowers;

Is Tribute to Inspiration – shares
Love that empowers;
Is a compilation of Short Inspirational stories
that shaped our faith with words of love and
comforts for hope, touching hearts & Tips for
Using Unconditional Love and also Acceptance
to Shape Today's Youth-is in 18 steps!
It Emphasizes, positive encouragement for all
and, is of a Brighter future for them; A series of
five books in one Volume, is a classic reading.
A true story of One Woman's miraculous
survival –My account's, a powerful testimony-
"Great is our God, and greatly to be praised!!"

Caroline Arit

Other Books by the Author

Ema, A. *Cross River State At a Glance.* Calabar: Government Printing Press, 1987.

Thompson, C. *A Daughter's Love: Remembering my Father, My teacher, and Friend(s).* Lincoln: I-universe, 2005.

Thompson, C. *The Joy of the Overcomers: Slavery from an African Perspective.* Pittsburgh: Dorrance Publishing Co., Inc., 2000.

Thompson, C. *Parental Influence Matters: The Positive Legacy of Good Parenting and the joy of Training Up a Child with Priceless Love.* Lincoln: I-universe, 2007.

Thompson, C. Priceless Love: A Matter of the heart and a gift for a lifetime. Lincoln: I-universe, 2010.

Greatness is in the Heart

A Tribute to Inspiration That Empowers!

Carol Arit Thompson

GREATNESS IS IN THE HEART
A TRIBUTE TO INSPIRATION THAT EMPOWERS!

All Scriptures from King James versions of The Holy Bible or otherwise stated; Scriptures quoted from The Holy Bible, New Century version, copyright © 1987, 1988, 1991 by Word Publishing, Dallas, Texas 75093 Used by permission.

iUniverse books may be ordered through booksellers or by contacting:

iUniverse
1663 Liberty Drive
Bloomington, IN 47403
www.iuniverse.com
1-800-Authors (1-800-288-4677)

ISBN: 978-1-4917-6772-6 (sc)
ISBN: 978-1-4917-6773-3 (hc)
ISBN: 978-1-4917-6774-0 (e)

Library of Congress Control Number: 2015907538

Print information available on the last page.

iUniverse rev. date: 11/17/2015

In Greatness Is In The Heart, Caroline Okon Thompson, author of four previous books on inspirational strength, makes a case for successful living through Wisdom, variously defined as "common sense, good judgment, or "the ability to live life skillfully."

To escape poverty, Thompson emigrated from her native home in Africa to the USA for a better life, but even in God's own country, the author and single mother of two children faced daunting challenges that tried her spiritual faith: tough financial reality and failing health. A woman of many limitations, she overcame those limitations to provide inspiration to her readers through her previous publications.

In this personal account, Thompson, weaves together the success stories of prominent figures and examples drawn from her own individual experience and spiritual journey. She posits that there was no other way she could have handled the trials she faced in her new homeland without Wisdom, some inspiration, and love, as well as an abiding trust in God.

Greatness Is In The Heart is arranged in 17 chapters, touching on many areas of human relationships. In this revealing book, those who are seeking to improve their relationship with God, their family, and fellow man will benefit from what Thompson has learned and shared about a godly life, about inspiration, about the love of family and fellow man, and the perspectives for sustaining one's faith when patience fades and hope appears elusive. Please, see also biography for curriculum vitae and /or track records for her other jobs.

E. Samuel Essien
Queens, New York

Dedication

To my glorious Father in Heaven and Lord Savior, I return all glory, and honor for; Your love and mercies toward me and giving me a second chance in life and being an —ever constant Friend and presence in my life-greatness, faithfulness, holiness, unfailing Love and Comforter. This is for Healing & Comforting Touch as my Healer whose, "infinite wisdom" predestines all!! I love You more and ever and more is eternally adoring You and for who You're is Life within!!

To the cherished memory of my affectionate parents and grandparents: You are missed but not forgotten: I remember that you were always there for me (through thick/thin), and doing the best you could do for me. **Even before my eyes were opened to see the world, you were there along with the rest of our family, sacrificing, caring, loving me with great joy in your hearts and** with love forever and thank you for you kept the faith and we have come a long way. **This is for your love from your inspirational words of wisdom; you gave me blessings of a happy childhood that have carried on to my life as an adult. You'll always be loved by me!**

To: the inspiring men, women, and children whose words of wisdom have given all of us a quality education and inspired me to launch this work of mine.

To my daughters: whose inspirations and love carried me on, and taught more beautiful lessons, powerful tips on using unconditional love and acceptance to shape today's youth. You've blessed mom, lots of love, loads of encouragements, end-less supports to cope in this journey we called life and: Comfort, you were a teen at the time, and loved to inspire me by saying, "Mom, I love to see you write and publish your stories. I know you are blessed, and have gone through a lot, like others! Mom, I see other kids and hear their stories and books by their moms as well!" I recall Pat and teaming together, with all the love, ideal ideas: "Mom writes! True Mom, you can! And, my part is easy too, when you write, I'll copy notes for you, simple!" Blessed your hearts!!

You have suffered with me and struggles always you have my unconditional love. Thank God having you in my life and your love daily fosters to inspire boosting my heart is Inspiration. I don't know what life could be without blessings; couldn't do this alone and, I love you with all my heart. Mom forever loves you, proud of you, your love and inspiration both becomes passion for all kids/youth. Forever love for: great inspiration. May God continue to bless you both use for His glory and honor, inspiring and blessing is my prayer and to keep you blessed for your loving support, and inspiring me in my journey with love that offered hope to forge ahead is sweet love!

To my nephews and nieces, whose inspiration echoes: "Aunty, we love you, praying for you and the family and for success, including your books!" Bless you and, I love you dearly too!

To President Bill Jefferson Clinton: Sir, I want to express my appreciation to God for you and your family. I am grateful for your kindness and love for humanity. And as I often think about the ordeal of my immigration, I realize that without your blessings, kindness and love and compassion, I would've been deported! **Your** thoughtfulness will always be remembered is a part of inspiration for this work, thanking God for my blessed former President of United States 1996 that He used as my angel! Inspiration is a legacy, and I find myself blessed as an inspired African woman from Nigeria of Akwa Ibom State, and dearly adopted country-United States of America, for inspiring me and glorying God through inspirational work for the improvement of humanity. My heart is proud of being a Nigerian African-American. Forever, I truly appreciate everything God has done in fulfilling Hs promises, all of this, and all honors forever go to His honor-glory!

To: President Barack and First Lady Michelle Obama and Family: Thank you for your love, to acknowledging my work in print, "Priceless Love" (2010, I-Universe). It was an honor, and I appreciate you and your great hearts of love. Mr. President, I thank God for you and your inspiration, your performance, and your great heart as a leader. As the first African-American President of the United States, your distinction as a world leader has made a great difference!

To: My Presidents of beloved countries of birth place (Nigeria) and adopted (United State of America) past, current, future, known

and unknown, and governors and people! I pray God to keep, bless and teach us how to love everyone same and serve faithfully with a heart of love and grace, to honor/glorify Him by each being responsible, accountable, great ambassador, all is patriotic citizens and leaders! May God's wisdom be ours every day of our lives, guiding and giving hope with our hearts filled with love for Him, and each other! Grateful and, inspire and hopefully you will join with me as well to celebrate this tribute to inspiration!

God bless us all! I'm hopeful your hearts will become also inspired to greatness as mine is as His loving, as we are all blessed to be the united people of the world as His children for the love given to us is awesome! Please, help me to promote this work; and donate for a good cause. It is for a portion of the proceeds will benefit charities! Inspire the youths, women, significantly impaired, less privileged, and more publishing, and lots of love-Caroline Arit Okon Thompson.

(Former NYSC Information Officer-Arit Ema, Calabar and Port Harcourt, Nigeria, West -Africa)!

Contents

Acknowledgments

Dear Lord, Heavenly Almighty Father: Thank you for sparing my life, inspiration, peace of mind, guidance, strength, wisdom, discipline, marvelous blessings you gave and for successful completion of this work. Every breath is for you and your glory, eternally. To all those who were my supporters and gave their time and talent beyond call of duty for my efforts- photographers or graphic artists, community of faith, prayer warriors, fans who love reading and promoters—you are all my appreciated friends. I give special thanks to: Ntiense, (my namesake-Witness), Idara/ Caroline- Sunday Thompson (Inspector), & our -entire family/Aunt Arit Sunday Udosen/family.

The Edebors (opportunity to write for the Christian Herald as a columnist) & I-universe staff- P. Hawkins, T. Mendoza, Jane Solas, Ken Barnes & production. Dianne Lee, you've blessed my life with this work beyond. Dr. & Mrs. Emeaba Emeaba; Mary E. Abia; CAC of Miami (First in Fl.) Hortense G.; Mr. &Mrs. G. Owor, Dr. Joseph Akpan, Pastor (Dr.) & Mrs. O. Essien; Jonathan Essien, Offiong Sims; Comfort Effiong; Offiong Edem; Tony Umana &family; Glory Anetor&family; Chief Usua Amanam, Dr. Val. Attah; Rose James; The Inspire Women Institute (Houston), scholarship/grant –training in ministry and I so very much appreciate your love. Thank you staff of Anon Hewitt/TIPP. Ms. Nadia, I have not met you in person with your love, I thank God your prayer and supporting me such love and concern for my health always you are in my prayers all!

My profound thanks to who gave not only time and talent but their love beyond the call of friendship and/or paycheck: Essien Samuel Essien thanks being there as among sponsors, you review as my consultant, awesome); Dr. Maurice Ekwo, reader great job; Mr. &Mrs. Benjamin Burum &Family. Ben, you are more of a good brother than a good neighbor, million thanks for typing this manuscript; Mr. Ekerete Udoh, you did an incredible job, so grateful your thoughtful commitment on such a short notice and Mr. Israel Chinyo Uhuegbu-your beautiful poem captures my heart beyond words is keepsake so inspiration; J.L. Davies thanks for the wonderful editing. I appreciate your talent and skills! Thank you Media, donors and buyers, whole sellers and retailers.

I wish to thank God again for my lovely dear, paternal and maternal grandparents and to our entire family (Okon Thompson Udoumanah /Emmanuel Udom (Ediene Obio Imo/Obotim Nsit); and all their extensions (for those living and to the memory of those that are dead). **To you my dear family...EkpeneIkpan Nsit, Etinan-Akpa Oboyo, Ediene Abak/Ikot Ansa Community.** You all have a spot in my heart. I pray God bless you and all of your works and show favor to you as well as yours and thanks is for the love that **you showed me appreciated with my love, respect, and admiration. A** very special thank you and same to all of us and to my dear sisters, Comfort & MaOffiong, I love you for you both were there for me as life's journey takes me through many places you dearly helped me out. And thanks, for being there for my children their best nannies in the world. You have shown me by heart of your true genuine sisterly love, and my brothers also you blessed me so dearly. I say everyday also May our dear God too forever reward you and yours. This for your love, and encouragement, sacrifice for me and my children everyday is my joy praying for us all blessings.

You're ever cherished my dear aunts, (Arit/Ikwo/usua my great nannies), were your love and blessings offered, I am proud of you and yours, and your thoughtful love shown will always be remembered! You've my love and heart with thoughtful prayers. Mostly, appreciated of how much suffering you endured, true love you gave me with kindness and of inspiration. Thanks, for caring to help me out with your sister, my sweet dear beloved mother in her golden age. Lots of love and I thank you all but w**ord expresses honors most our God who loves us most,** of joy! Sincerity of your prayers and love, kindness and for all your inspiration, for me also all inspired me and, I am very grateful and much indebted for your supporting me daily God knows it all too!

May God bless you with His richest blessings, be upon you for all that you have done and shown for me and blessings and love, keep you and answers to your needs and yours everyday of your life. For, all you did for my children, showing concerns from your hearts and never –ending support. You are indeed my dear supportive family, sons-in-laws, siblings, uncles, aunts, nieces, nephews, and cousins, you are my angels that God brought to my life and, I sincerely appreciate. Thanking God is every blessed day for being a part of you and for your love, sweet support, all is of prayers and never ending love, it will always be cherished; I love you forever as my dear ones.

Grateful for my supportive family's inspiration and gratitude is everyday for my joy is full. Heart forever with praises and thankfulness to the Lord is all and of my deepest love too gratitude is with lots of love to God's glory and honor! Thank you everyone, includes whose time, support, talent, friendship is beyond the call of duty inspires me is by reading this in manuscripts, typing, help to sponsor and those who couldn't but encouraged with words of love. Everyone includes fellow Akwa Ibom family, Nigerians, Americans, others. (Young and old) black/white and wherever you come from, are my worldwide-friends, part of my blessings and extended family as brothers and sisters and neighbors. Am Glorifying God is all what my special thank you is phenomenal blessings; joy in whatever we do we are all of His. Love inspires to empower and that is where my happiness comes from and wants my life to be an honor to Him. He has done, still does is so much for me. I thank Him for blessing all of us is everyday His love satisfies me is my time to celebrate Him and show how much His love is. Inspires my heart overwhelms with joy of excitement of His words spoken through to my heart is to love us, regardless of whom we are and where we come from. Borderless love is of God for all so this includes everyone. I thank God for the new President Muhammadu Buhari of Nigeria. Also, Governor of Akwa Ibom; Happy for the new regime as was for old regime of former President of Nigeria and as first from the minority States, G.J; Past, present and future governors of Cross River & Akwa Ibom States.

Love & thanks my love is, to the glory and honor of our loving God–Caroline Thompson!

Foreword from the Editor

I must say that my meeting the author, Caroline Arit Thompson, was purely by chance. A friend of mine was originally commissioned to edit this book, but an unfortunate family occurrence kept her from being able to complete the task at hand. She called me and asked if I could take over the editing for her, and I must admit I was initially hesitant. My consulting business had been keeping me busy, and I was traveling quite a bit. After some thought, I knew that I couldn't turn my back on my friend in her time of need, so I agreed to take over as editor of "Greatness is in the Heart – A Tribute to Inspiration That Empowers!" As I started editing, I became moved by the love and compassion that Ms. Thompson expressed in every single chapter of this book. Her relentless quest to share with everyone the love and the blessings that have been bestowed upon her is amazing. I found myself becoming inspired by her optimistic outlook on life and her love for all mankind.

I am honored to have had the opportunity to work with Ms. Thompson in bringing her dreams to inspire others to reality. She is a woman of honor and grace who I am proud to call my friend. Though our meeting was not planned, I cannot help but to realize that is was in God's plan to place such a wonderful woman in my path. I am confident that everyone will become as inspired as I have by reading this book.

J. L. Davis
EDITOR
Canal Winchester, Ohio

Foreword

I have known Caroline Arit Thompson for close to a decade, and I am always struck by her sunny disposition and the unbridled optimism she projects. Even when the horizon appears murky and somewhat gloomy, she will convince all around her that there is a bright light at the tunnel – illuminating and directing, shaping the contours and leading the believers onto the boulevard of hope and success. The key ingredient she always emphasizes is faith and a heavy dose of hope.

A writer of boundless energy and creative depth, Ms. Thompson's current offering **Greatness is in the Heart: A Tribute to Inspiration That Empowers"** follows her already established pattern – a classic appeal to the innermost layers of our altruistic depths.

In a world where accent is expected to be placed on rugged individualism, according to a certain form of political/social narrative; where the communal ethos are being derided and laughed at, where looking out for the little man is considered a wrong tack to follow, where the poor and the harried are supposed to be left to their devices and a kindred spirit is supposed to be subsumed by the all-embracing forces of 'freedom', Caroline's book tells us, we can be both: ruggedly individualistic yet community minded.

The book enjoins us to be thankful for everyday blessings, to be enveloped by the unblemished and ever-glowing color of love, to be optimistic, desirous, without being conspicuous, to give the best in us to others, to inspire without being judgmental and condemning, to motivate without being condescending.

Drawing from the fountain of her own experiences – both personal and professional, Caroline Thompson has given us a book that I believe will advance the best instincts of common good that is embedded in all of us.

Indeed, "Greatness IS IN THE HEART". Parents and their children will benefit from this captivating account of love beyond words, and I strongly recommend it to every reader. Hopefully, you will find the book as riveting and inspiring as I did.

EKERETE UDOH
PUBLICIST/EDITOR-IN-CHIEF
THE DIASPORAN-STAR NEWSPAPER
Queens, New York
(2015): Senior Special Assistant (Media) and Chief Press Secretary to the Executive Governor, Udom Emmanuel (Akwa Ibom State of Nigeria).

It is a great pleasure to provide foreward for, "Greatness is in the Heart: A Tribute to Inspiration That Empowers!" It has come at a time when the world needs some form of inspiration (such as in words, books, people, events, etc.). The author herself has related how she has been inspired spiritually by the words of wisdom from Scripture, her parents, grandparents, teachers, friends-at work, and most recently, by the President of the United States of America, Mr. Barack Obama.

Love, wisdom, and faith are necessary requirements for anyone to be inspired. In the book, love is referred to as "The Heart's Power." Love plays a significant part in our lives by helping to build our hearts with strong bonds in friendship.

With God's love, blessings will come to us and fill our hearts with joy. Wisdom is to the soul like health is to the body, and it is no wonder that the wisest man on earth (King Solomon) asked God for wisdom that inspires inspiration. Inspiration encourages the heart to think wisely, and faith, as we know, can move mountains. Remember, great strength comes from faith in the Lord.

Knowledge is power, and when you are inspired, you are full of knowledge. When we are knowledgeable about God, we are inspired, loved, happy, and there is joy within us. Surely, happiness transcends into our character, which determines our passion and who we are. It is in this book that wisdom, gratitude, peace, joy, faith, love, patience, trust, obedience and honesty are all tied together to show the path to be inspired. The scriptural references, and others inspirational words of wisdom, life experiences of the author, and others, is including the (2010-2015) First Lady of Nigeria's testimony make it a book worth reading when looking for an inspirational springboard. Happy reading!

MAURICE E. EKWO, PH.D

Preface

INSPIRATION IS A LEGACY

"Greatness is In the Heart: A Tribute to Inspiration That Empowers is a book that transforms the Human Experience, not only an inspirational story that shaped our faith, but also empowers. A story about God's Miracles, Love and Goodness that has transformed my life with inspiration, and Overall, it is a story that shares the wisdom of a transforming human spirit and addresses a variety of topics of interest to all ages. Wisdom, as love and as always professed, is a glorious and essential gift; it's a valuable heavenly gift and that offers hope and encouragement to all who treasure and beneficial of powerful inspiration, especially to the broken-hearted. Thus, it should be highly appreciated and mostly-valued; should be nurtured for it adds sweetness to one's soul.

As our healing begins from there in the unequivocally, Proverbs states: "Know also that wisdom is sweet to your soul; if you find it, there is a future hope for you, and your hope will not be cut off" (24:14). Awesomely, is well said! Oh yes, if you ever want something to inspire you and heart encouraged with emotion fuels of passion for hope, happiness and greatness, wisdom matters big time! It is a heavenly and rare gift of life from above. Sure, there's hope right there for man to eagerly seek after the path of wisdom. How? Friends, you need to grow up with the goal to be wise and mature, inspiration.

It blesses to bless work(s) for you! As, it is written in the book of proverbs: "He who gets wisdom loves his own soul; he who cherishes understanding prospers" (19:8). Apparently, that says nothing more than there is dream for us and prospects with a future, if we give our hearts with love to God! My dear friends, young and old, inspiration makes life bearable as much as love does! I strongly believe that if there were no significant value and benefit from words of wisdom, the psalmist couldn't have shared his experience with us for motivation/encouragement.

But out of the abundance of joy in his heart, he encourages us by sharing this marvelous thought of his inspiration: "Your commands make me wiser than my enemies, for they are ever with me (119:98). How about Job, a man who patiently endured hardship in his turbulent years? Definitely, he successfully applied a heart of wisdom and came out with this testimony: To God belong wisdom and power; counsel and understanding are his" (12:13). And, to that I say, amen!

Yes, he waited patiently as encouraged humbly in wisdom. Remember, Job had his own wilderness journey, or moments of trials and tribulations, but by faith overcame, seeking wisdom from above. He did not faint but kept on kneeling and praying, believing, thankful and more hopeful, and leaning solely on the ultimate source of Inspiration – The author of wisdom: God Almighty of heaven, and earth, the Creator! Over the years based on personal experience, I have come to discover that many of us don't realize the value in words of wisdom, is for joy and for us to experience God's love/ peace and that is the secret of happiness and success is by simply of being obedience to the spiritual words of wisdom and that is so sad that they can't draw strength. From the power that is relevant and inspiration from Him is what inspires us passion to stimulate our thoughts and encourages think wisely out from that thought is highly motivated and changes.

Inspiration encourages our hearts and one word of wisdom can change one's life for best. Remember, Scripture(s) teaches us that "the fear of the Lord is the beginning of wisdom: and the knowledge of the holy is understanding. For by me thy days shall be multiplied, and the years of thy life shall be increased" (Proverbs 9:10-11). Most, pleasantly, and is awesome marvelous and heart warming is that wisdom is of God. James took the time to explain in-depth, and let us know that: "The wisdom that comes from heaven is first of all pure; then peace- loving, considerate, submissive, full of mercy and good fruit, impartial and sincere" (3:17). Those attributes are all true love and characteristics of what God requires of us to use with-practical wisdom for our successful living. I am sure many will be curious to know, what inspiration is and may love to know after reading this inspiring work why it is a legacy with a tribute to cherish and is passion.

I believe many will want to know what Inspiration is and after reading, "Greatness is in the Heart- A Tribute to Inspiration, you perhaps, may be also asking what is so unique about it that it compelled me to write a whole book about it? I am delighted you would want to know and so, let's start out by defining inspiration for clarity. What is Inspiration? Well, since inspiration is my legacy and passion and matters so much and encourages our hearts to think wisely, is best for us to begin with the Living words of the Words of God. And, the richness of His amazing grace, the richness as His power of inspiration gives me direction and inspires of my heart passion and with encouragement and love that is empowering and it is amazing how you are blessed to hope.

God's love inspires passion and encourages and gives direction and one word of His can change one's life forever and divinely, is everyone and we all need a little inspiration everyday. **And Second Timothy 3:16-17 has says, "All scripture is given by inspiration of God, and is profitable for doctrines, for reproof, for correction, for instruction, in righteousness; that the man of God may be perfect, thoroughly furnished onto good works" Wisdom, of God is of encouragement is legacy of inspiration "furnished unto good works". Power within us is greater than entire world; Inspiration, regardless situation's where there's hope is Joy as is faith in God is the power. Inspirer's victory power, within offers love, joy and peace to us!**

Inspiration inspires as it empowers: *Second College Edition -The American Heritage Dictionary has this to say as well too on* **Inspiration:** *"Stimulation of the mind or emotion to a high level of feeling or activity. It says: 1. the condition of being so stimulated. 2. an agency, as a person or a work of art, that moves the intellect or emotion or that prompts action or invention. (3): "Something that is inspired; a sudden creative act or idea (4). The quality of inspiring or exalting; a painting full of inspiration! (5). Theo. Divine guidance or influence exerted directly upon the mind and soul of man. (6). The act of breathing in; inhalation".*

Pretty much numbers four and five are what mostly what shares this thoughts and just reflections of loving things you do with passion and love and joy as well to enjoy and that is what makes this work fun writing and, as I stated from the dedication to acknowledgement and entire reading, is gift and a legacy with passion that motivates me to do, is by inspiration. Stimulating me and what I never thought was possible and, you and I, and God He is doing in and through our lives daily to enjoy mightier things within us to inspire our hearts. Through those wonderful words of love all are His spiritual words of wisdom and it is can meet us at our points of needs and supplies us with what makes for hope and inspiring to boost hearts, motivating and inspiring is also stimulating and are capable of shaping our faith and that is the power of love His works. In words and actions is what makes inspiration a legacy to cherish and what gives hope is of joy, every little bit of effort counts and that is power of inspiration to me is of God's love also are divine blessings that stimulation awesome words when read and use them accordingly works too.

Appropriately is a legacy to cherish and that wisdom depends on how and when we make good use of them then we know that is powerful, and beyond human imagination as it is not just the word that we know shows wisdom. But its application and acknowledging my Creator is who makes me to know how that as it works and when. I give my special thanks and when we apply that makes it is application has it all that is what inspires most and here again how-in **Webster's Thesaurus Dictionary: "Inspiration (syn.): Creativity, aptitude, genius, originality, ability, faculty, sagacity, talent, proficient, master, gift, adept, intellectual, etc. We all can take any one or more of these words and define inspiration in a way that best fits our own hearts. As, is it is inspiration is joy to me legacy and a gift, and it can be that for you as well, if, you long to have a purposeful and meaningful life of Love great blessings and, am inspired as empowers.**

They are all viable ammunitions for our security and what we need to overcome all of our situations, and become more prosperous as well in life great love and achievers. I believe it is good delighting oneself in wisdom, those practical words are comfort and love are joyous for us and gives direction, hope and empowers us with the spirit to enjoy freedom and communication of love is of inspiration. Benjamin Franklin beautifully encapsulates this thought "The door of wisdom is never shut." The book of proverbs has over the years been helpful, tremendously and in teaching us, it also trains and educate us to delight our souls such an endeavor, investing with words of wisdom matters lucratively and, sincerely speaking, this to say: "A fool finds pleasure in evil conduct, but a man of understanding delights in wisdom" (Proverbs10:23). God's Word!

That is the ultimate truth and sure! It is absolute inspiration is from wisdom of God and for gaining knowledge and wisdom as it inspires and it is also pleasurable to have! Equally, the Psalmist concluded that: The mouth of the righteous man utter wisdom and his tongue speaks the truth (Psalms 37:30). Inspiration's legacy and of passion to me for it works and, there's no iota of doubt that, a presentation of this magnitude encourages one's heart of powerful commitment with diligence to seek that from the ultimate Source! It is important acknowledging the essence of wisdom for insights and gaining a knowledgeable understanding of what matters most in life and in an effort to build us up not just our character and moral values, but all is to give us a better future and hope as wisdom is of God. And who encourages and shapes our faith, inspirational all words of Wisdom have values that are more. More than gold, is lasting, rewarding and worthy as great investments. Friends, humanly on our own wisdom, we can't make through life of success.

Yes, not of our power successfully for, none is really wise! I like the way James-a prolific writer of immortal Book of books (the Holy Bible) puts his bold question across wisely to us as mankind and then, follows-up with a good suggestion: "Who is wise and understanding among you? Let him show it by his good life, by deed done in the humility that comes from wisdom!" (NIV3:13), please refer, for there is power of love, words of wisdom empowers power of God's inspiration's legacy to cherish and that is truth that never ever fails and endures through eternity!

Friends, as reflected on the topic of this discussion, are to think through the prospects of wisdom, and power of love and inspiration that comes from above and us as well moreover, see where the piece of the puzzle misses and/or fits in squarely. **Dear friend, enjoy and stay bless till the next edition,** and is in this series also. Of five books which will be even more empowering as is in this preface all and are life-changing than this more editions as well. Is in the special introduction is next. Thank you for being a friend with love from the heart and a transformed mind; Best wishes and remember, Love is the heart's power and Love that empowers and, that is all about what the love of God is to me most exciting and lovable too! Please, stay tuned, keep love and support by reading and sponsor, promote it as well donate to a child who needs your helping hand and share the blessings of love worldwide too. I am very grateful, that this is blessings and for us to enjoy and benefit and is a series of five books one volume is all classic reading, and great for all and, I am grateful that you all are working together with me and, again thanks!!!

Carol Arit Thompson.

Introduction

LOVE EMPOWERS

"Abide In My Love!" – John 15: 10

**Every time you smile at someone, it is an action
of love, a gift to that person-Mother Teresa**

Dear global family and friends,

I am so grateful for this opportunity, and delighted writing this with you in mind as you are part of my blessings. Mostly, expressing my deepest gratitude to God whose divine love and blessings are unfailing. In your hand you are about to read another inspirational book by the author entitled, "Greatness is in the Heart-A Tribute to Inspiration That Empowers," and celebrates all is love! Shares how life works for those who believe in a loving God and appreciate Him as His Words as children as His children as well as family and Friend of all in the world! It is, this work is fun to write as everyone is involved and this is for appreciation of love and all those who have been there for me and supporting my effort with your prayers, thank you for reading and for celebrating with me, unfailing love of an incredible reputable God forever, victorious is everlasting, is a loving Father.

For, no matter what the pain may be there a cure and assured, am sure you know! Friend is sure you know there is always a cure for us no matter the situations, joy and love that unfailing Friend gives to us is everyday blessing. Our beloved heavenly Father Offers life with eternal joy; and peace that is more is hope for the hopeless and a refuge for the helpless, unloved, sorrowful, oppressed, downcast, hungry and, for those disappointed and those suffering and all that we need He supplies them; from the same power is with hope and love for those who are sick, He healed them.

And, He set us free life, for us is beautiful and is for everyone who loves Him and though we may be suffering unjustly in the hands of the wicked ones and of any kind of sickness; but He does delights in taking care of all of our needs all supplies, provides all provisions readily made available. My heart as it is blessed, it wells up in praise to His Love and Spirit guiding me and is ushering me from day to day as I feel His love in me and imagine for humanity and comforts us; truly is bless to be able to love each, inspire and heart uplifted of others, love means compassion is companion is and being a merciful heart and to the needy and being there for the broken hearts that inspires and motivates my heart with joy, to be more than grateful for God is love incredible.

For the terrorists are invaders and it is the real enemy as attackers, and as well, it could be anything and is that includes illness and/or humans beings! Regardless, it is relevant for us also to stand up and take a stand and fight against it any foreign bodies all are to be dealt with them. And intruders that want to invade your territory and anybody and don't allow can be in form of your unfailing health or anything and someone. Thank God for that He doesn't want it to be part of His children, and inspiration to know of what matters most, so let's stand and not let anything to invade and take control over us you rather war to win is by prayer and standing tall and strong.

God loves us in faith and glorify God and use His name. I do and don't let it destroy, but I first seek inspiration and power from above. Consulting Him is to grow and is to overcome of all those obstacles is by holding to God and is alive is He lives inside us always, I live by that faith. Faith in Him is the fire for it is, "Those who have faith are blessed along with Abraham, the man of faith" (Galatians 3:9: NIV). Living life without love by words and action is not living real life. Living by sight and not insightful is down right of ignorance and Life is all about Him. And of love is all that we need and inspiration that all is all of which it is all love is faith in action too.

And words and deeds God's Love for He gives us and offers us grace for hope and faith too. Assures, all our blessings all that is in His hands and heart for us to enjoy and shares as well with us His words of love and power that is insightful is love of God is the message for all of us. To benefit from and surely when, we place our situations in God's capable hands, we can trust to be blessed that something mighty good is going to happen. For, God listens and answers prayers. And intercedes on our behalf also (Philippians 1:7-9), assures me that there is power within me!

Something good is coming from Him that it is guaranteed sooner or later you will be as is blessed more than ever, and it is enjoying daily is His blessings and none does He ever withholds from us for all are in His heart for us grace and unfailing love all too. It is enjoy and be happy for divine blessings are all a gift of love and we can celebrate love and life as well as our salvation is a gift and joy all are free and forever, is all secured because God loves us and His word(s) secures. We are always individually as well as collectively and we are stronger when united and that love brings us together His family and friends we are. Is awesome and ourselves together we can feast is of His will that words of encouragement, are a challenge all is great ideas, and best wishes and happily. He is in my business supporting me and I see believing in Him makes me who I am also.

And that is joy is to write and publish and to bless me and us all and others for hope and, it is of encouragement it is mostly healing that is what I received from Him too mostly that is for my joy is full and that is more than enough for me to be of thankfulness for I see how much God loves me and is so loving and so gracious that power, inspiration and hope from God is and of His tender whispering voice. God has blessed me and is of the tender voices of all is also love of my dear young ones and also of wonderful kids and other children likewise us as adults has inspires.

Yes, while in this journey of my heart is also full of great joy all is inspiration that moves my heart. I daily wake up to thank God and for us all is being blessed and all that God wants for my life, my being a blessing and serving Him is the purpose of my inspiration that is what warms hearts! It was that power of their language of love of my God, my children that hope to be there for me. I am thankful that I listened and sure, God is awesome and can you imagine blessing us. All, and me to borrow from their strengths it is grace inspiring me to challenge and boost my life. Happiness is God helps me to be of hopeful and to be strong for them and me thank God for love and faith. That is joy is steady and undying faith! Faith is love in action, words and deed, is God.

And, I don't know what my life could have been, if I didn't call on Him trusting and sure, everyone who calls in the God's name by Faith to truest and God gives peace to me and now the love is the language of my heart is and is my empowerment, a big break boost that gets me to the next level inspiring! It is both what a legacy for me to cherish and His Love is the heart's power. It is always of joy being a blessing and being of gratitude that is gladly for me to be blessed and to be inspired and is of deeper joy for me serving God, and acknowledging all those who have been my blessings in my life, and from God, family and friends and all have both of my personal and also of professional interest at heart and love as such are a result of this is work of God's the Love and loves us much on our side. And, team effort made all from friends and family and from Him to me and to you and all of us!

Those are why I am relying on Him and are expressions of truths with ability to bring us complete and lasting spiritual transformation when life tossed us also; It is so devastating it could be of poor unexpected health and as well a number of things and sometimes it is man created. It's not right that always we blame it all on God, but that is not true for God loves us and given us all what we need to use and for the pursuit of our happiness. Sometimes is to blame us as the human is to know that though, when it comes to natural disasters and its occurrence as human nature and as well as uncountable situations like, our sudden unfailing health and the loss of our loved ones as things those are beyond our control, we have to accept them, but others constitute(s) part of them.

Part our situations and, I am speaking from my heart! It is the grace for, I have had both natural and man created situations both also shares inside. You are already in the reading some. Now and, you will find in details as I was one of those who severely suffered also emotionally hurt as I was scammed and duped sapped and my financial handicapped too. It was man created not God. But, thankfully God is awesome power and is with God who loves me, I was blessed to overcome both circumstances both my physical and emotional health were as such, limitations.

Thankfully, I found the cure for both my situations, emotionally and physically and it has been a miracle! Is a testimony how God manifests in my life. Powerfully, and how grateful I am, for I see that is the remedy, beyond my expectations. Love of God is curative and healing power. And both of my physical and emotional health; He cured as well reversed them and, as well was in 1997. He went with me straight from my treating physician's office, from stress test straight to the fourth floor which was from my office at work place and, I never went back home till after one week, God's Healer. I was given six (6) months by my physical treating physician to live but God is so marvelous and incredibly and miraculously changed that is inside and what is inspiring my heart to be highly motivated, daily wells up in praise to the Lord God Almighty, is who heals.

The challenges of life and sometimes are quiet very much unpredictable and those often times are also unspeakable through it all, God is more than capable and this are true testimonies. God is with us has always been there and will evermore and that shows His love is a blessing and divine intervention is the favors that I have received and His love never fails is the focus theme for me. I say, glory be to God for His love never fails me yet and, is by His infinite love of grace. Mercies of greater grace as it is will never fails for, it turned out that incident was emergency.

And, was not a matter of thing doctor's visit, something went badly wrong, and I also so badly wanted to get out there and be inspiration esteem you as His is the joy, Love came down again! God's joy and more, I pray it flows, and thanksgiving the glory of God, shines upon me. He gives me more to hope for and this is the benevolence of His grace! That I continue to enjoy daily with all too and that is moving and apparently the wonder of His good work! All of us are blessed is much more than, is evidently what power of His healing love that is another important victory and testimony in the chapter by itself and breakthroughs that is what is testimony for this.

This is introduction and begins with love and thanks for me is of great joy deep down and that alone can be so exciting experiencing the healing and power of God my greatest physician. I am greatly indebted to Him and am beyond words and so am grateful for there is someone whose love compels me and is real and a true Friend. There is a power within in my inmost being and is the power that is greater than the entire world and you and I whose love is unfailing and ignites.

Love that won't let me go and my Healer who shows compassion on me has motivated highly shows me mercy and grace that cures and ignited my passion more and it is important, for me to share my story of how I found the cure and love that inspires me to love beyond word, race, creed, tribe and tongue and culture and go beyond those barriers. I am blessed truly to be in harmony with His love and am of hope and joy with my deepest gratitude and can't be complete without being grateful and that testimony of how my personal treating physician as human gave me six months to live! But, my God and my beloved Savior as the Giver and gracious is power is my awesome incredible miracle working heavenly Father and Healer says, is not what He said!!!

It is to be reversed order, because only His Word stands forever. I have life abundant and sufficient grace and it is with multiplicity of love and He gave more years and is of joy, life for us to celebrate with it now seventeen plus and many more to love and serve Him as His blessed me and this His lovable child, years and time are absolutely only in His hand and His love is joy. And, that says, who God is and power of greatness. He also dispelled all doubts and fears those of human's obstacles. Posing severe impediments, and rescued my life from all of them as it is.

I share is the story of my experiences with my faith and how God has worked with me as I'm one that did overcome by grace of God and, He also gave me all simple diagnosis and made me more a blessing loves me and am more than blessed, His grace, and that grace can overcome. Any of our conditions too, provides any believes! I am to testify and share God's grace and love it overcomes anything you can humanly think of and inside this book its deals on it step-by-step; with eighteen steps-powerful a strategy of seventeen chapters of how we can achieve excellence and all that we need through that Love.

How to find healing and contentment in the midst of trial, is in a series of five books and that is also to show the power of God's love and inspiration and lesson is joy and power of love. As well how my tragedies were turned to triumphs. Triumphant and He reversed of the cycles of my health and always. I am sharing the joy and for others to benefit and know with God that has enough all things are is of His power as impossible are always possible with Him. Testimony of my own personal one-on-one encounter with the power of the human spirit He is wonderworking spiritual power Love. Spiritual is everlasting Father and Power and Love who loves like no other.

No more beloved! I shall forever love and no one like my God (P.T. L). Who says there is no God as well power of inspiration as that power and love of can't prevent my panic and/or to moves the mountains of life and I want to also know? For, I was told to be diagnosed with quote and unquote according the lovely nurse, my doctor said to have told her, "Thought, I have a light heart attack!" That was man not God's thought and I was glad being home with my family, in 1997 and shortly because God is my greatest Healer. Is my Physician, is Savior the Redeemer of my soul; I see salvation of His redeeming Love vested on me as He visited me and inspires me of my heart not to worry but to be happy and be thankful and He abides with me everyday long too!

After that gave me knowledge and wisdom to change doctor immediately and that is the grace of God my life was spared and this is the work book of all His manifestations! Power is of His glory and the benevolence of God's grace that I continually enjoy daily and He revealed too. He is a revealing love to me more that, I was on the path of glory to becoming a woman of God; and like Abraham, also a true friend of His, and as such I was being tested by faith! Imagine that as you woke up and nothing happened and on your way going to work and you become so sick? And went there and you passed for to routine check ups, and wound up stocked a minute later is in a monitor, told that it was, "I think you had a mild heart- attack!! God forbids that and turned to happy hearty heart and gave me more life and to share of His goodness that inspires hearts too."

I thank God for He loves me and sent great family and loving people with good hearts of love to be with me! That happened to me it was in Miami, Fl. That was, at North Shore Medical Center and is Hospital both same vicinity, thank you, Lord for reversing death to life; six months, to be all of abundant life and grace of your love as benevolence and I continue to enjoy blessings from 1997 to this blessed day and it has been His desires that I live to love and serve Him more. As, it is His will that stands against my treating physician's as human being we are all helpless.

And His words evermore, and I thank You Lord my refuge and underneath your arms are fortifying me and working as well as my fortress empowering and strongest Love ever known to man, "The eternal God is your refuge and underneath are the eternal arms"(Deut.33:27:TLB). Sure, is my refuge! Told me, while there in the hospital, "Don't worry about anything, instead, pray about everything; tell God (Him) your needs and don't forget to thank him for his answers" (Phil. 4:6: TLB). That is what exactly that I am doing and, I also thank Him for these and those that were there with me and how appreciative and excited that I am because after one week, I was released. And, He was with me all the time and is over seventeen years since that ordeal.

It happens and this is to show that six months given by my treating physician for me my heavenly Father reversed it and because my life is in His hands and time and not man's will but His will and that is all about the difference between God's love and power and that of human. It really goes to show unpredictable by human being, can happen but, regardless of the situation, where there is love and faith, there can be victory because only God has ultimate say is who has power is created me has that power to determine anything about my life. I thank Him for my life. Am a child of God overjoyed, is faith/love to Hope/deepest gratitude!

To begin with I am a testimony for I was born blind and so this is all about testimonials as I am a miracle child of God and so many situations has occurred and blessings also given to me. Is of strings of victories and so I love for you to share and celebrate as we are going to be hearing and reading more and more testimonies in a special chapter of most and some of those as well for God is so faithful and so good to me and my family and friends all over the world black/white us.

We serve an amazing and an incredible great God. He is, "Alpha and Omega" (beginning and end). And, for sure His, is the best pathway. As, I have stated in my case is joy to know and have Him and so much those formative years those guidance and counseling from my family as it is blessed; I grew up some more understood more and very easily cherishing Him more and more that love is what motivated more my faith that and more, in my childhood when I heard of that great news too, of how I was born a blind beautiful adorable child of His and miraculously as He took pity on my parents and grandparents; tears and family too and relatives and faith family of their tears and fasting and interceding cures me and is was my first of His gift of love miracle.

I remember how I was blind and handicapped but God rescued, I also already saw God's love in my life and I said, signed me up, and sold! I am sold out for Him and sure that is what I can never ever forget and I forever will treasure cherishing Him, family and friends and tradition of my faith in Him forever more for His being so good for my life and healthy heart is just that love inspiring to motivate my faith more. We, all of us are blessed capable of loving and can be great at any age. I didn't have to be told twice, when being told I knew there and then, I was born and destined to love and serve Him by serving His humanity with love and that is my gratitude.

And whether young or old, you can be great and capable as well cherishing to love and is to serve that is God's way is best is for us all and as well scripturally is a noble thing of joy and confirmed "But, they shall serve the LORD their God, and David their King, whom I will raise up unto them" (Jer30: 9). God uses anyone, chooses any person and at any age and blesses also. I see what it means too, is to look to my Friend Jesus and, He is the King of kings am His daughter and Friend to look up to Him only and between Him and you making up your heart and mind to serve. That is a choice for you to be all that God He wants you to be and loves for you that God's plans is the best and in all, He wants us for Himself, planted, is wherever also we are to bloom!!

It apparently, says more and sums, "Greatness is in the Heart- A Tribute to Inspiration That Empowers as Sub-title shares experiences with my faith, using both personal anecdotes, and some third-party stories to illustrate how God has worked in my life and given me inspiration in all that I do. In my life and has offers me a second chance with hope and love and His inspiration as well is about my miracles that I do receive with divine favors is given to me by Him and so I have found that before Him and man and that is what resulted this work and it explores as well. Is all inside the doubts, fears, and perplexities that I had experienced in my various life situations and sure it illustrates how I found comfort and guidance in the Bible and through prayer."

Healing and miracles that is also as one of the readings most featured. As one reads will also observes all that being proven proofs that is provided with very good personal examples. It is to show the incredible power of God and as well the incredible power of prayer and what God is capable of doing for us through His Healing Word and leading of Holy Spirit wonderworking! Each of the situations is throughout in the text and is adept using also my personal stories and is to illustrate key points. All are very vital information to us to note this is the salient point, and is by living that faith by love and hope and joy in your heart, and mind and spirit that also matters.

Is for our success, stimulate our thoughts also is engaging our minds. Documentations of sources vital much as it is possible and the content all are valid, original and informative, racy, is readable and, family-friendly to inspire and engage us as stated my sincere intent is in helping all readers in finding inspiration in their daily lives; Finding empowerment, love, joy, happiness also blessings all I have been privilege to share of based on my own eye-witness account as inspired. I will forever glorify God for His love is excelling! Joy in my heart is the Saving Grace I found.

In one of my books, *Parental Influence Matters* published (2007), it is dedicated to all of our parents and mentors and friends is of joy to have that Love of God, shows that power of their positive influence in our lives any child is to be grateful for them and, all those who rally around to help raise up a child is a great thing. Blessing and is joy when that child can find favor before God and man and that leadership quality and success is the gift from which first comes from the love of God to them for theirs is joy, wisdom to apply the words of God administers to them and together with unconditional love. You will see there is a chance and there will also be a positive influence and a brighter future and hope as well is joy, future and positively is giving hope and is of joy to a child and that is surely hope with a future is something to love and thankful forever!!!

That's the power of inspiration too, for there is more to be thankful for and happiness too. There is a chance and hope for any child who listens and pay close attention to their counseling and guidance resulting from words of God's love through Godly parents and mentors you can as well see the prospects with faith in God no matter the circumstance that we find ourselves there is hope and victory for us. Parental Influence Matters, I thank God for my family raised me up in that faith and also gave me a love that is priceless and unconditional for they endured with me as well my disability and that is also the very book that documents this testimony about my healing.

Miracle of God's love for my sight was the first testimony that I wrote about in the book. Hope in Him for faith matters and of His power, I am blessed am the healed and restored woman of God's love and of His working power He is all I need Love that endures evermore that is sure! Is so awesome Love is our God. Beneficial of His love and power works wonders and that makes me and it is very much awesome and authenticated God is good, keeps His promises and daily as well for He celebrates me that is everyday very relevant! Is well with my soul, is joy so much for me to be of deepest gratitude and He is the remedy of my soul and very much is significant to be happy and excited. And, I wanted to share how I found the cure to my own situations that were so hurting and heart breaking and His Love is hope and solution to my situations and that power of inspiration to bless and is encouraging and I found divine favors is being Encourager, is daily.

And a divine intervention that's His power of Inspiration ultimately means a world to me is God is all. Finding solution and something that is healing will also be helpful to all of us and, as I am blessed from it I didn't' hesitate thought about us and of it all is for us as what will be used by God to heal, and helps me and my family and friends is great for me to share worldwide for people too are hurting to know where to find be all blessed that is my prayer. And, my wishes are that it will be a contact point everyday, I pray God for us, and for healings. And as often said, "It takes only a moment to be kind, but it result can last a lifetime;" It is that is so true and is why love is the key and theme and the heart's power and my passion and it is compulsive compelling.

Is my commitment helping people to find inspiration in their daily lives to live life fully, and happy that is my sincere intent of this, also testimonial is what makes for my love and joy it is sheer joy and of my heart and is for gratitude. Is the memory of my heart is greatest hope that Love thrills my heart me most to be alive, to be a blessing and inspirer, is God is awesome. And I was in a near death situation and out of death has came a new life and faith is increased daily is even more that also is of amazing grace love, the blessing. That's everlasting is the living well, it brings to my life, joy! Friend, God has done it again for me. As this is attested, and you can read the above mentioned book and see in chapter one is page 14. I am a testimony as happy survivor.

It shows my Father's love also and this is shows faith is of God is that faith in Him what is what matters most is that love in words, actions and deeds is with a brand-new joy and brand-new confidence to me to share with us all and that love is my story that is power of God my Joy. He is the greatest source of my inspiration. And this all that turned to glory makes me to become happier and is to be more than thankful also for He gives me testimonies after my ordeal turned story around is now glory! I am more than grateful, super excited and overjoyed though naturally am a happy person. As is of my norm, for I was born as well that way my passion is to bless us is to do what He calls me and that is by grace/faith inspire and Love and serve, but is by His Love!!

I survived being scammed and duped of $11,000 dollars 2008 by a dubious conned artist. I was also being told 2010 by Hematologist, "Caroline, I think you have cancer" and that power of love of God changed that too. And, being told of my knee was to be amputated because of being a situation unknown and bad prognosis of my right knee. Now thankful, it has a name and before was named anything including it to be cancer. Name that was scary and God is love and the greatest is Joy is Physician as my God is who reversed all of that and 1987, was with issue of blood is in testimony chapter too. All through grace and this is another defining moment of my life as is my hopes and dreams that all were shattered became real once again as He answers me and is being most grateful and happier as well that is most exciting through the grace and abiding love of God also is of my deeper joy is and a greater cause for my gratitude, is testimonies and thanksgiving!!

And is of love of the abundant blessings given daily that include of supportive family and friends and marvelous of opportunities of His limitless blessings and gift of grace and talent and skills and mental discipline, and with faith all. It is possible to overcome those stumbling blocks. And with prayer, believing by faith both of the uncountable, natural and of human created, cured. He loves, healed and cured and dispelled of all the doubts, fears and perplexities and turned it to passionate purpose that is what inspiration is gift; and nothing beats sharing your happiness with others and giving glory to the Lord, God Almighty who made all this to happen in my life, is joy.

Many of you now will be familiar with what your gift is and please find ways to live it is your life and go about as well being productively in service and reach out and touch others lives. Is the best of gift and to offer and am glad that even with our broken hearts, we can serve God is a blessing. That is the right thing to do and, healing balm not to cluster our minds with negative thoughts as well it is how you can hang in there with the love of God and together with support, of your family and friends and mostly, with you willing to open your heart and let the Lord have. His way for His loves and abides in you and to fulfill His purpose in your life that, it thrills most will rekindle. A sense of gratitude in you, my happiness is what God has done and not what I did for Him is my redeemer and Ebenezer and you have heart of love and inspiration that is given to you is progress and is inspirational stories for hope and the difference is there God is awesome.

It's **"Thanks be to God for his indescribable gift" (2nd Corinthians 9:15).** Yes, it is a moving experience more heart of love is with a sense of purpose in you and, is you are not only taking care of your physical body, but, also mind and spirit and that is a real vitamins to help us is for heart healthy, is love and faith and that is of victory rich there. Is by living that life of hope in you is by faith, is living in the freedom that comes from being confident in God's love that is inspires my passion and more ignited me to do more is love! Your heart will rekindle of more of gratitude and thank you God will be part of your joy everyday life is that is moving with love, is appreciation and asking is the question of what the true meaning of a gift is? He is to me A Gift is a present; and, we are all gifts of (God's) love to one another, and that is what you are to me.

And that is why in dedication page it features as well in the acknowledgment. Scripture, teaches us that, "A gift is a precious stone in the eye of him that hath it: withersover it turned, it propereth" (Proverbs 17:8)! This is my forever, eternal Father's love and gift of love is power of God and inspiration always my Jesus and Master and Savior that is my greatest Gift is evermore, and, "A man's gift makes room for him and bringeth him before great men." (Proverbs 18:16). Is of joy as shared pretty much a joyful and joyous present to me is! When life seems too much of a hopelessness and tough to bear, God steps in, is joy and to be rescued and blessed and loves. We will be chatting more on this in other series living a dream and is achieving success through love.

Love makes a life beautiful and happy and resilient and more useful and, isn't God good? Only one that is more than deserving of my thankful heart, as trusting that same foundation is the Faith and my Lover is as it is my All. In-indwelling, the sweetest name that I know; Jesus is my world also life, my true Friend; to let me live is to invite us all that is, all of us to experience that excitement and enjoy with me "Evangelism is one beggar finding bread and telling others where to find" as often said, and that is what this is all about God's love's and power in my life that are miracles! And how He has blessed me with all the joys that life has to offer and sharing that also!

Hopefully you will make every effort to use yours as well and, be a blessing to others and share your love daily. Love is amazing and, bearing someone else's burdens that lightens mostly of our loads and finding happiness doing what you never thought were capable of doing in your wildest dream, let alone in your faith journey. How I derive my joy and happiness more because of making others happy as well as I am is even happier how God is blessing me makes me forget about my situations and be about helping people find inspiration that is God's love and joy and is amazing care for me that power of love is, joy unspeakable; Marvelous is God and in making us be purposeful! As well I couldn't do it alone without your support and prayers that love inspires.

Absolutely, "A single bracelet does not jingle" (Congo Proverb). Yes, is as simple as that, for I couldn't do this alone and without Him and sending great friends that are from my family as well of others to be my gifts are my blessing! The following Nigerian proverb sums it up: "Hold your good friend with two hands." All these are of God's love in the power of inspiration and has that is in meliorating the heart and it is as such is launching all, dream comes true but not without His love and power making it possible. And people like you being there as my supportive system family and friends all praying and believing God for me to make it and my children also helping pushing and fostering my efforts with love to get to the next level is of love joy of all networking that also makes power of love and inspiration to be my blessings and supporting that power is a gift of grace and love from above for it all begins from the heart that loves and cares as He gives.

They help me and encouraging me to write sure inspiration does inspire heart is a legacy! To cherish and again, Friends, I wish you the best that life has to offer, with greatness each heart, and remember love empowers- so count your blessings and use your God's given gifts too and to cultivate them all to their maximum potential. Thank you again, and enjoy this gift of mine. All is I love you, God bless us all! Happy reading and enjoy and pass the love on! And, I am hopeful that your life of your hearts after reading will become as blessed as I am and excited, for you are all part of my joy as is blessings and daily prayers for love amongst all of us, and I thank God for you and this blessed day also being a great day of joy and for us all to read to celebrate His love.

And, for the fact that you have decided to join me celebrating and appreciation Him and of Love, as well and, decided to join also on this quest for greatness in the heart and so the Love is the next chapter for us to read and Love is the heart's power. I am very encouraged. So, friend love is obvious please, let's each be of hope and happy and as encouraged by Him daily, as this is His gift to us and there is also more noble Scripture, His is love that conquers says simply this to each to make more thankful sums, A find proof here is for you too. All what we went through all were rough all of what I overcame is marvelous and I am now is a living testimony to what God has done for me, my family as a happy survivor is what makes thanksgiving and my testimony.

It is apparent that I must return my thanks, is to encourage others and that to me is what a joy for a moment and this rare privilege and, I am honored and being alive to have this chance. He is blessing us as shared and joy is being alive safe is due to God Almighty and Love and so in my life is a defining moment and most deepest gratitude and in defining love my oldest daughter she says with love is the peace is obviously, and that is also is the language of God's Love always is everlasting God. He is Inspiration and Peace always, and my daughter reminding is to me this life is all everything love is true and peace and of Love is all about God's Love to us all!!

Nothing as peaceful as one of God and experiencing that peace of God awesome what she knows and has received from God's love and is experientially as she has tasted too much of His unfailing love. Is we all been through together in the journey as the joy is arriving is where that's God's love, demonstrates to us His power takes us and it is through it all victory is of God's love! Is the grace and joy that faith is what makes us. This is how she puts it in her words based on her insights and wisdom, **"Mom, Love is God's language, even though many people in the world only care about themselves"-Comfort U. Chevannes (2013).** I continue thanking Him for my life, my family and friends all of us and those blessings are of joy's experiencing peace in heart.

God's peace and love for our daily living that Love is all we need for our lives. It just that goes to show that parental influence matters and faith in God is the power that always helps us to sing through the storms. Is the blessings is there for us God's unfailing love and divine power is the divine intervention and we pray that love and breathe daily and His inspiration surrounds us is like the air that we breathe. Is for its manifestation in other place that needs is relevant peace. I see and feel deep within me is joy of God matters is to know Him. More and more is joy of hope is amazing grace and how to appreciate Him and His love and for life and inspiration that is most what world needs is, especially in moments of our unexpected. You will be fine with His love joy it is hope and, so is for individual as well collective, blesses is by faith comes victory no matter what your situation God will be there and see you through so far that you believe in Him is Love.

Love is theme features more topics and variety as you have seen the contents and is richer by faith is and wisdom is of God! I couldn't be healthier and happier than now making a big deal out of Him is all that I have to do as I am blessed to be His poem of praise and for His glory an honor! As, I said earlier in preface it's of fun to write about all of His love is testimonies to the power of the human spirit and all are truths and no additives and adulterated in any form or way. He is a living Power and eternal there is deeper Joy in my heart is awesome. Wisdom is of God and inspiration legacy, for the knowledge, Love is the heart's power is the Joy is divine healing!! Is divine health that Power is of God and always He is there hidden blessings and marvelous and this work details it!! Shows also there is hope for us, regardless of the situation God can cure it.

All is well, for where there's faith there can be victory and in the name of the Lord that is what this work demonstrates from the power of God's love that empowers me and it mesmerizes my heart overjoyWhat saturates thought is love, is a legacy of God and is to give back is for Him more and more, that is what by grace, faith and peace; Is all working and how those promises are amazing also all of it is fulfilled. Is a testimony and sure is that power of inspiration is am paying of this tribute, for sure when I remember all the goodness of the Lord as He spared my life and is still doing in my life and family and all by grace and love. It is evidently is beyond measure and everywhere, God's with us and gives us the Love and graces my heart with His love and power is what can I say more than to render my heart with passion that can't be substituted and I share of love. And the best of everything is He illuminates paths that we trade too and covers us also with His love and blood, protects and preserves, endures evermore, covers us and secures everyday!!

Oh yes, covers us well with His blood and as the banner over us is love, He is a good God who cares for His own, and carries us through anything that posses hindrances as He overcomes those for us is anything and/or something or someone that terrorizes, overcomes all on our behalf that says more than Conquerors with His love and wisdom is power Of His inspiration and Love. Is all is what matters most that is Joy as excitement of its discover is amazing grace love growing and maturing in such for me my heart is overwhelmed of Hope, Redeemer, is Remedy of my soul my Joy and Inspiration. He loves me is everything I ever needed is just I wanted my life to know Him better and love most. Amazing that Love Empower and, shows the greatness and power all.

Is this is the life and passion for His love did it all. He sacrificed all for me and now time for me to return and all my love and life I give for He first loved me and gives all of His, so that I can give of mine as well there is no more beloved. Please, refer the Books of (Colossians 1:27; 3: 17; 1 John4:19). How much Jesus loves me as my best Friend, Redeemer, and the Blessing of my soul and fills my heart with His love and joy so I must praise the Lord for God also is good to me as well as my family is everything. He is so sweet and kind and love and caring and all He is amazing is Love everlasting and miracle's that abiding Love and Faith that empower Inspiration!!

Son of God that God He gave me all of His love. And my family and much is that Love, for our acceptance most. And, for our security all is well appreciated. I know that is saying over and again thank God for this is victory is for us as I see how much you love us and care everyday He is Love, and is the remedy and, also I received my healing, it is all blessing all as well as I am personally grateful for that truth and my miracles are all based on facts as all are as is and see it's abundantly is of God's grace, and I invite you to please join me in thanksgiving. God first is the celebrant and for my overcoming is that my thanksgiving for Love is the best thing that ever happens, is experiencing God's peace is better than life itself and, idealistically, the Lord is good!

Miraculously out of my greatest nightmares something such as this comes out it was such meant to be and God's purpose! God has purpose is far greater than what we imagine. There is a greater cause as for me my deepest gratitude and reasons my testimony is the way and how God manifested His love. Healed and transformed and brought His love and Majesty to this daughter of His that to me is very special and loveable and gift that offers me all the joys that life to offer. This is the result of my faith journey, it was not in vain is blessings out of burdens and something beautiful for I benefit from the joy and the power of that exchange and my heavenly Father helps me ride on now on now is testimony a story of love that prays for me and with me and inspires!

That is the power inspires of my passion and rejoicing and triumphantly the blessings all of words of God it is of all inspiration, inspires and encourages the mind transform and renews. It educates the heart and renews the mind transforming my life as am living this triumphant life and blessing that love is everyday is who guides, inspires, transforms. I am blessed empowers is by God who loves all and He loves me most and His favorites loves me I am for real. Father's favorite, prays with us and is for us and teaches us as well, how to navigate the twists and turns of life and, heals and anyone, who is calling Him, will be as well saved those are all His Words for me, life it testifies true testimonies to the power of the human spirit and inside this you will find more testimonials from me and others and seventeen chapters each with inspirational stories.

Jammed pack with spiritual punches is love and this is the end of series one of the five series of this work and as stated this introduction.

That is also thanksgiving begins with love and thanks is of my deepest gratitude. No matter what is the cost, I will always obey Him and do the work; He called me to do that is of my –inspiring hearts to find inspiration in their daily lives. To live life fully, as am blessed, I'm being thankful. And, very willing to carry out my call of duty as assigned to me and is specially, inspiring youth, as well the women(young and old) rejected, abandoned, desperate and lonely as broken at hearts; and the poor, needy, discouraged, and all helpless children and disfranchise people of this world this is for them to cheer up with hope all.

Also, elderly, disabled and single or married this represents all they are hard working the people and often are those abandoned and abused more than others in the world and is a great thing to do. I am challenged by those that have crossed my path to be a blessing and thankful to God and everyone who has supported me and inspired my heart with their witnessing too for me from my great-great to great- grand to mother and all the women, that are in the Bible and now to be of my generation, my daughters and younger and those to come and after will always bless the name of the Lord for what He has done and will continue doing in encouraging and empowering.

Mostly, while on this journey all! I am thankful for their inspiration and mostly is for joy! As our God is awesome is super marvelous inspiring my passion for helping people to be happy, joyful, hopeful, more confident, resilient, purposeful, encouraged, is inspiring theirs is as well is of hope for them is they will also bless others' hearts. It makes a difference in the lives of people with any condition, situation, disabilities and those that are helpless this is also what is dedicated to them this chapter is to encourage all of them and also celebrate women (men) and those who are inspirations in my life. And also a shout out to all Single mothers to stay strong and hopeful, for you are never left in your life alone in your journey, God loves you and knows all about you!!

Yes, Is so much a trying moments and you can live and survive with Him by your side it is so, possible to make it through those tough times and days that you wonder and doubt if, it is. All hope lost, is not at all, trust for you are not forsaken! Is to also survive and with triumphantly become all that God destines for your life and He has blessed you and yours and everyday is of Blessings that He gives is for you to rejoice in

Him and wait as well and don't let your faith fails you! For it is well and you are blessed and, so Is with God who is in you! Thankfully, of my joy serving Him makes a meaningful difference in my life. And, also those of others that inspires me.

More to aspire for greatness and His love inspires as it empowers and transforms and you never know what tomorrow will bring your way, so live its to fullest, love is a gift is of greatness is that is in heart is Love and Power, and I am most grateful. That He sends me His Son, people of great hearts of love to be there for me just as blessed as I am is a beautiful thing to reach out in love and touch those of others, with love also. All who needs help the most and of joy for Giving comes from the heart and giving is a great life is giving something back to bless us all and make others life happy as well and life is more beautiful to be a blessing than being a burden. Available and able to be there for those who need your help with inspiration and thrills is this journey too is amazing grace love and fruitful journey! I am more than blessed through Him and love to bless.

It is surely sums, "Greatness is in the Heart-A Tribute to Inspiration That Empowers is a blessing, story of love, how much God love inspires to empower and transform and brought me ashore. From where I was from a very long emotional journey; I am more than grateful for what I am most grateful most of all, I must thank God for His Son daily and, is above for all what He has done for me and mine, not what I do for Him for He first loved me! He gave me His all That Friend's of the friendless; Comforter of those, who are lonely and grieving spirit and lost souls is Lover of the unlovable, Encourager is everyday life as He is a blessing. He comforts me through His presence that shows is alive and is within me in my life in inmost is of my being. Love that is uplifting heart and soul is there is hope and joy and with Utmost; is gratitude considering all this.

Also marvelous of all What God has done for me and all of us are of deep joy and utmost is of my deeper gratitude. Is He is greater more than thankful; I am everyday too is of Joy and, as my daughter, daily reminds me this though, l know is really already all what we live and we also do trust in too is sharing Him as ours as He is our Living souls is daily cup of tea and bread and is butter. He carries us through all those insurmountable mountains. Toughest journey; She tells me everything life is love and love is all about God and that is His language and had been there for us day and night and more too, it is surely wherever life takes us through He's always there! Thick and thins and He is and why as she says her motto: "Peace of mind is priceless!"

God is that inner strength, and Peace is healing power and I found profound thrill thought of hope and life both by grace/faith. His Love and brought us home safely. Always and, this is so awesome me to be growing in God's amazing grace love is inspiring Love story and blessings of God amazing power is joy everyday is for my thanksgiving. For He Loves and both is joy and is of excitement that love empowers and secures us and protects us throughout, is He is an abiding Love that is unfailing, never disappointed us ever and never will He is unfailing Love and, as this testifies what makes me alive and to be more than grateful and happiest illustrates how much He loves me as always. During and after a wild wind and the blizzard turbulent weather of my faith journey; and there is evidently one more proof a testimony after the tedious winter storms that is we have to be thankful and reflections is appropriate and to me being thankful and to encourage us and others more to be of hope is joy, overtime is faith increases. So, I praise Him … "He sends springs into the valleys" (Psalm 104:11). I am still basking in that supreme bliss, is eternity too!!

I saw it, "They flow among the hills" so even in the desert love and grace abound and it is all that goes to show, there is hope for us that, regardless of the situation that we may faced us is have faith in God and trust to believe and obey His will and victory is of certainty. For me and mine is we have been there is together and is through it all is more to be more thankful for God is an awesome and amazingly that Love endures for us a lot and of all together and is also, we have seen of glory and salvation to rejoice be glad in the love and power of his greatness. Greatness is of God giving all of His love to us!!! Together we have been blessed and of all, as seen blessed.

God as a family, us we all have a testimony and joy received more than also anticipated, all is a gift of God's love as well grace that glorious lovely glory of being alive is of God and is joy in Moments of trials, spirituality it works and prayer and love are also is invitation. It is also joy, if you know how to reach to His love, call Him is available anytime. If, it weren't for God's joy and grace and love in 2008-2010, that I had experienced the worst of my calamities as all is to be shared in details, my whole life's all as said and read was a twister, could have been worse but for love and words of His unfailing love that brought me hope and joy and healing peace too.

All is with inner peace and strength all with His presence that is commuting is the touch of love, is my life all, so comforting for one to know and able too to love and relate with eternal heavenly Love. That is the healing balm and love is chamber is of heart is of life and that makes me whole as love is heart's power and that is true Love is alive! And again as Nigerian proverb sums it up for me is joy: "Hold your good friend with two hands." All these are of God's love in the power of inspiration meliorating the heart and this is all results is also love are action and joy for launching all of our dreams to come true! Is in your heart is everything will become inspired and transformed of His goodness is joy-greatness as His loving us is awesome is how to become, that love for others and for us as well to be the united people of the world is my daily prayer too.

And wishes too! It is to share and inspire as well uplifting spirit as encouragement also to help everyone to know more about their blessings and the power of that empowering Inspiration. Greatness is in the Heart and a Tribute to Inspiration that Empowers sums them, have to read my 2008-2010 too of both incidents is more to read inside as well testimonies all from Chapter eight all are analyzed to simplify more is in a way that all readers will enjoy. Inspiration is a legacy too is to be cherished. Celebrate more and am so glad that inspiration is great and comes from above; as is also us and better my life and is showing more of appreciation is by sharing and loving of us more is of heart's as blessed, opens me up more to be ignited to all the joys that life has to offer!!

It is greatness, goodness, holiness and faithfulness, of God in words, actions and deed is He loves us, and keeps us company as we walk the road of life and in my life I have seen love is one beyond marvelous for Him also is best. Expressed with deepest gratitude and affection in the heart that is in my deep down is what it is, then lingers on more and more and is most. Most lasting than anything else God's love us most and lasting is everlasting and amazing grace love is joy as benefits of that moving experience. And of expression of love is so fulfilling and power to me is to be a living testimony! Love is of <u>God great Force also</u> is the <u>Way and Life it inspires my heart with passion that is all these are</u> <u>love</u> <u>and a tribute to inspiration, Love that empowers me.</u>

There is no comparison is just marvelous to thank Him though many of our books are also inspiring us, but, it cannot transform and heals us. For only God's love does; that grace by faith what is profound. Faith is another aspect of life and your inspiration that power I got and all in all that I do, I am so excited, is for everyday to me a day of thanksgiving! I must do this is to give thanks and is what I live for daily being His poem of praise and joy is And to serve and love, and never could I ever be satisfied or happy, if not shared the love of God and joy and grace also and testify always is of His goodness to me, I am to glory in Him and honor and bless Him publicly always.

It is appropriate thing, so that is everyone has a little gift of His love and benefit from! Is a blessing assigned to me that am more than capable to do it is the Lord's gift who performs also is and nothing as bad as being disobedience to my Father's will, is joy and of immense gratitude. Sharing to do and a blessing and is of joy to do and I treasure best is the advice and suggesting is to adhere doing Father's mission. Believe or not, those things that we do on our own power and not trusting God's will to carry them out as our assignment by Him are among sinful lifestyles: "Whoever does not love does not know God, for God is love," Joy is doing is His will foremost! This of my pleasure is God has given me the joy of life and my heart is full of joy as it is always fills with love and joy for everyone you know and those that you don't, is excited to love always.

As empowers, I know, it is good to one another, it encourages is with strength to go on, when all else is lost, and fails, gone and everyone you need may be gone and the only One that remains is the love is God. That is God loves, does not depart(s) from you and I. Am blessed with His being my blessing. Having Him is love for eternity and I have my compassionate traveling Companion is through eternal life and, so far is for me there is no more beloved than He is and all that there is, for, "Whoever does not love does not know God, because

God is love"(1John 4: 8). So, I celebrate my love first for Him with my gratitude because He first loved me and there is no more beloved than God and that is what this message is to who suffers one thing or the other.

And also those going through situations, any of racial/tribal discrimination, likewise any prejudice, not to give up on hope and don't let your faith fails you that is the last chapter, in this work to read and know that we are not alone in our life's journey of life there is help and hope. Friend, God has been so faithful to us and He loves us so much, so compassionate and a merciful loving to us is a loving Father who never changes but so much cares, and invites us to: "Abide in His love!" And dearly that as well gives us grace to endure and the strength to be able gives us the enablement of ability, capability, talents, wisdom, power, knowledge, and grants with peace.

Is the most is life's richest blessings and love richest joys and blesses us throughout our journey. Entire lifetime and has given us power with authority that can win for us everything and all that we need. I have and that is hope for me, for He blesses our hearts with love and laughter. As He teaches us *how we can overcome obstacles and achieve for us our greatness. I am* Sure with His help we can find the answers to our missing puzzles of life and may not always be the way that we want it to be always, but that is best for us! He the throne of grace and mercy is sure for us was always there for me and mine and as far as I know will forever be there. He is our everlasting Love, desires for us to be steadfast, not shifty; sure the shift is the exposed.

Exposed shifty is not, the best of life, neither life but, "Honesty is the best policy," and it is best to practice loving more than being hateful and I am thankful for the power and greatness. He is Hope for you and for me, that is much and is how much this is an inspirational story that is of joy and is with educational, powerful Ministry of love and showing mercy, is through infinite love, of mercy and grace God bestowed powerfully upon my life and His grace lifted me up too. Is with joy, for He anoints me and entrusted with the responsibility of reaching the world through love all messages of this work is words of God's mouth for there is essence of life to do the right thing more than and better by far than roaming around and causing havocs to fellow human kind.

More than the wrong and love is and world is in needs love and truth and inspiration that is empowerment right there for us. Our peace comes from the love of God and trust in Him and, a word of life is healing is truth matters. Trust in God and in Him for refuge is there. Happiness is of the *Lord God,* is Almighty and joy also comes from within and likewise of real happiness and we need to remember, to make us like Christ, and "we shall be like Him" (1 John: 3:2). "All things work together for the good of those who love God" (Romans 8:28). Joy is God, He brought life to me more to hope for and strength to my heart, living that is high energy. Is the heart's power; There is power in us is the most liberating and lasting spiritual power ever, is for our Freedom and all that becomes this is moving passion and experience is a gift of God!

Is God's of love to able inspiring our hearts in finding inspiration in our daily lives that is intent of this gift is of God, this little inspiring work, evidently shows God is faithful and keeps to His Words and so loving and kind and loving me so much and my sincere intent writing this work is for all and that is the purpose, for encouragement, education, evangelism also useful for family and friends. I am most thankful for there is joy for us and hope and peace of mind that is and you can be truly happy. Regardless, of the situation where you are so far you have faith Love within can overshadow you with unfailing love, and there will be always victory using His name.

And where there's love and faith is joy and victory. Here is a testimony to the power of the human spirit and God abiding and unconditional love as He is the blessing of my hope and is hope exits and love empowers is through grace and Scripture. He inspires my passion and to do. More than ever thought, in my ordeal, He rescued and as read heals and inspires, and empowers. And helped and trains and guides and transforms the emotions in my heart, life remarkably, and changed, re-shaped me to become that vessel and poem of praise for His glory and honor. I have a testimony, I am a testimony and I have seen the power and goodness of God. It is to speak up.

Both more of His Greatness and Great Healing Power and Comforting Touch all for me and also my miracles He performed and from my infant through For, I live daily by that faith in Him. Faith is action, God's in word and action and deeds. I am when faced with the emotional roller coasters turn to Him, life of looking more to Him is of upward than down. That is saying it is all is to cast all of your situations to Him, pray fervently and read the words, those love letters. Are words of unfailing love is reading; Praying as well with praises and thanksgiving, and when once inspired is inspirited is we can trust that whatever happens it will turn out for it to be for our own good is for motivation (Psalms 18: 6/143: 9; 138:8 & Phil, 1: 7-9; Matt.11:28/Pro. 18:10).

Those are all of vitamins for body, mind and spirit and that is what faith stands for and is as walking in love, trusting and beholding His beauty and this is for my past blessings, is present. And is this tribute all is joy to be thankful is current and future is in advance thanksgiving and all will be permanent all blessings according God's will and for, I know the best is yet to come and His promise to fulfill. I know that, as it is from generation to generation. Another, sharing love, faith and friendship and blessing others is in continuity and is also of joy and by offering hope and love form of kindness is by encouragement and not always by giving money to someone is.

Always, love is words and actions and by deeds also, is it small or insignificant as far is a genuine from the heart of love and sincerity God uses of heart, it goes a long way to encourage. Inspiring one another to be encouraged obvious that says, "Love makes the world go 'round!" It may be a sentiment always, but is the truth, love is the greatest and who is with love indeed of a little love and kindness, especially given to lonely heart and needy can make(s) life to be bearable. Is true one can bear with it, is as well healing to be better and is all about the heart and thoughtful mind and willingness to share of one's heart, that makes for hope, and how precious can that be?

Awesome! It is great for is and can fill emptiness of a broken and grieving soul, is always amazing grace as to how God works in us and grace that heals and restores and is comforting and fulfilling and that is His love gives me hope and joy which also brings inspiration. Warmth to my heart and fills with love and joy and, as the wonderworking in me is that Power. Love is what it is. Lingers on and that inspires of my passion is of more as, I am motivated by it. Is that faith is more as ignites my heart is highly inspired motivated is willingness of the mind to be is quiet heart and mind to hear from above and to do always as my calling and is my passion.

And as well is a charge to obey as a call of my duty, am only a choice. It is not my will but my Father's will and is joy for it love for my lifetime and beyond; I am truly blessed to be so revealed of His love and of His Holy Spirit to become that love for others and a messenger and His lovable child and this is so gracious; if we are willing to trust and obey His will and follow is awesome. It is accordingly, that is what makes me alive and happy and, to love Him evermore. I and, more in my lifetime that is in every aspect of my life through eternity and I thank God for Jesus my beloved Savior, Mentor, Friend that He gave to me is everyday joy in my heart. I thank Him for being my Blessed Redeemer, Salvation, the remedy of my soul and healing love eternal.

And one who died for me and to forgive us of our trespasses; Wash all our sins away and fill us. That is the amazing; believing in Him is a blessing to me Yes, is and inspiration power of God all unconditional love. Love is the key to use and unlock is the gateway of freedom and that power is unmerited favor is Grace. Grace of God, it is as well is by faith also where there's cure, that God is more than able! And, He is as well delivers and sets free by the power of God, I am so blessed, healed! Cures and saves me! Moving love is experience and passionate Love always.

And blesses as I'm truly blessed and led by leadership of His Holy Spirit and that is joy is; Living triumphantly, is that shows how much blessed that I am filled full and sanctified and anoint with power is a loving God who never changes. He keeps His promises and makes happy and nurturing me in the light. Illuminates my life and mind is of His words all are the blessings. And confidence that I have, for is who inspires hearts and guides and leads us and stimulates our thoughts and gives us the life and grace with strength; I am here to testify for it is one of the key most powerful emotion as that fuels me to ignite my passion is positive and highly motivated.

Education is educating heart. It is The heart is and encouraging the mind to be willing to aspire for greatness is of God and His words educating the hearts that passion emotion is positive passion makes for my hope and joy. It is the happiness and joy gives me of this opportunity with a chance for God's love is a gift for a lifetime through eternal life inspiring being wrapped with His love, Words give me life and hope with more encouragement, and future is brighter with hope too. Is His word(s) helps and builds and shapes our faith and is healing Love, and is also great for us. It is so very good for us, the soul and builds us of our self-esteem, and gives courage and as well as mind is renewed transformed that can be so remarkable for anyone who wants to be a blessing.

As well is for, public and human relations, is so good in business both private or personal and professional or public is rewarding for and joy is to live a life of love by faith and hope too is awesome finding love, joy and inspiration is same affection for everyone! For me to find Him to care and love and celebrates love can be marvelous and so amazing that is. Friend, did you know that love could be transferred? Oh yes! This is how God helps me to help myself, and my family and friends globally to give of hope, a little gift of love something back to my community and, is also the world in general this is a gift, I inherited from my ancestors is passed down says beyond.

Beyond every reasonable doubt we are closest to God more than we know and loved, are capable than we know too is love that binds us together and in our hour of trial, can still find joy. His love brings to strengthen us all and love brings us together and through the power of God's love is words of inspiration and that of human, encouragement from God uses both also for our healing too. It is also of our community as well, for friendship is coming together. To love is joy for us to share, and so I am grateful, and I love you all and for your love and prayers support me.

My being a part of solutions than problem is how much love is and God inspires hearts as well transformed. He inspires and, with not of problems, is love that blesses how much as I have been truly blessed and, very thankful for me is lots being given a part in sharing blessings of this wide world ministry of love, showing mercy having a part, I am so thankful for that is power, am so grateful for God loves me so, much beyond gracious. Love is of God and that is the Spirit too. Uphold, and that works from inside to outside. The wonderworking always that is only material of faith and, currency of life war against indiscipline and intruders don't just make it personal or possessive, demonstrates is love acts of unselfishness and I thank God that we are given of His.

The power to be able and use lavishly to cultivate it with the authority as given to us and nothing beats living in grace and faith in God and that is amazing too as bless we are by my God to us is to achieve greatness and make a difference in the world also, as is universal love's just as is, simple as all are supposed, be great leaders and followers; as a man or woman, boy or girl you are destined of God well equipped is to be and to love and capable of loving and standing tall for what is the truth. We all are to love, be loved and blessed and that is of what inner joy is deeper.

Deeper joy and strength that inspires heart is with harmony and gratitude to be lovable is to be kind and just being alive is enough for me to know that power is of God and inspiration too is His blessings. Joy loving God and others back and is happiness and more resilient, purposeful, successful child of His also, that says that to know that we can learn to our potential and capable than we thought and seek further no more but is within! I am capable of loving Him back easily. I can easily love all of us because He loves, of what He has done for me and family from infant, childhood, through adulthood, keeps and making me happy and the joy in my heart reaching out, to touch others has been taught by Him most inspire and reaching out and through love find Him. Nothing beats finding your Spirituality, is meaningful!!

Always, being all is always there for me and mine all and answering our prayers always. All seasons, anytime, anywhere; God is everywhere and He is good so much am blessed to know and love and joy is to serve Him humbly is by my serving you and of all others on His behalf is so cool. Too, for He first loves me and you, God loves me much and being His responsible and lovable daughter is of joy for His love grows and matures me to be happy and successful that is He loves and blesses and values this child and joy of being His evermore and serving too is my pleasure and reaching out through the power of His love and words inspires me is how to love all of us. We all are blessed are to be just His loving and caring children, black or white it doesn't matter. Are stronger when we stand together is genuine love is one of the things that brings us.

Strength is togetherness, loves and inspires is valuable to show love, respect to each other and inspire and blessing me by His love, the encouragement and love of God's words, is power. And love and inspiration to me, God knows about each our situation and the intentions that is a blessing we get from our faith journey and is to be thankful in everything and that is what we are encouraged to hold unto; His unchanging grace and love. Is to be strong in faith, prayer, keep it up and loving and serving and trust, "let love and faithfulness never leave you; bind them around your neck, write them on the table of your heart" (Proverbs 3:3). That is what I am grateful for!

And that is also what we are encouraged by His words to note, no matter what it is He is with us and has been a blessing to me the joy of my heart, is learning, knowing more about love. And more about Him, knowing Him is better than what I had endured and more gracious power. His love gives me all the joys that challenges of life and journey are hold to Him and hold tight; to His unchanging hand and His unchanging love and power, love and grace all are unconditional and effective made so easy all that I was imagining and overwhelmed dispelled as changed, from story to glory. His grace' glory shines on my face reflections is on joys and love and peace, and is honor of God to keep me steady in mind and my heart alive, with eternal peace inside, is thanks!

Thanking God for joy and inner peace is for strength, hope, healing and comforting touch and for family and friends and for all. Also of joy there are so many things to be thankful for and, the list is inexhaustible there is nothing better than that love within me is happiness, hope and that I found a profound thrill and there is none like His love and power and inspiration. That is all we need peace with God is a great gift, is God provisions and resources are available. And, working from it is awesome blessings and God is so awesome and what remains is the joy to love evermore and with my love and thanks is that my heart couldn't hold than wells up too in praise to acknowledge of Him and I must return my thanks with love my open hands and heart to bless His holy name publicly. I receive with more gratitude, more blessings activates is thanking.

I lift up my hand to Him is from bottom of my heart. "Praise the LORD! For it is good to sing praises to our God; for it is pleasant, and praise is beautiful" (Psalm 147:1). I Believe in my great God, awesome is He and that faith that was first in my ancestors still lives on me is what I breathe from is the heritage and family of faith. My loving caring faith of my family dear descendants and loving hearts is always, what God keeps it refresh so that others will be blessed as well from is a deep well for those who taste for the living water is from the cistern that never ever dries. I must be thankful and, though, the devil when I was sick deprived living my life by unforeseen circumstances of life, and it was grace by that faith which it endures and, that inspires and increases as God led me and kept my faith refreshing it and for my hope is in Him overcome.

Yes, as I am an over-comer with joy. I am grateful that He touches my heart and teaches me always show me how to love you all. It is joy to know Him and to have and to be steadfast in trusting of Him and you know, that being scammed and the unexpected illness is often what can make life turns to a total around about as often, said, true "life turns around". Sometimes, is of a three hundred and sixty degrees Fahrenheit and what you can think of is not so pleasant. But, that is just a test of our faith and so it pleases, God to do His will as He sees fits and, knows all about your situation is what I am thankful for. As sees fit for me, and is much appreciating all the ways God influenced me in my life and is journey and tested by faith and I was blessed by God's love.

He helped me and healed and sustains refreshes and renews and satisfies me. Please, help me do the math, with all what I am blessed, how much God so loves me as 1997 was also serious one another trying time and tougher year, as well was physical situation; I landed at North Shore Medical Center. I had never knew what I was going to face, either; All I knew God was with me; also went in there and was in there with me and, that is all how much God loves endures daily.

He is for me and beyond measures eternal One is precious Healer. Mighty power that is He is the Word and His word is life; it does not only give us knowledge but more than that, yes! Is life-giving most love that is healing saves lasting spiritual's transformational power His Love! But, the dupers and those living fraudulently and thief is their work of hatred that makes them so very happy, you are buying trouble already for yourself and family, what you bargain. I am not a judgmental moralist or perfect but, believe or not, there's a living God of justice as much and He is the judge and does not stand for wickedness and rudeness and disrespectful behaviors either.

And, is against wrongful attitudes, victimization, terrorism, duping and fraudulent cruel acts and malice and deceitful behaviors and lies to scam all and, so we have to kick against such behavior and practice and wickedness only thrives when people fail to stand up and boldly speak up against injustice. The truth is all we need, too. And, it is the only way out is the solution that is ultimately that is better what matters in life most, and that can help and sets us absolutely free. And in helping we find as well answers to our human situations, individually and/or collectively.

The truth is the solution and love, is what we need most and is more to seek for and that is the answer that we are seeking to achieve peace and progress in our society. It is from seeking and inspiration both is from God, that is sooner and later, need is and the most important always. The need is there for we need order to achieve peace and also for our society love is the answers both is answer to our situations. The need is to pray more, for revival as only God is capable and He is our greatest Revivalist and let's pray for more to hope and enlightenment and education for us that is also a very important part of life and also all are what we need most is love and prayer.

That is repentance too is great. For people to come to know God is His blessings what we need and to do mostly, pray, for it's good to pray and intercedes for one and all that God will help us and arrest and bring them as cuprites to repentance. Culprits that most is they need help to be touched by God's love, they can repent. And, be inspired by words of His truth. Why love and inspiration is so crucial is all beneficial, so is for us and the world as a whole and that is the best.

The world is in need of more good people than the wicked bad mean creatures. As, is all over places today we see those worst than yesterday and so many are worldwide terrorizing all is people wrongly is Left and right young and old; on the other hand, "we are to tolerate the good and the bad and grow together until the harvest time come" (Math. 13:30). That is inspired to fight war against anything that it raises ugly heads to torment, invade, don't let them invade you or yours. And or your neighbors and friends known and unknown are to be our "brother"/sisters keepers.

As your territory, stand and hold tight to God's unchanging grace and apply the tools as given and it is effective and believer or not, God listens, answers and sees all our tears and heals us as well through the Words and the incredible power of prayer can also moves the mountains of our lives. And so, we have to tackle the enemies and prayer is best tool for spiritual warfare that is something as well what is workable, and is not a fist fighting and prayer is for us to be of serious commitment. It is for a highly emotional situation and likewise physical! For me prayer that what results this action as it resolved and this is my public thanksgiving and also is testimony is for others to know God is with us even in the desert He too, fights our battles and abides with us.

Scattered enemies and their plans thwarts and returns their negatives to them and that is it becomes destructive themselves and they are exploiting all that is good theirs. And so I thought I let you know as we are living in a time that the terrorists are on rampage and destroying others is actually themselves and all that is good that God has blessed them with. Is so sad and that could be all something for us to be really think about the point of greatness in the heart. And they need power of inspiration for hope and it is only in our humility before God that greatness is revealed and that says seek, hook up to more with what is more inspirational and significant spirituality is that is the way that we need to stand in the cap as intercessors and life as I see needs more love; and inspiration for overcoming is always something for celebration and thanksgiving always too.

I especially want to take advantage of this time again thank God for grace in fervor, and of giving me this moment, keeping mostly, and enabling grace in strength and for opening doors for me. In my journey is the opportunity, for me to successfully complete my education; Leadership training certification program, as am trained for ministry and more to be thankful for everything. In my life and all situations also happens for a good reason(s) and is for increased and growth and prosperous living is and for God inspiring my passion and in my faith journey mostly, blessed to love and blessed me serving Him is love of the Lord. March 13, 2014, unforgettable was another.

Indeed, defining moment in my life, when, I received certificate of successful completion from inspire Women, accompanied with a congratulatory letter from Mia Kang Yoo, who herself is very loving sweet Vice-President. I graduated from the Inspire Women's Leadership Institute, Houston and that is awesome work of the Lord of the grace and divine favors and that is exactly. What happened to my life and blessings and I had no idea the Lord has always surprises us at the turn as

I know Him had knew about my situation and my heart's desires as well my passion, as I had prayed how to make me happiest in my journey is gave me my heart's desires but, I had no idea this was His purpose for me to take me on this faith journey; met me at the point of needs!

Please, see details in chapter six is even more testimonies inside, how much God loves me and loves you and how it is possible too is an inspiring story how He works with me always. God knows how is all, He is who blesses and in every details of our lives and gives us, our heart desires and knows how to do. Placed me in the right place is also His timing, right people to be in my path, my blessings in an unknown moments and steps ahead of me has me covered as well. Made provisions for me where there was no more hope and filled of the emptiness of my broken heart. He made a way where there was no way fill His providence and is all for my joy and to be more thankful and how grateful is my heart and, for successful completions of the program too?

I am so blessed and am excited also for all of you and don't forget love is everything and it is the heart's power and is a blessing from above and what a joy for to be so favored and very much grateful I am appreciating of God and of us and too is as I am and for my God and children and from home and abroad everyone. I have been loved and inspired and from the children who love from Mom's heart am always greatly indebted to you. And, do give some love also to our most loving greatest Dad is God of all our great dads, is for you keep the flag flying and I love you! But, please don't forget is God our Almighty heavenly Father who does love you and most.

And, for my lovely children is thanks again is for you foster my love and borrowed me of yours from endures is God loves you and gives you grace for your joy for me that is both of you, it was "I love you mom!" For, it is, love fosters the inspiration. It has also becomes my- passion, I love all kids/youths very much! Forever love from Mom, and I may not always say that everyday love you to know is to you are but now you know! (Pat/Comfort), thank you making me proud mom as well creative mom that is inspiration, fostering love of which you both inspired me with love!

I don't forget God's our Love is hope and faith in action, words and deed and calling on God, is believing in Him as well as those who love believe in you and I a believer and is to thank God; for you are blessed everyday of the year and is evermore. This is for all ages and love is for us also! Is true love is of God and that capacity is to receive openly from Him and saturate one's thought for Him and He gives us all and is all for us a gift to equally treasure appreciatively and I receive daily and is my responsibility that I give and grow more soaring is daily, is His kindness.

His love and words of love and spirit of love, I am confident that is also all what matters and makes a great difference for we need each other. His love is my joy, power and is secret code is and grace. That is the gateway from Scripture and God Himself we can find love and joy and inspiration is and wisdom and matters and comes from God only and His love overflows as is a blessing is joy. Joy that He gives never ends with family and friends and sharing that love is joy!! And of grace is experiencing that peace of God within my heart the gateway is a greater grace. Is the mercy of God upon my life and that overshadows our lives has all that and is a blessing for His Love is beyond measures and best Gift is a Friend, whom no one else could have given me as He does, for there is no more beloved than He is and friend this is the thought that is all Love!

And my spiritual growth, how my life has God's joy and hope and happiness as well love. And fulfilled purpose, happy ending in the wilderness abundant of His love abounding there is! It's hope as well too! Grace is sufficient in my faith journey; this is how much it is happy ending is of deep joy and a beautiful ending and all my heart wells up in praise to the Lord Almighty. I am thankful for all that He has done as continues doing testimony as, Mia wrote: "Dear Daughter of the King! CONGRATULATIONS on completing Inspire Women's Leadership Institute. You have achieved an extremely important milestone in your walk with the Lord, and we rejoice with you for your faithfulness to God's calling on your life…" Mia is a lovely vice- president of the Inspire Women, Houston. There more on the testimonies and in this work and subsequent ones.

She is also among many of my blessings God-send to me so many angels my life is truly, I have seen the glory of God the best is blessed wherever, He sent me is to be and, is to bless my heart with joy and love and peace that is the most thrilling part of His love and He refreshes my heart; love fueling positive passion and renewed and transformed of my mind; brought me brand-new confidence and also brand- new joy with love and laugher is also is everyday. And of that is my hope and faith is powered. It is motivated more my faith is of God's love is His inspiration is my empowerment, for my heart is full of joy and self- improvement of my personal enrichment.

To be enriched and professional and spiritual growing me mature and joy and this was a refining moment of my life, successful completion. Chapter six has details story more on that as His love is and speaks to heart more inspiration. Is by love and inspiration, is a teaching moment between Father and daughter and, how much of His love empowers and this is how much what was hopeless is hopeful and He worked through me and others to see how it is love and joy more than enough blessings for my daily blessing is gratitude. So I continue thanking God for my life, and also what I am enjoying is benevolence of His grace that I have as well continue to enjoy.

Is every blessed day is with family, friends and all. My family is all known and unknown and also the beautiful people of my life as loved ones home sweet home, and my dear countries. Is to everyone how grateful that I am and happy and mostly thankful for there is no one like God is ultimately is who loves us most and always gives us the best of everything and everyday joy.

Friend, watch out second series that love is continuity and for now so long and we will be starting with Chapter One is coming your way soon as is Love is the heart's power. Healing, I see is the wonderworking spiritual power of God. And is all there is in life that Love is what can endure, and wins for us anything as God's purpose is for us to be in health, happy, productive, as well successful and purposeful, enjoyed and share love. He is the means and methods is by grace of God and quite a moving spiritual experience that there is no word for me can better ever that describes and, I can't sure why I am lost in transition of right word to describe wonder of God.

His love is so marvelous and who can describe that in words adequately, no one that for sure but thrust is Love. Who reveals all that is Love and I needed and is that is my path to trade as assigned to me too. He listens and answers our prayers daily and this is for my every answered prayer and also every miracle this is the day of joy the "D day." Today is a day of joy celebrating my love for and of Him too joy and love with public thanksgiving and, would love give everyone a little gift of love of His to be enjoyed all of us too together and that as given have to bless all. I am grateful is I have to is must do is seen is who is surely my Almighty, and He is, "My beloved is white and ruddy, the chiefest among ten thousands."(Song of Solomon 5:10). That inspires my passion and rejoicing and triumphantly the blessings all of words of God it is inspiration, inspires and encourages and educates the heart and renews the mind transforming and am brand new too!

And am living this triumphant life and blessing is who guides, inspires, transforms. I am blessed empowers and made whole is God who loves all and He loves me most and His favorites loves me I am for real. Father's favorite, prays with me and for us all and teaches me as well the secrets of contentment and all are inside this you will find more testimonials from me and others and is including this introduction as a special chapter but both combined and each with inspiration for us all.

Everyone is welcome with warm heart; this offers us faith, hope and love. Be it young or old, needs Love, helps with anything they can turn to Him and use those powerful words. Easily, than clichés are words to overcome are all capable is power the love, God is Love and praying the word's praying His will for us, and it makes life more bearable much as His all is love, and joy is, I am the healed and I am returning my thanks, for there is hope and, victory and something to be thankful for. That is the Lord's Healing and Comforting Touch. And we all need and that is of encouragement from God Almighty and from the Lord's God is sustaining power is amazing grace Love is that Love is incredible and God for daily shines me my face as am able to take a bold step of faith. Moving forward by stepping out of my comfort zone, using those words and at mention of God's great name and all using them powerful Source and resource resources, as I have gained much is from His knowledge and is the wisdom.

That power of inspiration. I have gained so much wisdom guided by His gentle hands and thankful also for my parental priceless love that they taught me about the love of God always. It is awesome and hopeful. Pleasurable and His wisdom is of joy has already put a blessing in heart and hands all that remains is to apply and put them to use. Is there to use them, cultivate and why don't you use the love? God's good and I appreciate Him for His treasures are infinity and joy for me is to open up my heart to Him and by embracing has also taken me to places that is marvelous experience, helping me to become a blessing is surely infinity, and how do you feel about God's graciousness? Awesome! It is and how do you use your love and potential given by God's grace to inspire you! I encourage friend, open up to power, infinity, and how do you use your love given by God's mouth and potential?

The power is given and, if you want to know how, where and what and who all says (Acts 1:8). Expect to be blessed and is experience the joy of the Lord!

That you possessed within is limitless potentials and some are never ever yet to be tapped from. Are you using it for your pursuit of happiness and self- improvement and for the benefit of others and beyond your family and friends? Use and are what you make of your life that is gift of love is available and Is all we need and, yet, is by choice, and is not by duress am blessed, to lean and learn is by grace how God's love inspires by it; I am able to do what I never thought. If you really want to know how, what, who and when to apply, is to ask and seek is how you will find is Him and have faith is favor the entire Lord, "The beginning of wisdom," and He abides in you!!! And, you're important!

And for me is thankfully, that He is all loving. And supernaturally caring and His love is, can be so infectious and magnetizes my heart is And, I decided a long time ago not to let how people see, think or judge to bother and to focus on how God loves and, how He sees of me. And that settles it for me, is sure rather than to be about what people think of me and scared me to be shaky and have phobias and get distracted. I look up more to Him and I rather have Him than all what is complicating to life and that is too much baggage to carry and the weight all God doesn't want us carry, too much and, so He simplifies my life and got me on board His side. And is away off from that entanglement of the world and hearty is to be contented with simple priceless love treasures of life I have peace of mind and that is, priceless, which is my daughter's her favorite motto: "Peace of mind is priceless" and name Comfort and, I couldn't agree more is joy to know.

Is a great gift of God and with faith that grace I am from much weight and the demand of this world and I am blessed being myself; cut my coat according to my size, is just awesome to have peace of mind, rather than how people see me is how does God, see me? Is a better question as periodically, I take time to evaluate myself and, ask myself, "How does God see me, and am I living the life that He wants me to live and do His will and not my will and not as others want for me to be, and do only for them and none at all for me and my dear loving heavenly Father who is the one that gives me life and the very present help in time of my trouble? That is my question?"

And supposed to be the first that is whom I am obligated doing for His glory and honor as such how does God see me not joining all kind of sorts of affiliations? Just for me to belong and identify with people who do not even want my physical, let alone my spiritual progress and don't want to see me alive? Productive of life, and I am to walk by faith as do well to, "Bear one another's burdens, and so fulfill the law of Christ" (Galatians 6:2). I thank God for Jesus to have a chance and taste of God's love and have blessings of joy that is with vision of hope with joy as well He gives me brighter future in my life, a cure for me is true genuine love and not fake/false pretense! That is a disaster, buying trouble for you right there and is best to do God's will first!!!

And, praise and serve Him for it is pleasant and, I cut my coat according to size and, in life or death His love abides and remains is joy, to be happy for His love is the greatest this is for all of us. All ages and all circumstance and for all professions and is a very good gift to anyone as is handy, family-friendly and racy, a great resource and fills with words of compassion and love, as we may know God is a great companion. His touch of love and joy and His warmest thoughts are always with us everyday to comfort us and am, so glad that He helps me writes my story of how much He loves me and love is healing is balm and unfailing and testimonial is of His Love!

It is to be read prayerfully to read along with your daily devotion- The Bible is all about God's love and human condition and is for our daily use and is family friendly as well this is also given by Him to us and is a classic work and more is a friendly reminder and aim as always is to inspire you and mostly, I am to glorify Him foremost and much grateful exalt you all, you're also part of my blessings. As my brothers and sisters both young and old is by extension and, all is of His gifts to me. I do this to glorify God and give Him due respect so this is my gift from the love of God and for this and more I give Him all my love and forever and ever more, I will love Him.

And, it's really amazing all He does for me is awesome. I thank Him for being my Source and means and strength and inner peace and healing and comforting touch and joy have given all of His love and gifts to me unique as the most pleasurable is everlasting is the Love and precious present; and it is borne of love of God and passion both spiritually and for our physical wellbeing. Spiritually my gift is my Redeemer and, and we are all gifts of love to one another, and from that Source too is my joy and happiness mostly to be of hope and aspire to be inspired more Salvation is by grace of God that I am here and made to be who God destined me to be through His love.

I know Him personally through His Son, and it is, I have seen the salvation of the glory of God I love Him so much and look what my Jesus did for me and, my family, I found my true Friend in Him to be all that God wanted me to be and shines me on with love come rain or sun, is nothing changes; for it is always Love everlasting and spirituality promotes positive love healing. That has Love remains is Love's power that have all the wealth of this world is my experiencing that excitement of peace of God and so, I am more than happy and grateful for life, my recovery and discovery, and His "loving kindness is awesome Joy!" The power and glory of God that is to share is awesome and what makes me and my heart rejoices and (Psalms 63:3), is there. He is the connector with the heavenly Father and I know for sure, we are all connected is by heartstrings.

Yes, we are all connected by the heartstrings and words of God is the linked the healing Word is by grace and, I see heaven and earth linked together in us is by heartstrings that is joy to know Him. Love of His Words of God are inspiration and all are powerful matter is of the heart and grace is through Scripture and through God Himself, is by the Holy Spirit. Peace, Joy, Life is all of them and, so life is all about Him, not us is Him first before all others. He is alive and real, you will find spiritual power it is the only way is through Him and, He is also who loves us most.

He lights us all through those words and more inspiration will surely come to you is with love and joy into your soul is but your heart, fills you with His love and joy is power; Inspiration is a legacy inspirits passion mesmerizes my heart daily and, faith in God only is of that power. Is what keeps you smiling and is through the love of God always thrills my heart. That inspires me is and makes my mind to be saturates my thought of more love for Him. And once your thought is in a good spirit and positive things placed in your heart it is clear and with pure and true love.

Is obvious for God is love. And the feeling, is so awesome experiencing God's peace also phenomenal never something to better tell or can it better explain it is out of this world, nobody else can better explain for you and/or details of the excitement or knew by description am sure is. Only feeling, for quality is not something that you can explain, is experiential and you can only feel. You must experience to feel and absorbed the present moment which is full of joy that is l am saying from my heart what I feel and one must through one's self by grace to best experience.

That is the thrill of life, as often said, "Experience is the best teacher and here is obvious. His joy is best to be acquainted and that is experiential traveling to higher level of thought and is knowledge that wisdom is given only by marvelous to be so is grace of God. That power is what is amazed and His Grace, it can heal and cures and overcomes anything for us. And restores it is sure and can heal and save and mends all what was broken and as fixing all is easy. It is what comes from Him of God's Love that I have that privilege of first hand is Power is only in God to trust and hope and, not on my power or yours is His. I am so grateful that my journey ends well!

And only He gives as your heavenly Father the Creator and, He created all the things that we have been enjoying! I am included and we all are beneficiaries of the grace of God and much as we are creatures, we are inclusive among all and are benefitted from that very blessing and are celebrating with us as well inspiring my heart overwhelmed with excitement is of the recovery is <u>discovery of joy and love and inspiration we all are blessed by God. Beneficiaries of His Love as He abides in us and He also who invites us to diner, that is abiding with Him and that</u>

blesses us. Is what am being grateful for me being His lovable as child and be us great and small, young/old, God loves us and has us in His heart.

God is who has the answers to our every need as Creator of heaven and earth made us in His image and, that is, "Marvelous are thy (His) works." Clearly as crystal ball (Psalms 139), see please verse, it is 14b! And that is for me is my thankfulness, I don't know about you, but I know for me that is what is for me is there is hope with a brighter future for me hope and joy and peace as it is the blessings that Love and the verse also is self-explanatory. It doesn't take a brainer!

Nor does it requires scientific/laboratory observation. It is just plain priceless truth and is the powerful Words of God's mouth and there is no need for experiment is spiritual, just to taste it and eat and you will be amazed. Taste and see for the Lord is good and trust and obey to do all as being what He says and that is faith is what takes experiencing that Love that is all is are about Him for me to claim faith: "For I am fearfully and wonderfully made!" Else, you be drifted lost along with the madness crowd to the wrong places and loss in the big crowd and that is really so sad, missing all the goodness and greater and mightier things God's has given freely always too.

It is my time to shine that light and tell it as it is the truths and all about those inspiring stories of heartfelt warmest love and how much God's loves me and visited me when I was His desperate child. Love is moving my life and is and this is all I have for loves, and answering my prayers and those of loved ones as well as others, miraculously transforming my entire world and reshaping me to become what He made me to be and, is resounding yes, that God loves me very much and answers and heals all my body and mind love is in these and, is what I can give back.

And, all is what I was given and, I openly received with love and gratitude the happiness and love and joy and am to give them back. I give and to the glory of God and as well for us and all to enjoy the benefits and as well for the edification of all those who believe in love the power is of His. Love and Gift of God and, I live by that faith can enjoy knowing that is everyday living it is to glorify Him. Affirm faith and power of inspiration all is His love, miracles of His power is what resulting this reading is, "Greatness is in the Heart-A Tribute to

Inspiration is happiness and joy is for us to enjoy together and celebrate as everyone is involved and that is why this is fun."

It is fun to write about the goodness and trust in God's and obey to do His will for has never ever fails in accomplishing His purpose for us (Psalms 138:8), please refer. I am sharing how, and show God's love has ability to deliver, heal, rescue, save and restore us and redeem as well builds us, our small faith can make a big difference. It moves mountains and it is a chapter same; Friendship is for sharing too all inside. For us to read more about what God has done and still doing and will never ever stops loving us as His own in trusting and doing His will and, pray. He has been very faithful to me is all by that faith to do His will only as I have benefitted and is more than blessed for my joy is of glimpse of hope for that hope exits and it is real in all of us. He is awesome God; believing in Him gives, "the right to become children of God" (John 1:12).

You have to first experience in order to better appreciate love as that Love. Power is the feelings and faith, is so great to feel that are to know that is the capacity for my life is of highest enjoyment and is clearly all that are evidences and so my soul is enjoying so much is question as "Who among us can say that we made it solely on our own power and strength? Can you answer to that honestly? Please, it is to remember, "A single bracelet does not jingle" (Congo Proverb). Simple and is plain priceless truth that is another answer! "**No man is an island entire of itself; every man is a piece of the continent, a part of the main... (John Donne)!**"

I love you to read about all the blessings that the list is inexhaustible and I thank you for reading and evaluate it on a case by case. I say basis, then you will know, where, what and who and, why and then see, why I am celebrating the love of God daily with love and thanks and with all of us. It is just a little bit at a time for this is a book that is going by series of five volumes and in one collection is still not to be all exhausted for more and more are given on a day to day basis and all is of joy receiving with gratitude. I am thankful is from Him to my heart is overflows His love and joy that can never ever ends without the blessings of also sharing and touching you and all others, is the occasion and it is this celebrates Him is more than deserving of my deepest love.

And my deepest gratitude and that is what I live for to love and thanks to Him everyday too. This is another opportunity to express my love for His never-ending kindness with eternal love and compassion. I cannot forget to be thankful and show my gratitude and I remember all what He did all! Again, I wish you the best that life has to offer, with greatness in the heart, and remember love empowers- so count your blessings and use your God's given gifts cultivate them fully all to their maximum potential. You will find that each chapter is with my appreciation and how the series runs is chapters one through five is ending of series two. Chapters six and special testimony to chapter eight end series three; Chapter nine to thirteen series four and then, from the Chapter fourteen to seventeen which is, Never Give Up sums it up, and each series, is all fine short stories and helpful and heartwarming and inspirational to inspire us and every series is a book of love/hope.

To be inspiring us and for healing and continues in the next chapters ahead are also inside inspiring, for regardless of our tears and pains and hurting remember, where there's faith is there can be hope and there is also victory for us and this the work of God and Is spirituality. For faith and for inspiration and self-help/improvement, all is motivational, inspirational is General and is spirituality is faith-based as my other books is great so is invitation and blessings is for the body, mind and soul is empowerment and is for everyone, any situation, is ageless. Family friendly is also for institutions and schools worldwide, from headstart through higher institutions universities and theological schools is God's gift for each, everyone and heart-warming, is what this makes it a must read for all of us, regardless of our spiritual leaning is all about love, "God's Love!" Loves us most it crosses boundaries, nooks, crannies of universe, transcends race/culture barriers!!!!!!

Friendship is for sharing and our codes of ethics require us to share vital information that is well useful and works. Poverty is also very much in high rise in so many society of the world in many places is due lacking love among them and not accepting the truth that makes free with absolute love. The limitations and many don't realize that Love is faith in action, words, deeds; And, I don't know what my life could become, while in the trail, had it not been for the love and caring heart of God and His love touching me, and is also by words of inspiration that inspires of my heart passion more and it ignited is more and motivates my passion everyday is an adventure and therapeutic, with love and gratitude, for there is hope for us!!

Power of love and inspiration sharing with you more testimonies interesting stories of love of God for us and I say Thank you Lord for this! To be continued friend!!! Thanks for your support and reading you'll enjoy and be satisfied with a rekindle' heart and All are appreciated and I'm so grateful that you care and love to read add this a great book to your finest collections, know is fun reading for family library for you and yours and generations to come and I thank God for you.

God bless us is so marvelous to know; that sums Love Empowers for there is joy and felicity of velocity is the happiness of the believer that is our: Greatness Is In the Heart: A Tribute to Inspiration That Empowers- A Tribute to Inspiration- shares Love that empowers is a compilation of Short Inspirational Stories that shaped our faith with words of love and comforts for hope. And for our joy, touching hearts &Tips for Using Unconditional Love and Acceptance to Shape Today's Youth is in 18 steps. It emphasizes positive encouragement for all; is of a brighter future for them. A series of five books in one great volume and is a great reading for each and all of us daily too to enjoy the goodness of the Lord God Almighty and is that power!! Please, pass the love on! Thanks and happy reading share with friends known and unknown all over the globe!! This ends our first series of the book/general Introduction!

(Note: please: You can read more from: *Parental Influence Matter; Priceless Love* and visit www.iuniverse.com and or dorrance.com; carothompson.com and or youthnfamily.org). Please, fund us for the translation of this book in various dialects, to help the masses and reach out more general population and help fund for videos and more).

CHAPTER ONE

Love Is The Heart's Power

"The greatest use of life is to spend it
on something that will outlast it."
– Lord Chesterfield.

The motivation for this book comes from a desire from deep within to invoke thoughtful words of love, faith, hope, and joy to help build our hearts with strong bonds in friendship also. Daily, my heart fills with peace, joy, and hope as I prepare to share these thoughts with you, as a dear friend to everyone across the globe. It is a joy counting these blessings, for my passion for humanity is priceless, and so is the power of hope, which greatly inspires me. This is one book which does not only inspire, but aims at effecting changes, and increases the depth our love for one another. Mostly, sound healthy, academic and moral influence at both local and urban cities of our society and the world as a whole for it is now my classroom, motivated by desire to help.

It is an opportunity with privilege for us to learn about the God's love and power, how is of inspirational and beneficial it is to support one another with compassion. The love to support a fellow kind for encouragement always is to the glory of God. There is beauty when we can be there for another and uplift the spirits with inspiration for hope. Love like Inspiration, virtually everyone can be elated and benefit from it, for we all can relate and use for our encouragement. Nothing beats brightening one's life with hope and puts a radiance of joy with a smile on your face like love. Think of the beauty of power of inspiration and how meaningful life when offers of hope with opportunity can go-love empowers to inspire the heart even more so than our faith!

During my time as a youth, the children of my community were more concerned with lasting and more valuable treasures from within. Some of these values included spirituality, compassion, kindness, responsibility, unity, valor, industry, ambition, and integrity, also all with appreciation and love. We realized that what mattered most was what was in our hearts and not the external beauty one may have. Our friendships were built with words of encouragement as we engaged our minds with practical wisdom, which enabled us to have a hopeful outlook on life with emphasizes on positive things and that encouragement to give us a hope and brighter future was most wonderful motivation with values on what is most significant and love and education.

As I write this, I am flooded with precious memories of the past that have made me the optimistic person I am today – one filled with love and compassion and unconditional love also. As I grew up, I realized that peace, happiness, and constant encouragement were the ingredients that resulted in lasting friendships. These traits definitely improved our quality of living because we were happier, more caring, kinder, and had an overall belief that a peaceful environment is of joy and could be achieved for all. The community that I grew up in had kind-hearted people who were willing to show their love and share their time with others. In today's environment, this is becoming more of a rarity. Many people today are more often than not filled with hatred and as unfriendly attitudes. It takes a heart of unconditional love, tact, wisdom, and inspiration, care to thrive in this world, because the heart needs happiness more than sadness and peace and love too.

A healthy, uplifting spirit and the ability to cherish everyone is the basic foundation that has enabled me to have such a positive outlook on life. I saw my upbringing from a very loving /interesting perspective. This perspective is uplifting to the spirit and is inspirational to note. It was absolutely a blessing which enabled me to have a happy childhood. Thankfully, the love in my heart that resulted from a joyous childhood resulted my dreams comes true too today in adult.

Unquestionably, it is rewarding to follow one's passion through the power of love is inspiration. It is also important that one does not fail to acknowledge the source of the blessing for hope. I am so grateful that I have not ignored the root of my passion; for the past ushers in the present.

Is those memories are precious and powerful for my hope in strength and faith as well. Remember that you cannot change the reality of what makes for your hope and happiness. Yes, my past influenced my future, but it did not determine it. Though the past cannot be changed, it can be referenced in a positive way. I say this proudly because I have profited tremendously all from the valuable lessons of my past that ushers in my present and given me the joy that is so profound. During my childhood days, these happy and unique are memories are ones that I will never ever forget; for they have taught me lessons of hope as well life as all raised my awareness on the importance of having positive influences, including the kindness and the love of God also.

The lessons learned were of great importance and helped inspired my heart with more of love and enthusiasm, faith enhancement is improvement in: quality of life, inner beauty, sense of hope is joy, responsibility, a love of faith, learning, reading, belonging, dedication, commitment, integrity, dignity, conscience, grace and practical wisdom. These blessings were inspirational, so fulfilling, and very important in my upbringing. It was better to be blessed with these traits than to fight over unworthy, materialistic things that were worrisome as problematic, so love inspires.

It is imperative to build one's life on a positive foundation, which I consider to be one of greatest gifts of love that lasts a lifetime. It is rewarding to have the ability to train children early in life for a positive, amazing legacy. By engaging those tender hearts and precious minds with the stimulating words of priceless love, the result will be a promising future filled with success.

It is joyous to recall and address these refreshing memories of those sweet hearts that were there to care. Caring pays, love is supreme, and a quality education and environment is just as important. Real beauty, I learned from my parents (a man and woman of wisdom), was not to be sought after in the outer world, but discovered in your inner world. Unequivocally, they were right: the real beauty that matters lies within us. It lies not on the outer surface, but inside, and by realizing this, one realizes that there is an overflow of deeper love within each and all of us.

As Scripture reinforces, "Put on a heart of compassion, kindness, humility, gentleness and patience. Beyond all these things put on love, which is the perfect bond of unity" (NASB: Colossians 3:12, 14). This is definitely what I feel to be true, because where else can peace, love, hope, courage, wisdom, and inspiration be found to show gratitude for our many blessings? Genuine love is all about the heart! Counting my blessings brings deeper joy to my heart as well is happiness, peace, hope, and encouragement to share with you all. Hopefully, we can all look forward to coming together instead of remaining divided, with inspiration guiding us in the right direction and love is always the heart's power and that too could be as well willing mind always.

What this peace pilgrim quote says is true: "When you find peace within yourself, you become the kind of person who can live at peace with others." Inspiration is love from within and is a legacy. Peace of mind is priceless and is given free to those who trust, "seek to pursue it," desire to maintain as it is a treasure, not necessarily to work so hard for it. In order for the world to have peace, there must be peace amongst us. By living a peaceful lifestyle and having a caring, loving heart, we can help the world become more peaceful. The goal should be to aspire for peace so that we as a people can enjoy living together in a progressive environment. Indeed, we can love ourselves as inspired, progressive, peaceful friends both at heart and action.

For the sake of our youth, living in a secure environment is good for them, so they need to be brought up and trained well with a civilized, sound foundation, because it promises us all a brighter and better future. Part of the reason we need to be open, sincere, and active participants. With love in our hearts is because a sincere, caring heart contributes to society and improves it. It is imperative to prepare our youth ahead of time because they need growing and developing a heart of minds filled with positive thoughts. Thus, we need to encourage unity and development. With actions rather than merely with words, and also become ideal listeners and communicators.

A child needs to be taught early in life, rather than wait until they are older and harder to manage. As the proverb says, "Early to bed, early to rise", which challenges our becoming more alert and committed to their good cause. The best of gift is our educating them on great love and greatness that comes with compassion for their achievements as investors. Are we ready to invest more love and promote quality education to help them and all of us together learn well? As often said, "Giving is receiving," that is an unequivocal truth. If we give them the blessings that comes with words of wisdom, blended married together of gift of love with the prospect of hope for today and tomorrow, they will not forget that and will have something substantial to offer society now and for generations after, which is a legacy with progress and growth for peace and success.

As the educator Immanuel Kant noted, "In teaching children we must seek insensibly to unite knowledge with the carrying out of that knowledge into practice." This is the best approach for the proper training, cultivation, and development of strong morals, self-esteem, confidence, and academic and leadership skills of our young. Certainly, as the saying goes, "An ounce of prevention is worth a pound of cure", applies when preparing our youth for the world that they will face. Early preparation instills disciple that enables our youth to be focused on hope, developing and enhancing their talents, skills, and aspirations in a befitting manner and way too.

Establishing, a unique and positive environment for their happiness results in happiness and progress for everyone, with future generations benefitting from a more positive society. With progressive minds coupled with growth and a peaceful environment, everyone's life will be prosperous. As a people, we need to work on rejoicing, hopeful and helping to uplift our hearts blessed with informed, knowledgeable minds. Unequivocally, love is the foundation for progress as; it's a worthwhile endeavor to aspire to love, to improve our attitudes toward one another, and to celebrate this tribute to inspiration together. Love, along with knowledge, perseverance, faith, confidence, and empowerment makes it all worthwhile, for it is ultimately for the common good of society, which is the thrust of this book, because nothing can compare to love. Love aims to stimulate our thoughts by inspiring practical words of wisdom, making us great happy people.

As a matter of fact, we are always in the business of learning, growing, and improving ourselves and our general welfare. Undoubtedly, unique individuals with great minds that think positive learn and grow. It is a good practice to promote. As the proverb says, "Great minds think alike," and as the slogan of the United Negro College Fund eloquently states, "A mind is a terrible thing to waste." Sir Winston Churchill puts it more succinctly by stating "The empires of the future are the empires of the minds." Hopefully, all minds are together joining forces to pursue love and peace in the world, but keep in mind that love and peace begins with our hearts.

Whether we are young or old, age is irrelevant, studies have proven that at any age, you can accomplish anything you set your mind to, if you commit to it, with passion from inspiration is joy, something unique can be done with a little inspiration to spark love at any age stimulates. Definitely, anyone all can contribute positively to the growth and progress of society, if inspired of love. Together, loving and caring hearts delight in having positive thoughts and to be ready "to ride high, rising and shining" above and beyond our tribal and racial slurs. When we possess ego-driven thoughts, we are not able to progress, and we eventually are drawn backwards instead of going forward. So we need love that is of joy and vision of hope with a brighter future works!

Remember that greatness in the heart makes unique individuals with wisdom, love, and kind and is of peaceful souls. Unity will eventually bring about peace, and it encourages success amongst our youth by enabling them to live, grow, develop, and harness their skills and talents to the fullest. In every heart/society, hope's prospects center on happiness, a blessed environment. Living by working in harmonious and peaceful community, which is what all societies strive for.

A blessed community is a society of growth and love that welcomes peace and progress. Peace, love, faith and hope go hand in hand in creating this blessed environment. Characteristics that are great as are what society needs most. Regardless of one's age, gender, and social status, race, creed, or tongue, we are all unique in our own ways and we all need love and peace in our hearts and environments. Love is always a matter of the heart, and it determines how one looks at life. We can be all achievers and innovators as well as great leaders/ followers as highlighted.

We need to live a life filled with love from the inside out. It is apparent that having love like eternal peace which is priceless on the inside, is more hopeful and encouraging to everyone, and also encourages unity. Absolutely, eloquently, "There is unity in strength," says immortal word of wisdom. This is what the world needs most, rather than us living in bitterness, division, discrimination all resulting from hatred, leading to jealousy, envious, greed and power struggles, being the world's products and most likely stemming from interest of selfish gains love is better. Love flourishes more with peace than with war and chaos, which brings about fear and can tear the world apart. Is bitterness, nursing hatred and spreading slander all over the place (Pro.12:22).

When our hearts are filled with emptiness, frustrations, and shattered dreams, this will be, only stifle the growth of love, happiness, and joy that is needed to avoid hardening hearts. Hearts that lack the necessary love needed to foster a positive environment can result in hateful living and violent acts. Peaceful resolution is about harmoniously settling issues with love, joy, and humble wisdom and taking responsibility as well. Knowledge and wisdom are crucial tool in life and, mostly helpful to us and constitutes of foundations in having a loving heart and inspiration.

As this proverb says, "Truth does not blush", and yes, unequivocal, is so true, as wisdom and knowledgeable insights can enhance our ability to understand how to harness our lifestyles to productivity and most importantly, enable our leaders to have vision that goes beyond politics as well as selfishness. Indeed, they can be all that, fair and humane, though politicians can love. The leaders that think only of their own personal welfare at the expense of their (his or her) own citizens (especially the poor, needy, and homeless) are only hurting themselves and everyone around them by keeping these citizens from the help needed to achieve love and hope in hearts.

We need peace to bring more love and truth into the world, and wisdom enables us all the process for peace and progress to occur. We also need more hearts filled with love and peace all across the globe. The power of love and peace is a force greater than that of hatred, and sure the worst thing we could do is live a life of destructive acts. But, By ensuring that the heart matters the most, we can stand united and work and grow as a people, with our actions reflecting the fact that our hearts are inspired and filled with love, for together we can. Yes, love accomplishes much as team.

When we have peaceful and loving hearts, there is always hope that fairness and justice with equality will be possible. Every human want a community that is of charity and justice. Where there is heart of wisdom with conscience is when things are done well and beneficial to all due inspired faith and spirit of love in oneness. Any individual driven by love of passion to care and bless to share is human, so loving heart of compassion is progress and harmony. Heart that cares is the real deal in my perspective. As John C. Maxwell rightly observed, "To handle yourself use your head. To handle others, use your heart."

These are words of inspiration that should be taken to heart. Norman Vincent Peale beautifully summed, "The most curative thought in the world is the thought of love." Life is meant to be lived with good thoughts and to benefit from the knowledge of these thoughts. We can always make something unique out of these thoughts, living prosperously to the fullest of our potential as purpose-driven individuals of dignity and integrity encouraging others as does self, which equals hope basically.

Hope, in general, lays the basic foundation for living a loving, prosperous life. Hope is positive and brings about a more meaningful, loving life. This combined with love, peace, faith, perseverance, and intellectual abilities, are virtues of the greatness in our hearts. Having the knowledge and the informed mind with the understanding of love is the power that makes all the difference. I always believe that "giving is receiving", as that is what I was taught and observed wisdom witnessed that from my environment where I was highly breed. Also, confirmed Booker T. Washington "Those who are happiest are those who do the most for others."

Once an individual is transformed into a life and heart filled with love, nothing ever feels the same again. He/she sees things in a different light – a light filled with joy with a heart that is educated and passionate. A heart of wisdom does matter most, with the blessing of love coming from above. God loves to guide and direct our steps on the path of His wisdom. Above all, loves to see us happy and planning and achieving our goals. Stay with directives of His guidance and principles as the by-laws of hope for success. It is a heartwarming feeling when we are able to plan and accomplish our childhood dreams. My heart is filled with joy and peace, with a deeper love of unspeakable joy, which highly motivates me and inspires me greatly in this interaction.

The boundless love that I receive from above is the motivating factor that inspires me to launch out on this mission by faith. All because there is hope, is certain that there is a chance with positive influence and progress will occur and, bound to offer encouragement too. As Isaiah 40:30 states, "But they that wait upon the Lord shall renew their strength; they shall mount up wings like eagles, they shall run, and not be weary; and they shall walk and not faint." True faith takes courage and is similar to a kite, with an opposing wind which raises it higher. As word of Scripture encourages, "Be of cheer!" Mostly, "Hem your blessings with thankfulness so they don't unravel" (unknown author).

I truly believe that there is inspiration in human hearts. I also believe that this comes from the grace of God, whose power enabled me to gain the wisdom I needed for my life. The ability to write and inspire hearts is not of my own power, but from the power of God. Certainly, God's love speaks wisdom and releases blessings to each life. Remember, "The tongue has the power of life and death and they that love it will eat thy fruit thereof" (Proverbs 18:21). His plans are for all of us to have hope and blessings, and nothing less than prosperous living added.

The power of hope being achieved with joy and peace is a wonderful feeling! Through the same power of inspiration, many hearts are filled with hope. He always surrounds us with His presence and loving kindness. As the saying goes, "Power belongs to God" (Psalms 62:11). He loves us so much, and He wouldn't give anything than the best of His love, which is the unspeakable joy I feel. There is nothing His power of divine grace cannot handle, as gift of love.

I am just so thankful that He trusts and honors me with so much – and He did so because of love! Being blessed was included in His biggest plan, and His love is destined with favor (Jeremiah 29:11). He is life's everlasting, peace and divine Inspirer, destined to give mankind a wonderful future filled with hope. I've always known in my heart that God has a lofty plan for us, but little did I know I was going to be this blessed with inner peace, strength and deeper joy.

I had no clue that His planning was in preparation for my heart to be filled with the love and joy that I feel as I write this. His glory in acknowledging the power of the greatness in the heart is a joy that I am sincerely thankful and blessed for, He has been so good and beyond love awesome. In my estimation, He has demonstrated His incredible and amazing love, which is and always will be unconditional. If we fill our hearts with inspiring thoughts, every heart will be as happy and excited, shower Him with gratitude and love - because hope and faith inspires us all.

In my heart, I believe that His love is faithful and everlasting, blessing us with the joy the newness of a kind, loving heart. Daily, His love gives hope through inspiration for the young and old. I glorify The Higher Supreme Being as the "Author and Finisher of your faith." He is ever-present, with His grace and faithfulness always upon us blessings, for us to enjoy all that is in His heart. His promise to us is that His strength can take us places – places we never knew possible. No one knows when and where the future will carry us, but there is joy when He calls on us to serve in any capacity. The power of His presence inspires hearts everywhere, is peace!

As a child I was always very curious and wondered why my family was always in the habit of offering the community their services, and even when some of them didn't have enough to eat, they still reached out to everyone with sincerity. As I grew up, my heart became wiser as I learned about love and serving with a heart of kindness. That is real greatness, all about hearts of love, for "love is like the five loaves and two fishes, for they don't start to multiply until you give them away." His Love is heart's power and peace (Ephesians 2:14).

When we teach children the lessons of life, we come to realize that, "It is more blessed to give than to receive", awesome know that "we are not called to live up to others' responsibilities, but to our own." I have learned many lessons of wisdom in my lifetime, but one thing I have never forgotten is my family's love and how they lived their lives with my best interests in mind.

Ultimately, in the words of Albert Einstein, "We are here to serve one another." Is a great blessing to be resourceful child of God and give heart of love these words of wisdom say, "Love one another as I have loved you" No love is greater than God's love, which speaks volumes. "I am among you as One who serves" (Luke 22:27). When hearts are filled with pure joy in being able to be faithful servants of His, we can all realize that, love empowers and unity is progress is sure to love is to reach our goals successfully. "Happy are the kind and merciful, for they shall be shown mercy" (Matthew 5:7). Absolutely, positive His love, grace, and mercy are unconditional and everlasting, and when we are kind, and generous with our hearts, we will always be blessed.

Hearts should always be encouraged and hopeful because He is everlasting Lord of love is all, whose glory empowers, inspires, and surrounds us with His presence and, loving kindness never ceases ever fails but flourishes, which is sweeter than life itself. More thoughtfully relayed inspiration by Henry Van Dyke that, "There is a loftier ambition than merely to stand high in the world. It is to stoop down and lift those around us a little higher." God's power is word of love is that brings healing to heart, health and happiness to you and I. Uplifting to soul and the joyous gift and voice, the unspeakable joy, which was mentioned previously, that is the blessing which inspires empowerment inspiration is powerful words can make life to be of more hope, anytime!!

God's gift from above is powerful and inspiring, and ultimately, His voice is within reach of every heart. He blesses every heart with hope for today and the future, and as in the days of yesterday, forever more continuously brings joy to every heart that is broken. His tender love is whispering voice it brings peace and rest daily from deep within. The heart moves joyfully, and the power of the spirit of the living word is alive and real. Your heart rejoices as you hear Him, and my faith makes me a believer of this testimonial. Unquestionably, life is beautiful you're of heart filled, "with all joy and peace," as Romans 15:13 confirms, "May the God of hope fill you with all joy and peace." The hope that He places within all of us becomes our greatest source of success. That is the great pleasure in life: fulfilling your purpose with hope and everlasting joy. We don't lose faith in hope; we depend on it with deepening love. God is the perfect source of joy for mankind, but that knowledge alone does not solve our situation as human beings in the quest for loving hearts.

Ultimately, there is the power of the inspirational words of wisdom, which is beneficial to life itself. It is more than we may humanly think, and the inspiration is a glorious gift that surrounds us constantly. This inspiration flows as a blessing in everyone's heart because God's love is for everyone. He is the sweetest friend of all friends, including the unloved. He is an everlasting inspiration of joy, and I thank Him every day for blessing all of us with grateful hearts, for He is worthy. To begin with, I didn't think living in the chaotic world; it would be possible living a life of love this much. He is the ultimate solution to humans' needs, and He is a problem solver of all things impossible are possible with Him.

That is why I proudly give glory to the Lord. He is capable of changing all of us from negative to positive. He offers hope, empowers informed minds, and transforms all lives. He alone has the answers to everything as he is the master Designer, the Architect, and the sole Planner of our lives. From His sincere heart, He transforms hearts to become loving, all by the power of His greatness – the highest in love and glory. His love is an inspiration to my heart is everyday joy He inspires all hearts and gives best to those who trust and obey His will believing! Simply put, those leaving their choices in His hands are greatly empowered, strengthened, and are encouraged. Indeed, with prayers, blessings of love, and encouragement, hope is abundant. He inspires us daily to be transformed – to have an informed mind and an educated heart filled us with knowledge, wisdom, and understanding.

I implore all of you to continue giving your love to one another for the sake of changing our lives and the world for the better. Encouraging our hearts and those of others changes an unreal world only dreamed about to a reality. As we work together as a team, we can accomplish more. As the saying goes, "United we stand, divided we fall." We should all be willing to help someone solve their problems, and we must remember to love genuinely from the heart, because its power provides unity and strength. I pray that this book will help those with dubious hearts realize that joyful, loving hearts will inspire them to greatness.

Ultimately, love from sincere hearts encourages our hearts and inspiration comes along as well with the love of God, everyone is blessed as that empowers us to become prosperous. We are blessed capable of loving, must be able to offer the necessary help to whoever is in need with it an opportunity to excel, because God's love and his love is ours, which transcends the human and race cultures. Regardless, of race, tribe, tongue, color or creed, our love should go beyond boundaries and given out of sheer compassion, and that is what makes the world to become a better place---universal love is good!

Genuine love of the heart to everyone who needs it, is offering help for hope and it goes a long way. It warms our hearts, and no matter how small of your kindness is love and love should be appreciated. As Mother Teresa says, "There are no great acts, only small acts done with great love." Think passion with wisdom to serve and bless! It is rewarding and hope when one can care to reach out in love and touch the broken at hearts! This proverb sums it up: "You can give without loving, but can never love without giving." Love is the heart's power, and that is what the world needs most: loving hearts that can love and give! Love that goes beyond words and without thinking race or tribe makes the world to be at peace and creates more and more love. True from the heart, love is for our empowerment, and has a lot of benefits that can open more doors of opportunities for us.

CHAPTER TWO

The Power and Joy of Inspiration

"I know God will not give me anything I cannot handle.
I just wish He didn't trust me so much."
– Mother Theresa

I pray that everyone who has the opportunity to read this book will be revived with the power of love of God and in finding inspiration in their lives. Educated to know God's purpose, and find empowerment and live to fulfill God's purpose. Finding joy of inspiration has blessed my life and that is what mostly is my passion and I believe, everyone can be blessed when inspiration is inspiring to grow in love, becomes unique, accomplished vessels used by God to lovingly reach out to all hearts that need their joy and inspiration. Indeed, is thrilling life bringing love and joy to ourselves and to others is a thing of beauty. I tell you my reason why? Because, a heart that is blessed love overflows and joy never ends with family and friends, thus, with a life shared brings joy, not only to you, but to others and is encouragement and empowering love well, inspires all!

If one reads inspirational materials daily, the words are intended to nurture and nourish hearts so that one can prosper from His wisdom. God's word, unlike ours, comes from infinite wisdom, and scripture is filled with stories of inspiration. He gives a love that comes from deep within and gives best to those who trust and obey Him.

Praying and seeking after "a heart of wisdom" will bring happiness to yourself and will enable you to be a productive member of society who can encourage others to build confidence and hope for their own happiness. A life of happiness shared not only brings joy to you but to others as well, and one who blesses another is rewarded with the joy of inspiration and power to hope, among other remarkable benefits. "Happy are the kind and merciful for they shall be shown mercy." Little did I know I was going to be blessed sharing this much with every hearts.

If you do not know where to turn to get your blessings released, do something about it to change your situation. Get on your knees and realize that you need the heavenly Doctor. Do not wait any longer to find your source of inspiration and creativity from love and of inspiration. All you need is a heart filled with delight and one who is willing to seek wisdom and to understand it that love, peace, truth, faith, and comfort and all with joy are divine blessings and are gift of love from heaven and comes with empowerment. As the saying goes, "ask and you will receive, seek, you will find, knock, it is going to open" (Mathew 7:7). You have a path to trail in the quest for laughter, faith, power, passion, persuasion, love, hope, and an overall productive life within you!

There is no need to look far, for the answers you have been searching for are right in your front and of within you. If you have been searching everywhere for this feeling of contentment and have not been successful in finding it, it is because it is found from within and not outside. It is not necessary to look outside for something that is found within your own heart. By realizing this truth, your mind will be set free from self-imprisonment. As I believe Donna Gephardt, an inspiring teacher, said, "A love of learning doesn't stop with graduation. Your whole life will be learning and growing experience, whose extent can only be imagined" She is right, "Life will be your classroom." I learned and observed many things about life is by inspiration and love is too!

This is what life is all about is to grow more by living learning is love of heart and, even democracy is a lifelong learning process. There's certainly nothing as powerful as an education, which infuses the mind with knowledge. Wisdom, especially which, comes from above, is much of joy and unique. It is never acceptable to ignore the many blessings that you have. You are all blessed and destined to become gifted and prosperous and to responsibly harness your gift for progress. The lives that we are given are meant to be lived with quality and purpose and to be lived without unnecessary pain, conflict, and waste. I ask that you please "use the talents you possess; for the woods will be very silent if no birds sang except the best."

Do not ever take for granted the potential that you all have, for it is your pride and will enable you to have a very successful life. Believe it or not, we are all meant to harness our gifts to their fullest potential. Be thankful to the generous Giver of these gracious gifts of love – gifts that are yours to love and appreciate. Once we have realized that these gifts are within our reach, we should cherish them and hold on to them tightly. We should all dare to always have joy in our hearts so that our happiness will last a lifetime. As the saying goes, "Happiness comes from within, and relies very little on exterior things, for it is in us; truth does not blush." Undoubtedly, happiness is a gift of love from above and comes from the peace within you. Joy is never found in material things; it is within us.

We need to bring more truth, love, and peace to the world. Wisdom matters and the gifts of joy and love are priceless things sent from above. The gifts that are bestowed upon us by God are all stored within our hearts. The heart is always capable of allowing us to live a happy life and to have an inspired soul. Writing this chapter has been fun for me, although it has been challenging and has caused me to reflect on a number of issues. Indeed, as I am writing this chapter I have stopped repeatedly and have been amazed over the joy that inspiration can give. I've pondered and reflected upon this thing of joy and the remarkable difference it makes in everyone's lives. Hearts that are inspired are blessed inspirers.

I realize that all of you that are sharing your guidance and wisdom are moved by the joy of inspiration as well. My own life has been impacted by some remarkable people, from the past as well as the present, who have blessed my life through inspiration. We need more people of wisdom to make the world a better place for us to live and prosper in. This wisdom has been passed down from generation to generation, starting with our ancestors, and is currently instilled within many of our world leaders and presidents, as well as everyday people such as you and me, making extraordinary things of our lives, and all because of His unconditional love and choices.

Humans, by nature, possess political minds, and many of us, especially in this day and age, are up to par with the politics of the day. Apparently, a lot of good things can come out of those who strive to change their environments with the offer of hope and opportunity to those who've been deprived of it. It fills my heart with hope and inspiration to have the ability to leave a legacy of hope, and though I have weathered many storms throughout my life, I am honored to be able to share my joys with you all. Those who are selfish and are only concerned of what to get themselves with their own gains and, that can make politics a disease associated with power and influence, though nothing is wrong with being a politician, but the one problem that is so much troubling, when not used in fairness and integrity to make life better for the masses.

"I, me, and mine" and money, more so than using politics to make a positive difference, and exciting living for all and progress to the "have not," as society needs help to be offered to the poor to have a part, just as the crumbs, that could benefit them; can be blessings of a chance and privilege as well for their growth and self- improvement as well for the society too. Overall, it is very inspiring to hear how many people were so interested in the recent United States presidential debates in their quest to gain even more wisdom. Everyone, from the young to the old is interested in learning from the knowledge and wisdom of others.

Happiness, like living faithfully, in part depends on taking a stand on your core beliefs, morals, values, and defending that which matters the most. In order to be able to do this, learning different viewpoints and opinions is very important. Words of wisdom that are spoken eloquently can take the heart to many interesting and new places, and like reading a good book, can take the mind on a journey the world over. Listening to gifted speakers such as former President Bill Clinton and President Barack Obama, among others, is powerful and fills my heart with joy!

While on the subject of President Obama, I must say that it has been incredibly moving and inspirational to hear the President in his many speeches that he has given. It takes a heart of courage to endure the challenges that he has faced, and I am sure that it is no easy task leading and likewise following, unless you have a humbled spirit and are inspired to make a change for the better. I am very thankful that the wisdom of God has given our President His blessings that are needed to guide his path with confidence and joy, for "Inspired leaders inspire others." It is a thing of joy, and in fact should be a responsibility, to encourage one another rather than giving unconstructive criticism, show more support to boost make it a dedication to inspire heart, bless.

Being blessed as one of your many advocates, I am encouraged by your inspiration and hope. Every individual is remarkable in their own ways with varying opinions, but many do not appreciate, those who are frank to be honest that, "truth does not blush!" Many individuals find that opinions different than theirs are not worthy of being considered. I especially am inspired by what offers more love and hope and inspiration these words of wisdom: "Ask not what your country can do for you" But what you can do for your country"-President John Kennedy.

He was right to encourage hearts to aspire for hope and greatness as, "Idle hands are the devils workshop", and I would add that so are idle minds, which is part of the problem with the world today. The loving and world's inspired first United States black President stated the fact, "You have no excuses not to change the world." Everyone, especially our youth, are prepared ahead of the game, so be ready to take the mantle of tomorrow's leadership with dignity and pride. Follow your heart diligently and make us all proud as our future leaders of tomorrow. My heart is pleased when you are achieving success.

As you read this book, please take that thought to heart, observed the philosopher Aesop, "No act of kindness, no matter how small is ever wasted." Our power is in the heart, and thought of mind comes first from the power of touch of love in the heart that is of compassion to care and to bless by inspiration and, then you can give of love by kindness and what is better like act of a kindness that encourages you to hope. You have a chance to excel and make a difference in the world. Think about how you can be an inspirer, who with admiration and motivation touches others with love, compassion, and empowerment. The joy and power of inspiration got me here.

It is very important that our leaders of the world walk "side-by-side" with everyone as a motivator and inspirer. What President Bill Clinton once said inspires and encourages me to this day: "We hold this truth to be self evident: All men are created equal and they are endowed by their Creator with certain inalienable rights that among these are life, liberty and the pursuit of happiness." Definitely, we have today in which to be thankful for the power of inspiration, celebrating it with joy, for we all are blessed to be inspired. Every blessed day is a day of hope, and that is why I use this and every other opportunity to be thankful.

Today, I am highly inspired by all the words of encouragement that I hear and by those who make use of their blessings to guide and encourage inspirations globally. We should all pray that the world become a better place for the leaders of tomorrow. Hopefully, this book, which is the first of a series of books about the power of inspiration, will give everyone the hope and courage to lead others to a better life. As a Nigerian-African American mother and sister with a mission of love, hope and inspiration for others, I pray that I can reach out to all of you so that your hearts can be inspired as well live life fully, mostly my passion for the youth/women too.

I have my reasons to mention those two groups, it is not a gender thing or favoritism, we are those who need more self-improvement as the ones tagged "Minority group," encouragement is what we need more to boost each other up that there is no reason to be limited by people who label and/or name calling. It is not at all a vain endeavor on my part, but one of idealistic values. As words of inspiration touch everyone across the globe, including Nigeria's first president from the minority states (Rivers), they offer more hope than despair. God's power of love is assuredly amazing. No one can make you feel inferior and tell you that you cannot do what God destined.

I am highly inspired by what God has done and put in His big plan and have you ever thought about taking delight in the simple pleasure of life to light up your world and shine the light for others to see the glory of God in you, and reflect who he is in you and who you are for Him and His glory? (2010-2015) President Goodluck Jonathan of Nigeria once stated this fact and has also said what is inspiring: "If our leaders at all levels, whether political leaders, community or religious leaders, talk more about those things that divide us instead of those things that bring us together, then we all will be encouraging younger ones who know little or nothing about the history of this country to do nothing differently."

I couldn't agree more, and our children need good advice and leaders for encouragement than discouragement from their elders and, peers the need to set great examples and role models with ideal that portrays good character and human dignity and pride and sense of belonging and acceptance to work on team effort and with unconditional love; to show more unity and shown to all, regardless of color, tribe and tongues with integrity and compassion, wisdom and faithfulness leadership and goodwill that will motivate and stimulate and give them happiness, more hope. It will be a legacy with a vision of hope and a brighter future.

As Governor Godswill O. Akpabio of Akwa Ibom State of Nigeria has said, "We are building today for tomorrow" (August, 2011 in Houston at AIDN). Sure, also we do should be inclusive of them with transparency and legacy as a foundation that is transferrable with skills and, thank God for His love and power to give us all. He gives all blessings that we need too to grow productively, and guidance to know when and how; Scripture is a love story of boundless love of God and how He loves and blesses all of us and we should demonstrate similar love to all is one way that we can minimize poverty in the world and offers opportunity for others to grow.

Lee Kwan Yew, ex Prime Minister of Singapore adds, "A Singaporean's ability to rise depends upon his innate gifts and his application." If you look at the history of very big and post-industrialized countries, some have faced what seemed to be insurmountable challenges, but their determination to make a difference has enabled them to overcome those challenges. Also, if you look into the history of American presidents and of people in general, you will notice that the majority of them have one thing in common: hope and the motto, "In God we trust!" Is the key word and power for the joy is to hope with a vision and future and idealistically application too.

This is from the inspiration of love from the founding fathers and what structured. Two of the most remarkable qualities of these people are their patriotism and their idea that we are all one. America's men and women, especially those in uniform, have more stories to share that are inspiring to the core. Ultimately, God's love is the heart's power, and nothing can compare to His love. President Mandela of South Africa shared greatness of love in his heart as he emerged from prison and led South Africa through apartheid, and Ghana's President Rawlings performed a similar feat. As Mahatma Gandhi said, "You must be the change you wish to see in the world."

There are certainly many leaders who are admired and who have been credited for having the courage to endure adversity in the face of those who do not have their best interests at heart. President Obama, who has been stressed with many of these obstacles throughout his presidency, has still been able to inspire others to achieve greatness. Black, white, young, and old, please remember that the greatness that is in your hearts is a vessel for progression for yourself and others. Please, never forget what President Bill Clinton said: "It is not the man with great native talent who wins but him who pushes his talent, however small, to its utmost capacity."

As these words of wisdom state, "Character and ideals are catching. When you associate with men and (women) who aspire to the highest and best, you expose yourself to the qualities that make men great." As reflected in my book entitled "Priceless Love", "A good cause is something to proudly identify with and cheerfully promote, and there's no doubt in my mind that proper mentorship will help to enhance our youths' quality of life. Surely, they are precious and full of amazing talents and imaginations; and want to see them unfolding those with enthusiasm, dignity and pride…with happiness for positive productivity (Priceless Love, p. 14-15).

Indeed, as you effectively apply knowledge with wisdom, and know how the higher the inclination to stay motivated and to aspire to greatness, because while at the same time becoming a blessing as patriotic citizen(s), you are richer by faith and when to use by all standards, that is far better than being abandoned to the mercy of the perpetual ignorance of the streets, and which can include drugs and alcohol that can virtually destroy a society and yourself as well most too!

Keep in mind that in order to keep hope and faith alive, one must be able to love oneself by the ability to live a quality life and to inspire others to live the same way, love God first and, "Love yourself as you love your neighbor," are words of wisdom and are the gospel truth! If you hate yourself to the point of living a reckless life and are self-imprisoning your mind fixed on the negative thoughts always, it is obvious that you care very little about yourself and future. If you care so little about yourself, how can you even start to care for others, let alone love them and encourage them with words of inspiration?

The deep happiness and joy that I now feel is something I hadn't experienced previously in my life. My joy has come from the enlightening words of wisdom that started to make small differences in my life and that was the gift of hope and love I was given and passed down from my childhood home love is the greatest. I was still thankful, however, that even though they were not rich by the world measure, small differences, they were meaningful, and as the proverb says, "Half bread is better than none." I was highly breed educated, enlightened hearts are aware that if you do not love yourself, you cannot love others, I will forever remain grateful to my family!

One must have an open heart in order to educate it. Words of wisdom that I agree with are, "We cannot feel what is in another person's heart." With that being said, there is at least one positive thing we can do, and that is to bless a heart that is in need of hope, with the ultimate message being love and inspiration that is the power and joy that we can all derive by blessings. I know that we can derive, "To handle yourself, use your head. To handle others use your heart." When you care for others, it shows that you have an unselfish heart that is capable of achieving you great things of the heart, soul and mind and body, with our hearts, we can educate, to inspire.

We can offer hope and encourage others to open their hearts to love and joy is by sharing. The life you shared doesn't only bring joy to you but others as well, and that is how I derive my joy is by making others happy, and I thank God for inspiring my passion through the power and joy of inspiration. For, helping people is more excited about Him and His love and thankful for the gift of life and even being more alive, empowering with ability to be resilient, happier as purposeful.

Never allow anything to take you off of your focus of achieving your goals. We all have been blessed and empowered by the grace and glory of God. God loves each and every one of us and we are richly blessed to give each other the power to live our lives to the fullest. Above all, by all of us leading the way to living a life with these blessings shows us that His faithfulness and mercy has always been with us. A friend once asked me, "Caroline, why is it that you can write but I can't?" I responded with a smile and this simple truth: "Thank you for the love of your nice compliment, but you blessed, are richly blessed as well with various talents and gifts."

She then went on to say, "I don't understand what you mean. What is my purpose? Is it to sing?" I was very pleased that she was comfortable enough to confide in me, and I realized that she actually didn't know it, but she was directly telling me what she was meant to do. I then said to her, "Please don't make life difficult for yourself, my friend, for you have just stated your purpose, we are all blessed uniquely and love by God and to grow and not stunted but prosper." I was happy for her enthusiasm and encouraged more to stay on top of reading more the words of wisdom and inspiration from above more for power comes from believing in the miracle of God.

Every one of us, you all are natural singers born with great gift and talents it is joy sings through the heart before it gets to the mind, love is the heart's power and love fosters my love of books as well in reading the Bible more than any other too. When you make the most of your God-given abilities, you are living a successful life in which the precious gifts that you have all been given are extended freely. God ensures that everything is in place so that when you are ready to tap into these abilities, you are able to fulfill your purpose in life and to help others in their quest as well of fulfilling theirs. In the other word, there is joy and power of inspiration; from above and below is same power given unto each of us to encourage and build each other up, thank God for that! And my heart sings knowing that Love and power of His inspiration too.

No matter how little your love and confidence is of yourself, you are all empowered with magnificent blessings! In order to see clearly, you need light, correct? In the case of unleashing your blessings onto the world, the switch is in your hand, ready to be turned on and don't hesitate to be of hope and courage and self-confidence, in one bold, courageous attempt, that light can be turned on and your heart will feel the power of the glory of God all by your faith believing Him! Be thankful for our precious Lord from whom all blessings flow! Remember, "Healing begins from the soul," and the inspiration and passion that results from Him this healing will overflow.

From deep within the heart, "love makes the world go 'round." don't you love empowers. The heart is where joy, love, and blessings are in abundance, and the heart begins to rejoice as it is happiness, inspiration, passion, and enthusiasm take over. However, happiness, much like joy, involves you making the effort to realize all that you are capable of. God's love for us knows no limits. We all have the ability to capture the joy that I speak of, but in order to do this you need the love and power of the inspiration to be energized with the passion to reach for it comes from power of God and His love, which is the divine guidance and number one principles for success.

The phrase, "To make the cart go, you must grease the wheel," is a fitting one under these circumstances. Rejoicing in hope is essential, and if you have faith in yourself and faith in God, your little efforts will be rewarded. Believe in the fact that you can achieve whatever goals you lay out for yourself, and that you can overcome any obstacles placed in front of you and succeed.

In closing, let me leave you with these words of inspiration, "…to be truly human, one must serve others. Everybody can be great because everybody can serve-" Martin Luther King, Jr.

Hope comes about by living with the faith that you believe in His strength and that He will watch over you. Trust, obey, and know for a fact that everyone is blessed with the potential to achieve all that they can. What Maya Angelou has said is true: "One isn't necessarily born with courage, but one is born with potentials." With that being said, if you feel like you cannot have what it takes to achieve your dreams, least of all, you can achieve all matters of the heart, trust in the miracle of believing in the power of God and His love you can be able to do the impossible!

In order to get your mind ready and your heart prepared for the blessings that will be receive, it is necessary to do your homework with the unique gifts that we are given love by God.

The grace of God; you are blessed to successfully harness your talents and skills. By daring yourself daily to do the best you can and to push yourself to persevere, you will have the ability to reach your goals. Trust that you have the ability to excel and to make a difference in the world, and that joy is the best wine for your soul. Inspiration creates energy and excitement from above.

When you achieve success, you have seen your dreams come to pass. Remember, when God is by your side, all impossibilities become possible. Ask for wisdom and an understanding heart, for "the wise man's path leads upward to life (Proverbs 15:24). Trust in Him that makes who His promise to love is with us, and that His hope is within us. He surrounds us all with His mercies, faithfulness and everlasting love, and He always stands beside us, willing to give our hearts the true happiness that we pray for.

Unquestionably, whatever measure of satisfaction and love that we may need, once that measure is achieved, it not only benefits ourselves, but it also benefits everyone around us. Amazingly, there is always power through His anointing and through His fulfilling our needs, including joy and peace of mind. God is the word, the light, the joy and the hope in all of our hearts. I am always amazed of His presence and how He appears in my life with such power. Thankfully, He is working daily, and I can feel the soul's soft whispering voice, speaking "peace with joy."

Through God, I am able to share my blessings with all of you and to encourage all of you that hope is within us. And, even in our greatest heartbreaks and difficulties that hope will never fails. Rather, it is on our side more and waiting to embrace and help us more to succeed. Most enduring love and peace that are of greatest help, and steps in to readily take over our burdens and that says, much more about the power of love and inspiration. Right there, that peace that is from above is within and waiting to be revealed and, is the peace, we should long for and seek.

Seek for His inspiration that directs as God is who surrounds you and me with love that is unfailing and empowering. Powerful, and full of glory and true love too, and action in words. He is author of kindness of deeds, and, is what makes easy and life bearable. Are you facing a life of struggles and need your load to be lighter? That is the only hope we possess, is in the power of God's love and inspiration, and faith in God is the faith that inspires, of cheerfulness. That is of you most greatest and most liberating transformational power, and glory to bless us, boast of too.

There is power in inspiration because it enables us all to rejoice and hopeful. We all need a faithful friend that is supernatural and offers something that helps us to dream more and, think well and, to realize that our dreams can come true. To be without the joy of inspiration is to live a life with no future. To me, it is emptiness or like living in a house without good books to read. Friend, be not deceived, God's Word inspires. His inspiration creates power too, and I'm grateful and hopeful that you will join me in this celebration of inspiration, and at the same time seeks for inspiration. And, May God bless us and encourage us to strive for greatness in our hearts, the joy to be hopeful, standing strong in faith, united for the common goal of offering hope to people and spirit to be passionate of your grace and offer love, around the world.

Please friend, do not forget that with inspired hearts of love and greatness come power and the joy of inspiration. Keep faith and hope alive and expect a miraculous breakthrough, because your time to shine is coming sooner than you think. Cherish the fact that you can share the love in your heart to help make the world a better place for all, and most of all, cherish the power and joy of inspiration, to be a creative child of God that aspires for greatness as well!

CHAPTER THREE

Wisdom Matters –
Greatness is in the Heart!

"When God measured a man, He puts the tape
around the heart instead of the head."

Reaching out with love and healing thoughts to hearts throughout
the world is my new assignment. Simply put, reaching the world with
healing words! Because nothing is more fulfilling as helping people find
happiness of pleasure in their lives. As I have quoted before, "Inspired
people inspire people," and nothing can compare to that joy in my
heart. As the proverb says, "A merry heart doth well like a medicine"
(KJV: Proverbs 17:22), is love there!

God still performs miracles today, just as He has in the past. He is
constantly speaking wisdom to us and spreading miracles along the way.
Ultimately, his powerful words of wisdom make miracles a possibility
in the hearts and lives of people the world over. Willing hearts that
are accepting of these words are benefitting the most from His glory
and power. He will always reach out to us, and His loving kindness
never ceases. If you are able to accept His wisdom and love, you will
be anointed the power of blessings, unity, peace, progress, and joy for
yourselves and everyone else in the world, for that heart is the chamber
that creates love and is speaks love.

Make a list of all of your needs and feel free to request them from
the Lord with the prayers of a thankful heart. When you show gratitude
for everything you receive and are about to receive, it is hard not to
celebrate with pure joy and elation when your requests are realized.
There is a caveat, however: The Lord answers these requests if met with
His approval. In other words, even if your requests are not answered to
your satisfaction in the time that you want them answered, please have

faith and know that God has not turned his back on you. He knows what is best for all of us and is only waiting for the perfect time to bless all of us; delayed not denied.

Once we are filled with inspiration, it embraces us and makes our lives happy from inside out is awesome. Everyone can have a happy life, but not everyone has the patience and the time to be of willingness to learn and know the wisdom needed to achieve this. The problem is that many people feel that if their prayers are not answered on "their" time, then God must not want to help them. This is the farthest thing from the truth. He knows what is best for us and what the best way to meet our needs is. He accepts us just as we are – flaws and all. We must be patient and know that God will answer our prayers on His time. Once we all come to this understanding, our hearts will be opened to unlimited possibilities.

The Lord wants to restore hope and peace, because He knows that this is what our hearts need. His words are simple: "My son, give me your heart…" (Proverbs 23:26). The following words of wisdom are very true: "Words are windows to your heart!" Maya Angelou, an accomplished writer and poet, said it best when describing hearts of love that give acceptingly and gracefully: "When we give cheerfully and accept gratefully, everyone is blessed." Gratitude to me is of Cheerfulness is a gift of love, and if you give your love to the Lord, life will be easier and better managed, if you just receive with a heart of gratitude is so obvious accepting with joy.

In regards to matters of the heart, time waits for no one. We must realize that these gifts we are given by God need to be utilized as quickly as possible to benefit everyone. Smile, and encourage others by being happy for them and their progress. Kindness is a gift, and when it is given, all blessings are bountiful and filled with love and happiness. By generously giving and accepting, your hearts will overflow with joy and satisfaction. Hopefully, you are appreciative and are willing to accept my invitation to join my celebration of the power of inspiration is daily.

It is important that we all have well wishes for everyone. Happily give your heart to the Supreme Creator, and understand that your inspiration and joy should be celebrated daily. Keep your mind refreshed for the sake of your body, soul, and spirit, and let your happiness shine very brightly. Be encouraged to stay on the right track as you travel the path to wisdom. Give your all to touch others with your gifts of hope and blessings, because when one gives their heart for the Glory of God, He changes sorrow to joy. Any situation that is plaguing us can be healed is with His miraculous hands.

We all face turmoil at some time or another in our lives. Adversity will always be a part of the world as we know it, which makes it imperative that we have faith of the known as well as the unknown. We must remember that love and peace of mind are priceless and relevant, and makes for the heart's greatness as well. We must remember to pray for both as we navigate through the uncertainties of life, for "the heart of man cannot be determined by the size of his pocketbook." Preparation must begin now for all of us to enjoy the fruits of our labor.

Today's world is in dire need of spiritual awareness, and instead of being bogged down with our physical worries; we can use spiritual insightfulness to give us a pleasurable life. Truth is this, "Awareness, adds quality to life," so feeding the soul with "good nutrients", so to speak, enhances ones quality of life. By devoting more quality time to ensure that our soul has the nutrients of wisdom, hope, and joy, we can achieve anything! However, as I have previously mentioned and must stress again, these blessings may not come when we are anticipating them. But, "when you put your energy behind something, the results will be powerful as you endure it.

Keep in mind that God's time is the best and that His time is not ours. His delays are not refusals, and we will never be denied, "For with God nothing shall be impossible" (Luke 1:37). His blessings are always beyond measure, but as we all know, timing means everything, so is joy is continue to be hopeful and wait patiently while working hard to achieve our goals. As these proverbs eloquently state, "Have the faith to move mountains", and "Faith is daring the soul to go beyond what the eyes can see." Remember, success is possible with hope, so remove obstacle.

When we pray faithfully and give thanks to all He has blessed us with, we will surely be granted our wishes. He listens and hears all of us, but answers when it is best for us. However, only inspirations of the heart give us the knowledge of such wisdom. Thus, as the proverb says, Knowing how to find knowledge is the first step to wisdom" and understanding and knowing and doing God's will, that is the knowledge freeing a person, application and it is in our best interest. To gain all the knowledge we can, is good but knowledge to use the word when and how matters.

Hard work and desire that comes with love and enthusiasm from such blessings can change our lives forever and can make us happy and productive. Certainly, "when love and skill work together, expect a masterpiece." The love of God inspires and motivates me to pray daily for everyone to be encouraged and to learn that inspirational wisdom can be achieved. All of the joy that I feel is made possible by His will! As is often said, "Prayer is a wish turned upward." It is always a joyful inspiration when friends are praying for others and uplifting one another to become better and happy people.

Let inspiration come from within – it helps build strength and joy and allows our hearts to be more willing to help others, for "joy is the ability to be happy in small things." I am grateful and thankful because "when you inspire others you are truly rich." From all indications, the inspiration of the word of God's wisdom is alive now more than ever, "...for out of the abundance of the heart the mouth speaketh" (Matthew 12:34: KJV). God is the best to be trusted.

The power of His presence is always with us. You do not need the world's approval, but only the approval of your Heavenly Father and the belief in His will! As the saying goes, "Experience is the best teacher." The Book of John 15:19 has the answers for you in the quest for faith that inspires us, so do not fear! Again, read with enthusiasm, and the word will enlighten and bless you. Enthusiasm matters as much as faith.

Nothing is as magnificent and endures forever like the beauty of God's glory. That inner discipline helps, protects, and rejuvenates one's body, mind, and spirit. His glory brings peace to the soul as the heart rejoices. Also, the contentment that I mentioned earlier is not so much about getting what we want, but is about the heart being satisfied with what we have. In my opinion, a loving heart and a willing mind equals a content heart.

The joy that I feel inspires me and makes my heart hopeful, so in every situation, whether it be good or bad, I have learned to live a content and thankful life everyday life is based on God. The words of wisdom that have helped transform me and has educated me to be content all come from the words of God's mouth most and as stated by Paul summarizes eloquently for me and to borrow from is this, "Not that I speak in respect of want: For I have learned, in whatever state I am, therewith be content" (Philippians 4:11). My contentment causes my heart to dance, singing beautiful song, and everyday! "I can do all things through Christ who strengthens me" as proven!

Joy and hope continue to eternally overwhelm me. As a wise proverb says, "Joy is the chief wine", and I always feel so drunk! You may be thinking, "I know Caroline, she doesn't drink! What you may not understand is that I drink the best wine of all, and this is the wine of joy. I am truly blessed to feel "drunk" as I write this book, for the pleasure that I feel in inspiring others is like none other.

Joy is the knowledge that He, who holds my today, also holds my future. Tomorrow is not in my hands, but I know God looks out for His dearly beloved children, and to Him I give all the glory and honor. Indeed, "Joy is the ability to be happy in small things," and that is certainty encouragement heals my soul. Ultimately, He is the greatest; greater than the power of roaring lions in the most mountainous regions. "He that is in me is greater than he that is in the world" (1st John 4:4). My Redeemer lives and faces the mountains squarely on our behalf with his power and might! All that matters is dare trusting and having faith in His power and trusting more also of the power of prayer. Indeed, no matter what the situation, there is no higher mountain than Him. Trust to listen to His voice and believe in His almighty power and infinite wisdom assures.

Nothing can take my focus from that path, for His is the glory, and His glory is the greatness in my heart! His beauty is the passion that fills my heart with inspiration and there is hope is unspeakable joy. Nothing is more blessed "when thou sendest forth thy Spirit, they are created, and thou renewest the face of the earth (ground)." Please pray and continue to pray, for is life-giving. He is the soul of man, the most special of all friends and our hearts will rejoice in His living word. It is true that no one knows another's heart, but nothing great has ever been as well achieved in my lifetime without His power of inspiration, which fills my heart with joy. The following is so very true: "A person's true character is revealed by what he does when no one is watching." My only choice for my life is to live by the will and grace of God. I am not bothered by what people may think of me, for His will matters far more than man's expectations. Judge, as you may, because I refuse to change! One's heart is at its best when at peace, Caroline Arit's philosophy. All matters of the heart come from your passion to love with faith and hope, but love is greatest of all above others and outlasting too: "Look to Him and be radiant" (Psalms 34:4-5). I feel that I have come a long way, and the thought of how far I have come makes me smile.

However, for some reason, many do not like to see me smiling and being happy, which is their problem and not mine. The phrase "Happiness is the Lord" makes my day every time I hear as He guides my heart in the right direction, no matter what anyone else says or believes that can't change my perspective and is a matter of the heart and choice just fine with me too. Indeed, there have been many times that we have failed because of a lack of a wishbone, or rather, a backbone. Wisdom matters just as much as a backbone does, but there are those who do not possess this wisdom. Please try to understand that "he who wants milk should not sit on a stool in the middle of the pasture expecting the cow to back up to him."

Again, all what these words of wisdom say is true: "Some decisions will give you joy or headache for a lifetime." Thankfully, wisdom is choosing joy instead of headaches, is inspiring and fills my heart with faith. Indeed, inspires, more love and hope of heavenly significant more than earthly worries, for must as I believe and exercise that faith it takes me to the next level in life and that of deep joy. Please understand that when the bold, courageous steps are taken to stake claim to wisdom, love, and happiness, one must believe that "I'm not going backward to the world but 'forever ever backward never', and am enjoying God's joy in my life heart and soul is awesome. I have heard people ask and tell me am fanatic, and too bad that is just me and am living the joy it is as asking and, "What is the purpose of trying to change?" These same people feel that it is not worth the time and energy that is needed to invest in changing for the better. I cannot understand why people feel this way. Ignorance is so stupidly expensive and that is not what I stand for. I stand for God's love, which is full of hope and abundance.

Who knows of someone who has felt the mighty power of His words of wisdom and would still want to trade in happiness for sadness? I am proudly different in that these words of wisdom fill my heart with joy, and I wouldn't trade this in for anything in the world. Life is not for worshipping man, money, and the devil doesn't give anyone happiness in the long run, but only fills the heart with sorrow and pain. Live your life as you were always truly meant to – by living happy and content lives with the blessings that God has given you. In this world, we all need to stand our ground firmly and claim our happiness, mostly as children of destiny, blessed heritage. Surely, it pays for as often said, "Nothing great was ever achieved without enthusiasm; it overcomes discouragement and gets things done. It is the magic (miracle) quality. And the remarkable thing is – it's contagious." Inspired words of wisdom diligently guard our hearts.

And strengthen it to extreme proportions. Embrace hope and eagerly look for the mercy of your Supreme Being. Wisdom, which is one of the many gifts of His gracious favor, is just so amazing but also goes alongside with faith, hope, perseverance, trusting, and obeying. Trust that His wisdom does wonders for the soul. Give all you can give to His glory and serve with love is rewarding and is deep joy from the bottom of your heart. It is for the best! "He is truly wise who submits to God's wisdom." Bear in mind, as I have said time and time again, that His love is Joy is He does everything in His time and not ours. We do not know when our time will come; only He does and knows it all.

In the meantime, rejoice in His name and believe that He loves all of us. What we can be certain of is that He has not forgotten about any of us, and that the greatness that we achieve in our hearts should be ready to receive His blessings. "Those who walk with God always find Him close at hand." God's love is always full of grace, and His wisdom has enabled me to gain a heart of wisdom, holding loosely to what is temporal and tightly to what is eternal. This love has blessed my soul beyond human understanding and is one of the most remarkable happenings of my life. Something that has been derived from heavenly joy and happiness should never be hidden, but shared with the world. Good news, like love, is too good to keep to myself.

The joy and insights I have gained from my journey have enabled me to live a happy life is prosperous, hopeful life. Genuine love is something that must be shared with the world to add purpose to one's life. I always knew deep down in my heart that when joy comes with the help of God, my life would be filled with happiness and celebrations. I knew this would eventually happen, but I just was not certain of when. This lack of knowing, however, did not take away from the hope and faith that I felt, in anticipating this remarkable event, and the inspiration also brought out happiness from within. Certainly, it's never too soon to invest in eternity, is the best considering the brevity of life.

The hope that we could all eventually be together rejoicing in the happiness of achieving, love and inspiration is what should keep everyone going on their path to contentment. By grace is joy in sharing inspirational thoughts and by touching hearts, we will have a world of peace and hope, for fills emptiness. What matters in stimulating the heart, is hope and wisdom. Promotes and fosters unity. What matters in stimulating the heart, is what is inside, which is a greater force than what is outside. Thoughts that inspire our hearts are motivating and educating to you and others. Please, never underestimate your power in capability, influencing positively and of helping to encourage/inspire. Faith in God leads to life of everlasting love and exercising works.

Daily prayers, along with words of inspiration, have helped my heart. My faith helps me achieve hope, joy, and peace, which joy radiates glory of God's love. Power of inspiration is of greatness in the heart of those daring to believe. With continual prayer, the glory of heaven will be upon us, and His power-filled voice will be present, filling our souls with His soft, whispering voice, and witnessed to His glory. We will all be assured that He listens and that He speaks of peace, hope, love, and truth. This makes my heart rejoice; for every day is a positive day filled with faith-inspired words of wisdom and inspiration. Each day is bright and beautiful because the feeling of His presence is so close to my heart and enables me to live a hopeful life. "He's King of glory, strong and mighty in battle."

Indeed, "Where there is hope there is life"; and where faith is also bound to be victory; is apparent that is my faith is secured in Him and no one else but Him and, His love everlasting is with kindness and graciousness. Throughout every blessed day, "my heart is glad, and my soul rejoices, my soul also dwells secure in hope" (Psalms 16:9). Hope in His constant love and joy. This is incredibly awesome and inspirational, for "a heart of gratitude is a heart of greatness and is of joy (Caroline Arit Okon Thompson, 2013). That is my philosophy, rooted in the belief that the best way to be thankful is not only by words, but by actions as well by expressing it to show.

Tell someone today how much you love and bless them by giving out your love and that is letting it multiply. That is exactly what inspires my heart when I read of Lady Dame Patience Jonathan's testimony. Happiness is of the Lord, and it was a great and powerful testimony, and that joy fills my soul with love and happiness. I am happy and thankful that she never forgot who was there for her, in her time of crisis! This is her inspirational story: "I was dead for 7 days, but God brought me back," Patience Jonathan said on a medical trip to Germany testimony. "It was a shocking revelation on Sunday at the State House Chapel in Abuja when First Lady, Dame Patience Jonathan, revealed that she had died and woke up after 7 days, when she was hospitalized for three months abroad. During a Thanksgiving, held at the State House Chapel, the First Lady praised Nigerians for praying for her during her trying moment, confirming that their prayers helped sustain her. She also expressed disappointment over those who had wished her dead, and she disclosed that she went through 7 operations in the span of one month, yet survived, even when the doctors had given up on her" (Isong@ yahoo.com). That was in 2013.

Today, I am very happy and grateful, because as I'm writing this chapter, other friends and families is also worldwide in many places black and white and (young and old), in different languages, also happily are testifying as well, what God is doing for them. In and through your life, I am happy for what God is doing mightier things for us moving. And his power of love and infinite wisdom creates joy and, passion. The Lord is inspiration and is the passion for everyone that has been touched by the power of His love and miracles abounds.

Much as His love and grace too, even in the wilderness, offered that blessings world-wide The Lord is doing great and mighty things, and will continue to be faithful and true to his Word. No matter what happens in the world. His goodness will forever be proclaimed and shared, for the world to know who God is as the power of His glory that cannot be shared with anybody. Let us strive to be all that God desire for each of us and, continue to pray for one and all. Pray for one another, and be happy as well for one another as well, most importantly, remember to praise the Lord and be thankfully, for what He is doing and in and through each of our lives, for God is good. The first Lady of Nigeria, Lady Dame Patience Goodluck Jonathan, many others all are inspiring my heart and is joy that, she took a bold step of courage and faith to launch out her faith, proudly testified. Truth is that, if we don't exercise our faith we don't get to next level.

She lets the, world, to know shows her gratitude and celebrate with family and friends. It is always so good to join others and expressed thanks and promotes the love of God's goodness and greatness with gratitude encouraging others as one another, she testified and, such blessing is impacting many lives. I am sure, not only Nigerians, but many of diverse backgrounds benefit is of grace God's abundant grace, as lives will be transformed and praise God too. This assessment, based on what is inside her, which is greater than what is outside, is to my admiration of her and that matters most, to share, is an encouragement to inspire others, expect your miracles, as well.

I pray the Lord answers us and, your entire request in His time and season. You are truly all co-laborers! Personally, is of joy to take delight respecting, obeying, submitting to the power of God and following the word of my heavenly Father with gratitude for there's is joy with hope. Harmony and love which comes from His love for me and my love for Him, which is graciously appreciated with gratitude, it is rewarding and, awesome too, when submitting to His discipline. Serving, loving Him, and worshipping Him with all of your heart and soul and mind and being.

Remember, "Greatness is in our hearts, and it is only in our humility before God that as this Scripture sums, "Who is the man (woman/child) who fears the Lord? He will instruct him in the way he should choose." (Psalm 25:12). So, it is I am instructed to keep my eyes on Jesus, and choose happiness, always with love in my heart, and humbly keep praying and moving on and to appreciate the love and word, and be of joy and expecting more blessings too is inspiration for it is when that greatness will be revealed too, revelation is of God what He does to those who love. Keep in mind that, "Love remembered is never lost," for, the life that you share brings joy to all.

And, happiness not only to you, but also to others as well and that is why, it is my time to celebrate Him, and, I reciprocate love with appreciation, as I remember how much God loves me and mine rightly, He is more than deserving of my own thanksgiving, and what He has done and as I continue to share continues, to love and increases my faith and blessings for He is awesome. I did pause and ask myself this question and is personal to me; "How can I forget Calvary; what can I do without God giving Jesus to me to show redemptive love is that, "He first loved me?"

I can never, as I observed many things and learned about life from my infancy and being raised a child of faith, messages of His love, was order of the day, Scripture Fills my heart with the joy of His amazing love (John 3:16) and now I feel His presence daily. He is near to me and all of His blessings that He has been the, loving heavenly Father, who bestowed upon me, all are proof of that(1 John 4:19). His love is real, and His word is power and unfailing for I know that deep down in my heart there is hope and joy in the belief that praying with attitude of gratitude. I am as I said from the introduction and having faith in God will result in the inspiration and love.

Nothing beats that capacity to love Him and also love of others much, yourself always. As the Proverb says, "He enjoys life who (that) makes others enjoy it." As observed by Marcel Proust, "Let us be grateful to people who make us happy, they are the charming gardeners who make our souls blossoms." And, sure they are and Scripture testify to that too in a nutshell, "Give thanks to him and praise his name"(psalms 100:4 (NLT)/(Phi. 4:6). It saddens me that in this day and age, still live in a world of more non-believers and this day of uncertainty more so than ever in their hearts is due to lack of faith and love and for what makes for hope inside! It pays to show gratitude, for the gift of life and that abundance that is coming to us from above is everyday love.

Else without which is empty inside and outside is hopeless and uncertainty for there is no anchor to hold to. It is crucial to seek spiritual awareness and to practice kindness in thoughts, as in words, and actions. My heart's desire is to do well, to be a blessing, and to invest more in the goodness of the heart's greatness as God has given me the power with authority and, a dedicated heart is such a blessing. That makes a difference, and love is usually the catalyst. I prayed that God would bless me with this gift so that I could make a life-long investment in sharing my joy and passion with everyone.

Anyone, that is god-send and who crosses my path is to be blessed and has given me that inspiration in all that I do and, how grateful that I am, for His answering. I am very thankful for this, and I am blessed to see my sorrow turn into the joy of writing another inspirational book to comfort hearts globally. I am thankful that the time is now to capture the joy of this moment. Sure, I crave more of the wealth of wisdom, knowledge, and joy that I have gained through this experience, but I also know that actions speak louder than words. I now see why my knee was situation, which was one of my worst physical nightmares is, endured, lingered for a reason and so, as often said is true, "Everything happens for a reason!" For most of life's events are what is unexpected and so nothing is ever guaranteed. As the saying goes, "No one knows tomorrow."

Being blessed to have been a rehabilitation counselor, as well as working in federal/state matching programs, and teaching in a county-based job, my passion was in promoting more of the youth programs that I came into contact with. My inspiration to inspire and motivate our youth, along with working for so many years with the National Youth Service Corps (NYSC), changed my life and further reinforced my love of our youth and being an advocate for them. Ultimately, I prayed for them, and as a public relations officer, as well as teaching the first grade and working as an educator and vocational rehabilitation counselor, I was so inspired. However, I was mostly inspired to become a school counselor and one of the primary reasons that I earned my Masters in the field, which fulfilled my childhood dream of counseling and helping others, especially youth. It practically blew my mind to be able to help people solve their problems! While helping these people sort out their lives and relationships, I persevered and prayed that I could be a success in what I love to do.

"Perseverance makes the difference between failure and success, and as rightly observes by this inspirational word of wisdom, "Courage conquers fear thereby masters it.""- Dr. M. King, Jr. Yet true, and, when the storm came, I found myself desperate and unable to accomplish even the most basic of tasks – standing for long periods of time, and even walking and sitting were a problem for me at one point in my life, fears griped me and I was afraid of the future unknown. I definitely believe that most of life's events are unexpected and can certainly shatter dreams. But we are blessed in that when one door closes, another door opens. I am definitely one of those who are more than happy to testify to that truth. Sadly, my plans were disrupted, and the health issues I had were unforeseeable, but faith inspires hope and gratitude, and I am counting my blessings with joy in my blessed Redeemer and His helping me to overcome that power of fear.

Wisdom matters, and is of thankfully, my passion enabled me to find a solution for my situation. I was inspired to mend my broken heart, and words of encouragement inspired even more passion, motivation, and enthusiasm. In other words, life's lessons can bring be what this proverb says: "Learn from adversity." I pray as blessed relating my experience and encounter with the power of inspiration, you will be touched, and realize also that for whatever situations, God understands better. Please know and appreciate more that God loves and thinks more of us, hears our prayers, and supplies our every need more than we even asked.

And, that there are blessings of His Power of Inspiration. Only God of miracle can supply one in need, grace to endure. The ability and favor of His grace to be inspired, and you will know for sure, He is the eternal living God. Inspiration fills my heart with the hope of being able to do what is best for me. Shedding a part of my previous lifestyle was an important step in the quest to be filled with joy and hope. At that time, I couldn't perform adequately at my job, yet I had a committed spirit that was blessed. I was determined to live beyond my limitations. As we all know, most of life's events are unexpected, but being inspired by faith and hope both does work to create passion and uplift the soul. Uplifting one's heart to think positive thoughts, and so is to aspire to achieve goals and dreams, comes from inspiration, mostly from that which is of above.

Inspiration benefits our physical, emotional, and mental health, and it inspires and also it is encourages the heart to think wisely. Thoroughly researching and finding out more about my health was a life-saver, which was rewarding, and it introduced me to my intimate friendship with inspirational words and the wisdom that comes from them. Passion comes from inspiration, driving hearts to be blessed with the discovery of joy.

As Solomon wisely remarked, "For God giveth to a man that is good in his sight wisdom, and knowledge and joy" (Eccl. 2:26A). That thrills my heart, for "He who pursues righteousness and kindness will find life and honor" (Proverbs 21:21). It is rewarding to think of the source of these words of encouragement, and it fills my heart with inner peace, enhancing the ability to joy in the love of God and live a hopeful, productive life. Behold that everything in life comes from both positive and negative rewards. Positive thoughts reinforce us to think as visionaries, while negative thoughts do just the opposite.

I am grateful that I resorted to the devotional Book of wisdom, which worked miracles and gave me the healing touch that I needed. It was incredible and it humbled my spirit as these words of wisdom rang through my ears: "Honor shall uphold the humble in spirit." The more you read, the more you become richer with knowledge and wisdom. You become wealthier in terms of faith and blessings, which is better than all the money in the world. Wisdom results in an abundance of joy, which is the blessing that the Biblical King Solomon relished in for most of his life. With joy comes of more of hope and happiness, and the heart who dares to seek after the wisdom will have a great heart of joy that is all about Love and Life is about choices, that we are making and as the saying goes, "Peace is goodwill in action."

Whatever decisions and choices you make in life should be based on your own particular situation and what is best for you. It is important, however, to keep in mind that no matter what path you may choose to maintain the same goal of pursuing peace, love, and happiness for the progress of us. All is the best peace is what makes you happy and so sad if you don't have love in you. It is rewarding to think positive thoughts that heal others instead of thoughts that hurt as that always is and break others down. Enjoy the pleasures of life, and remember that an inspired heart knows joy and love is the heart's power as is all is well and, that the fruits of our labor will soon be realized. It will be a banquet that we all will be able to sit down to, as stated in the Book of Ecclesiastes. Chapters are all very familiar and mostly from Chapter 3:17 to be very specific!

Unfortunately in this day and age, many of us do not care to stop and listen attentively to people who possess wisdom. I implore our youth to stop and listen to those who have authority over you, even those amongst your peers and those who are younger than yourselves, for you can benefit from their wisdom and good advice. It truly pays to listen to everyone, especially your elders, for they have the knowledge and wisdom to inspire as well. All of us can have loving and caring hearts if we apply the words of wisdom, for the inspiration we receive from them give us direction and as my folks used to say and true, counseling is a community affairs and elder song.

I believe that thoughts of wisdom are crucial to the heart and are an integral part of our community affairs. Thankfully, in every community, there are those who are blessed to have the knowledge and wisdom available to share with others, which helps to mold those who are wise enough and willing to listen to the guidance of others to lead them to the path of creating happy hearts. I am grateful that today the Book of Ecclesiastes (KJV 3:1-22) educates us even more.

The Book of Proverbs speaks eloquent words that give wisdom and inspire heart, hope. Ultimately, "To everything there is a season and a time to every purpose under the heaven…A time to rend, and a time to sew, a time to keep silence, and a time to speak; a time to love…, but for a man to rejoice and do good, And that every man should eat and drink of all his labor, it is the gift of God…Wherefore, I perceive that there is nothing better, than that a man should rejoice in his own works; for that is his portion: For who shall bring him to see what is after?"

By appreciating and treasuring the pleasures of life, we can learn to grow and mature by the lessons learned from these pleasures. I have said this before and will continue to say it: Hope is the power of inspiration that brings peace, joy, truth and comfort to your heart! Having hope and love for the Supreme Being is what matters most and what is most relevant. His word offers hope, and encourages as well as empowers all of us with an unspeakable joy. His joy comes with strength and the commitment of walking in His light. When we listen to His words of wisdom, our hearts are filled with inspiration and trust, which makes life a lot easier.

The Book of Proverbs very highly recommends wisdom: "Say unto wisdom, Thou art my sister; and call understanding thy kinswoman" (Proverbs 7:4). Those virtues and benefits of wisdom enhance our understanding of it. By applying this wisdom to your life and to your heart, you can achieve motivation, which leads to knowledge, encouragement, and a successful life. Practical words of wisdom are worth being shared with everyone! All of us have the capacity to be a blessing and grow above the poverty that you think, is something impossible. Indeed, if you are moderate in your choices, and think less of piling and cut your coat according to your size as well, it is part of the solutions to curb some of excesses of greed and lust. Being richer by worldly things is not necessary, more than eternal significant.

However, if you can afford, and still want to measure up with those you have seen and want to be like some of your friends, and you have no clue to how they get it, that is your choice. In fact, the choices we make can be good and some very bad in taste and action too. You can be richer by faith, love and wisdom and greatness is being secured in the faithful love of God and sharing whatever blessings that you are blessed, is just as fine as and better than being richer by cheat and cunning and deceptive means and duping, senseless means and what can being a scamming scammer fetched you than the life to live of wisdom of God with better abet life and conscience and peace of mind which is priceless. Decency comes with hope and this is in many productive ways too, encouraging and is something to be thankful and share as joy is for love is of empowerment and something to claim for us and our children is there too, Joy is in the heart!

God lives in our hearts, and there is the real happiness, is of the Lord, and Joy is the most inspiring of the blessings as the "the chief wine;" is to the soul that healing begins in the soul for our victory, and that is for spiritual growth, which is word of wisdom, and inspiration of God that is the ultimate. You don't have to live a life of yoyo, and abet always on the duping and cheating, getting rich by being liar and lazy and disobedient always on performance merry –go round and, looking for who to make an easy target and prey to consume. Robbing, or stealing from where you did not sow but want to reap, please, don't go there and don't rob yourself of the blessings that God has given to you. Remember, greatness is in the heart and, it is in our humility before God that our greatness is revealed. If you can't get off the wrong track, ask God for help and is great seek for wisdom and, and be secured of His love and words of wisdom; romance your life with words of inspirational wisdom, you will get love of a lifetime, as the, "truth shall make you free" (John 8:32). There is no question in my mind that this conversation is going to be helpful.

To every human hearts is all about the joy of inspiration and the tribute to inspirational as words of wisdom inspire and that impacts all of our lives. These words keep my heart moving forward, for I am a friend of all of you who wants you all to be happy. Ultimately, "Wisdom is to the soul what health is to the body." Hopefully, you are as inspired with this discussion and feel as blessed as I do. Please, don't forget that you need the power of words of inspiration to make remarkable discoveries. Have faith to dream and faith in God. Faith is knowledge within the heart of wisdom; is of God's love and that is who moves. Indeed, you will read more of this in the next chapter that follows, which is why, I wrote this book with you in mind, as you are all a blessing of heart, where greatness lies.

CHAPTER FOUR

Why I Wrote this Book with You in Mind

"You have no excuses not to change the world."
– President Barack Obama

Everything in life matters simply because it all comes from the heart, where our greatness lies within us. It is no wonder that we are encouraged to be motivated, alert, and watchful, by "guarding your heart with all diligence, for from there comes springs of life" (Proverbs 4:23). Inspiration, as I have stated previously, comes from an informed mind and a heart of wisdom. It takes a pure heart of love, wisdom, knowledge, understanding, faith, courage, and hope, and of perseverance to excel and achieve our goals.

In order to rejoice in the hope of being successful, one must possess integrity and honesty to be able to start on the path to a successful life. With patience, faithfulness, and perseverance, there is always, hope for one to excel. The power of inspiration is definitely an essential proper is ingredient, but character and hard work is a stepping stone needed as well. By living our lives in the path of the Creator, one is destined to be creative and prosperous. This means to live our lives appreciating what we have instead of dwelling on what we don't have.

Be inspired and always mindful of both God's gifts and talents, for His very presence is a motivator to achieve greatness in the heart. His power is amazing, for "there is fullness of joy in His presence" (Psalms 16:11). There is nothing more glorious than to hear the "still small voice" that motivates us to greatness and gives us faith and spiritual growth. With those priceless words blessings come "more and more in knowledge and all discernment", which all of us should take to heart. It may sound unbelievable, but, it is true that there's an anointing power of inspiration that helps tremendously in our quest to excel in life. The fact that God wants us to prosper and rise above our calling is a joy and a blessing in and of itself. It is a wonderful experience when one is "full of joy" and ready to seize the opportunity.

Simply put, I feel that it is a privileged, rare honor to be able to demonstrate our capability of living up to our responsibility of a purpose driven life. It is a blessing to be able to reach out and touch one another, for that is the joy of living our lives to the fullest. The Psalmist David said it all with these words: "Only the fool hath said in his heart, there is no God" (Psalms 53:1), and "God has spoken once; twice have I heard this; that power belongeth unto God" (KJV 62:11). Believe that by following inspirational words of wisdom, your hearts will be filled with hope and joy. We all know in our hearts when we feel the real power of His presence, so much so that we dare to celebrate that "unspeakable joy." Make no mistake about that that soft, tender, whispering voice is speaking daily.

It speaks words of peace from deep within as we rejoice in the greatness of our hearts. There is hope for fellow man, including you and me and that is why I am writing this book with you in mind and, I love you and want to encourage you to not let adversity keeps you from your goals, and to remember that daily prayer is an important first step. This book is proof of that as it is such also of a wonderful feeling when our prayers are answered and we are able to each be of inspiration and is to do what we are passionate about. If only all of our hearts would surrender to God is the faith of our Supreme Being, is God Almighty Creator of heaven and earth is the things we could accomplish would be limitless, including peace of mind that is priceless and of unity.

By believing in the powerful, inspired words of His love, we would be able to live in a world free from wars and disasters as well as have all solutions to personal situations always too. Much as collective and can you imagine the power of love that inspires of hearts to be hopeful to be happy and resourceful too? Can you imagine how peaceful and loving the world could be just by listening to Him as well and following his commands? What comes from above worth more is be not deceived more than all the gold and silver, rubies and diamond this world has to offer us and that is the joy of find inspiration and love is in our experiencing and marvelous to know love of God is to know power and is to experience God's peace and gazing at the beauty is amazing.

Is grace love and power that is, if only all of our hearts would surrender to the love by our being faithful in Him for He is the only Supreme Being, the things we could accomplish would more as well be limitless potentials is by believing the powerful, inspired words of His love, we would be able to live in a world free from wants of this and that for He is enduring and outlasting Love to personal situations and collective consciousness and responsibility that is relevant to us. I asked over and again in quiet contemplation of self how blessed we are and yet how poor many are desperate and, that is because of many being wise in their own eyes and not fearing God too.

Can you imagine how peaceful and loving the world could be just by listening to Him and following His commands? What comes from above is worth more than all the gold, silver of this world has to offer me and His message is a message of hope, love, happiness, faith and joy.

Also, I want to stress to you all that nothing is impossible when we believe in Him and is certainly that, when all else fails us in the world, His love remains. The power of inspiration and love is real and alive and lies within our reach, enabling us to achieve our goals with confidence. With that confidence along with the faith in our hearts, every hope and desire can be achievable as with us God knows that we all have dreams, and by having faith in Him and trusting that He will guide you to realize those dreams enables us to be happier and more purposeful is closer to Him more we love more we grow and more we soar and more we believe and receive and live it!

His higher power, wisdom, and strength are blessings to us, and He is a loving and kind gracious God, willing to give each of us our blessings in due time. Once we all surrender totally our hearts to Him, His grace and love will always be with us. You will never be alone, and when you come across challenges that test your faith, God's faithfulness and loving kindness will bless and guide you through any storm. He does not want His beloved children to lack for anything, as and He will provide all that we need to flourish. Is of joy to acquaint oneself with Him is peace.

By expanding our horizons with the power of words of wisdom, we are able to show love to Him our desire for progress. Remember, all of the joy and knowledge that we share with others is for His glory and honor, and I pray that we will not be discouraged or stumble in our journey and I pray may He please always bless us and all our families worldwide and friends for they mean a lot to us and that is so sweet to know that we can overcome with His love abiding is awesome to me. The following verse of one of my favorite songs says it all: "I want to scale the utmost height and catch the gleam of glory bright; but still I'll pray till heaven I found, Lord lead me on to a higher ground" (Oatman). "Wouldn't it be nice to strive and celebrate Him together everyday fellowships with Him and fellow kind in love, peace with joy and harmony as untied?

By the grace of God, myself as well as all of you can continue to be blessed with the hope and joy of accomplishing anything we set our minds to. We all need to know that His power of inspiration creates knowledge, wisdom, faithfulness, and an overall wonderful life. He is more capable than any of us to heal us and to restore hope, even turning our situations from perplexity to prosperity. No matter what you may be feeling, whether it is sorrow, pains, or tears, He is as is there for you anytime, day or night. He will comfort your heart and turns that sorrow into joy. And gives us happiness, is when we are at our lowest point, we can still cherish the thought that we will eventually have the inspiration and joy that we all strive for. Even when you are sick, is He will love you the same, and will remain by your side, constant as the North Star's marvelous!

What I believe that we should all hold dear to our hearts is that God loves us dearly and is our best friend in times of need as well as in times that we prosper. His heart is faithful, and He makes sure that we are all surrounded by His presence and loving kindness, "Steadfast love and faithfulness will meet; righteousness and peace will kiss each other" (Psalms 85:10). He is God the Kingdom, the King of Kings, and the Power and the Glory. His love surpasses all and anything we could possibly imagine, and I am so blessed to have found this faithful friend. No one can love and inspire as He does through His kindness in words as well as His actions. There is great strength in the power of His presence, and yielding to Him in obeisance is not weakness, but is the greatness of the heart expressing meekness. As the proverb says, "Joy is the chief wine," and that joy is a powerful tool in every willing heart who submits their strength to the control of the Creator. It enables us to realize that He knows everything about us and is inviting us to be renewed through His love and power working within us. I thank Him from the bottom of my heart for not giving up on me and for inspiring my heart even more.

Trust your heart and know that the words of wisdom that you hear have the power to inspire you. His kind words of love have filled my heart with hope and have helped fill a void that only He could fill. Once I was filled with this inner peace, my heart was transformed, creating inspiration and joy as I cherished His will and expressed my appreciation and gratitude. This is a triumphant victory that I will always celebrate!

As the saying goes, "In a battle, the heart will win over the brain." These words of wisdom have become an undisputable truth to me. One can indeed create a deep sense of joy and live a beautiful life, even when it seems like things couldn't get any worse. Remember that when all else fails and when life is filled with sorrow and pain that you will eventually get through your trials and tribulations, and once you do, you will find joy. By listening to inspired words of wisdom, we can find joy and inspiration within us to excel in anything we do. We can learn from life's lessons, whether they be good or bad, and we can grow from them that positive greatness that you can achieve rests squarely on your shoulders in that you must make the effort to search and find this joy that may be eluding you. That power of inspiration is obvious power is part of reason is that love of God I am empowered able to write and encourage our hearts. Word of this Scripture inspires me as well: "Do not neglect to do good and, share what you have."

Initially, you may want to ask, why do I have to do good or love one another as myself or share what I have, after all is my gift for keepsake? The catchy area is do not neglect or fail to be obligated by love to care and serve, is just my interpretation. Does it make sense? Sure, knowledge and wisdom, I have gained from God's guidance, am great and healthy enhancing grace for love, which makes it a privilege, not of my power. But, all glory to God, His ability enables me to doing this out of love comes hope for all. So, why should I keep to myself, and be selfish of what I have been given of God's love?

I am obligated to give away love as well for it to go around and multiply. The name of the big game is all about sowing and reaping to spread, multiplies and creates! Showing is reaping more love generating to cultivate more blessings for all people of human races. Above and beyond after all, you gained more than shared, is a blessing for your investment in sowing is never wasted. Rather, is reaping bounty harvest; matter of commonsense, thought about this, and which speaks specifically, of understanding, with insight, takes God's Knowledge and wisdom.

His is how much I leaned and how He loves, is that love is great and opens many doors. Is it possible, since we live in a materialistic world, the like liken ever before as selfishness rules hearts? Is there any fringe benefits or not, to you and others? Yes, focus on God, and let Him take over your world, and you will see miraculous blessings as He models for you. He is the just and eternal perfect role model, one that is ever faithful and, ever loving and kind as a lavish Giver, who changes not in value. When you love God, He nurtures and nourishes and fills your heart with joy that never ends, and you can never lack in all circumstances of your life, He is always there! That makes for my joy and obligation, of pure joy to encourage all of you as my brothers and sisters. It is my place to inspire and help by being there to uplift your spirit, support you to find and express that joy that you are longing for, because once you find it, you will see that greatness is in the heart.

Ultimately, there is a power of inspiration that comes from within us, but it is not of our own power. It comes to us from God and flows through us performing miracles and enabling us to reach far in realizing our dreams. This great friendship we all have with God can fill our lives with such happiness and joy, and is worth sharing! The bottom line is that everything we deal with in life is a matter of the heart, and the love that our heart can possess is powerful. This book takes a critical look into what lies within us and what lies before us, and attempts to reconcile the two. There is a need to educate the heart. It is inspiration that serves as the catalyst to launch dreams. Inspiration does matter, and is a powerful blessing, helping us to live meaningful life to its fullest.

Using God's given potentials and to create inspiring, and successful life as you love that is fulfilling and, it is not the words we know that shows wisdom, mostly it is how and when we use them. To me, always inspiration is a legacy, and in the wake of my experiences in life, I realized that the title of this book can be none other than "Greatness is in the Heart – A Tribute to Inspiration".

Hopefully, this book warms your heart, fills it with inner peace, and gives you the blessings, power of love of God and ability to achieve greatness in your heart. Please read this book prayerfully with an open heart filled with love. The inspiration that you will gain will empower you to overcome pain, sorrow and worry and will enable you to celebrate the many victories that are about to come your way. But, as a friendly and sisterly reminder, do not only pray when you are despair, but pray always to give thank and express your gratitude, because kind heart is what brings more blessings. Be thankful, acknowledge, grateful for all the blessings of your achievement in life, and the wisdom that you have obtained from God's Supreme Being!!

He is the One, who gives all things great and small and offers us all hope, and so my dear friend, when we are blessed with the power to do good works for His glory we are working and also blessed able to leave our mark in the world for future generations to follow. "Evangelism is one beggar finding where bread is and telling another beggar about." May blessings inspire us to have hearts of love and joyful, hopeful, and thankful hearts this power of inspiration ministers to; I pray May God bless and also gives us peace, and helps us to use our talents to better the world, bless all we meet to love too!

I am thankful for the power of inspiration that writing this book is being able to share my experiences with you. I want you all to think of God's love and how it inspires people of all ages and racial backgrounds to experience joy and peace through grace and faith that is what Love is is of God makes me. Greatness in everyone's heart's will make the world a better place to live in for His immeasurable love knows no boundaries is of joy also. Stay focused, as the next chapter ushers us into another story of boundless love, resulting from power of God's love and is for our inspiration, to educate the heart. Educating the heart that fills with love is joy in encouraging the mind are great blessings, for awareness matters and adds quality to our lives and that certainty.

CHAPTER FIVE

Immeasurable Love

"God loves every one of us as if there were
but one of us to love."
– Augustine

God's love is an eternal love! His grace and mercies are unconditional and everlasting to everyone. When you long for someone to share your life with and help you through the ups and downs of your life, just count on His immeasurable love. He alone understands your plight in life, for His love is the one true love that is genuine and TRULY unconditional is Joy to know it.

Once you pray and begin to have hope and faith in your heart, you can leave all of your "baggage" behind and be satisfied in knowing that He will always be there for you. Believe that anything is possible and trust in your faith. Everything works by faith, but never forgets most is to acknowledge Him, thank Him, and tell Him how appreciative you are of Him. My experience has shown me that doing this provides one of the greatest sources of encouragement to continue on the path to a loving heart. He is "the rose of Sharon" always will be there to see you through.

Ask Him what you need to know, and let go and let God do what He does best. His love is immeasurable because He needs nothing but for you to accept His will. His love and care will make anything possible, and the beauty of it all is that He can make anything within your reach. I prayed constantly when both of my beloved parents and other beloved ancestors passed away as well as other situations that plagued me, including my health. My family members were my earthly rocks, and when they returned to their sole Owner and Creator, I was left at the mercy of His will always done and anytime and everyday and everywhere blooms (Song of Solomon 2:1).

I mainly wanted to know how to survive in an orphanage. My heart was so sick, but I didn't need a doctor to cure it. The truth was that my heart needed to be filled with inner peace. You will read more of that journey that I took to find the doctor of all doctors – both physical and spiritual, in future volumes of my work. Amazingly, right when I needed Him the most, He was right by my side, which is one of the many reasons why my heart belongs to Him. He is an on-time God and never ever fails me and brightens my life daily and always there is joy in heart.

Matters of the heart, including peace of mind, can be answered by God with the promise of happiness, contentment, wisdom, knowledge, courage, grace is and understanding. He is our best Friend whose wisdom is infinite, surpassing all others. He has an abundance of everything, with the ability to successfully bless us all. His grace and love are immeasurable, and are given to us for free from the heavens above and that love is reviving the heart and mind is reined too.

As amazing as these glorious blessings are, we must keep in mind that we need to utilize these blessings wisely. The talents that emerge from these blessings given to us need to be properly harnessed (Exodus 31: 2-5). Regardless of any situation that we may find ourselves in, we should be encouraged in the fact that there is always hope. Learn and grow from Him and prosper all you can!

More than anything else, it is imperative that we remain hopeful and that our hearts are filled with love, obedience, confidence, and joy. Simply put, we are never in this world alone, for we are closely connected by loving and caring spirits. Love is the heart's power, and we should band together using this common bond and follow Him as good sheep should. Our Shepherd will not let us walk in the dark when we follow Him unconditionally. We are blessed and connected in many ways, including our thoughtful prayers of faith resulting from the power of inspiration. Everything falls into place when we have faith, love, and patience. Depend on these qualities to reach all of your goals in life.

A heart that is dedicated to service and prayer, along with the attributes mentioned previously, results in a peaceful way of life. The power of inspiration can encourage us to step out on faith and live the life of our dreams. Our overall well-being depends on many areas of our lives, including our ability to believe, trust, obey, and above all, hope.

These words of wisdom reveal the ultimate truth: "Hope deferred makes the heart sick, but a desire fulfilled is a tree of life" (Proverbs 13:12). We should take delight in hope to be rejoicing and dancing in God's love, for His love and grace are wonderful blessings.

When we realize all that we can achieve, we are assured that we will be filled with hope and are able to use our blessings to their maximum potential. Keep in mind that joy comes from above and that you can achieve anything just by listening. God speaks His words of love directly to us and to our hearts. I have benefitted in my life by accomplishing goals that are possible on a human level, and nothing has compared to the blessings that are received when wisdom and knowledge come together to bring joy to one's life.

The beauty of God's love and glory is amazing, and once I began to absorb His power of inspiration, I find that He visits me more often than ever, showcasing Himself as the Glory! He is with me daily, comforting my heart, and I am so grateful that He is the Power and the Glory whose boundless love is immeasurable. If you receive God with a heart filled with gratitude, you will receive abundant blessings and love. We will always need Him in our lives, and we should embrace Him with open arms.

Recently, as I was sitting alone and feeling very lonely, I silently said to my heart that I need a friend wish that I have a faithful friend who is caring and that need, a friend who loves and to take long walks, who loves to talk, and can stand with me heart-to-heart in prayer. So, I said I need a friend again and I said a little love, and sweet prayer, praises of joy overflows my heart with thanks. It wasn't a dream, but real that love follows, before I even concluded, look up guess what I saw? It works, heart warm feeling, you cannot believe. But, believe or not, God then appeared and gave me more love than I ever bargained for: Inspiration. I saw the love of God in my life, moves in all kinds of ways in my heart and through songs, praise and worships, prayers and, more inspiration overflows, I felt the excitement and of joy was presence of God.

His love gives me inspiration with a passionate love in my heart. That passionate love of God's immeasurable, is the kind of love that daily gives me the vision of hope and joy and peace. It is the joy blesses more than I ever dare in my wildest dream, which is the very love that kept me alive and is the very inspiration, that opens my heart to Him and healed and moved, turn around my life and shows me great and mighty things that I never knew joys were waiting to be revealed too is love that transforms and by the Holy Spirit!

Inspiration is in every man's heartbeat, and it enables us to realize our potential to the fullest. Inspiration matters, but keep in mind that it is achieved not through our power, but from the power of God. His love has no ceiling nor ending, and does us no harm but good with love of the riches and comforts of hope and abundant living. God's love gives us the power to have a full and enriched life with pleasurable lifestyles and radiant, and it sure put a smile on your face.

Ultimately, God wants us to enjoy life and to speak and act on His words of wisdom. The Book of Ecclesiastes cites clearly that this understanding is a priceless truth. Amazingly, His love is given to us so that we may succeed and enjoy our happiness. You may have heard about the various ministries that offer prayer, hospitality, encouragement, and comfort, among other offerings. I feel that these ministries are the springboards to the quest for joy and peace. God's love and inspiration manifests itself to fill our hearts with passion. Through the power of inspiration, principles of perseverance, working hard, and being smart, one can overcome those little poverty, laziness and ignorance are enemies that we can do without, when we turn our eyes up looking up more to the Lord God than anything else and that is the beginning of progress also.

A young lady recently shared with me how she discovered so many products in Nigeria and had a desire to invest in those products, but was discouraged because she did not have anyone (such as a godfather) to help her with the funds needed to invest in these products. It was sad hearing this, because it sounded so similar to my story of the past and how I wept because there was no one there to support or promote my work. It is very difficult to find agents and the publicists who are willing to assist a self-published author with financial difficulties. But, I knew that was blessed enough to do these work, that I must never give up promoting its good cause.

I have always had faith that the day will come when the doors of opportunity open up for me, and it wasn't long before the "Inspire

Women Ministry" organization discovered my hidden talents and skills for writing and my passion for Youth Ministry. The staff was so inspired with my books and my column with the Christian Herald entitled "Word of Wisdom," that the vice president, whose name is Mia, contacted me, and that blessing was followed-up with inspiration that I received from Tatiana Fox, the young intern and part of the publicity staff was awesome!

I was even more overwhelmed and excited when I heard from Anita Carmen, who is the inspired founder of the organization. She told me how happy she was for me and I felt her love and compassion! It resulted in me being awarded grants both for promoting more publications for youths as well as the organization sponsoring my leadership training. They were more than happy to assist me in any way possible, and showed me that immeasurable love can give us the love and will to accomplish anything that God wants us to do and be and encouragement makes a great difference in any human's life and that is the power of inspiration that is so passionate it is!

Within the organization is a remarkable program for all age group called the "Inner-Circle, which is made up of inspired mature women (both young and old), People who values power of God and inspiration. They are blessed inspirers, and we all are happy to share in the blessing of the authentic friendship. The beauty of it all is that, we meet monthly as part of a "spiritual spa," for inspirational teaching moments and devotion. When we meet, we feel the joy of sisterhood as our hearts are filled with warmth and love. Listening to inspirational music and the lectures ministers from the words of God is crucial. These are shared by the generosity of graciousness of seasoned inspired mentors as teachers of love and words of God are all blessings.

Some of the fanfares of the moments and important that wherever we meet we pray, first, is important and as students, the staff is always there to inspire our hearts and their support gives us always to me is inspiration is having them makes us happy around us is hopeful feeling for it is because of their acceptance of us and not just me. There is no more room in my heart for the rejection that I felt in the past. And all my feelings of loneliness have subsided thank God that His love conquers. When I am blessed to be around the women of this group,

I feel the love of our dear heavenly Father around us; for I know that He is watching over us and blessing us daily is what I really love about the group is the fact that when we unite as one in prayer, we all feel of even more blessed that we are recipients of God's immeasurable love and unity of strength there.

Indeed, we need each other, and helping each other out is one of the treasures of the authentic friendships that we share and is in building each other up stronger. Our great Provider will make a way for each and every one of us, "For with God nothing shall be impossible" (Luke 1:37). Encouragement, we are blessed by the joy of knowing God's many gifts and how to share those gifts with love to family and friends, because "those who are happiest are those who do the most for others" (Booker T. Washington). When you can believe in life being honest with heart of love is of joy that is for yourself and is apply yourself to the best of your abilities, the rewards you will receive will be a life changing that is right there you know the truth is the only solution.

Being honest about what you feel and God's Joy and Words of wisdom that I live by is to help inspire others are to "know thyself", because even though you need to know that the source of your power comes from none other than God, you must also be true to yourself is true to Him. When we know how the power of inspiration can help us/others, we can use this power to bless. One another while warming our hearts at the same time and that is the purpose of a loving life is a great heart embraces love, inspiration the time one gives and the hearts touched in the quest to inspire others, not just you all blessings. Let's Let's inspire us! To be honest the challenge here is to encourage ourselves and others; to stay positive and true to God, self and others and that love for us to continue is pray for one another daily and, encourage and comfort with your/our love, is so thrilling.

Is a blessing the joy of finding <u>inspiration and love with joy from above is awesome daily for it is a moving experience</u> it is such a wonderful feeling to have a positive heart and to use that heart to bless one another with love! This is how I have come to develop heart of habit of loving of joy curling up in a favorite spot daily and immersing myself in words of wisdom and reading as and studying. I also love to listen to songs of praises as part of my moments of devotion. It is so beautiful knowing that God loves you just as you are and is so true this, "people will not be judged by the way we see them but by the way God sees them." America is a praying country much as Africa and has huge hearts of love and so is reaching out for me is with social and economic services for us all, is that is part of my saying thank you Lord God is of joy that is blessing America is a blessed nation and, I believe it is why her motto is, "In God we trust," and how she is ideally she does things for people who need help, wherever you come from accepts.

And, support can make a great blessing and that matters too. But, truth is that in any of us human life and is with God's help, this is what and how much God loves us. Is you and I are and you're His, much as I am too. Love is the greatest and love is the heart's power is the simple, but God gives us great opportunity to express our love and skills and talent as God's given potential and life is of God. And His love prevents and endures everywhere for me and is something to be more than thankful and God has truly been good to me everywhere and everyday. I say God bless America and also He has blessed Africa. Blesses me to be thankful that there are people, who are hearts of love in many places around the world, and programs aligned for us with Him for us, in America, you are blessed in a special way that is everyone has a chance to benefit from program.

As you have read, and for rehabilitations as such you can be thankful for life and, also of such available programs in vocational rehabilitation insider as someone who worked there in the system, is what I know, what it does to people. And how blessed that can make for it makes very much a difference for someone and needy to take it to heart, and loving to do something for you and also for others and yourself is happiness is of the Lord God is making a difference in a needy person's life and love is hope more and don't put down yourself in the face of odds of life is see possibilities and don't be bitter and love is help for hope! Is reality is that, I don't dwell on the past, but I think positively and move on is how I am an overcomer with joy and is better for life.

It is a blessing when you can be available to do, when you help another person and better self even in the midst of your trials and react proactively and not reactively that is the life to live. Is the best step and way to go, and <u>I say an Amen to that and in my life as privilege</u>

in America to work in the capacity as a senior vocational rehabilitation counselor for over a period of twelve years is am being thankfully I, have reason to thank God for America; you see and know that's is part service makes is a whole lot of a difference and helping out too much in many ways people is challenging can make life a blessing is bloom wherever you are so is great difference in life.

If we take time to be thankful and thank God for giving us the advantage of what God has provided for us too and, it works by faith and a combination of passion and confidence in living that positive energy is heart's placed in positive things is of good thoughts and love is of hope in Him is inspiration wisdom is of God.

And, I thank God for blessed we are by my God first and our family and neighbors as all friends. Loved ones and from where I have come is also love of God for me too started from my birth place and is my proud home too as America and in my mind and prayers everyday. I cannot forget it; I thank God for more of His abundance is to pray that a time will come when we all can shine the light and rise up to our clarion calls and do more to take care of the responsibilities that we have to give, and of those who are needy and helpless and children and the adults, especially of the elderly and give them hope; It's by helping is in improving our lives, children and adults is as well the elderly and it can be helpful and great help in education as rehabilitation is education.

All is blessings as life- changing programs that offers hope and, I was determined to find solutions. To those battles as acute and strong as mine and put a stop to it, it was relevant for me to take initiative for it was my situation too to do this it is a gift what God helps me to take a step forward and He gives grace as well guidance on how to be! And that responsibility rested on me as life is nobody will do it better for me and that is why, I start this introduction with love as well with my thanksgiving and also is relevant to begin with love and I thankful for all what God has done and given me and overcoming those hurdles as those were of serious life's challenges were.

All were one of my biggest obstacles. I found myself wallowed always in an unexpected agony, one after the other. That was part of not for me to handle in the first place and, also not my portions neither; I couldn't and still can't handle other things in my plates all those bigger all than I can bear; It is to thank God always with me and loves me too much, and is true, as I have said am favorite of all. You can see there are evidently and you have read them He loves and does me well that is sure! He can't give more than I can handle. So, as always came through for me is as He is my Father and put me in His care is a path that He walks me through the wilderness and so, for me God answers prayer and listens too! And, for me is a promise Keeper and Blesses for He is there is always is for my rescued and refuge inspiring and guidance as He guided and, He told me, "let go and allow Him do it all those hard to do!

Lovely and tenderly told me, I will be handling, so put in His things to do basket." Gladly, I did without any hesitation this outcome is testimony and one more another proof to the Great Healing Power of God and He raise me up a testimony and never to forget who, what, where and how and why and to whom should I be most thankful, all that is something to find out more also. Power of God and one more to show no one else can do it but for His love and grace that shines upon us. I saw utmost and loving Father Works as He is, was with me and best Friend and had prepared me with His heavenly radiance today and tomorrow that will shine me on and is eternally. He did my heart with more sufficient grace as is the Love of my life and Joy of my heart. God has given me victory and I will lift His name up evermore forever that matters in my life as first is crucial, is who saves my life and met my needs in any hour or seasons that means is a world to me. He made me happier. He only met me most when in my needs of joy this to begin the testimonies with thanksgiving and that journey ended.

Joyously, but one thing for sure is, I must be clear that it wasn't all that rosy initially for it started with what was hopeless and difficulties and was so hard; One emotional, but with utmost gratitude to God's glory. Thanksgiving, is adoring Him, every blessed day is demonstrating His love is Excelling love and power is everlasting and is a God that is revealing Love as well God of hope and love is also joy, justice, faithfulness, holy is He the One only supernatural Being. He God is of power and not man and He doesn't see things as man and purpose for our lives is love, so is everyday and is far greater beyond ours. I am grateful for that is beyond human imagination and, please, don't let them fool you, for God is alive is also real, hold on tightly to Him God's love, for His words are unchanging love and, when things happen the way you did not expect do leave it as is there and don't question so much but pray more and all by faith have hope is there.

It is more by trusting and believing Him, when He says He will plead your cause don't you worry, so take it to Him in your prayer and on bended knees, all is well and working best to it. Most and trusting more and more in Him for the best is about to happen and yes, hang in there and holding tightly, is expect His joy and peace is more than abundant it is a good thing to know Him more personally, is how and when we can use the wisdom so, is to let go and look up! I'm encouraged by the Lord's healing love to look unto God's unchanging grace and also leave all as is all in His hands and this is of a aim to help us as well to inspire and to enlighten and encourage all those out there who are being of despair and know the joy encouraged and hopeful is inspired.

You more of who have similar grief and situation is as shared and never give up on hope and keep up the faith and do praying for love is the will of God that offers joy, and we can be as shared also always conquer the enemies but, must first find strength from Him is by faith that He is the power within in your greatest moment of agony is no matter what time! He is there and are you relying solely only in Him it is there and you going to be just fine and He is going to inspire you to be of hope and joy with happiness His inspiration inspires and that encourages the heart to think wisely and transforms the mind stimulating the thoughts. The God of all-redeeming grace and love and power is who comforted and inspires us all and, I am one of those, as such you are blessed thee in the good company's hands and, the best is yet to come is in God's power and is He is who blesses, that each we may be a blessing and in His tenderness hand and that is Only Love!

Truest and that is who measures you; if you are one of those that are faced with moments similar situation as shared. I have for you here something, I love for you to know that fear is not our portion, but faith in God! FEAR merely: "False evidence appearing real," you'll overcome as well, and God doesn't want us fret but to be happy and cheery! It is not up to man, is up to God! Your limitations and all that are what you go through not measuring your life and are only God's Love. And all your circumstances, He takes charge if you believe for says leave it whatever to be cherry and trusting more in Him, and please don't give up on hope either! Rather than give up is keep it alive and don't cry more than you should, but don't cry anymore and don't let your faith.

Faith in God fails you! I am sharing the power for my victory and for God will never ever fails you is a promise Keeper and, is as I see is Forever Love. He is the greater Grace and Mercy. The one and only Remedy, He is and that says, "The grace of the Lord Jesus Christ, and the love of God and the communion of the Holy Spirit be with you all. Amen"! (2nd Corinthians 13:14). Don't doubt what that power of God's love and words can do is a blessing, If you do are the one to fail you instead, don't and limit yourself to people's opinion rather than relying upon God's words more is the best to be strong as well for He keeps promises. He is who encourages always.

Please, let us be hopeful, and it is joy to beware of the simple priceless treasures of life; they are much more are all powerful. All are spiritual principles of God, not just mere as often said to be just saws, clichés and is more than that, are as Spiritual words of inspiration priceless. Treasures and all are divine blessings are a gift of love. As are sure also life savers and, also this is the doing of the Lord in my life and, love and power and miracles and as He is over generous! Please, don't buy trouble for yourself and don't pay back with revenge but pray more and keep forward is than to fret, is you keep moving on up. Is the prayer more and trusting in God is best and, better is more than able to deliver those trusting in Him; He is, so let go and let God handle.

He is the best and being the One; and in handling all your situations, for it is the best for you will be satisfied as well, marvelous is; if you are hurt by anyone, when you allow Him and trust, you will be more than happy. Finding, divine favors all for your victory and there are also as well miracles on your way. Is marvelous, and greater than you and I, is also as well a miracle working God of wonder! I found that, if you allow God have His way in your heart it is, you will be very happier and healthier and filling that with love, and joy is there are all great things of the heart with hope and in His love and inspiration you will be healthier, happier, satisfied and more.

Purposeful and, I see that is than wasting time to attack the enemies with words of mouth. Friend, please use the amour that power and potential is spiritual! I am telling you as I have seen the most effective means and methods to be wonderworking and its spiritual power and that is it are what God destined for us to use in accomplishing of our goal and love is the heart's power and I found a profound thrill, the way best of approaching God. It is through our humility that He is in every way that is the best in understanding our situations ultimate is He, problem sovereign Solution! That is what I found healing Love and there is hope for us and, this book has proven.

Been fun to write because He is the one who inspires my heart and fills me with love and joy is with laughter and inspiration in all that I do that overflows is I am thrill is to leave it there! And friendship is for sharing and fellowshipping together as well is happiness and is of the Lord. Remember this always friendship and love and faith matters and it is what makes life bearable as and is also what crowbar that is and the only way is with His grace. Faith in God that is awesome is all by God's grace is by faith is how to respond to those situations. It is in our humility before God that greatness is revealed, for sure as well, "In my distress I called upon the Lord, and cried out to my God; my cry came before Him, even to His ears!"

There is hope daily, in His love His presence brings me love as His words are of unfailing love comforting it is touch of love and joy and happiness and healing and power and strength and grace is where to find with words of hope and love comes. Powerful words of unfailing, unfading all everlasting love. But, we need to learn that is totally dependability is total surrender and, how and when to apply those spiritual words and achieve positive results inspirational words are very important to life and is like the air that we breathe and it educates the heart and helps the broken. Is joy to know it and He says for us, "To stand fast in one spirit, with one mind striving together for the faith of the gospel" (Philippians 1: 27).

Is so good there is nothing in life like one to know Him and yes and yes, what we need is God as His love is inspiration and, God has purpose is best, far greater and bigger than what we are His love and inspiration of God to, "be kindly affectionate to one another with brotherly love, in honor giving preference to one another" (Romans 12:10). A cure for me is God's love in my heart and to love and serve and to obey and do

His will in my life that is all about as well true genuine love and it is not fake and/or false pretense and to do otherwise is to say you are on your own the wrong track take that to heart and note that is a disaster and buying trouble for you; I cut my coat according to size too! My size is love God and love fellow kind and do my very best to inspire and encourage my heart inspires as given and be able to serve others and He wants me to serve Him is humanity and is to love. Love all and surely of suffering comes joy and, God wants.

Us to love and look out for each other! Peace within is what I have, and from that comes with spirit of love and, His is of that Joy you are always eager to use that power of love always. It is that capacity to receive, give and to also too grow more and receive even more than ever and so it is of spirituality more for the physical too that is the same of the enrichment personally and professionally and He grows us in His love, and bless our hearts with love and happiness is also, God blesses you and I to grow in His is God's amazing grace love, that is when it is so simple.

As it all that matters for you can overcome anything that bothers you, for it is of God's who is in you is the power that is more than capable to overcome anything but is by faith. If you believe in God is done. He'll help you to move past those obstacles past and live of life fully and moving forward. Is you can overcome all is with God's help daily is with you; regardless of what that it is, even of one's self imprisonment among others and that is what makes for my life being well and happiest is, for I know and prosperous is God empowers and divine guidance is the first key source to go too if one thought saturates love for God to tap from the limitless are potentials.

Can anyone share of His glory? Truth is there for, Nobody shares His glory and that is all what cuprites need to understand that no one shares of God's glory and is no match for Him as it is neither here or there is Almighty God and thank God for defeating them and, I'm forever will praise for being our God who never fails His own people! The culprit was out to hurt my family as I found out that he diverted my money to personal use and thought it was over, and laughed, boasted, but, did not know it was not over that indirectly was buying trouble more for him and his family and friends with all that his dubious motives and agenda just to hurt and to cause me trouble. Behold sooner realized that, "Many plans in a man's mind, but it is the Lord's purpose that will stand" (AMP: Prov.19:21). How grateful that I'm for the goodness, greatness of God's power. As this work demonstrates the goodness and greatness of God is a testimonial also.

It speaks for itself that there is something awesome mighty about greatness of God' love as well His love to us demonstrates that it is, "Not by might, nor by power, but my spirit, saith the LORD of host" (Zechariah 4:6). Too, my job is to sing and rejoice for God dwells among us. This is it for us is soaring and prospects as the power and decides the best, we can bloom as well. He is who gives grace and heals and abides in us and that is the good news for us and your life's pathway is all as well, scripturally is all awesome love, is a noble thing and is the gift that is God shares with us and here His word says categorically to me, as His beloved daughter to "Sing and rejoice, with all of us and this is what says all evidently, "the proof of the pudding in the eating."

True! "The LORD God is my strength", He is also my Salvation and Redeemer and I will always love Him much more says, I am His lovable daughter, (Caroline Arit Thompson), and am to, "Sing and rejoice, O daughter of Zion: for, lo, I come, and I will dwell in the midst of thee, saith the LORD" (Zachariah 2:10). All quoted is in black and white, and again we know that it's not something hidden and not my word either. And, again and again says this also is what great joy is for me, to share in this world wide ministry of love of God to His humanity and carry out the duty that I am assigned inspiring hearts to live more fulfilling lives. Heart of love, is a dedicated.

Heart and mindset togetherness is of faith that inspires heart and am inspired by blessings of God and these are all of us and am so grateful we can learn to our potential and be kind and so is love being blessed by God, is what works and so, am hopeful that you will find satisfaction by reading, Greatness is in the Heart – A Tribute to Inspiration and rekindle a sense of gratitude and find your blessings and dreams to come true; and May God grace bless you as well and meets, and as well each of us all, and at our point of needs accordingly. For, our satisfaction is life is only guaranteed by Him is life and grace is given to us through the power of the words and that through Him is struck me most as love is all is Only by God's grace that I have come this far.

And achieving success in my life and in my faith journey is exciting and I am humbled as I never ever anticipated this much graces. I am enjoying so many blessings and graces are with it is His love in my heart and I am truly blessed. Blessings, I never thought in my wildest dream is as read, I never that I never thought, let alone in my faith journey is all beyond my expectations. And, is exceedingly abundant is of my great pleasure joy is to love all, is of God's love and grace and endless mercy is always to be, is an honor, and gifts all for me to see, and walk and find that I am more capable than I thought, and, I had also doubted, while there in the trail of my trial too.

But, even thought that I am not capable, and there look all these receive all these miracles and of great blessings and mightier things and also given to me as well everyday is a blessing to me it is that is daily, dearly as all are inclusive is from Him to my family and friends loving ad caring and showing His love evermore is for His humanity is all gifts of God and that says all is well about the title of this work why greatness is in the heart; it is relevant for me to share of His power and greatness with a tribute that and, I had argued that, our greatness is in the heart that is the conclusion, also with love being the heart's power and is obvious power being He is always.

This work is authored He is and with enough narratives and emotional power to stimulate thoughts and engages our hearts and minds and encourages our hearts. Inspires us and with God is of course that is we can do all things through His power with authority that He has given to us with potential and He is who else would? I say and do overcome and soar beyond those obstacles that impeded and my limitations were critical and, significant impediment is what obstructed and can you imagine the power of love that inspires, empower changes everything more confidence.

And is left for us to find and I found and joy and is to keep it burning and brightens us up for God is all that we have and nothing else is as better as finding what you were hoping and the thing is the best is joy to be thankful for that gleams of hope and it brightens you up is your hope is all ups and radiance smile when you had flood of tears is amazing grace love that is all need is of inspirational and empowering and restoring and working for those who trust and believe God.

"No one has ever seen God; but if we love one another, God lives in us and his love is made complete in us" (1 John 4: 12: NIV). And, I am glad that God lives inside there is Hope is for me and also revealing to me things that I never knew in my wilderness journey and that sums our, "Greatness is in the Heart!" A Tribute to the power of love and inspiration that God has love is manifested in human hearts right here on earth is a blessing and my conclusion that love is the greatest and answer and solution is to all situation. Please, refer (11Cor. 1:20; Heb. 6:17-19; Acts 1:8; 26:6/7; Gen. 28:15-22). God has love enough power and He is truest, not forsaken His own children. And He is mine to be proudest of His child that is favored this much and His greatness to share goodness and give thanks with love and thanks. That power of His love, inspiration what results gratitude, for is awesome to magnify and for me lift Him name up higher and higher and that is happiness is living every moment with love, grace, gratitude and for my joy is full and, the very best of everything is the joy of finding love, inspiration and to do what I never ever thought.

After my ordeal that is possible but it is for God is Joy. Joy is alive and is living the life of love, reaching out to touch one another, am grateful to happily inspire and cheerfully is true Love that is what I experience and feel in my heart is God's Love and truest His love and compassion is what makes life more hopeful and bearable is the joy being alive is wonderful. That Love is powerful and inspires ones to be happier and stronger and more lucrative, and loving is a spiritual experience and essence of life living, loving and sharing. Our friendship in words and actions; Mostly, is being thankful for what God is and has done and that's so gracious. This is gracious what Scripture encourages is living with love and a purpose.

Inspiration and gaining is pleasurable and very impressive and that is power with wisdom and insightful knowledge and is all God He is a promise Keeper and, says to me, my dear lovable daughter, Caroline Arit Thompson today, "See I have engraved you on the palms of my hands" (Isaiah 49: 16: NIV). Knowledge, wisdom all are given is also are what first originated from God and Love, for Authors is God, who is saying love one another most that is compassion is love we are to share and love as well as caring is well comes from Him and is from the heart always so is all the strength, that I have need to keep moving. Love comes from the heart of God to us is love.

He daily abides and is the greatest. And love is ultimate is the Only gift that we owe and none other than that, is apparent you cannot withhold love as it is given of God's love, is the best. Is the best for everything and a gift to give away and love empowers, giving energizes as we give grows, and we together enjoy the progress and the process is love is expressed is from one heart to another is joy and mutually is sharing and cooperating and giving to support and uplift each up as that is what friends do is in interceding for one another lifting up in prayers and sharing love.

Making each other happy heart and inspire strengthen when in moment of trials and that is the best and is freely given is likewise nothing else more for me to offer than to give and as to receive it more than is giving to those in need of hope and encouragement for their happiness as well also. And I celebrate my love for Him for His Love is in my soul, and is praising the Lord, my God and my Father the one who Fathers me too and reigns both in heaven and here on earth is Lover. And I thank Him for He gave me a very dear Friend and Comforter His Only Son, my Inspiration blessed. Awesome is for me and joy and happiness and success and my gratitude are my spiritual experience fire that is joy is to find Love within and that power is of His that is how power works it inspires of passion that can't be substituted. Inspiration is my legacy and passion His Love is compelling me and that is empowering me. Empowerment! God's love empowers us.

Blessed me is my life and my faith in God inspires more and God gave of heart of His is power and love and joy and hope and inspiration and life that has blessings of hope with it is my life is with a vision of hope and more to be thankful for there is bright today and tomorrow also. And, yes, a brighter future and joy at the end and more growing in His amazing grace love that too is a great thing is good news and what a joy and blessing to be a part of this as well blessings of Joy and now I am as well to share that faith and love and friendship as a happy survivor.

I am thankful for God allowing me the gracious blessing of my having a part in this world ministry of love and showing mercy and inspiration, as a woman with a vision, with a mission that is also one borne out of sorrow. Is power of love and always is inspiration from the love of God and fellow kind as human kindness that is to cherish and values too. And, as well purposeful living always, because God loves has given is joy of my life and after so many years of sorrows.

It is joy and what a blessing(s) and the hope difference now is something happens to me and when that love abides life becomes a masterpiece awesome living and mesmerizing that is am dancing and romancing also. Friend Seek for inspiration for there and only God gives is of eternal peace that is everlasting Love. It changed my life and for my happiness, fills my heart with His love and joy that never ends. It's amazing is of heart of love and graces with love and blesses with joy. Love is a great gift is God has given to us and it works best hand in hand with grace and faith always is of profound joy is enjoying today is because love is the greatest power is within me that healing and curative thought. It lies within you is good for me is to know God personally better is best.

Better life is God and He is greatest of love, is empowering is strongest and He is who gives us life and is peace and His kindness is all that moves and inspires that is serving Him is more and love is the key, see the remedy also is everyday joy. And believing and receive and live and love's access is the code love for He opens me up. And, His love is of one's heart and mind and, dedicated when you let God into your heart and to be the guide into your heart is Joy fill, I pray that as you read that "Out of his glorious riches he may strengthen you in your inner being, so that Christ may dwell in your (our/all) hearts through faith" (Ephesians 3:-17: NIV/ Hebrews12: 1-2)!

Oh yes, and what a joy there is that Love? He is such marvelous Lord God is to me is the best Encourager and greatest source of my faith. He is a Gift that has no comparison. God uses both supernatural and well are as well is the natural to also bless and heal and blesses us and that Greatness is in heart and that power is Love. His and Him only can heal us from the inside out and transforming and, I found cure and more is a blessing for the body, mind and spirit, very exciting and also important is to have faith as well love in our hearts and faith that is all showers with prayers and there is hope for us so far He is the Lord God all He is Mighty and faithful and from God to us and our entire neighbors is and that is love is, "Freely you have received, freely give" (Matthew 10: 8: NIV), is my gift is of grace and is joy for me to give it away to multiply.

This wonderful gift of God's love is further expressed in the Book of Numbers, for "the Lord bless thee and keep thee: The Lord make His face shine upon thee, and be gracious unto thee" (KJV: 6:24, 25). That assures me that I will always have immeasurable love, I am more thankful every blessed day with the joy in my heart that Jesus is a friend who knows your entire situation and even of your faults will be there and never depart also and still loves you anyway.

In your heart's desire for a brighter future, there are certain things that you should pray and pay more of your closer attention to. Daily reading and prayer are required, and you must remember to glorify God's immeasurable love that thanksgiving is very important in every way as situation. Most importantly, you must pay critical attention to your heart and to use all of your blessings to their maximum potential. Be encouraged by doing this, you Will be a success. It's by believing and believe is doing by faith and action is love and trust God to and putting your little effort all, you Will be a Success!

CHAPTER SIX

Nothing Passes God – A Legacy to Cherish!

"The best inheritance a father can leave
his children is a good example."

As I am writing this chapter, I am aware that on a daily basis, people world-wide are living their lives with mixed feelings. I am happy about this, but at the same time it saddens me. Sorrow can be very overwhelming, and a time that I know I have felt great sorrow is when I have had to let go of loved ones. I am vividly reminded of my dearly loved earthly rock, my physical father whose motto throughout his life was "Nothing passes God."

He was inspired by the wording and how even though it only contained three words, it said so much. He lived his entire life glorifying God. He would tell me every day, "God, who loves us all, gives us the power to do anything, and we must be thankful and abide by His word." He cherished the power of God and talked about it constantly. He was a blessed man and those who knew him knew that he relied on the faith that "Nothing passes God's love and power."

My father constantly acknowledged the supremacy of our Creator/Protector, and he knew that God would protect us all from the dangers of the world. I admired and adored that inspired spirit that my father possessed, and I knew that it meant more than all the money in the world. My father's interest in the power of inspirational words of wisdom and his passion for God left a legacy that is priceless. Words of encouragement, enlightenment, and most importantly, prayers, were expressed on a daily basis by my father as well as the rest of my family. We always love is how we were inspired and motivated glorified the Maker from whom all blessings are possible.

As I watched and admired my father for always serving and being devoted to our Creator, I felt blessed and it gave me joy and inspiration. It was a worthy legacy that I proudly emulated, and it encouraged me to pray daily and to be blessed. The joy of knowing that nothing passes God's power was amazing! Both my paternal and maternal ancestors were special in that they were Godly families. I am so proud to be identified with their roots as well as their spiritual awareness. Certainly, we are defined by what we make of ourselves during our lifetime is love.

These words of wisdom are so true: "Children act in the village as they have learned at home," and "Charity begins at home." Also, "Setting a good example is the best tool a parent can have in raising children." Indeed, "The only two lasting bequests we can give our children: One is roots; the other wings." Education is the most important aspect of society, and your character is your destiny, for good leaders are always good followers. Good home training can be great educational material because it opens many doors of opportunity for generations to fly and soar – both in academics and in character.

To become a leader and a patriotic citizen in any society takes hearts of unconditional love, perseverance, compassion and acceptance. I always admire great leaders of wisdom who are real men, fathers, and role models as they speak to children to inspire them to live life to the fullest. Great fathers, to me, are considered admirable leaders and inspire not only their own children but other children as well. In my opinion, the most important blessing that these men possess is the fact that they have the ability to be excellent guidance counselors for children.

We already know who mothers are and what they can do, so we won't even get started on the many praises that they deserve, such as being the heart and grace of her family. Even though this chapter focuses on fathers, I have to still say thank God for our sweet mothers. Of course, we all should be thankful for our fathers, but keep in mind that mothers are just as noteworthy!

As these words of wisdom state, "Nothing passes God," and they have resonated with me since I was young. Today, I see it as a source of my strength to persevere through the many hurdles I have had to face and overcome during my lifetime. The memory of my father gives me a soft spot in my heart and enables me to count my blessings every day. Likewise my mom's too.

This legacy of blessings that I possess is something unique to cherish. It has been years since my parents left this earth to the care of the ultimate Father, but because of the unique characteristics that they possessed; I am able to reflect fondly on each of their personalities. It is difficult to express in words how my mother gave us tips for survival in life, among others. These tips, which were the formula for survival, were shared by my father as well. My father taught me to keep faith and hope alive, and of all the things I learned from him, the most intriguing was that "Nothing passes God." These words are meant to tell us to keep living! Life may be turbulent at times, but if we keep pressing on, we will all be blessed with God's favor.

Perhaps you have read "The Christian Herald" September 2011 edition (Vol. 8 No. 4), and you may have stumbled on the interview I had with the inspiring Publisher/Executive Editor Tina Edebor on this subject matter captioned: "Christian Herald Columnist's Gift Acknowledged by President Barack Obama." It was heart-warming to humbly present our President and world renowned leader with my book "Priceless Love", and I am proud to say that he is a great father to his children and other children not just his because has compassion towards humanity always. I was so overwhelmed with joy and happiness to talk about his role as a positive image to them.

Children that need role models and who want to become positive vanguards and leaders of tomorrow are blessed to be touched by President Barack Obama's words as well as the way he lives his life. He sets an incredible example for many of the desperate children and families of the world to emulate, and I have heard many children as well as parents sing his praises. He has been praised the most for his positive image as a loving father to his two beautiful daughters, Malia and Sasha. He reminds me of my beloved late father that I testify about him always wrote a book about, titled, *A Daughter's Love —Remembering my father, my teacher and my friend(s)*.

Although my family (mother, grandparents/ other ancestors) is not with me and I miss all them dearly, I am thankful that they lived their lives with love in their hearts. Even though they are gone, they will never be forgotten, for I will cherish the legacy that they left for me eternally. I have great memories of them and am constantly reminded that God's blessings enable me love to continuously relish in these memories. Reality is though hurts when we miss loved ones, but comforted to note, are rested with heavenly Father and owner yet, and never left our hearts as my heart love lingers. Their priceless love and vision has guided me through a happy childhood and that in turn has resulted in happiness in my adulthood life and that is of my dedication so sweet.

Is of sweet memory and I be happy and can honestly say that I could never have known how my family's legacy of true contentment would become a valuable asset to me if I hadn't been so blessed and love listened and paid close attention to my father's teaching me words of wisdom and mothers and grandmothers are wonderful great teachers that God blessed of us all is to cherish! Today, in both lean and prosperous times, I know that "nothing passes God's power of provision." Thankfully, my devoted parents knew that children should be trained to serve as leaders and vanguards of tomorrow, even before society ever suggested it. We were grateful that they were blessed and enlightened enough to share their guidance and counseling to their young.

Like most great and inspired hearts already know, their commitment and responsibility is always and was to train a child to be the best they can be. These words of wisdom are very true: "Train up a child in the way he should go: and when he is old, he will not depart from it" (Proverbs 22:6). Is a workable solution and that is the joy of parenthood teaching them is the best and, this wise saying from the Orient echoes, "The tribute to learning is teaching," all education.

Nothing passes God's power in wisdom when it comes to parental priceless love and of it is their guidance. I am so thankful that my memories of childhood are pleasant ones. It is joy is so very important that we have happy and healthy childhood, for when one can cherish devoting quality time to one's family; it will lead to an honest and good heart loving is so marvelous and is a thing of beauty. If a child is devoted at a young age to having a loving heart, then he or she will be blessed and will have a great and flourishing life. What counts most is to listen to words of wisdom at a young age and not to ignore them, for that is the key to the joy of future and your inspiration is motivating hope with a child's future is that offers hope with a brighter tomorrow.

Daily! Above all, the key to success is through courage, perseverance, and consistency. I have learned many of my parent's examples about life, and I am so very appreciative, for hope is living that power is, "inspiring wisdom can change your life forever." One of the many lessons I have never forgotten is my father's motto, "Nothing passes God." We must prepare our children today for tomorrow is to be successful in life by teaching them inspirational words of wisdom, is which mostly come from God's word. Whether or not you are a believer, it will help to build the child confidence and character in a child believing and living that hope in heart, mind and spirit.

Throughout our lives, we can sometimes fall into the trap of failing to care enough to listen sometimes but is there the word sticks in us and drifting too are of many reasons. That can be caused by a number of things, such as trying to make a "quick buck." But when we totally as going after, forgets to listen constantly to the nourishing truth, we are also forgetting that wisdom is to the soul what good health is to the body. Truly, nothing passes God's power and His words of wisdom, and we are all defined by what we make of ourselves during our lifetime and love is a blessing when given unconditionally and is priceless to any it makes the world a better place as you blessed openly and warmly receive with a heart of gratitude and use wisely that is priceless.

It seems many people today live dangerous lives with hardened hearts. What makes it even worse is that these people are liars and do nothing but corrupt others, which makes the situation even worse. It makes it harder to trust and differentiate between someone who is blessed with the spiritual gifts from God and someone who is simply trying to "get over." At first, is difficult to tell, let alone believe; who is among the specially gifted whose mission is to uplift people and is the time that we live it has made it so. Bottom line is that we must be careful in who we trust.

Even though it can be difficult to tell who we can or cannot trust, please take the chance to get to know our faithful leaders – teachers, pastors, evangelists, apostles, prophets, and many others, young and old, across the globe. God does speak to us through these groups of people, and some may be familiar friends and family members, while others are blessed encouragers, inspirers and messengers. But please keep in mind that no one is assumed this role, for they are appointed by the power and authority of the Creator Himself. Do not forget that greatness is in the heart! Please, act upon what the Holy Spirit reveals to you. "And the peace of God, which passeth all understanding shall keep your heart and mind through Christ Jesus."- Philippians 4:7.

If someone you know is blessed, make sure that instead of being hateful towards them, have love for them and cherish them. Be encouraging to them by praying for them so that they continue to be uplifted. Embrace them and enjoy their fellowship and gifts from God, for they were given these gifts for a reason, as it differs from innate gift or talent! Our Maker has the power to anoint those He feels are capable of carrying out the duties of being anointed leaders.

When one prays consistently and is trusting of God and willing to water the seeds of His words, he or she will be inspired, resulting in the "unspeakable joy" to fulfill their purpose as destined. The fruits that the Spirit bears are many, most importantly being love, and anyone can achieve it. To the world in general that is not something to hear, let alone welcome shared. Well we all just need to believe that if we work hard to be the best we can be, we can be at our best not just physically, but spiritually as well. It is our path to tread! It's both for success/progress.

Think twice before you act out and try not to belittle someone for that really goes to show of your belittling yourself and where is your dignity? This only shows that you are filled with ignorance and that you have a small mind. Think twice before blackmailing and humiliating all those children of God as they are chosen loving hearts. These same people that you may hurt are the ones who are blessed and who are placed in your life for a reason. Please, do not get into the habit of participating as well wrongly accusing these blessed individuals! God uses many media.

Yes, to spread His messages of love and wisdom and hope that is to say that truth is this. Whether it is imparted through dreams, words, or a fellow human being who is chosen vessel as kind enough to bless us, and this individual could be either an adult or a child, it is best to show them love and respect for they are doing their assigned duty and it could be written or spoken has God's purpose as ambassadors representing Him and that is what many don't understand and sad that is. Unfortunately, these individuals who are blessed are often disliked, is shunned by many. Are, often the real ones are doubted by many. They are many times confronted by others, why?

Doubting whether or not they are the source of these power-filled gifts that we aspire to have and keep in mind that we should always be grateful and happy for others' progress, as they are just as grateful and happy for yours. I am reminded daily of lessons by God's love to be grateful for His blessings here on earth and for the promise of eternal life and that is the thought to be in place, as the ultimate. Else, you won't see the blessings of what His love is doing in your life. His love has taught me to be friendly and creative and bless people and hope this chapter finds you excited as I am. And, what a blessing to know that nothing can separate us from the love of God ever and is faith endures. Evermore, He is the Lord is and continues to be faithful and true to His Word also.

And, is the same chat, I had with Anita Carman, the Founder and President of "Inspire Women Ministry" (Houston, Texas), who inspired my heart with her warm, encouraging words. When inspired my heart, was of joy with her note which said, "Caroline, I am happy for you." It impacted my life, so she is one of my role models, and will forever be friend inspirational friend of mine, along all her staff, as blessed people that are happy, humble, and have loving hearts. As they are filled by the Holy Spirit and love others to be hopeful and progress they are all blessed!

To be happy and be purposeful too, which Anita Carman, founder of Inspire Women's Institute, fits in my perspective description of genuine love and kindness, is measured reaching to touch others, shows compassion and that love is by words and actions not just boastful mouth. I see, think of just saying and not doing and as you read in the acknowledgement and introduction. As well, she is "Investing in women who change the world;" That is her mission statement, and I am so grateful to have part and included, and I never knew or met until after I was granted award for scholarship and grants to further my education in the program and, that is known her, through that generosity of her heart and she is someone who helped me with encouragement, inspiration.

And offered opportunities for me to do what I had thought, I couldn't do but God put her in my path, as graduated, from the Institute, August 2013, it was the final day of the program and it was another turning point in my life is student's beneficiary and, I successfully completed one-year ministry program and that was divine fervor and God used her and met me at the point of my need. In case you are wondering why I continue to acknowledge her, it is because of how I was in need God blessed me in my life's challenges and journey, has surprised me with all of my needs supplied what I cried and wondered where will I go and what shall I do? He already did!!

As, I never knew put that helped with the training and paid for tuitions and books and all gave me, scholarship and grants, and I am grateful to God and for what He did surprised me with the right people at the right time is of God's grace and grateful that Anita was the vessel He used. She did together with her staff, thankful that nothing passes God and uses all others to bless us, is not just our biological family members, how His love empowers is in so many kind of ways and positively influencing our lives, I could share miracle after miracle. This is the answers that is to share may surprise you in moment of trials and temptations but God is real and I see the power is of love, faith and inspiration with God's miracle of love and power that, I am thrilled, is being fulfilled! He's moving one more time in me to fulfill His promises made for me and His wisdom.

I accomplished and developed skills and more inspiration to aspire with hope, living both my heavenly Father and earthly father's hopes and dreams! Fulfillment is of joy to live fully your dreams and life to the fullest with success and progress, of existence, significance and intention! Is a legacy, and I am here to serve God by serving others and my life does matter as I am a child of God, "For I am fearfully and wonderfully made: marvelous," is to attend and obtain quality. Is life to live well as in education to contribute to my community, society and make a difference in the world Moreover, for my self improvement, and happiness as the life I shared I have fun-time!

With my heavenly Father's blessing and am enjoying but not being selfish for it does not only brings me joy but, the life that I share, also brings joy to others as well when joyfully give it away that is love. When we look at life in that positive perspective of wisdom is from above and that is not obtained from the academic. Is classroom but from that of heavenly delights. College of eternal and beautiful words of life it says common sense is not all that common, nor is it easy to understand, is not by sight but faith and is by grace to appreciate that education as is Tip-Top. But, by walking with flaw thoughts, you won't! These Scriptures confirm as it teaches: "A man's gift maketh room for him and bringth him before great men" (Proverb 18:16).

Girls, all are inclusive and my primary intent is helping readers find inspiration in their daily lives is all women blessed much as the men and children and everyone young and old too. I enjoy evangelism as the best of business with my heavenly Father, reaching out in love to touch. Touching hearts with His love and words of life is inspiration for courage and comfort for hope. And I am thankful for His inspiring my passion and blessing to obtain a certificate in Leadership. That is an added impetus and gift enhancing in my professions and in this writing, speaking, and in the building of a ministry that will globally inspire and impact the spiritual lives of our youths. And, all families, with a legacy for generations after is what a joy, it was a dream come true and of my late dear father, Papa Okon Thompson Udoumanah Ekanem Abasiekong of Ediene, Akwa Ibom State of Nigeria, has strongly encouraged and inspired my life motivated for serving God!

Globally inspiring people and helping those in need, reaching out in love and, in through literacy, in reading and writing, and teaching mostly our youth, and inspiring all hearts to aspire, find hope and inspiration in their daily lives, is a dream come true for me, for which I give God all the glory. And, more than thankful for, yet another chance helping people live life fully and inspiring the broken hearts to build toward the future and ministering love and mercy, this is for all women as well, since it is my passion, with a spot to help us to be inspired despite all hurdles and abuse. Group often exposed ridicules and all kind of abuses and so it is also dedicated to us.

And, to the young and single girls, ladies/moms to you and May God be with us all, keep moving and don't ever let them scare you with threat that, you can't overcome those situations! For yes, you can we can make it with God by our side, and I have been there and done what were my hardest challenges, and, God showed me the way and told me, I am loved and capable than. I was challenged and, it is very possible to overcome as well. That being said, I take great pleasure in thanking Anita Carman repeatedly from the bottom of my heart and staff and for all blessings.

Inspiration encourages faith, "In the fear of the LORD is strong confidence: and his children shall have a place of refuge. The fear of the LORD is a fountain of life, to depart from the snares of death" (Proverbs 14: 26-27). I was sharing thought with a friend of mine overheard someone says, "Those who only hope are hopeless." I said is without taking action and making a little effort. This is lesson on how to defeat odds of sufferings and find help through God's grace. I shared that is faithless who are hopeless and loveless because for me and you, there is hope for us and rescue, and survival. I encourage, continue to hope for with Him, no one can be hopeless. When you do pray, trust and claim victory and take step of courage to launch out in faith boldly.

With faith, believe, apply your God's given gifts, and be thankful for those who believe as well in you as well, that you can and are supporting you show how much they love you is your gratitude to God and serving God that brings back joy life. And that is freedom because of living in the freedom that comes from being confident of His love inspiring our passion to do more too! I am so grateful to God and faith of my ancestors that I continue to relish and in the joy and hope in God's love and happiness is what I derive everyday from that sweetness of my loving family.

This is my story of power of inspiration, power positive influence and faith in and 2012, how, I was one of those nominated and awarded a grant to enable me to publish more books for our youth to read and to be nourished with, especially the youth in Africa (Nigeria), and inspire victimized women. This is a blessing beyond words, for I am now able to reach out to the youth of the world. I share my story of hope and let them know that they can have a brighter future, and with hope in God and a little efforts they too can have a chance, and all that remaining is to be thankful and of good behavior pray more and believe and follow your heart and instruction also.

I have also received education in leadership training, which was another blessing for me in my journey from the, Inspire Women's Leadership Institute, have successfully completed the one year program as today I am certified and awarded, Inspired Women's Leadership Certificate. As a leader with hope as the best self –defense is hope in God and, not in you, or someone else. Else, will be hopeless! I am more inspired, through help of God, and with these blessings, I am able to fulfill my father's hopes and dreams, and God's purpose for my life to be transformed by the love of God as well, by the Holy Spirit to become that love for others and reaching out more as others as reached out to touch me, I know that God has purpose far beyond what we imagine.

What others may think negatively of us does not matter, shouldn't stop you from moving. And that is as shared faith in God does matter, transforms heart and, emotions by the Holy Spirit. Eventually, result is you will become that love for others. I am committed to reaching the world through the gospel, by inspiring hearts, nurturing the spirit and changing lives through creative expressions of faith is all, and that is my divine calling and using inspirational words of wisdom. Is that healing journey that transformed me and others the world over and, building a community of authentic love and friendships through God words is a gift. It is one of the best gifts of love as it is and divine blessings are all by words and actions and sharing love is my mission and, I have prayed for grace and the strength to endure and carry out His assignment to all parts of the world!

The "Inspire Youth and Family Global Communication Foundation Ministry," I thank God for open doors, ministry my late dear father wanted me to carry on name was inspired as is by him, but not knowing how I would be able to do it without his presence was scary and, God is good did it in His own time and way. He wanted me to assure him that I would find a way with prayers and of God's help and of love and faith to do what he couldn't do: serving humanity is of world-wide and spreading the words of love of God too. So, I went to school and completed my degree programs, in sociology from Spelman(I thank

God, proud of school/motto: "Christ Our Whole School For") which was the best thing I could do in my quest to fulfill my father's wishes, for he was illiterate. But a blessed pious man of God loving God and fellow kind and very generous and giving to all by treating others with love and kindness!!

Daily, I find myself thanking my family, especially my father, for wishing the best for me in my life. I know that in order for me to excel and to be unique, I would need to attain a level of academic excellence. One of the most important things I have been able to do is give back to my community and to society in general. Regardless of what area I was to be blessed to excel in, he always emphasized this: "Diaha (first daughter), make God prouder and make me, your mother as well as siblings and others proud and keep the faith and remember your grandparents both the paternal and maternal set the passion which were all evangelical and pastors and evangelist also!

I want you to be an investor not just for you but for others to grow and prosper with love and eternal significance." Growth is love of God and grace, like happiness, progress, receiving a good education, and establishing a faith that is ministry were my family's business, as relayed in my third book, Parental Influence Matters (2007)! It was very challenging trying to live up to my father's dreams with all of the emotional, physical, and intellectual battles I faced in life, not to mention being in a foreign land. I was constantly worried, especially after being scammed and duped of all my life savings by fellow Nigerian(s) and from my very own State, which was when my nightmares real financial battles began. I realize now that those hardships were necessary for me to appreciate the value of life and the positive changes in my life, that were to come into my life as a woman with a mission, rather than of sorrows. God's good prepared for the work ahead.

Unquestionably, "To accept God's will is to experience God's peace"; Scripture reveals to my knowledge, understanding, courage and wisdom that is it all that of God, "He who has the key of David (is) He who opens and no one shuts, and shuts and no one opens" (Revelation 3:7). Ultimately, when God says yes, no one says no, and reverse is once, He says no, no one can say yes, either! All and all, He holds the key for all our needs and releases all our blessings in His time and always at the appropriate season and timely reason too so clear. Because, He lives and holds key eternally and, we can also be empowered of the hope and inspiration offers ability too. Is to release what we have, glory! Power belongs to Him who loves gives every tools to work.

Through it all and by the precious glorious grace of God I am thankful, for my late father. Also, for my entire family and my sweet late mother and Anita Carman, and all those inspired all the women who came to be my friends and my rescue as the biblical Barnabas (an encourager), is that love of sisterhood. Anita invests in women of all ethnic and economic backgrounds, and is the founder of Inspire Women's Leadership Institute, Houston and is a place for inspiration and, "develops women to have the spiritual fortitude to define, pursue, and finish God's mission for their lives; with an emphasis on how God's word teaches to transform emotions of loneliness, rejection, and fear to respond to life's changes in a way fitting for the daughter of a King." I am rejoicing in my God's and praising Him for love and comforting touch!

As Anita wrote in one of her books, "Transforming Emotions in a Leader's Heart," "Each of us must settle in our hearts what God has entrusted us to finish. What you must think about is how you will feel about your life the day your time on earth is over" (Anita Carman.2007. pg. 155). Indeed, our greatness is in the heart, and the truth is that progress, love, unity, cooperation, meekness and working hard, smartly is part of what shapes us as human beings and gives us the enablement to choose, what makes us to be happy or to be sad the entire lifetime. My passion as is I have God always shows, teaches, and leads us if we are willing to trust and obey His will.

In every aspect of our lives, young or old, you can be great and faith in God is keeps us and, makes us strong and more resilient and purposeful living that is my observation and, it is so interesting to note that one does not necessarily have to be perfect to be spiritual, and you don't need the highest or terminal degree and or have to come from affluent neighborhood before you are accepted and welcomed and celebrated, but God loves you just as you are and willingness of your heart and mind. Just strive to be the best you can be, and be determined to climb each step with the realization that, as the proverb says, "Practice makes perfect." It is more important now than it has ever been to continue in your quest to have a loving heart, no matter how many times you may fail. You may even feel discouraged by others who have ignorant minds and who are trying to bring you down. They may label you being a "sick" individual who should just give up.

We must all keep in mind that the message of hope is to be shared and to never give up. Sometimes, our daily lives can become so busy that we tend to ignore what our hearts are trying to tell us. The power belongs to God, and He speaks to us to inspire us to encourage us, others to have a joyful heart. One of my own gifts given to me by God is in literature evangelism, which inspires me to write to inspire others, and surplus is motivational speaking as well among others. I know that we are so blessed and given potential and talents and gifts of grace to use by God.

In your quest to have a loving heart, please pay attention, listen carefully, and use fervent prayer so that He may release His power unto you to harness your productivity. Yes, you can be empowered to lead a successful life. This success can come about in unbelievable ways from the heavens above us, but you must pay attention to and concentrate on God's words, for He speaks to us daily to enlighten us and to instill greatness in our hearts. His purpose is for us to bless and to be blessed! It is not possible to fake any of God's glorious power, He answers us and prays.

He prays with us and for us and He answers also the prayers of the righteous and pure in hearts and that through inspirational moments of sweet fellowship, as He prefers to deal with us on a one-on-one basis. First and foremost, He prays, inspires, teaches, disciplines properly trains us, that is to ensure that we are being properly developed and equipped to pass His message on to others, anoints us. Scripture is filled with incredible stories of children being used to accomplish God's purpose, such as in the case of Samuel, who was a child dedicated by his mother Hannah.

He was given to serve God and dedicated, his mother love for him was inspired more for what God did for them after so many years of her sorrows. Her prayers were answered, and the son was blessed and anointed at his tender age by God, but young Samuel boy listened and asked wanted to know who is calling and the voice of joy was of God's (1 Sam. 1:27-28). Likewise, in today's world, we must inquire of and know whose voice we are listening to and to remember that joy is better than heartache. For more, please see 1 Sam. 2:1-10, 3:1-21, and Isa. 40:8-31.

One has to be anointed by Him in order to be able to help others, and we must wait for Him to decide when we should be anointed. However, many people are impatient and want to be able to preach to others, but this is not the proper way to go about it. Clarity does matter! Pray and ask Him to bless you with His power-filled voice and it will come to pass. God is real, in the business of making impossibilities becomes possibilities into miraculous happenings in our lives. He is a trusting God who sends words of wisdom to those who have dared to listen to Him to be able, to make a public declaration of our anointing, we must be properly equipped to guide others in the quest for a loving heart and it takes faith and that faith is in God is immutable and it soars.

In addition to what I discussed above, we need to establish a deeper, and be more serious meaningful life of hope and build is intimate relationship with God spiritual growth is given by His love and that grows us mature. To achieve this can come from a number of ways, including prayer. Paul's exhortation encourages our hearts to continue in prayer. Does any of you remember or know of the one thing that he encouraged and told us to delight in doing? If so, please remind yourself of what he says. If you do not know, bear with me, for I will share it with you here shortly please.

Scripture teaches and corrects anyone who doubts like Biblical Thomas, and that is of certainty states, "...that power belongs to God (Psalms 62:11). That is an ultimate truth and what we need to keep in mind today. Please, don't hesitate to get down on your bended knees and ask God for what you need. If you are asking, on bended knees doing what it is simplest as always is praying His will quite simple: "Praying always with all prayer and supplication in the Spirit, and watching thereunto with all perseverance and supplications for all saints; that he might comfort your hearts" (Ephesians 6:18-22b). Nothing passes God's love and power.

It is which inspires and motivates and joy is to listen, trust, and be obedient to Him and it is to keep pray and work and work and pray and watch, serve and trust and, "Nothing passes God and is so true. Keep in mind that the goal of inspiration is to comfort our hearts and inspire also is to comfort the wearied broken hearted and The heart is not only the most important part of the human body, but it is also the most intricate complicated one, as well as the one that needs more love, peace and joy that never ends and as always, in my curiosity, also wanted to find out more.

Reading the definition of the word "heart," I came across words such as middle, center, sympathy, nucleus, midpoint, sentiment, core, feeling, midst (Weber's Thesaurus Dictionary). In Webster's Dictionary, heart: 1: hallow muscular organ that keeps up the circulation of the blood. 2: Playing card of a suit mark with a read heart. 3: whole personality or the emotional or moral part of it. 4: courage. 5: essential part—heartbeat n—hearted adj. And crucial to know and glad. The quality of the heart matters the most, because life and death results from the heart both be it in our physical as well as spiritual matters, no matter how one looks at life, everything is about the heart, which is why it is so important to have a joyful, loving heart is peace of mind to have.

And, is priceless always to find out more about one's situation and endurance and rescue is. Love, like kindness, comes from the heart, but so does bitterness, hatred, and envy all that too. It is of urgency now more than ever to pray continuously to achieve greatness in the heart. Love your heart's power and who, says, "Love one another," and cherish its greatness. You must also exercise your faith and resist the devil, and continue to be happy with open hearts and dedicated mindset. An informed mind which is knowledgeable is all key, for we need to all be receptive as everyone life's is interesting when we know the love of God and trust and obey the blessings are awesome that is the truth of the matter is that faith in God is essential and needs to be cultivated.

In every human heart and, amazingly is, "One single grateful thought raised to heaven is the most perfect prayer" (C.E. Lessing). Is the truth and gracious to Be determined to give Him your heart and to strengthen your mind, because in order to be open to the gift of the Holy Spirit, you must have an open mind and open your heart to receive and it is that capacity to receive and give and grow and cherish the way out and that is the ultimate and everlasting treasure, priceless. Love and gift of His word is wisdom is eloquently all knowledge and power and but "It is easy to condemn something not understood." The most important thing to learn from is of God's power is of grace is inspiration is that God can inspire all of our hearts and minds and transforms us.

It is a comforting feeling being blessed with this knowledge, and I hope that you all will pray to seek the wisdom that He can give you, His wisdom is all and love and I hope this wisdom given to me of His love and inspiration will bring you great joy. Get the knowledge you need by reading the Word, and remember, always that "Nothing passes God and is a legacy to cherish of His faith and, sure true that, "Nothing can make a person happy, but what comes from within." I wouldn't be this blessed had it not for the grace of God touching my family to be of His heritage.

I wouldn't have been enjoying as it is all is nice to be blessed in knowledge that inspires faith like our forefathers had? The truth is that our heavenly Father wants us to distinguish and when we look back on all the big and small ways between cheap thrills and meaningful, lasting rewards, such as love of God and family of faith. We must use our love beyond words and take positive actions, and also go after knowledgeable insights, "For the Lord is a God of knowledge" (1 Sam. 2:3-4). Be thankful for life each day, and all of its blessings that come with it shaped us.

Be happy and remember that His love has no end and faith in God is the currency of life. I am grateful that His grace and mercy is unconditional and everlasting and that His love travels the world benefitting everyone, mostly those who are caring and cherish Him with their hearts of love and deep abiding faith and courage to endure. It is that power of inspiration that has helped me to write this book that you are reading and all of this takes faith and His love, resulting in His power of inspiration, which warms the heart and makes all dreams come true. Nothing is ever done by our own power alone, so we must celebrate every day, for the power belongs to Him and it is better to celebrate with family and friends and no matter where they come from for we-His!

When your prayers are finally answered, celebrate the joy of inspiration because it brings about even more blessings. Cherish your heart's dreams for success the pursuit of happiness. As the heart becomes more grateful and inspired, it becomes a heart of greatness. Also, please keep an open heart and informed mind and realize that when we receive joy in our hearts, we are able to possess the power and confidence that empowers us to lead productive lives and purposeful. Is the joy of inspiration enables us to realize our dreams and to be happy, my gifts are of great joy for me as great blessings to me that I cherish and to use and glorify the One who loves me most and, in blessing others and that is the source, I derive my joy everyday adventurous daily!

Blessings to me that I cherish, because they are divine blessings, and as a gift of love of God and is from above, it should highly be appreciated, are for us to use and bless each other is by our words and actions, and we give them the same love and gift, to inspire and make them as happy with hope as we are inspirers. And you should cherish your gifts as well. Please, cherish with the vision of hope that blesses us more than you ever, can imagine in your wildest dream.

That inspiration helps us strengthens each other for nothing passes God's love and, is the only power that is strength to those who are weak and are broken. True love, kindness, gratitude, and patience and joy are all are all productive qualities cultivated through power of inspiration. Hopefully, this chapter, like the others, inspires you and, also stimulates your thought for you to start your quest for a heart of peace and love and also for His marvelous love joy, so that you can make the best out of your life and make it as productive as possible, and you never know it is by God's grace to be all that He desires for you to be and, many times that comes to pass always!

CHAPTER SEVEN

Faith Can Move Mountains

"God plus one is always the majority."
– Evangelist Billy Graham

When there is faith there can always be victory for us and that is what power of God gets going for us and we have love in our hearts, and we are able to promote progress and cultivate a life of faith when we keep steadfast love in trusting the real, "Author and Finisher of our Faith". It is in trusting in the loving heavenly Father who never changes and His love never fails either. I had been blessed made a testimony to the Great Healing Power of God and that has been the joy of my sharing truth the power of the spirit as you have read all along in inside and the previous chapters are not very different from this but to share my joy of building relationship and of friendships with God on a personal intimacy for my spiritual growth is always exciting to me.

Nothing works better between individuals than a friendship with understanding mind and trust, simply because it promotes deep-abiding faithfulness with unity and love and harmony too. Honestly, God has made us and the whole world in His image, and that will never change. The Book of Ephesians encourages our hearts to cherish and emulate all that is positive. Seriously, I have come to realize for my own testimony that there is none, and no other way safer than to be true and humble to our heavenly Father, in all we say and do, faith in God is very crucial matter.

Please, remember to keep joy in your heart, because it will result in a positive energy that will light a fire in within and under and around you well others to obtain that same joy you possess, we need deep abiding faith with joy. It is what makes the heart and in order to obtain takes love.

Always open your heart and welcome the sweet spirit of your Supreme Power, who is your Redeemer and Saving Grace, "Remembering you in my prayer" (Ephesians 1:16), He says, we need to all listen out and hear His distinctive voice, for it will make a tremendous difference. In our lives, only the Divine Inspirer can motivate a man's heart to greatness, and this inspiration gives birth to inspire hearts and that is positive outcomes are good for the heart, for they bring us words of encouragement and to others and their happiness, and they in turn become motivated by your example. Yes, you can live your purpose with fulfillment once you stop going through the motions and begin to think more about the joy of giving God first place and with praise's faith is.

The power of inspiration does wonders for the heart and God's words all along stressed is more effective in expressing and testifying about what you have witnessed and convey that to the people with confidence. I am so thankful that I have been blessed with this gift, which has also enabled me to make my dream of uplifting others through my writing a reality. I truly believe in the truth these words of wisdom makes is obvious that God does not mince His words and says: "I love those who love me. Those who search for me shall surely find me" (Proverbs 8: 17).

"In a battle, the heart will win over the brain." That is another words of wisdom that is simple as well to note and words of God's love and power is in our faith to believe and look more inward.

This inspiration has enabled me to obediently follow God and to continue my service to others, even through not many believe in the indwelling healing Word and life-giving Spirit of God but we can look times of extreme illness, ask one's self who heals and rescues us with life? With hope, there is joy in the heart, and we are then able to inspire and motivate others, giving them the faith that they too can have a heart of wisdom. There is always something in life to be loved and to be hopeful for, and gratefully, the heavenly treasures of life are priceless extremely.

Inspirational is the glory of the Lord shall, endure forever and James 4:8, encourages us. These treasures, though they may be simple, are priceless treasures of inspirational words of God wisdom are spiritual weapons and soothing is powerful and full of energy and passion. That can help you achieve your goals and are all healing and a gift of love by words and actions to draw. I have seen and, "Draw near to God and he will draw near to you" (Jm. 4:8: NIV), sums the truth.

Unequivocally, inspiration has made a believer out of me and has enabled me to trust my faith, for it has helped me become the best I can be. I'm more than thankful, and I pray for more of that sustaining, everlasting, spiritual energizer, the oxygen to keep me healthy and thoughtful of others, so that I can be more of a "blessing that the world is waiting to receive," Jill Briscoe challenges, and so to encourage our hearts more as the writer of the foreword for Inspire Women Ministry's textbook by Anita Carman- Transforming Emotions in A Leader's Heart. Yes, faith is power in action and it can move mountains, and it is a joy to think of all that is possible because God is in it and of it as Author ad Finisher of our faith. This is certainly my life and what I was destined to be! I am a daughter of destiny as my Father is King of kings His love empowers.

There is definitely an abiding happiness in my life now that I am so blessed to be able to experience the thrill and joy of the power of inspiration as He inspires my passion. I want part of these blessings to be given to you, because as these words of wisdom state, "Happiness adds and multiplies when divided with others." I continue to hope that everyone is given the best that life. Can afford them, so whatever status your life may be in at the moment, think positive! The best way to forget your own problems is to help someone else solve theirs. It is my pleasure to write share these tips to help you overcome your obstacles and to be able to live your purpose, which is a life, filled with love and joy and greatest expressions comes with love and that is greatness.

Gifts of love are the best to share with others because they bring about more rewards that can be shared with even more people. Make the most out of every potential opportunity to share all of your gifts with others. Everything in life has the ability to turn someone else's life around, especially when used properly at the right time. These glorious gifts of grace are given to us for our happiness and prosperity, for our education is not complete when you finish school, lifelong.

As I have previously stated, it is important to pay close attention to the power of love as inspiration. Spend quality time investing in learning more about this power and how to use it to your fullest potential, instead of being amongst the busy-bodies and gossipers, find your purpose. And look for opportunities to discover more and explore to see what makes you time-wise and be the person you were blessed to be a blessing, inspiring others and to be happy power is within us. And is heart, nothing improves one's own life like exposing yourself to those qualities that make you great by acts of goodness, and that responsibility is for the good of self, family, others and it comes to society and progress of everyone's growth and happiness when we all bring something.

Is awesome to contribute as a person with an identity to the social and economic growth and to make the world a better place than when we met makes us all feel good about ourselves as well as others and those are the people we are blessed with and also part of our progress and that is why I am blessed and am greatly inspired, which has made a profound difference in my life to share what I have been privileged and blessed with love in my life, joy is celebrate with us all.

The following words of inspiration are so true: "Character and ideals are catching. When you associate, you associate with men who aspire to the highest and the best." This is an absolute fact of life, and if you simply believe, your faith can move any mountain is victory. By just imagining positive thoughts, you can be inspired to greatness, because you will be exposing yourself to the qualities that make you want to aspire for the passion of creativity. You will want to be amongst the great men and women you have been exposed to in your life, even reading of them and, about their qualities if you continue to dream big and work hard, you can hopefully join them. Change the world as well and also love to make it better than what you have met awesome.

Please do not forget title of this book: "Greatness is in the heart- A Tribute to Inspiration and of certainty is that we all are ambassadors in order to achieve this greatness, it is imperative to have positive thoughts, to count your blessings, and to continue to be encouraged, for there is inspiration all around us. It is indeed a blessing when we are able to have greatness in the heart. Because then we are able to reach our fullest potential, God's good keeps us blessed and love us all! The problem is that many are lacking the knowledge to use wisdom correctly, but once this is overcome, true happiness will become a reality. Faith matters and we need inspiration to spur our motivation with passion, helps us rise and shine for His glory and honor and for edification is all hearts can be more than hopeful and grateful for life is not about us but about Him for fills us!

Always be encouraged to follow your dreams. That means using the knowledge that you have gained from school along with the knowledge and wisdom obtained from God. A quality education helps us to make the best use of the potential that we possess, and sure although our performance may differ amongst each other. It is important to remember that even though we may differ as far as the quality of education that we have received, the end result will still be the same: A grateful, joyous heart filled with love, happiness, and inspiration can move mountains and can subdue all the forces of intimidation and move passed the odds of life and feels hopeful.

Do not let your fears and worries scare you into not realizing your true potential. Instead of thinking negatively, think positive and be gracious. My work is a blessing, and it results from the boundless love of our lavish Giver, who I love endlessly. This is why each chapter stresses how important the power of a great heart really is. Like many inspirational writers, my passion for writing has become my way of life. I have seen it as part of my therapy, and for me, just the thought of knowing that my friends around the globe are being inspired by my words gets me even more excited and inspired.

One of the most important things we can accomplish by having a loving heart is to share your inspired thoughts with others. I have had such moments that have made me so happy with fulfillment. Recently, I received a telephone call from a good friend (Ini Ebong), who is a nurse with hardly enough time for herself, who managed to read one of my books entitled "Parental Influence Matters." She informed me that she gained so much knowledge from reading the book and that she felt very blessed to have had the opportunity to read my inspirational words. This made me very happy that I was able to inspire her, and it motivated me to write even more words of inspiration.

By doing this, you are multiplying the love that is in your heart and sharing it with others. As the Yiddish proverb says, "A wise person hears one word and understands two." Do not let fear into your hearts or give anyone the power to cause you to fear, because your heart will deceive you and make you believe that you cannot turn your burdens into blessings. Think of our Supreme Being, who always steps in for us, and if you believe, His love will be boundless and will fulfill your life with joy and beauty. Do not be afraid to have love in your heart and do not allow any deception in the heart to wear you down. If you are afraid that you may have limitations that will crumble your world, you will end up with a hardened and bitter heart and it is best not to worry to be. Do not think of physical, emotional, and/or psychological situations!

But think more of love and positive in your heart because life's situations are far more of diverse. Remember, nobody knows what life brings next and only God knows and thankfully is of faith, His inspiration is all around you, and before you can move others, you must be moved. It is in my daily prayers and wishes that we can keep that spark in our hearts aglow to be inspired hearts by the word of God's wisdom it encourages, us to be alert and alive and cheers us on and is keep moving and as often as, "Labor to keep alive in your heart that little spark of celestial fire called conscience." Keep in mind that wisdom without conscience is fruitless living what a joy.

Please, keep faith alive and strive for love and happiness, for none of us can love without the passion to do so given from love of God. Greatness is achieved through the grace and power of God, for it takes passion and love from Him to make your life a success. Indeed, you cannot love without giving your heart solely to your passion. That brings this question to mind friend: "Who and/or what motivates your passion the most?" Is it reliability of God's love and power?

Know the source of your motivation, for it can make you stand out and make the world a better place for all to live in and enjoy. I challenge you to double your joy by sharing it with a friend by either calling, emailing, etc., and let them know just how excited you really are to be doing what you really want and loving what your gift is doing to help others. Channel your talents to give hope and happiness to others! Daily and I count my blessings; I thank God for the blessings of helping me to seek for inspiration from Him and guidance words of His wisdom too.

By daring to love yourself for who you are and by utilizing your potential to its fullest is an unbelievable feeling. I always feel like I could never have too much inspiration. If anything, I am greedy for more positive prayers and results. By hearing more words of wisdom and encouragement, it enables me to be a better person with an even more loving heart. It sounds good to the ear and warms my heart with love and wisdom. The Bible has something to say on that too, Psalms 25:

12-14 (KJV). "What man is he that feareth the Lord? Him shall he teach in the way that he shall choose. His soul shall dwell at ease; and his seed shall inherit the earth (shall lodge in goodness). The secret of the LORD is with them that fear him; and he will shew them his covenant" (KJV). I am constantly praying for more blessings and favor in order for me to excel in such a way that it glorifies our Father in heaven. By praying and continuously learning and growing, I am able to have a life rich in faith.

I am able to give more blessings to others, and it gives me an extremely rewarding life. As these words of wisdom say, "often your faith in an uncertain result is the only thing that gets results." We all need to pray for the strength to be able to use our blessings to help not only ourselves but to help others as well. If you trust, you don't worry, and if you worry, you don't trust. What else can be better than doing what is encouraged by "the man after God's heart; for we must wait on the Lord: Be of courage, and He shall strengthen your heart" (Psalms 27:14).

Our greatness is definitely derived from the heart. This book discusses genuinely how the power of God's wisdom can inspire us all to have everlasting faith. This wisdom that we thrive on impacts everyone the world over and is especially important in the quest for greatness in the heart. For those who want to be more empowered, please have an educated, informed mind and a heart that is dedicated to love. Love is amazing, and you are all unique in your own way, but you must have love in your own heart to be able to share it with others. It is crucial that we live a healthy life, because that is also the power of inspiration. Healthy living does matter!

Happiness is crucial for one's own success, whether you are young or old, and everyone deserves to be loved and to live a happy life. Happiness is not limited to only the rich, so please keep this in mind as you strive for a loving heart. As the proverb says, "The great challenge of life is to consider what is important." Cherish the inspiration that is in your heart and continue to move forward and celebrate the joy that you receive from your daily blessings. Also, remember to continue to be blessed with daily words of wisdom and celebrate the jubilation of greatness of the heart. Dare to be a great mind with a loving heart, one who can be in control of doing what you are destined to be. As your purpose is fulfilled, your joy will be celebrated.

In this book, you will have a thorough knowledge of the power of inspiration. It will offer you the unique opportunity to learn, grow and enjoy future inspirational readings. My belief plays a vital role in my life, and is amongst the most important characteristics I possess. It is refreshing to my heart to have the peace and joy that the Lord has blessed me with. Indeed, "Great strength comes from faith in the Lord" (Zachariah 12:5). With this faith, a life filled with joy, happiness, and prosperity are inevitable.

We all know that we are better as a people when we receive bountiful blessings because these blessings give us a successful and purposeful life. We should all learn to live by a leap of faith, and to realize that God's favor is free and never waivers, and His love fills our hearts with grace and joy when cherished and appreciated. Bear in mind that "It's in our weakness His strength is made perfect" (2 Corinthians 12:9).

What I have written in this book comes from my own experiences; I do not know of your experiences. It takes a lot of faith to be able to give your heart completely to Him. The greatness that I possess in my heart is all from faith. As someone who has triumphantly excelled over many of the challenges that I have faced in my life, especially the fear of losing my health, I have my faith to thank God for getting me through those difficult times. I have fought the battle of poor health here lately, and even though I have not completely won the battle as of yet, I know that I eventually will.

All of our lives need faith, hope, and some sense of inspiration to overcome life's hurdles, and to bless others and their happiness as well. We all have a story to tell in many dialects, tribes/tongues the world over, and if we listened closely, we would find that each story speaks volumes on how important faith really is. Some of these stories are more inspirational than others, and you may want to cry over them or they may inspire you to change for the better.

Listening to others' stories of faith has changed my entire outlook on life from negative to positive. These stories have changed the way I look at things, and have given me even more inner joy and happiness within my heart. My once faint heart is now renewed and restored with a better outlook on life, which is made possible by the power of inspiration. This very power of inspiration shared was a victory for me because it enabled me to receive the joy I needed. That is through healing thoughts, which was the therapy that was much needed. I had to acknowledge of my weaknesses as well as my strengths, which overall made me a better person more than ever.

Despite the obstacles that we all encounter, it is important to remember that overcoming these obstacles enables us to gain the insights and knowledge needed to embrace our Supreme Creator with faith. As Jean Baptiste Massieur has stated, "Gratitude is the memory of the heart." I am so grateful that the power of inspiration has enabled me to win many victories and to be empowered to transform my life far beyond what I ever expected. Michael J. Fox, who has inspired me with his words of wisdom, had this to say: "I am careful not to confuse excellence with perfection. Excellence, I can reach for; perfection is God's business."

God's love is the greatest and the most supreme of all loves, for there is nothing like the kind words of wisdom that He whispers to me that brings joy and inspiration to my heart. As I think of God's love and His faithfulness in His words, actions, and deeds, it melts my heart. My Lord and Savior, who is the chief Inspiration and Motivator, is a blessing that I am thankful for from bottom of my heart. The Book of Proverbs teaches our hearts to know and take note, heart is appreciate, "from the fruit of his words a man is satisfied with good, and the work of a man's hand comes back to him" (Proverbs 12:14).

Some using bad drugs, being bad character are behavior. Bad behavior is tripping and as new waves adopting and that is adapting to life of influence of wrong people pills, when we have the best as is best words of life (pills of wisdom); best to crack the words of love than those illicit drugs and substances disaster. It is destroys and ruins life, takes you down hill and, is sometimes Peers' pressures all is to belong and, to identify with wrong groups and being bad uncontrollable. To be among, the group thing! That is belonging, "am grown, big and bad;" Is so mean being you belittle yourself, and disobedience is what takes you on a wild ride wrong path. We all love you!

Is to know that because love can bless you but there is someone who loves you best what you are doing discouragement for at end you will be wasting all the great things God has blessed you is so much potential in you and you there lost as one buying trouble for you. That is also as it is a very big price. To pay and wasteful of your precious life, be it young or old know that God is in us all and loves us and want the best for us. He is who loves us most and gives capacity is all is that we need, is awesome when you let Him to abide in you that can give you many more joys.

His is blessings than to let the world mess you up and it is pressures that goes with each passing day and wrong peer pressures and disobedience can be very detrimental and is, if you let them, and don't listen to change your ways and manners also a good habit is best to learn, and to listen to your Godly family and friends and God is who guides and direct them, please take it to heart and in prayer, that is inspiration that will help you and a true blessing! Be observant, of the encouraging voice of the Love within and, I am not saint! But, I know is better to learn to take it to heart and the right path of life is, for lost time is never fun, nor found that time awaits no one.

And, is a not glad tiding wasting all you are so blessed with and time is precious already for yourself, you can't blame it on others, let alone God, for He has always blessed is who dearly loves us and wants the very best for each of us! I can only size every opportunity to be, to give encouragement and pray for everyone for it is all what I can do. And, is offer of heart of love but can't stop you, or tell you what to do! I am just a good friend at heart and knowing that lost time is never found easily with us all, and God has also so much, blesses and encourages as His gives us all the means and methods, has given us the capacity to think through things and reasons, too.

Our hearts and minds thinking also is to think over and again, on those as He encourages us, "Honour thy father and thy mother: and, Thou shalt love thy neighbour as thyself" (Matthew 19:19). That what God's words says and it is this precisely clear, mostly all is the ultimate words of love and inspiration that can give us a little something to boost us up, and stimulate thoughts to think wisely. Truth! But, my friend life is a choice. It is, is up to you to do you good one, for as often said, "The ideal we embrace is our better self". Word of wisdom that is what makes for my hope and words of inspiration blessed my life, mostly, is that which comes from above. Can give happiness mostly, for it doesn't consist in things is joy within is deep down that is for happiness.

It is in thoughts and is happiness of the believers, is that there is something more than gold is the words of God in the hearts of men and it is that power of faith song is, also words of wisdom and that is a blessing and, a great gift of love that comes from God, sang through my heart and inspirational. It does me something marvelous is healing and not only from receiving also of joy giving is pills of wisdom is and joy without which, I don't know what my life could have been and I thank God from whom all blessings flow and I am enjoying every bit of that very benevolence God's grace.

Everyday, is a blessing(s) and is all the day long, and if, it weren't for that greater grace life living within in my inmost being. I wouldn't have pulled through those obstacles and let alone to think positively and, focusing also. In my mind, talk less writing another book edifying us all and uplifting our hearts and spirit also, an is am thankful that is to glorify God and lift up in His Holy name is a blessing nothing short of a miracle and from burden to blessing and given by a glorious grace and that of enduring faith is a blessing and that is trusting in God's love and power always.

He only is who is of understanding more about us and our situations than anyone else so is God who and shares in our details is His grace, love and power; His love is inspiration. All has been awesome to me and who God is faithful and awesome to glorify; He loves us, and keeps us. He is that compassionate companion and as we walk the road of life and my love for Him also is best expressed with deeper gratitude and affection in the heart that lingers on more and more and that most is most lasting than anything else is most lasting soothing and, so amazing the benefits is awesome of that moving experience is and that and expression of joy and power to me is to be.

A living testimony that Love is incredible great God a Force and inspires that all these are from the joy and power of God and took place in my life and, is divine fervors and interventions is and great mystery to better explain how it works. I can only be thankful and it thrills is hard to and I can't keep this to myself and hide those blessings is of joy and the best is for me to express my love and nothing than sharing them to bless one and is all for us too enjoying together and it is by words and actions words being express that celebrating that love of Almighty God and that is for He keeps steadfast and faithfulness meet us and peace will kiss each other is a great thing, is the words; Bible says, to let our light shine and confirms "Let your light so shine before men, that they may see your good works, and glorify your Father which is in heaven"(Matthew 5:16).

It is my time to shine that light and tell all about those inspiring stories how God's Love is moving my life and is and this is all I have and answering my prayers and those of loved ones as well as others miraculously and resounding yes, that God loves me and answers and heals all my love is in these and, is what I can give back and all is what I was given and openly received with love and gratitude to give back and to the glory of God and as well for us and the edification of all those who believe the power of His Love and Gift of God and live by that faith can enjoy.

Is to glorify Him, Affirm faith and power of inspiration all is His love and miracles of His power and trust in God's and obey to do His will never ever fails, in accomplishing His purpose. (Psalms 138:8) and shows God's love has ability to deliver and, our small faith can make a very big difference. It moves mountains and it is a chapter, same friendship for sharing too all inside is for us to read more about what God has done and still doing in my life and family just to trust! In trusting God and doing His will and has been faithful to me is all by that faith to do His will is and is glimpse of hope for that hope exits. It is real in all of us is best of His love what measures.

Our life His of true Love is what comes from the heart and measures of our true colors is that Love and gives us the joy is of God daily inspiring each of our heart and springs from soul is a blossom! Great for self-esteem and satisfies of each soul and to be contented in wherever place that we find we are of hope and is rejoicing and be happy and contentment in Him and mostly be. Thankful, everyday for me is a day of joy and thanksgiving and, nothing beats power of love and great strength that's it comes from faith in God is my testimony and that says, all the time my life is blessed for God is awesome and illustrates that power in everyday living and in my life is body mind and spirit and faith is its vitamin for I can feel the love of God in my heart and feet always!

Indeed, I feel and our greatness is indeed in the heart, and the truth is that Power of God is what overflows us progress, love, unity, renewal, is by faith, cooperation, meekness, and joy to obey is praying always His love, is follow instructions that of hope and, He offers us inner peace. And strength with healing and faith in God is action that is be praying and working hard, but it is smartly is also of joy is part of what shapes us as human lives and, a little effort is being together. Is better and is that spirit of oneness and love and power of inspiration that also has blessed me is of joy from that has resulted this work and all is by faith is that Spirit of love of God gives me all strength. The enablement to choose, what makes hope makes us also to be happy and controls us!

Unless, you decide chose to be unhappy and/or to be sad the entire lifetime and that is of your choice but not, to blame it on God and or anyone else, but blame yourself for failing to obey to do as He Has given us all grace, love and power as well potential and power with authority for pursuit that of our happiness and that is of my passion as is I have God's love always greatness. I am and this shows, how? Teaches, and leads me and can be for us, the most motivational power!

And, only a choice is if we are willing to trust and obey His will and follow it accordingly that is what makes me alive and happy and want to love more and, in every aspect of my life that love manifest and God has blessed and shown me His love and divine fervors, interventions story follows and inspirational and my friend (young/old), you can be healed and happy and great and can shine for God and love and, by confidently also by trusting faithfully everything works is all by faith.

Faith in God is what makes it easy and it keep us going strong and, makes stronger and more. Resourceful and resilient, purposeful by daily living that hope in us is by faith in hearts. So, in my heart there are blessings something more than gold Word of God inside. Observation and, the greatest gift of God is peace and joy of living that life of hope in my heart, mind and spirit is what make me to do this is it even happier and success story for that is the secret rightly indispensable love is it, power of faith can move mountains and we can do things never thought of being possible. It is so interesting to note that one does not necessarily have to be perfect to be spiritual, neither by forced to believe in God's love and power either, it is not by duress too.

But believe or not, faith in God works miracles and because, based from my past and to the current situation and life's experiences how faith has produced meaningful result is beneficial God has done it as He has manifested in my life and those of my family and friends and is all joy and happiness as well and miracles of His love and power is relevant and remedy as is significant and I wanted to share how I found the cure to my situations and that power of faith is to bless us. I am blessed to, find a solution and something that will be helpful out of it all is well and healing. Help me and my family and friends worldwide to be blessed also, what makes for love and joy.

Thrill to be a blessing and, I was in a near death situation and out of death came new life. And as well brand-new joy and brand-new confidence to me to share with us all and that love is my story that turned to glory. Makes me to become even happier; I am naturally a happy person, my norm. I was born as well that way and my passion is to bless and serve humanity and mostly, the youth and abused, mostly inspiring women as once, I was one of the victims and, today I love to live a successful life as such, inspiring us. I always try to do my very best and was determined to find what makes for hope and it is what matters most, really instill in me a passion to love and goes beyond words of mouth but shows more by actions and God's works in mysterious way too.

And extra mile and, I believe in making a difference in world and my dream has always been to contribute more. This is how God helps me to help myself, and my family and friends as well is globally and beyond too to strengthen us and it is also of our community as well, society, and so I love being part more of solutions, and not of problems as I have been blessed gratefully. At the back of my mind always how to be among those making a positive difference everyday is what and for the world to become a better place than what I found too. Making others happy and hopeful and purposeful also all that is always of my passion is the dream of my life as always.

That vision is part of my forging ahead is of joy and even in difficulties and no matter of where God places you can be contented with His love and that is how our salvation secured that is always pray to God to help me, hold unto His unchanging hand, and follow wherever He leads. For me too and I found divine favor and, I have found a profound thrill before Him and man as is joy too, and inspiration is thankfully, born into a pious and God fearing family and as community of love and faith in God that inspires my heart motivated. Many times when they prayed, and do also read Bible and sang the songs, and was filled with the power of the Holy Spirit, I wanted to so badly to grow up faster and get to do more and be like them and thankfully they blessed me.

I am blessed today ready by same means and, the methods of His love power of the Holy Spirit, was guiding them same that has manifested and it was what had healing and vitality in all their lives daily. Their joy it was and of vibrating voice and powerful strong and fervent prayers. I knew then as now that their strength mainly came from above as it was, and the higher power it is and inspiration of the Almighty God and that charismatic power and, I didn't know much more as to how to explain, than being excited and, I was always glad and enjoying as well their prayer.

It is awesome to see and so interesting to have love that is never-ending and, for inspiring passion and helping people be happy to see and resilient and carries over, I say that, is awesome! The way I was raised got me started on this my faith and how wonderful to have loving as well as beautiful hearts to wish you all the love and joy in the world and as well inspire journey right from the word go, and God already has ordained me to do this in His big plan! Knows all of us as always and also what is best for us, is the best also, for leaving everything in His care and power. And trust His plan is greater and better and is also bigger than we imagine in all circumstances is to please do leave it there and, He is in charge of it and has the solution and answers too to all!

I know, that though taken in school so many classes in Biblical studies is well and though it is so right and from my elementary to college, but there is nothing that beats the one taught that I had learned from my home upbringing is best of spiritual, He leads, guides daily, bless all of us and teaches well as well anoints and know how that is important; taught us how to read and that is the knowledge the education, is best of which is what is inspirational and you have teachers great love and thoughtful warm and kind in modeling and coaching and inspiring and nurturance I was inspired. Through loving care and guidance love for the Lord was the passion of my family. And that is the faith that I continue to enjoy in that it has never really left me; I am blessed from them.

Is how much of God is, so good to me and, He keeps it refreshing to be a deep well where others who thirst as those that are hungry for living well of life, who thirsts can be refreshed and, I surely grateful that daily refreshes and graces my heart with His love and empowers me to be of hope and keeps my faith. His Love is Power and of positive influence and for inspiration, I thank God for happiness, growth is as well and success this is where God needed me as well to be and to be inspiring hearts to be cheery is of hope, for helping them to live life fully and happily, and as well successfully, fully also encouraged, motivated and purposeful and happy too as I am also.

THE INCRDIBLE POWER OF GOD/ POWER OF PRAYER both also is of immediate solutions to both problems relayed in my case. Above and all that was left was pray as well that is what my Father and my Lord and Savior and Redeemer recommends us to always do, and He has delivered and helped along the journey. As I felled in love with Him headlong; I felt His love and mercy reaching out to me and family and Friend, and my God is real and alive; If any of you find difficulty in life don't hesitate to call and He will answer anytime you is on time and in any situation and place and that is answer. Turn to Him is the way out and what you need to read and is with love is Bible is all about Love. Love of God is the truth; I encourage us to read the Book(s).

Both are all about God's love for us and of which we can learn more about our situation, is endurance and rescue that is all miracles and is clear and very precise and beautiful! It all deals with inspiration and how we can gain help and better understanding about us, of who we are and whose, and what and how and where and when also as well and how too use and discover that blessings that can heal and empower much it empowers to stimulate us; as it is everlasting it what has lasting spiritual transformation because of the capability and spiritual power that comes with it, is the joy of finding love and inspiration. Awesome is Book of books and that Love inspires to empower me and training me well is Love is God and says, "Pray without ceasing" (1 Th. 5:17); In the Book of Luke 18:1, "….men ought to pray, and not to faint!" This is my joy of inspiration as passion, assignment, God loves for me to do all of what is in the Book of (Mark 16:15-20).

It takes a man/woman of faith and child of God is by faith and prayer and reading those is our trusting more and believing. To take steps out of courage is joy; it is to be of perseverance. It in facing life's challenges and able to embrace of any change as life's challenges and is not an easy thing to handle and I saw need God is all we need, and His inspiration is and love all very vital. Is His Words of love that showed me how to do things I wouldn't ordinarily do is love and, I am grateful for His teaching love to me as it is how to bless and we are in this journey together. And, we can make it together turning to Him is the how. I am bless am able to take a bold step of faith step out of comfort zone too is by courage of His love and joy with self- esteem, persevere.

He is always giving us generously the grace to endure and has given us the words of hope this is evidently to show confidence that He restores, re-shaped, builds my life and more is self-esteem and He took my hand, guided in His words is, I couldn't make it on my own strength and there was no other that way that I could be this much blessed and taught how either this lessons. I learned than for me surrendering all of myself. As well of my life's situation totally unto Him in reading and fervent prayer and entrust that is I know for us to call and, He is waiting and wants as well to heal and saves us. And, can restores anything that is broken it is all of great joy such, is love empowers! God is and His grace is sufficient and love abides is all of it how is surrendered.

I emptied myself to Him and my life, is awesome so blessed for God loves me more than I love myself everyday, I must offer my gratitude, for I know for sure! He is that is my Redeemer lives within in my inmost being and His love is better than life to me surely that is as well and is the wellspring of life that is who inspires my passion and mends my heart and inspires my heart of passion and educates my heart and thought. Oh yes, renewed and taught me how to love and when and how to apply the words and to study diligently day and night and, I have to praise Him forever; For His help and I feel of His love and powerful hand on my life and His presence goes with me is a thing of joy. Also, of my broken heart mended, is awesome and my life as I said repeatedly has literally changed.

Is, so remarkably, transformed says is miracles, works and much more than we think and know that also works and for my miracles and all I have received more than love, is beyond love.

Gracious is our Redeemer than clichés more love, is God's words that and is strength and, power, it couldn't be any other way better than this it is and God, I couldn't be happier than now and healthier is either of any, other way than my God there is no more beloved than God. And so no alternative for me than this way was my choice and nothing else ever is better best than all I have and this is all I ever needed and will ever need and that God's love is Treasure; He loves me and Treasures are of eternal living my God and words of life that is I could soar and is reaching of goals is ever all needed, just that is for my life. God is the strength more than is sufficient for me and love is with that hope that comes solely is from Him, who else than Jesus saves and that?

His power is inspiration that comes from faith in God? And as such, is God's my choice and His idea is best. I have is ideal, all and of greater and deepest is abiding love and great and deeper joy and "Great is the Lord and greatly to be praised" is just that for me and greatly daily. Is praise by me (Psalm 48:1; 148:1-14); His love goes with those who also love, who loves Him and also love His words and, I determined. And, forever is to obey, to follow Him, no matter the cost and there is always joy at the end of every journey that may have started hopelessly and it is. Is all this testifies are truths to the power of the human spirit of God and of the ultimate love and is joy for me His love and, His ideology greatest love and is greatness and Joy also Peace is too!

Loving is the kindness of God's love and greater achievements. That's greatness is He, and, peace of mind that is priceless, so good for me to know Him is you can experience complete fulfillment and love and receive Him that is what amazes me most and life is hopeful and thank God for everyday is a beautiful day of joy and a blessing to be thankful for and am so glad being blessed growing in God's amazing grace. I am, For His love, is my hope, guidance and blessings. He is the Way as Power that gives me grace and opportunity to follow, works wonders, blessing of me to live triumphantly and He is alive; it works for me well and it is well with my soul also!

My hope is in Him and faith that is amazingly increases for more both also is inspiration as I have found what been experiencing God's peace and this is for the past and present blessing, even for the future. Ultimately, our salvation is sure as His words says, "For I know the plans

I have for you, "declares the LORD, "plans to prosper you and not to harm you, plans to give you hope and a future"(Jeremiah 29:11:NIV). "And he himself has promised us this: eternal life" (1 John 2:25)! Always, is where I had been, to where I'm now writing this, I say, God, I love you!

These happenings in my life and more than worthy for me glorifying God and I have to in every way and daily I must, greater cause for my gratitude and so many reasons far more beyond this is just a minuscule. Imagine all that I have gone through and to find myself here, growing in God's amazing grace and life filled with His grace and love and joy and happiness and power is when I think through life and of all His goodness and more are many more my blessings coming is worth and sure is beyond marvelous is our God! I have seen and daily receiving is so precious. And this is gracious! His works in words and actions as well as and in deeds! "God demonstrates His own love towards us, in that, "While we were still sinners Christ died for us" (Romans 5:8).

That is what sums it all and I'm thankful for God most, for He gave me all of His life and love beyond measures and that is His giving me His Only begotten Son that is love excelling and gracious and that has blessed me too throughout my life and grants me life's richest blessings and love glorious and sweetest joys. So, also I am to graciously loving Him more than ever and He is more than worthy all for me to delight and celebrate is joy that Scripture teaches us, the ultimate of love is expression of love. Faith and hope and Love is true and pure and kind and love is great the greatest of faith and hope (1Corinthians 13:13); Greatness Gift is that Love is gave us liberty.

Absolutely, I don't know about you, but I am speaking from my heart about Love that is also in me is in the heart and, I found that Love also is the heart's power and working within too. In me His Love is inspiration, its legacy and faith is that the currency of life, God's wisdom also is as well the, "infinite!" Lord of Love of all and is surpassing all others and that is so wonderful! Of all that is in His heart is a blessing for me to appreciate is divine blessings are all a gift of love and God is who gives us everything that He has and, thanking Him for helping and giving me my healing. His is divine love for divine health which is of joy, knowledge and wisdom for you also.

Being blessed is healing and power, for our blessed Savior and Redeemer has introduced me to Father! God's love and has given potential sure all, blessings are in His heart for us too to enjoy is who gives us all, and given grace, blessings with power, and authority for us to use, is to claim and for the pursuit of our happiness. All is to use that is wonderworking spiritual power it is what can also win for us our health, security, peace of mind that is the most important power. Our contented adjustment, for the pursuit of our happiness always the sky often said is the limit!

But there is no limit with the love of God and joy of growing is not being afraid anymore. But more is abiding faith. That is increased over the years and it is awesome to know Him more and more and insightful through grace and joy is in openly receiving His love and kindness with love as well gratitude, is well with my soul for knowing Him personally that is most! More than, gracious is better is encouragement that is to learn more about Him and to receive more as there is power, in knowing the message of faith in God is the strength from Him that I have more than. And all are divine blessings from His love and kindness; peace of mind that is eternal wealth as is peace is greatest need and for happiness the heart, mind has and, that transforming spiritual all.

A happy heart is a willing mind and without which that peace is divine fervors and must. No one could ever refute His greatness that it is in the heart and hidden deep inside caught my attention and breath and nothing can transform any human's life like it or not, than God's Love. Power is the graciousness of God and also love and inspiration that of compassion and as well is all unfailing love are demonstrated in words, actions and deed as my life has changed and also, is my perspective remarkably and God's peace and blessings are everlasting spiritual transformer!!!

I thank Him for blessings and giving me all His love and maturing me for my spiritually is growth amazing grace love always His love is and what is also that is compelling be the person that He destined me. His of love matters as it is what it is and is my life that to me means a world and had blessed me always wanted me to be in life a blessing and, to tell the world that is we are blessed as one in Him as a large family of His too and the love that is can also effect changes too in our lives with love and peace that no else can God is an Inspirer, most definitely! He is all there is in life and holds and hope for us is joy to be what you and I, were destined and I'm very proud.

My Father's little girl working as His ambassador and working with Him in His vineyard and am His poem of praise; I just want to praise Him day and night morning and noon all that than ever and Him, happily love praying, praising serving, worshiping and obeying Him as His love is so amazing. And joy is my relating and sure that is Joy is my heart and adoring Him. Everyday's a blessed day that is what this is also about is living in the Lord's presence to love day in and day out as the living Joy is definitely, is working in the light of life awesome demonstrating Love.

He is the most, His Excelling love and power as who is Everlasting Love, a loving Father and my Almighty God as well also that is a revealing Love and He is the Lord God of hope and justice and fairness and I have seen His glory shining. I have seen best of life is the light through Him that is so much inspiring me. His presence in my life; He is who illuminates. He has been so faithful to me. Holy is supernatural God and Words of God's love as well and power also that is what together revived and cured me as I had said there is no other way, I could have made it on my own power for my ordeal that did have commas, started on the "brink" of hopeless and, and is as seen ending being healing and all transformed into passionate purpose. And hope is this is a message of love, hope, courage, faith, grace, gratitude, and healing that is what is all about Love.

Is what the love of God has, and is all of Him and about Him, all that we need and power of love that God celebrates from which I am a living testimony to His Great Healing Power, I do. God is and Words of love is also all inspiration that is something interesting for is good to us and is for healing and living daylight and miracles and also what makes of remarkable recoveries and also more than ever transforms with exciting more are discoveries for our growth in God's love. Amazing that's I see is inspirational that as God uses many media to spread His message of love!

This is the priceless experience and wisdom, and, we can gain help, and knowledge and understanding. Wisdom and help from God's

Word also for our situations and only God has love that is of ultimate power and words He alone can see us through, when we experience suffering and is joy is to dig deeply into our situations is find more with spirituality is looking up to God.

Find out more about the miracle hope too and know about our situations and as well how we can endure is through the grace and the power of God is also joy to endure and He is the love that endures, and rescues, that can help us knowledgeable about who we are and education. Surely, that can help us and it is by His guidance and blessing of His word of wisdom and power! Many has sadly due to greed have abandoned their God's given blessings and potential to chase after useless things and lifestyles as well as the things that are not helpful. Is waste all their time, gifts and talents possessed, could have applied to better themselves lifestyles to make them better people and happy. As often said, "No man is above the law" is so true and God words of wisdom.

It works and has power and is the blessings and guidance but some are yet to be there and to give thought about. <u>There is a God of faith</u>, hope and love and how grateful that I am, living in that faith and though, I did suffer as a victim of which a fellow human kind, did create stumbling blocks and you can is clearly here see how God didn't leave me and my family alone. Never left me stranded and them going astray and, why I am saying thanks You and I love You Lord many times and again too. It is to me, is wonderful and marvelous and is not enough, and I can never ever graduate from thanking Him and imagine as me being this blessed and happiness is why it is not enough and am so glad that God loves me as well Yes, being thankful for evermore is to God.

He is so good to us and, that is let God be praised in my life from the rising of the sun and setting and know I am human, in my flesh alone, if I walk is to stumble and fall. But I thank God for who He is in my life and, for giving my Friend and His Only begotten Son who is Jesus to me My Savior is who came for me and that power has given to me hope and is a favor of God's love. The grace of God and is Joy. And by faith works for me and here greatest love demonstrated also and this work is fun writing reading and to write is that is my redemptive Love and Holy Spirit is directing of great joy to support and hold me on and also inspire my heart with passion, blessing!

He blesses me and fills my heart with love and joy. He gives me that blessing of joy for me to hope more than despair awesome with love and joy and surely, "joy unspeakable;" Though I am human but God He is supernatural and loves me and is strongest Love that is who gives me is grace with His blessing as well guides and leads me daily and let me live and see the good that comes out of unfortunate situation. The unexpected circumstance is made now become from my burden blessing. It is faith and is His is that awesome power is Love that God is amazing endures His love for you and me. "Beloved, let us love one another, for love is from God, and whosoever loves has been born of God, and knows God" (1 John 4: 7/ 8). That is God's words inspiring me.

That is for my closing statement is and that Honestly nothing endures like God's love and nothing beats living and loving and relating and serving God and empowering and celebrating is a thrilling joy is love is the greatest and love empowers much as it inspires and fills the vacuum of a lonely and broken heart is encouragement in other words nothing beats living in the love of God's freedom that comes from being confident in God's love and with that faith in God's love!! Is good being one, "God fearing," and you will find favor before Him and man and is joy finding Him and love is with ample blessings, before Him first and as well before fellow human blessing is because He is with you as well wherever you go and come what may God will never forsakes.

God love embraces you with warm embrace and throughout there through thick and thin and His love endures it all the way God is with you there, even in the wilderness and is His Love. And Joy He abides He uses His Love makes my life bearable and how will you feel within being healed and transformed by the love of God and by the Holy Spirit to become that love for others? As well all wounds caused by human God healed and as I said earlier, sees you and with you and loves you is just as you are and those situations already He knew all about you and a loving God rescues you as who has done for me what I couldn't ever? As well no man could ever have done.

For me, but He did it and has been so given me all of His that love and that is all that is in His heart for me also and for my happiness and prospects and what should I render? For me is to be proudest of Him and boast of it and appreciate look after all this marvelous blessings all are divine and God wipes all my tears away and of the trials and tribulations, He picks me blesses. I say who else can love way beyond measures as He is awesome and excellence is supernatural as God and rescue miracles all I see is for all He is and are I will glorify Him as He is my Salvation. And, I thank my dear Father God is who touches and is healing touch that Love teaches me more secret wisdom and now my heart is one that is always fills with love and joy because all is of joy.

He inspires and filled emptiness is with joy, love is even overflows and joy never ends is I am so blessed for it never ending with family and friends and all His of power is of His Power. And love, inspiration and in all that I do daily as I see the glory as God shines face on me is Love and power of words is both garrisons me and wraps me His love. I am blessed and surrounded by His Inspiration and the leading of His Holy Spirit. I am led of the living God around secures me and mostly enables me to become the person that He created me to be and taught me more words wisdom is of His love and power is to reject failure and defeat, and fight against the enemies also and use tools that power that hidden "Sword of the Spirit" with healing and comforts is of inspiration for me that is beyond human imagination as is true Love as awesome God and He always loves.

Steps in ahead and, delightfully fight my battles, cancelled what was not for Caroline His lovable daughter's portion. As I am His lovable child as and daughter of the King and He is also is so. I am also to be very proud of my Father God who is the Almighty and helped me and said such negatives propose by human is not for me, but purpose she will overcome all and He will as fulfilled only His will to be a blessing and lives for Him and glorify Him and that is already has been done deal. Taking place His plan for my life and this is already like am in heaven also it is!

I may be here physically on earth and in my heart, I feel that power of His and a child that is always with Father's everlasting joy and not man's created though is born of human but God's given and created too in His image that is ultimate and this is how God remembers me and mine. Is my family and friends! He remembers me for good with my family and joy to have goodness a blessing all of God and community of supportive family, and circle of loving friends to celebrate. Along with me and all to enjoy the blessings also with me and the love of God's infinite love and is the greatest greatness. Power and love that are surpassing and always something to be thankful for everyday and is all the day long for, I must not forget to thank Him who is life and joy to me.

I am for everyday thanksgiving and have done me well in the past and present and will be forever and it is for ever and evermore as my Father's love is unfailing and through eternal life. I know is He abides with me and is in all of us. And still continues is the Life and Truth and Light that gives, me hope that can help us to find answer to our unanswered questions and solutions is personally, is God has influenced my life with love and happiness and kindness and miracles has been so good to receive. feel that within. Using inspiration that comes from Him and that is the greatest source of my inspiration. He blessed more and is with my wonderful supportive family.

And my friends from across the world and that means sure truly blessed that is He is the Pillar of my life as well the remedy of my soul as well has daily blessed me and this is heaven on earth as God's love manifest in human hearts on earth and l have seen and by using that power in the name of the Lord and that heals and helps me to break myself loose from the bondage. Those hindrances and stagnation and help me to reject defeat, fear and doubts and perplexities that and more and God helping hands has brought me the victory for He fought my battles with His good angels also fought l defeated and you can imagine the joy of being able to overcome is awesome.

Is so powerful and since I got the victory and I am blessed and obligated to love God and fellow kind and must have to share also the love, useful information to bless those who need help and get them too to be aware of people who are conned artist, dangerous and deceptive and also heartless. Same time is to educate hearts and inform the minds and, of the dangers of not taking a bold stand and firm is to stay focus on God is to focus more on what is good more than on evils. I have found that in the hustle and bustle of this day and age, is of modern technology many lost it and fabricating stories as well exploitation, can do havocs, worst, they lied against innocence ones as they love to cheat and is to get rich fast and quick way by duping and scamming always.

They live by deceptions, want quick fix, for theirs is living on ripping off people regardless of circumstances surrounding, they do it anyway and all is because they know how to manipulate people minds and, lied and deceived and scammed and duped. Convinced, friends to believe them and that is what they think is okay to do, they gang against the ones they hate and their friends, is who believes them of stupid compulsive blatant lies, that is those who want to listen and hear. And, often they will sympathize with heartless sick inhumane people. Sickening as pride of their hearts deceives them. Thinking they don't need God and, also think can run others lives, when to begin with, they can't control self. They can't of themselves and their lust is greed that is so sad.

Situations that they need to take care and work on ask God for repentance what they need first, is God in their wicked heartless hearts. If you can't take care of that flaw mind of theirs is business foes are that is what is all their thoughts and places them on high risks and I pray they leave people alone it is better than hurting people. Find what occupies yourself that and is should be positive thoughts, and that is most important than bothering innocent people and taking from them by deceitful means and malicious dubious intent and exploiting fellow kind is what I pray.

And that is May God touch them their hearts to turn from their wicked ways for they are hurting of themselves and families. Book of books says, "Be not deceived; God is not mocked: For whatever a man soweth, that shall be also reap" (Galatians 6: 7) The entire chapter can teach us so many lessons of life and how to achieve excellence Bible is all about God's love for us and is lessons of love and wisdom and on how to overcome any situation God can help overcome all for us. It is most tough thing many things that culprits do are thinking that is hurting just victims but that is ignorant minds that is flaw thoughts what they don't realize.

Is that, "When you throw mud, you are always left with dirt on your hands," is proverb is words of wise wisdom and is. Please, culprits leave alone hurting others and take care of your family and if you can't do it for every intentional problem you cause for people downfall sooner than later will backfire has time for pay back all of us know that God is no respecter of any of us, no matter status that we all may be claiming. So, why not work and do the right thing and you know that hurting others is not the right way; is not right victimizing and scamming and duping, lying and causing hurt and pains to others and you know right from wrong, but you still do it as well and, anyway that is certainly, I have to tell others of what my eyes have seen God's love the goodness of God many abandoned their God's given blessings and potential and are in the habit.

Panhandling and disobedience and not able to use what they have it so big and great are happy to be chasing after useless lifestyle sad things of evil thoughts and minds and is waste all their gifts. And talents possessed all are and it is what could be very rewarding if they could have thought(s) wisely about all they are blessed with in life, to appreciate; be thankful as well satisfied that all could have all been applied to better lifestyles. And, to be enjoying all the blessings and to live of it happily and is better of themselves and even blessing others and celebrate as of it that is what God love does for us, God <u>loves for us to do what is of honor, be contented, and thankful.</u>

<u>And, responsible and productive, supplies us with grace for we are not called to live up to others responsibilities, but to our own and in pursuit of our happiness so is reaching out to share. It is joy reaching our goal and by love out to do good unto others is a blessing there is in life love and goodwill and we can all learn to our potential and share of that life and joy with blessing are gains more than hatred and bitterness and I pray for them that they will recognize their</u> malicious intent and mean crooked as ugly ways to cheat and lie and duped and devising illegal means too.

And, I say thank God from whom all blessings flow and to God be the glory for the love that is to grow and soar beyond obstacles and the healing love and power that inspires of heart to be of hope and, "Enjoy serving the LORD, and he will give you what you want"(Ps. 37:4). The desire of my heart God has given me and please, do like you would want others to do unto you do to them and please, I employ you to read and don't cause people havocs anymore and but use your God's given potential and gifts of grace to wisely, enhance your life and come to God also.

And know that love matters more productive and rewarding is significant and, I don't think many people realize that power of inspiration and repentance that is a must with thanks is the, "Do unto others as you would have them do unto you." That is the ultimate is the golden rule that is Scripture is a noble thing to do is being of His love and directives and is the best of all too. Love and show passion to God and compassion to a fellow kind and please, don't think that this is my words and, it is not, I like to refer to the Book of Matthew 7:12. Sure the law and prophets to commit to life, not just memorizing and am grateful for God's, all have seen that Love of God.

And, I thank God for giving, "Draw near to God and he will draw near to you" James 4:8 testifies His giving to me His the grace as much as strength for me to come this far as is from my journey of faith to endure and, I have to thank Him more for His faithfulness, taking over all my life and situations and overcoming all of it for me and, that is God shattered the thoughts of the culprits. It is and destroying how they thought evil against me and their negative minds and also all their plans thwarted and, it shows God loves me much, turned all that to be for my own good.

That says we ought to love Him more, and more, I am mostly and that is a success story. It is to do what is good to us and to others and to do good is to be kind to all us, we should and is a great investment do good more than that wickedness of heart that is destructive is laziness also and capitalizing destroying others and what do you gain from others and when you hurt them that is think about it and love is key? And is so good to care, rather than being abusive, exploiting is hatred and, let alone maltreating, all are His own children, and why do you walking all over them and hurting? But why is it what culprits capitalizes doing and they don't realize that part of law?

May God to help us all and you to, "Think twice before you act;" If you don't believe in God and continue culprit is yourself you will be perpetually committing those crimes and as you dupe and delight in havocs more and is; if you knew that God watches over His own children and is against that lifestyles and that havocs. I pray that you will come to know Him that havocs you do and think you are smarter than God is a disaster right there is no way that you can not answer is pay is the heavy price for ruining people and depriving them from enjoying the fruits of their labor and give the children opportunity to be children and live happily and stop worrying about.

The turmoil life and their future because you took from their parents and them and family their hope was shattered and the impact was the scars that you left and was right there lodged like a bullet in the heart and mind too, I felt like I was robbed at gun point what that culprit did to me and my family and I left him to God to deal with him and all of them that pestered my life are being rewarded accordingly. It is impossible and thinks you can hurt run or hide and ruin others; run over people and invade their lives, cheat innocent people, both young and old and deprived them of their joy as it is God's given love as blessings and what is all their hard work earned too.

It is that they all devotedly forget of their pleasures and them aside and put their efforts to do from all tediously is toiling day and night to fend for their family as well future; all you don't mind but maliciously deprived them from their enjoying, even those disabled, how dare? How do you not think of all their suffering and that work with all amounts of efforts and sweats from can to cannot, but they don't mind forgoing their leisure forsaking all of it and pleasurable moments, even deprived of it and their time to spend with their family, loved ones, mostly of those young.

Children; just to have food on the table and shelter over them and working daily to make ends meet? For, it was a service their security, safety and something for their raining day! But, why do you hurt them and their family and friends and not thinking about what they go through and can't you just work and hurt of yourself and family leave people and their property alone? Why others and not yours why did you take advantage of their situations made sad and frustrated and don't care about them? Is it right for you to rip from them to be miserable and as I thought all about those moment these were some of the questions and, I thought about when the culprit(s) who so wrongly invaded us took what was not theirs from the wrong way and is greed and lust.

To get rich quick and fast way of enriching themselves by duping, causing all heartaches! What does not belong to you is not of yours, and don't hurt people. Please, don't expect to reap from where you did not sow in life. And is so wrong stealing from others those are all who are struggling, let alone to take from the poor, disabled, elderly, disadvantage children, and these some of them orphans, widows; widowers and singles parents and any human married or not it is still dead wrong too to go after people and take from them what it not yours and you did not sow. And, why do you want to reap from it? Love is all we owe each other and living that their mean behaviors and attitudes of lies upon lies and sneaky, lust and greed all they do is God watches.

He is watching all and they want more than they can afford. Just to hurt and harm people feelings and lives, then brag about how they victimized and hurt, abused people, but, they forgot truth is this, "The eyes of the Lord is on the righteous, and His ears are open to their cry" (Psalm 34:15). More than grateful He sure listens. He listens to me and mine as well He shows, healed and delivered me and made me alive, from the hands and mouth of the lions is dubious thoughts.

Their selfish hearts and pride is hunting them <u>and theirs more than they had thought, it is victory for me and my mind is joy is to</u> talk about power of God's greatness as I am blessed. That God is who is looking out for me and mine, as He answers, offers ways and reaching out for us and provisions made richly too in my reaching my destination, and healed me and taught my heart. He teaches my heart how to have joy, the humility of faith of my sweet heritage and family of faith, like all of my ancestors were and blessed is all family and of other faithful siblings is all.

Including of Brother Job, Jacob and Isaac, Abraham and David too lived that same faith for it pays to trust in Him more and sure loves us as dearly and is this is for the love of God and for the Lord's Healing and Comforting Touch. I feel obligated and to share about power is deep down in my soul is has Spirit that <u>has power is what matters to</u> us anyone is to seek from God's love and it is power! And, also examples and that is inspires by faith that does not waver and, it shares truth in love as well because God's love and can carry us through anything is by his grace.

I am grateful for God loves me and teaches me how to love and I am capable of loving us all And is blessings and moving power is awesome is of the grace, as I found the cure for my health as well all situations and those calls to mind happiness and thankfulness, serenading heart all to and this is Hierarchy is favors, for His greatness is in the heart and love comes from heart is Same with giving and am giving glory to the Lord, whose Grace lives within and lifted me up! For as is am forever blessed is am favored by who reigns Supreme Being in my life Lord's all is so first credit as Healing, Encourager and Comforting Touch! Foremost, for me is to give thanks, too to Him. God loves and created me in His image, prays and Intercedes for me and also at the same time as He always was listening to all the conversations that culprit was talking and how of a manipulative and took what was not his own from a struggling single family/a disabled person.

He is precious and today still working wonders and He is as well is of Love and beyond measures to us all so all those matter it says any those who are hurts to call on Him and abounds of love evermore for He delights to hear from us and hears our prayers day and night. He listens and loves to hear us call and waiting and is job is to heal and inspire and bless us, am grateful for His love letters for us to read and digest. Is and each is joy and a full doze of God's Love works is Words that contains His mind, am thrill for the Lord's sustaining me is the love's medicine we as well have to have and there is none greater and than Him and also taking that love medicine is daily over dozes. And along is with fervent prayer daily is of faith to spice it up as gives us hope.

It is secret of success is spiritual words of wisdom and powerful. Please, take the time to be inspired with the passion for inspiration, and use the talents that you possess in spite of your situation-cultivate and use it to glorify God and also improve of yourself make a little change and is reach out and touch others. Having faith in God, moves mountains! Blesses and brings joy not only to you but also to others as well makes you even richer by faith and happier than ever is joy. Having faith in God, moves mountains! And remember, "Jesus is Lord" (1 Corinthians 12:3).

You even can do your best at a time when you didn't even think you could, with Him; He is the "Author and Finisher of your faith", so, stand firm in your faith, for there is power in wisdom and countless blessings to enjoy from above!

Testimony

"I will give thanks to you forever" (Psalms 30:12)!

Love, is experiencing God's peace is progress in the world
is blessed being contented so love is a matter of heart is of
joy and testimony is all Gratitude Matters!
- Caroline Arit Thompson

Everyday with my love is I must thank Him. This is miniscule is of my humble of heart is a gift of sacrifice is in lieu of my heart of heart of deepest gratitude and to Him being personal. My All is that I need, has given me joy and given me the grace, ability, capability, potential, gifts, talent and life to do and live for Him! What I am is all so much blessed and passionate about is to love Him more and more and serve as I am sold out to Him throughout and that passion can't be substituted. My passion for God can't ever be substituted and chapter also inside for God gives me is life to me and is my blood line also to walk in love, bless and care for others, give my heart and love to grow and is with peace of mind and hope and for yet another opportunity to inspire!

Of yet, another moment too see this manifestation is by faith as this a very blessed day of my life great joy to testify and glorify a loving God more than I give Him due respect and my life and love and all of my being and all is for His glory is joy being a blessing is awesome that I am. Honored to be as He destined me to continue to enjoy; He gives and saves me my life is truly am blessed. And to be of use of God more is than what I give Him is my being hopeful and it is what money can't buy and talk of my life and His unfailing Love is a God of love and fabulous super. Giver is He, is to be highly praised, and I am inspired and make this proclamation publicly of my faith and love. To begin with I thank Him and that grace and, I also thank Him for those as well.

And this is for, happy survival of that ordeal of being given six months shared earlier in the introduction chapter of my 1997 situation and this is my testimony in continuing to be, thank God for His love and power as well my family and friends around the globe and that includes all and my dear supporters as well who touched have blessed of my life with joy as human those are beyond my immediate family members that care as well for me in my journey and includes, Mr. Donald Strozier, who more than my supervisor (boss man) that we love to call as we never have seen such human being who loves his staff and to show love and compassion and kept my job for me and didn't mind doing anything humanly possible for us and protect us as his family at work.

I thank God with such caring human kindness and indeed always our angels are disguise sent from above. Looked out for us, and Don was one as so caring and I remember that as well as he told Beverly Croslin, co-worker to take me right away; To my personal treating physician. I recall vividly as Don said, "Sister, I will manage the office!" That fateful day of my fainting and gasping and God is so good. She was there also with me as well throughout, walking and holding my hands, praying with me and was worried more than I did for my health, and droved me there. And turned that it was very long day, but didn't mind to wait till after my emergency admission, thank you sister Bev, my senior colleague and that love of acceptance is what makes love real.

Is a blessing, is inspiration for more when it is understood as love and compassion and we can care for one another and regardless of whom we are, where we come from and what race and dialects and/or nationality, tribe and tongues and creed is love that comes from genuine heart of it is joy God's too. There is no such thing, but love that is for joy supports and is encouragement. Also that is love I am blessed with people of love and kindness of hearts that is being the legacy. Love of God of human kindness and pure genuine love and no adulteration that is grace of God. Wherever I work and a bloom is because God loves me and inspires passion and is divine favors.

Sure is before Him and man and I thank God for His compassionate that extends to us as one of the means is communicating love is a blessing expressing in words and actions am sharing friendship that cares and reaches beyond and above our immediate family and our mutual friends only that Love abides and dwells among us and that makes us to love beyond words of mouth as demonstrated and is to show that love of God is within. Am to thank God for my life and for the benevolence of His grace that I continue to enjoy with my supportive family and friends across is the globe everyday is a blessing with love. And thanks to the One who loves me beyond precious the Redeemer lives and so the there is no Friend like the Lord, God Almighty and I thank God it is mostly for Jesus. What will I do without Jesus? Nothing! I thank God for sending me a Savior.

And love letters along with it where I can read and find blessings. Thank you Dr. (Mrs.) Inemesit Abia, you spent more out of your time with me until the day, I was discharged and so were also great friends and people that I met and the nurses and all others which were there with numerous doctors and all staff in one duty or the other all were too. Thank You Lord and for all also for my family and friends and journey being another one more proof that you are the Lord as Almighty and Greatest in heaven and on earth you are the one and is and was and will ever be. The eternal Rock of ages and only Supreme Being and thank for raising me up a testimony. This too joys of my heart your Great Healing Power and a heart that is blessed with love and laughter.

I want to say, "Lord I love you and I thank You and for all you have done and are still doing and for those journey that together you were special things of your heart and blessings for me and my family and friends evermore and more is my priceless treasures of life that God gives so much treasured and lifetime of keepsakes and especially, deeply grateful that peace is joy!!!! Did you know that God will not break His covenant with you? "My Lover is mine, and I am His" (Solomon: 2:16). Take it from this child of His and blessing is in my Father's care right from my beloved mother's womb, He loves me and I was celebrated by the love of God and ever before I was cured of infantile disease to able open my eyes the gift of sight by God's love is, was Grace.

Again, I had lost hope, suffered of issue of blood in 1987. Dr. Eric Archibong desperate and confused but as we trusted and prayed miracles came through God-send intern physician (Dr. E. Ntekim) at midnight hour, when I had given up hope, at St. Margaret Teaching hospital, Calabar, Cross River State of Nigeria was the venue. I survived major surgery and everything successfully done. God was in it and we were all so glad and thankful and discharged within one week. But, sooner immediately admitted back as I went home and forgot God had spoken through channels at Qua Iboe Church, the word was delivered. But I got home, sadly did forgot rules had not followed it precisely, probably misunderstood that's interpretation; I almost died right there, before I knew.

I bleed profusely and wound up readmitted. And, it was God whose power saved me. It is and that is was by grace that I survived that was a blessing for us. Is Prophesized Words of God's mouth should not be taken lightly or for granted. Not all fakes! It is worth being so thankful for that means and is apparent that is for my thankfulness for my hope is in God and my faith also is. There in His heart, loves me and He says that He has a special spot, told me how much He loves me and is confirmed precisely by what He has done and I feel as all inside of me is so much love and full of joy. And have seen by all His words, actions and deed all is by grace and faith always.

Always grace both of His love and, I being touched by the love of God and Spirit says all is there and there are many ways to find comfort in life, and many of them are not of the what it is as all others is world made and so to perform, we look for love in the wrong places and drug to be enhancers to perform, but sadly, it is not there at all. It is all about Him and the heart and that is the reservoir of everything. That is true and is real is about the love of God and given only by Him. But, that is not the way that the world approaches things and this is what God's word says, "Be not wise in your own eyes; fear the Lord, and turn away from evil" (Proverbs 3:7). That is of the ultimate treasure and truth it is. Finding power, freedom and joy with peace is not there in the world is in us and, it eludes them. It does because in the world is identifies with the outside more.

Yes, is than the inside what is joy inward, is most important. Yes, it counts most. Looking for it is within is in our reach and not far is to turn to God for help and He will leads and guides and directs you. And, is what comes from within, if it is of God's love and will, that makes love is most important; is what the world needs. Most is foremost love and to have that God's Peace is first peace with God is for free within and is for process as well success, their healing and peace of mind, and successful life is much more than all the world it is everlasting and those who wait upon shall be blessed renewed and inspired and transformed. As, I see the remedy. My mission is borne out of sorrow and nothing beats that hunger and thirst.

For me to fulfill what I am blessed and destined and also I have tasted, seen and received of the Love of God and found the Lover of my heart as well remedy of my soul is the power to bless us! He is who Heals, redeems, restores, saves and revives and re-building is possible with God as it is always. "For with God nothing shall be impossible" (Luke 1:37); my recovery is joy from life's intensive battles and wars, and it thrills my heart experiencing the secret of wisdom and finding joy and love and maintaining also. He is my blessing in an hour of trial and it thrills my heart, victory is of God and you are made stunt and avid believer of wonder of the miracles of God's love and power also. Power and love of God is curative, everlasting and everything.

That as well that nothing beats that love and power like this mother, sister and friend with my joy of finding God in my life with healing and power is joy and my strength and inspiration is He is also inspiring my passion as I drink from the everlasting well that never ever dries. It is a blessing is with love everyday to be a blessing to all of those who are in need of help for hope. And, to relief of the burdens and find happiness is that power. I am inspires and, I am so grateful for His healing and comforting touch and that is with a mission born out of sorrow with intent of my making sure that others find inspiration in their daily lives and are encouraged as I am and be happy as well too as I am so thrill and excited about what I found and received beyond belief and expectation and nothing more for me to do than being more thankful and sharing friendship's joy.

I say, there is none like God and nothing to be compared, beats that capacity to receive His love, and give and more grow more in His love. Nothing beats that capacity to receive, and I cherished so much to be healed, find empowerment and to live life fully, being that I am blessed and given inspiration in all I do so I live; inspiration is compelling love that also am commanded to love and bless others as I am is thanking God a verity of reasons and is of encouragement and is all Love is to one another as given and is by grace and whatever we do is God is by Grace that I am alive and to be. Here are some of the testimonies: Have you ever been in a spot of challenge and begin to think what you should do? What is the best and so forth?

I had been there very many times and that is; my life, confused and, I almost lost it in my mind too. Really, how could that be? Yes, that is in year 2008, my heart and life as well crashed. Thoughts and heart all far as all my hope was lost. I was duped by a professional conned artist. That I had no idea and the wicked heart, exploited, duped, scammed as numbed flat broke, of my entire bank account! Really, if not by the power of glorious grace of God that faith moves all of the mountains. It is always thanking Him what I start with thanks to glorify the blessed Lord is my God! And like the Psalmist me too paused and asked "How can I repay the Lord for all of his goodness?"(Psalm 116:12). No word fully is, than for me to thank God for His love is goodness.

Who rescued and I thought that maybe God was far from me, but I didn't know was there all the time! Oh yes, He was there all the time looking, working on my behalf for me and for my best. I did not realize down there in the trail and that moment of desperation and, despondency of all it is great things of the heart were waiting to be revealed for me and I had no idea. Thought of hopelessness is you got to understand why. Please, understand that my mind in deep thought was afar and I have to show and tell how much God loves me and you and think of us and our well is being everyday, God's grace that keeps us hopeful and blessed my life and inspires of my heart.

He keeps me alive and gracious love of God's guidance and words of wisdom and faith is a blessing and but for that this will not be feasible today a great story of celebration and thanking God for being raised a child of His faith and am blessed by Him, that faith, victory testimony to the power of the human spirit and why faith is the currency of life and keeps me going and God cares and carries me along with Him and cried with me and wiped my tears. I cried from sunrise to sunset numbed flat broken, and was helpless being broke, cleared, cleaned of my entire bank. Accounts and life's savings and my retirement all of it everything that I worked a lifetime for it; what was for my children of today and their future and other family members and others it gone.

I have to say, yes, I did feel so much pain and hurts and grieve and cried but God healed. Being truly been blessed by the love of God to overcome and it continues to generations. And is after love and helps more with that is a reliable and unchangeable God keeps promise with me is so does His love only constant is His Word lights and shines through me to make a difference in my life, is also for family and friends His calling for love goes places to shine into dark corners. Helping those in the dark world and, I am enjoying being of more hope as He heals, helps me to become-transformed by the love and that love for others and understands many things of heart of spirit are for physical growth as well heals. And emotionally to be renewed mind, otherwise you will be in the dark, awesome is our God and truth is life is so difficult, not to be in your freedom.

God gives special blessings to those who trust and believe in Him, who are humble and give grace to us and integrity is awesome and character of excellence, which I find sometimes, I cannot stop thinking over and again and being more than thankful as well, and I will never stop. Glorifying Him for simplifying my life and making hard things easy, heals and helps me to learn. Lean and know more of Him and am a better person, re-shaped and inspired recovered; discover His purpose for my life! Over and again, am like why have I been so much favored and blessed? Though faced with so many stumbling blocks, but through it all, my wonderworking God has a way of showing divine blessings and makes easier as His love is best expressed of compassion.

My difficulties are resolved by God and, I love how my children they didn't mind to bear with me and even as kids. I saw love of God in their eyes and hearts, was hope holding on and in as much inspired more as all what we have been through, I bless and give thanks to God for us and on their behalf. My love for them, is to show love forever and ever, to God for without their tender love, cheery smiles, inspiration, joy by the twinkle of tender hearts that inspires my heart. Of hope to be strong and be there for them, I will not know what to do in my life when sadness.

It crept into me, and I thought about life and that dark moment and great difficulties too! And, I thank God for giving them to me your love, and inspiring my heart, as each day made me more of hope. Comfort,

God has guided, helped, and blessed us and, and finally your prayers for me (your dear mom, to write-publish) as you have prayed has become a reality. Thank you dear and Pat you did it healthy and helpful to believe in the power of God and pushing mom all of you blessed me and, it just goes to show how much dreams come to pass. When we continue to pray and believe by faith, live by the love and guidance and rely on the wisdom of God and do His. It is His will and obey is follow His precepts, miracles with effort. A little effort is better than none. And hard work pays, but mostly knowing how and when to apply the word, God loves us dearly!

Is a smart way to overcome when, we grow in the love of God, delightfully doing will of God, and praying, believing and to be thankful and hope for the best, "God works in mysterious way", He uses both supernatural and natural means and methods to heal us and ordinary people like you and I, are often channels used. I see angel's everyday and God; He answers our prayers. His grace is sufficient and best to put your heart into good thoughts. And your mind to be also is to be alerts. And though may be at the same time preparing for worse, but most live by leap faith, keep hope alive and pray daily be in anticipation, trusting and praying and watch, keep loving.

And, as well rejoicing and, the willingness and anticipation to live with openness that is a blessing peace of God is joy that, I am blessed and being thankful to God, through the power too. It is joy for me is awesome of more praises and thanks, is joy worshiping and believing that God is able and blessing me is and how blessed we are as His and I thank God over and again praising Him and I also thank you for your inspiration to challenge my life. Everyone and, girls and boys; and thanks you both as you encouraged Mom to write, Comfort and Pat, "Bless—that's your job to bless. You'll be a blessing and also get a blessing" (1 Peter 3:9: The Message). Shine the light and show and share it with the world the blessings of God's and power of His wonders and love.

Let them to know it is for our achievements and glorifying Him is through eternity and so more and more testimonies. Surpassing is of God's love and that is understood by us as well for no one loves like He does and even more provides healing, joy and inspiration with strength to us is everyday. Ref. Eph 3:18. But, truth stands as and is that His Love is excelling and surpassing. There is nothing to be compared among others is, exclusive love for me and from Him. Existed, before I was even born and those of my beloved family as my loved ones and all others as it is of God's who brought me to them back alive fought. He sure did me well and those battles and wars both and calms turbulent. Raging wars and battles all that I went through in my life and He sure comforted me too and, using all of His love and power too Love and wonderworking spiritual is His power has won it for me and all victory is mine and all glory His that makes life bearable!!!!

And His love bears it all and that captivated me. His love is captures my heart and you have seen His greatness and power demonstrated is there is noting else that I can add than what you have read than being more than thankful daily. The monsters all are being defeated, and all subdued is including is all those Egyptians and are banished and this is to show us of how love is empowering and is much Love of God conquers too and victory belongs to God for He is Power. He prevails with my faith is victory. Faith in God is strongest in God's joy and this work and is a testimonial, and He gets glory. All the glory and honor He's and the occasion celebrant as He is a great God, is more than capable and grace of God is power is an incredible great God is more.

Yes God, He is more than deserving all honor and so, it is reasonable for me and to do as I give Him all is accredited to Him and I give all my love and, sure is thanks, for, my Friend and is big Brother Jesus, inspires me always with His love. Sums, as well that is ultimate truth: "The Father himself loves you. He loves you because you loved me and believed that I came from God" (John 16:27: NCV). Divine Favor is the glory all and my life and love, being all to Him and is for Him to have and keeps that includes my strength. For Healing and Comforting Touch and all blessings; I have miraculously accomplished through Him and what does that show and as well it mean to me? I ask, you, my friend and how will you feel too? Yes, imagine if you were as blessed as shared, let me answer it yes, I do want to answer also too.

It is very quickly, is more love and more hope for us, increased faith that too is important. It is faith in God matters most is powerful and, helps you to sing through situations and inspires and well is strongest love and, is empowering and, I dance for joy and hold on to God's unfailing love more and am just so happy, to all greater grace and peace of mind and, that is resulted more strength as I have life and even I am blessed to become more resilient and useful and joy is from grace of God is growth in my relationship with God is that love with Him is the most significant.

Happening building me up, maturing me is in that relationship with God's marvelous and above experiencing God's peace in my life. That is wonderful and out of this world, truly is like never before! I wish you know how I feel inside of me and His words of love all are everlasting as inspiration that is all liberating and is most as well transformational power and the most it is healing and comforting touch, has power and it tells it is truth that shows me, "Greatness is in the Heart-A Tribute to Inspiration That Empowers the best means and methods! The winning power of God as right as life's approach to get personal with God and in relating with God on a one-on-one is the most. Effective means to me that is all I need love of God. Best a vehicle of which we can understand more and a better way to know how trusting in Him most is more enduring love.

Power as well is for me to love is a total surrender, to believe in the miracle of God's joy power and believe in Love! God's all that and we need to call on Him more also is it is the word of God in the heart, and is the secret wisdom and an encouraging touch and is from Him. Friend, believe or not, we all need a healing touch of encouragement from the Lord.

Is necessity of living it as life of hope in heart, mind, and sprit and results "unspeakable Joy," That love is what empowers His Love is the power of God is my joy as inspiration and the promises of God stand firm from generation to generation is Unfailing Love and the Lord is God. And, is life-giving Spirit of God is and I love Him as is more and, more and I love to share of His love as well joy for me to love you and be able to serve as well much the most I love what I saw. Hidden inside of me God is awesome as my joy is full to find "an anchor of the soul," Pleasures!

Is pleasurable what application of those spiritual words is doing is for me and my life and freedom is the divine love and joy and is all of my blessings and pleasure to share also with you, most pleasures is about the power of God's love! Wisdom all from the love God's guidance that has recued my life and is being blessed is more for healing of any persistent infection is possible. For the Lord to reverse the cycle and provide healing instantly and/or according to His will and timing, which is the best time and, is working and that is He is who healed blessing my life daily.

Well what offers me hope and courage and that is for perseverance and I found profound thrill from His love and power is grace and faith. It is well and as always is most beneficiary and workable solutions and that wisdom is of power of God's word and as well His presence is what lies all within is in those are all our needs and to pray and claim it as is! Praying the will of God is words of God's love and always unceasingly from those words, what works and results actions is by living by faith desires living in the freedom that comes from being confident of God's love,

We have in society more wicked, of heartless human beings and we need that love peace of mind from above and it is possible, if we seek with quiet mind and heart's all possible to find within is a blessing and within reach and, I thank God for that peace of mind and gift of his grace and faith. I am, for little did I know that a married man with family and children lives and is that can exploit others and living to dupe and lied just to live off those that are struggling and also are barely making ends meet. Their survival is through working hard and a life is lived also by grace is from paycheck to paycheck is grace of God and the benevolence that I am thankful for is life.

Human being creating problem for another fellow kind it hurts and, I was a victim of such duped and scammed and left dead broke by a **tr**aditional chieftaincy titles (Ukai/Mkpisong), that is in 2008 and puffing culprit, him pompous and so arrogant and claimed to be from Akai-Offot, Akwa Ibom State of Nigeria. He <u>lied and</u> scammed and all was to use, enrich himself and enjoy with family! Culprit and his friends were happily teasing and mocking, laughing at me and were doing as well laughing because took advantage due to my medical condition that I couldn't walk, drive and couldn't do much for myself is when culprit duped me ten thousands ($10,000 U.S. dollars) for landed property first time, then told me about shipping bags of rice took $1,000 too.

I paid 0ne thousand dollars in addition that is tricked me for another money and that said was for bags of rice, shipped and it is till today not even a bag received by my family back home. In Nigeria and culprit told me that the rice arrived was there but all was his lies sooner than later caught up with him as well and he was exposed. All along had played the game of "catch me if you can;" So them say! King of kings is His lovable and valuable. And mostly thankful that my Father's love is always as is with me unchangeable and no one messes up with me His own child all of children, and let alone Him and you can't do so go scot free. Sadly, that is what the culprit (s) fails to realize that one day, they will be exposed.

Is positively, one day all that the culprit took from me and lied to people about me even denied of the money he took from me fraudulently as conned artist was all revealed all what God did too! Culprit couldn't lie again than admit owed me $11,000 (eleven thousand of U.S dollars). Dream for our future, all was gone overnight because of the wickedness of scammer and coned artist who professionally exploits people from Nigeria to American and took fraudulently from us. All what I suffered from working day and night and building little by little culprit(s) took all.

All we had and that is though that culprit took as wicked dubious heartless human being that is okay. For God did not forsake us, nor allow us to be defeated but so sad, that a family man and able bodied can't go to work and support his family than fraudulently to go after people and as well live on exploiting and scamming and duping and lying to take the little that they have all. Taking from them and innocent people just to hurt them and that is what happened to me and my family and that is I had no idea but now I know that in the world are people who are out there to ruin and cause problems to innocent people due to the wickedness of their hearts. Human could!

They be heartless and obvious there are and could be even a married man with his family living and has children but lives that all he does scamming and targeting people to fraud that is what the culprit who duped me and lied and told me about property for sales available in Uyo did exactly. Uyo is the capital of, Akwa Ibom State in Nigeria and tourist attraction city and icon as a great place for tourism and economic prospect and business and family friendly environment and I didn't know all what culprit was up to and posing in public, was not real human and that is was to fraud me and, I thought I was getting a good deal with the property, when said was available.

I was interested in purchasing because I needed something in a decent place back home to build. I had tried in the past and where I got a piece of land was made a federal highway and wired around with electrical transmitters all dangerous from all indication hazard did not work. And, so it was not fit for building as I was left with a little piece to begin with. But, I did not give up hope. Yes, I did not give up hope that one day, I'll be blessed to have a place and build by the grace of God, for we all one day will love to bless people in our native home as well as we do in our adopted country. That has always had been my dreams and hopes and prayers to have it too.

A decent one, a place of mine in my own State of origin for my family and friends and it is till this day that dream has never changed though, here I was being thankful that I am blessed with a new property but I did not know I was being set up. To be scammed and taken for a wild ride and I had gone through marathons of from being duped, being left dead broke a church rat as nothing was left penniless and was desperate and broke but, God loves makes me am still alive. I cannot even begin to describe the unfathomable love and imagine what God has done for me in many miraculous. Shows up for me took over situations; He offers me life with hope and healed and transformed and then He employed! Love empowers and, inspired that is why I thank Him.

There are many more blessings for me to be thankful for this is for me are blessings and miracles again. That are shared inside are most grateful too! I am for my many miracles that I have received and others more and another one. And that is when, I was told by the Hematologist in 2010 and about also one more proof and proven and evidently, this goes also to show me that power of faith too. This life, and daily as well as I still continue to enjoy the benevolence of His grace from Him and love of family and friends and grace that faith as I continue to enjoy as read; it is with a deep joy in my heart and is also with, family and friends am given inspiration from that grace. Is hearty is of God's love is the greatest source of my inspiration, and also is all of His blessings all that is in His heart for me to enjoy with all of you and you are also blessed together.

Part of my blessings is all my family and friends and all I am happy and with the ability, to use this gift of mine, from Him and with capability all are great gifts to me and divine grace is blessings are a gift of love to share. His love is and in God is my miracle working spiritual Love is the strength too is the working power and that all is in testimonials, including, how I survived. Through the power and all is that Love's God healed me and answered all of our prayers as all is specific requests and petitions were made on my behalf and asked for my healing! I did also ask from Him too to also bless me and to, please touch me with His Healing and Comforting Touch, and He did so all as it is are for every miracle and answered prayer to be more than ever more.

I am eternally thankful, and can you imagine all these? As, I said more miracles after one a routine blood work and how I went for the result and scared to death by the doctor's report for it was negative report that results that was scary result. The results and so bad the doctor couldn't handle and/or control self; and I believe he was also so worried and concerned for me. At first it was hard for him, to release the words then, he said, **"Caroline, I think you have cancer!" You read sneak peek introduction gave a clue, sure of what God can do changed things around!! Indeed is a Healer as I recall how hematologist was shaking and scratching head and body. His body language shows effective communication something negative, I knew already why. It took him so long to tell me, I have no strength, nor knew what to do, let alone what to say than for me to pray in my heart all what I could do just that, Obviously, I was so miserable.**

As a child of God, yes, at that moment; but very blessed for one thing I knew where my greatest strength comes from was a matter of just a heartbeat and just prayer away and that happened. God is who listens and answers, blesses you and yours sure believing totally in Him and takes faith in believing that God is able the eternal living, lives words evermore. And, do you know those who reminded even though, I got the negative reports from doctor about my health, but still I could think more positive than let the negative gets best of me?

Comfort, oldest daughter, spouse is, Devon, my supportive family praying with me always I was of inspiration for me from friends it makes my day brighter than being caught on what the doctor told me. It was a moment of great joy and inspiration with love for me recalling.

It was, after reading the love letters that God sent to me, my daughter and son-in-law Devon both as well expressed of their love. And, it goes to show me that I am so truly blessed is joy to turn to God and also be happy with your loving family and friends and also all is rallying around you all are legacy of it inspires us is our gifts from above and that is worth being thankful for everyday. And their love always from genuine hearts it warms with joy always shows love of God is what makes life more being less than alone and that is the manifestation of God's love in us here on earth He is with us. It sure warms my heart, makes a big difference and less than alone they were there and as well inspiring and spending time with me is the joy of finding inspiration.

And of favor before God and man is always love is in the heart that is of inspiration and it is of a love that is never-ending support with love and family and friends is of God's love and for me and also it was of great joy. Indeed as they were encouraging me with words of God's love is as well and praying with me and makes me be so happy and were god-send blessings and this my inspirations is and sure is love story of what inspiration brings to our hearts when cherished also!

They prayed with me as all believing and it is not the will of God for me to go through all those calamities. Yes, they prayed and cancelled all the bad and negative were replaced it with all positives. And, like never before and were saying, "Mom God forbid always. And my daughter, I was so surprised, I say yes, Lord thank You Lord I was amazed has never before seen her to be so powerful, she was so filled. Energized, praying and speaking the words and prophesying that words of God will take over and God is real for it manifested! She was in the spirit and moved powerfully as we all prayed and agreed and in one accord with God by our sides, speaking also is the words and, so faith like love matters and praying together as a family makes a big difference."

Prayer is the solution in our moment of crisis. Praying in the spirit and believing His love and claiming all words that believe for in His will for us is praying the word, in His agreement. We were holding hands together, lifting up holy hands and thankful for everything, that prayer it worked as it resulted action and that God is awesome. I keep thanking God for Comfort and her spouse as she prayed so powerful shows the divine favor and of steadfast in our trust of God and that prayer my daughter presented on my behalf alongside her spouse who also is a Youth Pastor. And, their prayers were answered. It was so moving, so encouraging to me always it is power of God made me stronger as well and happy to have them around me was joy, and so we have good.

God reasons for gratitude is experiencing the power of God and testimony is all gratitude matters for time praying together In an agreement and that means a world to me much as they are my blessings and angels are around us in many places as my inspiration God answered us and He heard our petitions made to rejoice joy love is the heart's power when we are in agreement! And praising God and He is our hope and the faith that we know and breathe that has made this also a testimony happenings in my life and this is the work of God, encouraging and always for us to be happy thankful is and is awesome is a faithful God. I am grateful and we also were rejoicing too.

As happily in the love of God, He listens and answered prayer; I was full of joy and also blessed to be hopeful! And very appreciative of God much of their kindness and sacrifice much appreciated the love too. Am appreciative of their time well spent with me and invested by being there for me God is appreciate of us also participating actively, we were in touch with God and it is join by heavens, by faith and praying also as well along with us we were His good angels also. Praising, and thanking God for all His blessings to us and we were inspired is joy to be instilled a passion to love as a family united in same love and is in faith the bond is of love and in faith with hope in God. That is the immediate solution praying and incredible survival skills and certainly.

There's no question in my mind God was praying and in agreement also with us I know is for sure without any iota of doubt with us and for us, and along with us His good angels as well! There was peace for me as well instantly it was I know that is His power. Peace of mind that is a serene the greatest of His gift is with grace and faith that we have in God that garrisons us daily is a mystery of God's love and inspiration and being together with the heavenly hosts praying. It is always something about soothing and accomplishing with action is so comforting the power of God and is blessing and incredible God and also resulting a remarkable power of prayer, is an incredible Love. Power of prayer is all of God's work and His words are His unfailing love also.

And problem solving is with immediate answer is to pray and ask of your need and be of hope as is specific of what you will love Him to do for you. He is always listening and is with us through Holy Spirit, and though we may not always seem to feel of His presence all at the same time, but He is there with us. And also an ever faithful present, continuously being there He loves us so much and, never ever left His own. He can never leave His lovable stranded works well for is daily is evermore with us talks and shares always is there, when you trust and love Him is joy!

He is the greatest Friend to have and is the Comforter and He is as well my Healer that is also everything is in one accord as I said that comforted me. Most and offered I hope and more to be able to comfort others as well what this work shares. I have received, Comfort my daughter to comfort me and my heart as human comforted is as well and as she was caring thanking God for me and spouse, both prayed same time and inspired and, of encouragement. Their love and time well spent with me helps sharing love is in words, actions and demonstrates that we are capable as well of loving back and my heart was so inspired; both also reminded me of the great love of God and of my faith in Him, to be of hope more encouraged that love is God who empowers us.

Initially, my daughter was frantic, when I told them of what the doctor had said. What the doctor had said, before I even went to do the oncology test was scary and heart broken so, she said; "Mom, I have to get you out for a while!" I knew her heart was broken. She couldn't handle, but very much she understood, as she believes in God in the power of God's miracle-fervent prayer the key and, all will be well. We went on a short vacation to Florida. Like it or not, was terrified, she and just couldn't be able to handle all the bad news, but could love me more by showing me that love and it shows how love is very much what can inspired and gives is joy! But, it is thankfully, she knew right in her.

Heart and mind that God was with us, and faithful Father as well and aware and we all to have a faithful and beautiful Friend whose joy is ours and daily that is His presence was our Joy. And is by strength with Him will be victory always from Him. For us all that we were in hope of that love an agreement and praying fervently works and you see how it results and the role that faith in Him plays in our lives and powerful prayer. It is as God listens, answers us, fulfilled His promises and it is that power and inspiration is an unfailing Love of God as is everlasting Love is and His hope, promises stand. I have seen and received all that gifts is of His; yes, Him is a never failing and dialing Him more that is hope, words of His mouth is awesome as all are inspirations.

All is also powerful and all unfailing and moving as well inspiring that makes me to be so much thankful, fall in love over and again with His Love has power as He is too. Surely, He is an incredible great God, it is what that says love empowers, moving and incredible Power and His is Word, praying is His will for us! His abides and, "From the lips of children and infants you have ordained praise" (Psalm 8:2). That God's promise and evidently manifested. I am very grateful and thankful is He gives us strength to pray, believing in one heart and mind, worshiping, also as family and praising Him also together that makes miracles is of God's love and power evermore.

As He is God and His love prevented me from anything that threatens us from escalating and/or to be causing us panicky! He is like it or not, loves and preserves like a mother's love and of great father's won't allow; a loving Father; He is unfailing and like the good old mother's hen also and won't let her dear child/children to be in any harm and exposed to the danger so does God's Love which is even everlasting protects us and covers us with joy is the blood of His only begotten Son. And, so happy I know His name is above all names and that is I say, thank You to Lord God and my Father's Son and is true, "What A Friend We Have In Jesus?"

Joseph Scriven is right and one of my favorite's music beautifully sang into my heart is everyday, is so romancing and it is so sweet to have and alright too to have my gratitude and is Hallelujah Party for my Healer! That soothes my heart as it melted and so inspiring inspiration! It is just breathe-taking. Listening to Him is what makes me more to be hopeful and reading His words of God is you feel so good is all inside of you and all is about love that my Master and Oh my Savior and His redemptive love is in remaking us is the love is empowering and how do you thank someone that gives you life? There is just no word or any other way than serenading heart.

Love of God is awesome Joy and Grace is sufficient, and gratitude all makes me happy is awesome is that is my spiritual experience moving in my heart it is just so much most is amazing love and is heartfelt. It feels so good to hear of sweet sounds of heavenly delights! Peaceful and calm is His love is a thing of beauty to behold Him too that is the most super exciting part of my lifetime joy. And that is uplifting spirit too as for me joy is to know that reassurance that I am His and of heart of joy, is to hear from the voice within as well and heard from the sound of music. It made me to be inspired and transported to a higher plane; else, my life would have been perished very difficult without it to deal with negative news from the doctor as well about my health too.

Conditions and being duped and scammed my life of last dime, dead broke as a Church rat and what a joy to be this much blessed and so blessed and given a second chance in life after all the odds that twisted and shattered dreams! There is Someone who loves and listens and when you talk and laughs when you laugh and cries when you cry and holds your hand also comforts you in your moment' trials. And, be yourself not someone else, for Almighty's God is the Word who does not waste words of yesterday of which was His Word is till eternity very relevant and ties that God He searches the heart, we all are chasing more after money than spiritual values.

All are bleeding in hearts and as we are a part of society that is in imminent danger today of destroying itself and all that is good. Hatred is preferred over love more and that is part of the problem of missing out of the one great value in terms of high standard morality is fading more and more away. Where is your integrity? Those nightmares are situations we all see more and in the wicked world due to heartless human. People, who just live in the world to obstruct and well just there living to cheat others from their progress, and exploiting the innocent's souls, both of their physical and spiritual blessings causing problems is worldwide web and entanglement also. Is the pathology and are just thoughtless, lacks "the fear of God" and are missing out of glorious.

Love and power of God who loves them and always want their best! We can experience God's love as key to success and peace of which Blessed of His is love is in the heart and we can only get blessed and transformed by Him when we open our hearts to receive of His love always. Who says there is no God? "Fool hath said in his heart. There is no God. They are corrupt. They have done abominable works...." (Psalms 14:1a). The faithfulness of God's love never ceases is new every blessed day awesome revealing love, sharing, His inspiration, as a God of justice and peace, who makes you happy and fruitful have been so blessed and thankful for this opportunity.

God did open the door me to go home to Nigeria with my family and more times needed the receipts and document to develop, the said property, in discussion in May 2009. Wicked cruel culprit pulled all kinds of tricks on me. Had thought the worst for my life is the very pit that they had fallen all with theirs mischief's and all are rewarded for the lies, secrets and mean game plan of dubious wicked motive and deceitful intent diverted my money for his private use and family. In Uyo, it did not hide for long before the culprit knew his craftiness that was thought will never be known was! I would not have been alive and I did not even realize that I was emptied of my life's savings and retirement money and future plans all were gone it was until, January 2009.

God is always with me and mine and that love is His way in my life is revelations and on time Savior. Time offs for the culprit. All along I thought the culprit had bought the property. So, I needed, and I wouldn't have known it was when I requested halve of my money, the balance for he told me the amount paid for two plots. Lied that one was more money acres and the smaller as I told him I needed a larger piece just one not two and remaining amount was left for some of my more urgent needs and one plot was good for I only needed one for me and the other for my son-in-laws and children said they will get theirs. That is when I saw trouble started there is money!

No wonder every time I asked for documents, the culprit cooked story or of this and that excuses. I thought he was trust-trustworthy and all along believe always one lie or fabricated the other was cooked, not knowing. If not about the lawyer having them it will be, his senior sister as and more stories and more but I was patiently waiting on the Lord. Each time I asked how come, I gave you money to buy property and you had called me that it was bought and, but why can't I have the documents and I need the balance to develop and let my family know about and what it is that I can't have my property and money back? I needed and it is the reason for them to know about and the place. And, always why is it so hard that I can't have the information? So, hard for me to get the truth about the place and, when I asked and is more stories and you can understand.

"Oh lawyer says, until when I am physically there as the negotiator? How come not yours is my property? "Oh, well you know that they don't know you in person, I did the transaction for you". What? But, am owner all I needed was documents you call and let them know I was going to be home is time for my daughter's wedding home; I needed to know my property's location? I was pleading for the documents! Instead of telling me there was no property, that my money had been squandered, diverted for personal use, family and friends interest and wanted their best with my hard earned money. Times and over and again, I have to beg tougher time to get the answers.

And papers, then, I told him please, give me the property' document, or return my money just simple is okay, for I don't like trouble and be kind enough to understand my plights and also health situation. I was frustrated and I had to share my story to bless others who may face with similar situation. Take it to the Lord in prayer and don't revenge and let it be handled by God for you. Always pray and trust for God's purpose for your life is far greater than human imagination. His plans are also bigger and never give up on God and neither your faith and hope in Him and is be patiently waiting for God's timing is not ours and His time is the best always, happiness is joy.

Inspirational words, God's love is marvelous and don't be afraid to seek help and support if you need, there's something to help. I did kind hearted someone and community leader told the culprit since it was something so sad and embarrassing a problem that he will give me the money and take over the property in 2009 that was the final resolution and agreement made but where is the property? That is when the truth was known thankfully by the mediation- party asking for my money. Thought witnesses to this testimony! I thank God on this case and up till time of writing this in 2013, (and <u>2015</u>), not settled, but I still thank God that I have seen His glory; He answered prayers!

Most despicable for the culprit lied some more to those responsible and reputable people handled and aware of the situation, they wanted to cover the culprit up and save face of dubious. Top the professional exploiter, scammer and duper, who is so proud of career of passion is there as well says doesn't care as has shame? No! I recall once that I asked for my money to take care of my family and to carry out the project money was meant. What culprit told me was, "What is anyone going to do than to talk about it. But God can do something though man can't! I thought about why culprit is going about telling lies and about business partner and that I never gave the money to him by hand and that is despicable! That is so absurd and is not at all funny but it sad and I wired money from B.O. A. (Bank of America) Miami to Houston bank same in Houston, to him as that was the agreement and it is not legal transaction? Then what is that thought of him?

Because according to him the culprit, he didn't receive the money with his hand from me, but from the bank. God saw it and also saw my tears and suffering that I have endured with my children and relatives and God always answers prayers and brought me of joy and more hope and encourage my heart and keeps us alive and faiths more with hope to be happy and stronger more this is with a greater cause for my gratitude is that He turns my life around and bless me more as well and that is God continues to be faithful to His words and no matter what happens He is God! Oh yes, and I thank Him and also thankful for those He sent to bless my life with, is awesome! (I want to thank Him for (Drs. Francis Ekene/Joseph Ibiok (Rev. /Elder); Good Shepherd Apostolic Church, Houston).

No one shares His glory nor more can manipulate God and this was someone that said to me is a trustworthy person and naively I believed him and at same time being someone from the same State as and is who has a family person according to him and a traditional chief! If what the culprit did was not bad and despicable enough, also he went about blackmailing my name and all is same among the very community and that is what many don't know truths about my situations, but love to talk about it. And gossip about me and many they don't like to see me rejoicing in the love of God and is what also what springs from soul as I find joy, I am thankful for God loves me most and rescues also is always so good to me and my family. In 2012, community, same my people (close to my heart), I love, and serve again, hurt and duped and I was defrauded again! All experiences I have among them with my people but, I thank God few of them. Goodness, what have I done to my people?

Nightmares all the time that I want to get close to be among them and I am being bitterly hurt? I had with that of 2008-2009. It was bad enough and worst ever to be done and heard too. And, 2012, it happened again to me and this was of Association and what many termed to, "No money to them." They are all after rich and famous all of them are groups identified and but, I asked why is it that I wrote a checked for $50.00(Fifty dollars), you took from the poorest to be among you? But you categorized me not being a part of you as I am not rich as you termed to be the poorest among you. Why $800.00(eight hundred U.S. dollars), by fraud why and again? Why is it me again as one of you I am from the same community? Many of them put it across to me alas well straight to my face "that it was no money?" A check for the sum of $50.00 (fifty dollar); But, is changed to become eight hundred? Is many are so wicked in the world and victimizers as it terrible minds are of terrible thoughts and process bad. Is of a handful and thank God, not all!

Big and bad attitudes are lifestyles that are inhumane and heartless; they love to hurt and don't like to see the people who love them as is, not one of them. That how don't want to see me survive, but God got me on His side. Bitterness is what I do observe, jealousy, malice, not always to mention of hatred, blackmailing us and that, of course, is part of being human is backbiting as gossip! You are victim, always the topic happens most not of their groups or friendship but when you are not one of them you are their target and they will smear you with all kind of things and is because you are not loved by them and that is how enemy is and how they see you as a threat to be among them too. But believe or not, God loves you more and more and cherishes and values.

And, so you're blessed and in good hand and company in your Father's great fold and, so don't let them scare you and neither let that bothers. Keep trusting in God and keep your chin up. While they are against themselves, when people wrong you, a child of God leaves it all alone. It is not your business because God is with you and in all that you do and blessed you and what it is matters is continue to love them and do good to them, grow in His grace, and let His love abides. Is more in you for, there is a purpose and you will be surprised and just believe when you call on His name. There is only one way to find hope living it and trusting by faith and touch by it is for all children of God to be of hope and know that there is only one way to touch Him is us to trust.

I always believe we can learn to our potential and benefit more of it from a little help of inspiration as something to boost each other up stimulating us our love and kindness in the heart. As thought is for us more to use and we have the power also to inspire each other also as love is what comes from the heart, of God is a revealing Lord Almighty and Giver and the judge. I saw as stated is revealing. In the introduction of this testimony is how what the culprit denied to his friends was on the open and was he confronted and confessed by his mouth and before people of reasonable minds? Yes, and that it is why, I am so happy that it was known, people with integrity and dignity; but is there any secret that God can't reveal, is there anything hidden under the sun and, can any do wrong and get by? No! And, I that is reason for gratitude right there and also all is thankful for everything is all about God, is not about us is <u>With God on the throne</u> and you do not know God searches the hearts and sees all things? He listens and hears and answers all cries!

I know that the answers are all thanking God for nothing is a secret before Him. Though, those who do not believer in Him will without hesitation answer that to be YES! But, think more deeply about it and, I thank God for everything and making me to realize His joy and love and power and the true answer to those questions is No! Scripture answers at its finger tips with the wisest man King Solomon says: "Let us hear the conclusion of the whole matter: Fear God, and keep his commandments: for this is the whole duty of man. For God shall bring every work into judgment, with every secret thing, whether it be good, or whether it be evil" (Ecclesiastes 12:13-14: KJV). That is what King Solomon the wisest of man read about in the Book of books sums!

Many manipulations and lies upon blatant lies, I thought I had real clean deal, but to my greatest surprised I had no idea. That people play costly games of faking and developing news and all kinds of make-believe stories. Being naïve as I am what did I know, and all my battles the toughest as culprit is the most exploitive human being and that which were so tough for me also to handle, but as so easy with God is what I am thanking Him, daily He prays with me and helps me as He comforts, strengthen and keeps me going is marvelous for without Him, I don't know how my life would have been to survive and endure in the situations that kind of hardship faced. And suffering He rescued me to be a testimony to His great Healing Power and puts new songs!!

The culprit pulled all kinds of ballonet lies, was emptied of all my savings and retirement and also undergoing near death medical conditions. January 1, 2009 is as fresh in my mind as if today but God is always a way maker doing marvelous things in miraculous ways and opened for me a way to go home to Nigeria, and the excessive excuses and all the blatant lies the culprit had masterminded against me as he wished me bad and now see God turned to be for my good. As a marvelous love, "It is God who works in you to will and to act according to his good purpose" (Philippians 2:13: NIV). I was homeless, and hopeless, but deep in my heart, I was though also a stranded and hopeless and I was, too sure that God is in my situation, and has taken over my case and, culprit did not know that, I was under the canopy of God's love, wrong person that heartless act was carried out with His child and that my faith was not in vain, had also increase even more!

I am a proud child of God, which was hurt and painful to see His child the, culprit hurting God not me. And the battle was not for me to fight. And I turned over to my loving Father on my behalf. I have always known the Lord fights battles for me and my family, good angels were also fighting. Especially orphans suffering and no other source of any income for their upkeep. All in tears and sad, as we trust the power of God and both at home and abroad, I had no means or way with support of helping them as before. No father or mother, young children depending on me.

God loves them as much He loves all of us and saw it all, my tears suffering and that is kind of hardship and all that victimization and hurts and pains suffered due to aftermath of that incident and knew about it all! **God has me on His** side and, my life and family all of us in His care and you are not to hurt a child of God. You couldn't return my money and neither show the property, but talking bad about me and bragging and painting me black and don't you know God is watching and looking that is what the culprit didn't realize that God says and meant what He is "Saying, Touch not mine anointed, and do my prophets no harm"(Psalms 105:15). And, you are pointing accusing fingers and lying against a child of God after you have took all that, she had as well others and don't know some day that you are going to be same fingers pointing back to you?

Severely disabled, but you took advantage, duped and took from where you did not keep, hurt and cause me pain and my family suffering. In my despondency and, garnished my money and left suffering penniless, homeless and helpless! How on the world do you think I am going to live and survive with my family? Imagine one was on severe medical condition and you lied that your family friend in Atlanta, GA, told you the brother has two great properties plots in newly Government developed area for sales and craftily, you called me as you knew it was your dirty game plan and wrong motives and deceitful devices you asked me more, "Caroline are you still interested in buying plots? You told me family the owner is your childhood friends as well your neighbors and the sister has been your good friend and why did you have to lie to dupe me and took from the little that was for my family to make them suffer hardship? And you have no heart.

They suffer along with me all that trouble we go through because of your wicked heart as you tell a lie and when you lied to me and against me there and told me there was a property for sales and knew what you were after my money did you know God heard your conversations with me and knew hearts and is in the details of all that we do and our lives? He was there for me? Is all about the heart and conscience, "God searches the heart" and, we are rewarded accordingly to our works. If there is no God, I will not be here and no one to turn to. Though many people have so much blamed me that I did not investigate and checked background of the culprit, they had a valid argument, because I do take people by their words, trusting them on first value; you have to investigate and know more and who or what is a lesson to learn from the past is what a blessing?

But, you may pause and wonder why a blessing is being that as it may, God's has purpose far beyond than what human imagine. That is the answer and simple is so is a blessing as nothing is beyond His power and for a cause in disguise that was for me to be who I am blessed to be this day; And indeed don't take my meekness to be weakness. I have been through hell and back to heaven! **Humanly, a**ll of us are broken, from the women, men, children, young and old, boys and girls and also the less privileged and disfranchised! Love compels and is empowering too to race for the goal and share this blessings. Please pray as you read, and spend more time with the Lord and on this thought as joy, is thrilled just as I am. My other testimony is worth also for me thanking God more on many more miracles that He has blessed my life with His Love and the wonders. **Love and wonders of His Greatness are powerful testimonies!**

2001 was another terrified situation my knee problems swollen and unbearable, severely excruciating pains, a lot knee was fluid, and sleepless nights, as I say couldn't sit, walk or to live my normal life. I was praying for healing, overwhelmed pains and wanted to know what was the cause, inquired to know more about and drastic measures was surgeon used the term for it was both physical and emotional health, medical related issues and my worst episode was emotionally drained and same way what I heard frightened as was scary. I was scared to death, was thought after orthopedic surgeon as the expert explained steps.

I literally was frozen and asked what, do you mean? Is saying if no improvement my knee will be cut because no specific name and prognosis is not so good, asked question for it is important clarity. *I have orthopedic situation and it is now diagnosed to be,* and is osteoarthritis. It has a name now isn't God so good? But initially, didn't, it was given any name and that is why, it was named all kinds of things, including cancer, and that was so scary and my knee would have been amputated. God's is the All in All as Joy/Healer! Actually, what we pray for and long to become if we trust we will find fulfillment by faith is by calling Him unceasingly.

That is what my testimony is so inspiriting and saying is the love of God and power that is preventive, curative is preservative power. He preserves my life as I had no idea at all on what it was looks as if you don't know what is going on around you, especially, at the end of the day it is your body and you only are you are one suffering and no one. And only one as one who knows where it pinches, but for God's is nobody else to share and who else can heal you better than Him! I was not going to have my knee amputated as my Father is the greatest Physician, He's spared me my life and knees and now I can testify one more proof and is He the all knowing all- wise is God that is the Blessing and my greatest is power and physician is He that overcomes all. Is God, He heals and that power is Grace is my wonderworking, that is the bottom line goes with us also.

And prays and intercedes and so good on your knees and pray and God is who hears and listens don't hesitate. Friend is good go on your knees, and don't let it happen to you. Take good care of your body and, don't let it be invaded, is like your life is being terrorized at the gun point and also as well being always run over when ignorance. Your life is basically invaded, terrorized and just know that when you let that happens life is actually running you, instead of you running life and that is why Greatness is in the Heart and A Tribute to Inspiration That Empowers shares of the power of Almighty. He is God that Empowers, the Ultimate Director of life and wisdom is His is for directs and guides and so love empower more by faith is to go on your knees and seeks first from God. And God's Source and is word is first source is of all human resources the best.

And of the best of books is the Book of books is read the Bible is my favorite and that is where For instructions, God is the Source and His guidance is also the first source to seek from inspiration that is prayer, His words are crucial matters of life and very significant and relevant is not by duress is a choice is Truth is this, I did not know prognosis of my medical conditions. But, I did not want also to be any burden too to anyone, not even family, let alone to the government, either, though a patriotic citizen who's contributed to the society and love working. Yes, as good citizen who always love to promote and endeavor to contribute my part to the governments both, in Nigerian and America. I love to help more, as it is better to give more than to receive and by it more giving, one can always as well be blessed to receive more rewards too from above.

This is it for increased faith, past and present events and my testimonies are all truths, the power of His Love. Truths to the power of the human spirit, is a book that transforms the Human Experience. Is achieving excellent through spirituality too both favor of God and of man too, you see that is given by the grace of God for always, He's of Love greatest greatness is who makes a way where there's no way. Celebrate it also as the Love of God and Love is forever appreciated. Life is all about His greatness, goodness and faithfulness and holiness that grace and joy all our Love and giving glory to the Lord is God and generally life is all about Him and, this is how His Love has manifested on earth in each of our hearts and is one's way to express it love.

That is of acceptance and inspiration is sharing it daily! The enemies they had their own thoughts and plans all more but God He is more than conquerors shows it as that is of refreshing. God loves so much and proven Himself to me and forever over and again to me and my family. And that is the love that is the everlasting Father and the greatness of God's saving grace never to be denied the only way and it is really that acknowledgement that has prepared my heart and inspires my passion more as read. It has ignited my passion more. Joy is amazing grace love to me is living that faith and hope and love and in spirit is this For amazing grace, I thank God and, for who He is in my life, lifted me up by His grace! I am eternally thankful for His using me for His eternal purpose. I know what God has done for me from infant and in my childhood through.

Throughout my entire lifetime and now in adulthood evidently is and my being as this is blessed and nice for is of warm thoughts. Blessing of faith is lifetime hope that inspires faith is a gift for a lifetime love that empowers and entire life is your love is goodwill is way of life and is the best investment in life is of significant value and I am for that as I am also a stunt believer of His love and miracles also and the power. I am, because of what I have witnessed, that is hearty is healthy is joy for God loves me and as such am grateful and so much is being very thankful for His daily provision, faithfulness, protection, grace, and mercy preservation Power is my God and is my life and in all that I do gives me inspiration. I say I am grateful for me, to see this day and am all joy my miracles also of sight someone who was born a blind little child.

God is awesome and to see is exciting sure! He is marvelous for me and joy to testify of again and over again and, like one who was unable too to walk but God made all to be possible is of testimony all is God possible and to overcome that today walking and, was also given only six months to live by my treating physician in 1997, and am still blessed and alive that story is in my heart is testimony is going to be all forever is everlasting and read in details in this story of love. I am grateful and also for He who is my God is who handles all my situations. Changed of that is miraculously to become from a timeframe of six months to become abundant timeless and life is a proven evidently God has the ultimate say the only power. His abundant Love is for me too my miracle working God and wonderworking spiritual Power and He wishes me nothing but the best and to live life fully and abundantly honors me to become that love for others His chosen vessel!

A loving and lovable and adorable child of His as is His ambassador, vessel of honor. Is there anything that is too hard for God to do? There are all is deep joy in my heart testimony and no limit is to celebrate for, is not up to man and here love is again His is a gift of life from Him and how. How much love and over seventeen years since that story that was nightmare took place in Miami, Florida. What I found myself is I was shocked as being hooked on monitor on the fourth floor at North Shore medical center and is Hospital, as is premises is consisting of out patient as well hospital. I was there for one week and that has proven over and again that all power belongs to God, He is my Ebenezer greatness is of God forever. The Master and Healer and Power is that can help us is to overcome anything and wherever it is so true for as you read I have been blessed hurts by people as well and sometimes is from left and right and to include your own community.

It could be so painful and worst but through it all God being so marvelous and has given a gift and me inspiration, grace with joy to endure and I can't even describe how happy that I am everyday. Yes, imagine being hurt and despite by people of your own community than those that are different of your color as we talk about decimation and racism is not different from tribalism. What that is what I have experienced myself and this are just few typical examples testimonies on tribalism as I thought about that and how much God loves me and mine and gave us victory is His by grace to endure and what faith does in God, can do everything by believing that with Him all things always is possible and well these are few testimonies what God has done and continues doing for me and mine and others am speechless.

Here are more of my testimonies and is going to blow your mind and heart up to be more hopeful, for God is a good God, looks out for His own no matter what it is: 2004, I was recommended for the Akawa Ibom State Association of Nigeria, USA, Inc. To be nominated for the "Award of Excellence". Selected by presiding committee as one among qualified five people. Nevertheless National Board chairman, as am informed told them I shouldn't be given with his personal reasons and imagine that is you're selected but someone puts a stumbling block on your way because of the position in the board. Well, what would you do if you were me? Let me say this, was fine with just knowing I was being selected satisfied to me grateful for it. I let it go and let God deal with that.

More than anticipated, is a good God works well according to His will, not my will it is outstanding God's own way appropriates. Is God of justice than what anyone of us could ever imagine, let alone understands too, it goes to show more God's power is action Love, as has final Word God has purpose far greater than what we imagine as Supremacy One who is greater than you and I so His plans are best always wait on Him, for is bigger and better. Very much so selected but deprived by my own people because their action/decision being based on chairman's of Akwa Ibom State of Nigeria National Association (USA), Inc. That is all about human being. But God's own time is best of time is the fact of life!

Fact is, also that committee members were there for a purpose, but only a few people felt bad that what the Board Chair did was not right and I did my part submitted on time complied with what was required of them and it was about my civic duties, writings, contributing to our growth is and progress of society, as well reaching out to touch other lives also beyond my call of duty and friendship is shares my leadership performance evidently proven by my track records then as now still same is the grace of God that anoints me and shines me on to love and serve Him. His love excels more and more for His grace is more than sufficient for me and mine for God's love never fails to see me and mine through and whatever fellow human does, be it as an individual or group unfairly, is not up to them but is up to Him. Human blocked so sad is a hateful human who hurts another human; But, it is important to stress, those hateful, who love to hurt others are doing harm to themeslves worst and; But, is solely up to God to deal with that, not me to decide!!!

God's time is the best and it pays to listen and, see how it plays out by faith by believing in Him. Surely, when His time comes, easily President Obama graciously acknowledged my work in print, "Priceless Love in 2011. God's time is yes, the best, that's His kindness toward me, and mine, is unfailing grace as the same love is of His motivation for us, as everyday we find His love and favor of grace to be everlasting and the joy as well daily!! As an exclusive blessing, 2011 was my year of His beyond measures gracious and precious visitation of divine love and restoration and reclaiming what was mine and my blessings and all what was amazing grace love of God. It is so as that was also featured in our Akwa Ibom Association's Newsletter by, Dr. Sonny D. Abia in 2012, as the Director of Information and Publicity.

The National Convention of the Akwa Ibom State Association of Nigeria (USA, Inc); held in Orlando, Fl. It Was, indeed a marvelous!! Another milestone, divine breakthrough in our lives and how much God cares about His own children and how awesome much as read that manifestation of Love and Power and Joy, Peace as it is!! Wonderful, is who He is as God is not like man. So good to trust be of hope, patiently waiting is best blessing!!!

God is marvelous and 2011 was year of my testimony. The biggest reclaiming what was mine and manifestation of God's love in another way is how much He loves; Truly proven over and again. Everlasting Father provides the best of everything taken from any of

His own and all is based on His timing. God's time is the best and, He also always stands true to His words. He visited, blessed me, in 2012 published in the Akwa Ibom State Association's Newsletter. And, yes it is Another breakthrough and that I say it was a great honor, a blessing, and of it evidently it was an eye-opener, what God is capable of doing always is best! Bigger and better and He is the best. I was inspired as President Obama acknowledged my work in writing. It is indeed how, "God works in mysterious way". 2012, was our bless year of divine's visitations and restoration. He did it again for us is gratifying to say thank You to Him over and again, immensely over and again to His glory and honor.

I have to, for He has done it again for us, moreover, this time more thanks and is the long awaited day of justice came to pass is on behalf of my oldest daughter. He is a great Defender, wonderful is our God of justice and fairness and stands, and is forever And ever for us to obey Him and proud. For His holiness and faithfulness and greatness that is all of which are He. The one is everlasting in truth and Infinite mercies with lots of love greatness is He is an unfailing love, and that means a world for my thanksgiving over again and for another miracle is a thing of gratitude. This again is in miracle as Never as the 1st and the official Miss Akwa Ibom National Beauty Queen and Winner, contested winner of the contest ever was she as Miss Akwa Ibom State of Nigeria Association, USA, Inc, ever recognized. But was always ignored because, of the plain dirty politics of inner circle manipulating things as well!

After, 1994/1995 beyond the crowning ceremony because of the dirty politics and inner circle of "man- know- man" and well human hatred, and jealousy as well tribalism always is among us, and she was ignored due to the controlling party of the event's by those who want always to be of something just for their groups, family and friends to be the "chiefs and, no Indians" having any part in the commonwealth's welfare. There is attitude of bias of "man know man game" that significantly plays a big part and so not just cultural issue and believe or not, there is victimization and tribalism among us and don't be blindsided about this attitudes always plays! That is the biggest, is the problem that features among us all's injustice and not just a thing cultural issue. Believe or not, people are victimized by tribalism and you will see to say God is so good-trust Him! And, be thankful everyday!!! I say God is good to us all the time.

Because in Orlando miracle happened that is one more proof testimony to prove as well that nobody can stop you, from being who you were destined, nor shares God's glory is impossible unless you don't trust to believe His miracle power and nobody can limit you, is true for not man who determines your life or your future but God, so don't be intimidated or afraid to speak up and stand for what you believe and is share your love and inspiration for others and your humble life of sacrifice to work hard also is in His care, not in human. I have seen so many blessings and seen God's glory. Is of the salvation of God, always trust in God is His loves, cares, be happy and more than thankful when you know Him for yourself.

I have seen as 1st contested queen's mother to say is trust and keep hope alive, trust and know Him more is about greatness of who, is the Faith in place and power that makes your hope alive and In God's love is to stand firm is and power is of God, for I have seen is joy, is hope for best and all is in due seasons and, I monitored pageant's progress. Following it up, being more of advocate of youth than just the National Akwa Ibom beauty pageant's first queen's mom, very much fascinating more am one of their friends also inspired fan. As a blessed mother very happy and grateful to God for all our children worldwide, as such all the contestants for the pageants are to be seen and treated as our children and should be loved and encouraged and promoted as ours and not to select and/chose by who they know is right to give them their due and earned right and not to be based on the order of the politics! Not, at all fair, is unfair to overlook the struggling children and deny them of their rights and opportunity, is the privileges as is given to them by God to do, and is not right is unjust to treat them differently from enjoying and, forces them to be discouraged. Times that I have witnessed how that was with my daughter and I thank God for giving her the grace to ignore and move on despite the fact that many among us tried to make her to be upset and doing what she loves her passion. I have seen of other children and how frustrated the mothers were as well very disappointed and sad as well too!

This observation is normal as tradition and always of joy and excitement to see the contestants being all joyous and glamorous in their evening gown and cultural attires and ready to deck the hall with talent shows. I have fallen in love as well and there is nothing as profound as overall winner always crowns with incentives. Although the runner-ups (1st/2nd) are blessed as well but not much as the Beauty Queen in terms of scholarship among other rewards and that is to motivate and that includes cash and free airfare tickets to travel to motherland Africa and pay courtesy calls to the Governor in Akwa Ibom State of Nigeria and learn more about the people as the fanfare of the event, I think that is amazing and though my daughter was not given such opportunity. A greater cause for more reasons for gratitude and blessed too as joy is: "Acknowledge the God of your father, and serve him with wholehearted devotion and with a willing mind, for the LORD searches every heart and understand every motive behind the thoughts" (1st book of Chronicle 28:9). Please rejoice in the love of God and no matter, read please see also the Book of Joel 2:23.

He honoured me and my heart is grateful for what God did for my child; And, of all the programs that we host at the Akwa Ibom Association of Nigeria, (USA), Inc. You know I am not going to lie to you, one of my favourite programs besides the ambience of getting together to enjoy each other, from diverse backgrounds, and embrace love shown to each by family and friends, is the Beauty Pageant is one most admirable. Important, is most inspiring moment for me to testify of the marvellous love and work of God more and more this is how He is doing greater things for us as what no one else could have done for me and my family, but He did it all, so is fun watching them. I love seeing them displaying their gifts and talents, are used given them by Wonderful and Magnificent; that is to me a great event enjoying mostly of the moment and much to be thankful to our Maker is appreciating beauty and excitement of participants and mothers always. It is rallying around to getting them ready what a blessing! That is awesome and all was privileged opportunity of a lifetime.

It's an honour so thrilling and joy that I can do this as blessed, I take this time to thank God and again for friends and family of His marvellous blessings bestowed! I am still thankful, everyday and moment is joy to remember how God' loves is more and is and my daughter won and how today God is still sending His angels too. It is amazing more, we have seen justice that was denied I had over the years and prayed for my daughter. Over the years, God answered. He answered us, is what moves me most is in the power of faith and prayer and that love that God's love to dedicate this chapter for the youths is joy, my passion blessings and much to hope for as our lovely children worldwide! And I enjoy them also; do love and entertain us many kind of ways that my inspiration, it warms me much of my heart very much in seeing how much God loves them. They are blessed truly and can see things more than we do, though they are little, but more visionary. I know, and farther more than we see as grown up (adults). I do know fact many times, their inspirations have, all as along said emphasis is on touching the heart is joy of love is heart deep down as Have, equally been helping by challenging my life to do well. I appreciate them all, Surprises for me something to do be joy is and my thankful as in my life their love inspiring my heart everyday is joy and that is why is happy! Always, need it is thanking God daily His motivation's Love for us everyday love is joy for and hope with peace of mind is His love is forever Joy!! There is nothing as profound more than seeing overall winner always given some incentives that is for encouragement. Both with incentives, in scholarships among others awards or presents to motivate as includes cash ad traveling tickets to abroad to their root as observed given to be inspired.

I am so grateful that God love for us is unfailing and that is His motivation for us all He gives in 1994/1995, recall that day was August 12-14, 1994, in Cherry Hill Hyatt Regency Hotel and Resort, Philadelphia and is something never to forget for it was a day of great joy for us, she contested among others all were our blessed children, hope and future and she won and to me all of them were wonderful too and winners but only one to crown!!

Fresh this day again is another typical example of what obtained also with reasons too being grateful to God even more than thankful am overjoyed everyday is a day joy for me is of rejoicing with my thanksgiving, I have a greater cause is miracles of God's love. Something to be thankful for in life as did again and over for us and this time it was during, the 25th Anniversary of Akwa State of Nigeria celebrated by the National Association and it was at convention 2012, Orlando, FL. As stated same done this time was program catalogue instead of featuring her as 1st contested Miss Akwa Ibom National, another person name. It is what was meant to be where she should, shows what always obtained as God's greatness!

Evidently this time it shows what God is capable of doing. No recognition and I had forwarded information to appropriate source as directed and coordinating persons as well even spoke with few of them, but there was never a say anything, to that effect done. As we may know, politics play out in everything; but what I knew most, is what God can do for us, by unfailing love will do, and that will be the best for us. When I mentioned to Comfort of the situation that her answer inspires me most she said, "Please mom is easier to trust as is, just let it be God to deal with that, and don't be worried!"

It is why I am grateful to the God whom we serve is greater, so leave all situations to Him, and nothing like a Friend who loves at all times and there for you when trouble comes your way and, there is to help you and inspires of your heart little part, pray to follow Him, the living word(s) pays, and continue to pray and show a heart of love and obedience with love all is well!! How much to appreciate that love and motivate others of positive challenges? All of them for it inspired my heart always. I give all of my love and life to the Lord God who has blessed my life with them. Knowledge for them to apply and with their talents and skills and that wisdom is of God and joy, daily am so happy for all of little ones all of them is globally!! God's so good and so this isn't for something just limited to my own family, and friends from motherland Africa and/or Nigerians-Americans. Nigerians or Akwa Ibomites, AKISAN youths of my beloved countries and family, every one of them as well others very deserving of as well. Oh yes, all the children of the world, what time is better than now? Of what is real good and blessed by God and powerful inspiration-matters. It is joy that's everyone! If you know how to appreciate, can impact to stimulate thoughts and is my moving spiritual experience. That is reading of words of love, really makes positive encouragement, to be my passion as a blessing. Is inspiration is love, is with gratitude, deepest respect, admiration, love of God, made my life to count and everyday.

Is of moment for me to uphold let nothing ever come in between to limit and/or hinder my appreciation. His love and for, I must use every opportunity everyday and to bless others and everyday, deserves to shine and grow and learn more and more, is I love to do good and wisely and to bless others. Mostly, is youths among my good friends who's devotedly, encourage my heart and I want to use this time again to thank God for them as am being blessed! They helped me also in this journey and I am so grateful that is what is bringing the best out of me that is how am being so inspired, to remember to write this thank you notes. To thank God, have love, faithful love, a note it is very well is a noble thing all because of Him! Even, of power enhancing their love in supporting me is of joy is everyday blessing is a gift of God. That brings us hope and love, all aspects of my life His and their inspiration, joy is there is the hope and of wonders of His hands and that is how much God's love, does me well and extended too from generation and to generations!

Comment: Who ever sure, would have also thought that a day will come for my daughter being eventually as well recognized and in her defence Dr. Philip Udo-Inyang would be the channel that God used for that miracle? It is nothing short of a miracle. He is God and His love can overcome anything of any obstacles through His power of inspiration this much is how God gives provisions for us also inspires our hearts to look more forward. His love for our infinite victory; provides us with unconditional joy; a glimpse of hope, good living, and better health and life, is healthy lifestyles; Joy as well and grace for victory, success and the pursuit of happiness is for everyone and there peace in the valley and what more is greater than divine well? I would personally cease this time to thank God again also for all those that supported us and all, include the Igbo/Yoruba Community in Miami, Florida; for being there for us even, protested on behalf of my daughter when victimized at the local Chapter. Yes, as she won at that time and in both pageants held there nothing like love of God in human hearts. They saw how she was not given, was deprived; God made a better way; Opened too another door that brought about National as the will of God and prevails; won the National. Dr. Philip Udo-Inyang then also as the National President; Mr. John Umoh was the Chapter President (Miami Chapter). There is a history!!

Mrs. Esther Ekong (California). I thank God for you as both played significantly great part in my life! Mostly that of my daughter Dr.Udo-Inyang made a very remarkable effort and that has set the record straight after eighteen years of her being one ignored by our community. The, 1st Miss Akwa Ibom State Association of Nigeria, USA; at first, I had deeply thought maybe to her root being descendant an Annang child and, from Ediene Abak, Akwa Ibom State of Nigeria. But, I noticed that it was more than that though tribalism, sure it plays among (Ibibio/ Annang people), always it is big time and It's sad to notice and that commentary is priceless truth (brothers/sisters fighting against/among themselves as well)!!!!

Yes, from my observation but, that was not it for it was more than that and a mother watching what is unfair done to your child is always heart-wrenching, such actions could be so painful, yet, what many mothers suffered in silence but I always following up with the "Beauty Pageant." Program; Mrs Ekong was the National coordinator, but in 2012, shared her story on how her daughter also another victim. That she is another of our precious child and another of our Beauty Queens, she was not even mentioned, talk less of her picture in the program, neither did mine featured. But, at least her name was mentioned is such moment on reflecting reminds us of that incident and what happened. Too many times and the real priceless truth as observation and, is about time that we stop. Something to think about and consider and how to rectify and make all of us as happy community and all I have is love and I thank God for us much to God for He did me good as well in blessing us all. Moreover, as a good organizer and so well, was Mrs. E. Ekong and, I believe there is need for Akwa Ibom Association of Nigeria, USA, Inc, to look into how, ought to admire dedicated efforts, and hearts devoted to the event as well and start as to do everyone of love and is of inspiration to me; see how much the love of God works and sticks around us to know He kicks against vices that are of destroying the very fibre of our lovely society and community that love, and unity as a lovely group and that includes everyone. Impacting negatively is too much of favouritisms, tribalism, hatred, malice, bigotry, injustice, racism all and more too!

But, sharing my story of how God used people to inspire, both young and old to bless us, and their love that makes this to be a work that being a very special project, as you have read also the parts those children played. This is for them, youths and today is vanguards always as well our tomorrow's leaders. There's hope this is for your inspiration, is not just adults only to be enjoying, but one and all, is for us and everyone. Children Read it as well much as does us as parents, is all for family and also all our friends (youths, teens, and young adults all are inclusive). Don't forget that both, everyone, Young/old, can be inspired and is why am very blessed and very grateful that God sends us of His love to me with His angels all around the globe and joy, to be there for me and mine!!!

Is why this is your special invitation to the world of a little powerful classic book, is giant and for devotion! Book is for, us is the time to read this right is so, fascinating reading that is much to enjoy the youths as much as their fan and devoted advocate, I do love you very much God after that long good eighteen years (1994-2012), her being ignored! God saw it fit to open all doors as well saw it all and, how some of my people were victimizing many of us and my daughter was one of them and to bring justice. Yes to bear! Is through the grace of God and using of, Dr. Philip Udo-Inyang as the channel to, demonstrate love by his words and actions. And spoke too in favour of my dear daughter and what a blessing and what a joy is that love and is a typical example of being is kindness to another and strongly believe positively, it sure impacted other children, who had lost hope in life to hope.

That is a blast!!! Blissful More and know, as well obviously, they're not alone in this world, though journey is of life's challenges, tough, when you have no god's father; but trust in God that so far some events/programs, that who have the joy, and hope is talents and skills as given from above can participate and excel. Oh yes, truth is there, says too as well that though more than often times are obstacles, but remember God's love and grace is sufficient more than all those, He is there always is Everlasting with us never fails us and He abides and there, (Mathew 1:23 shares of it and John 21:7) sums, "It is the Lord!" Intercepts on our behalf, regardless of your big obstacle, believe that there will be victory for you! You believe; "Be an example to the believers with your words, your actions, your love, your faith, and your pure life" (1 Timothy 4:12(NCV). I always will have a testimony to the goodness of God and soft spot daily is encouragement for them as youths and my passion, wishing those best of everything life has for each and all daily is to be encouraging them. More and more and that are my joy in this journey. I'll be following pageant a wonderful program especially to see youths' progress. Inspirational as well, so exciting, for me is joy being given the love. And Is joy God to see how much also, blessed allowing me to be a blessing, part of team, and my contribution is through literally work. Tool, is inspiring of all hearts. With words of comfort, love, joy, it offers us hope and peace is for hearts and to be, uplifting! Hopefully, you will read, to learn, grow, and good to know more as well of its source, of joy about that power of inspiration and can come to the realization that what is hard, is made simple by the love of God and, is a special book for a cause and this shares!!!

Love that empowers it's. Also great for our healing- Blessings and for victory! Though many over years attempted to frustrate my daughter's efforts and mine, you have read throughout, we have reasons for gratitude, they all failed!!!!!

All have been defeated foes and mostly I thank God for her, she was tried by many of my community and those that we dearly all love and, they were those that tried us most! Most of them were just out to make us to despair and sad, bitter and/or have any negative experience and impression, especially, during her tenure as Miss AKISAN; yet, God granted her grace to endure much as I do know, and so grateful God's is so awesome blessed and kept her strong!! And courageous in moving on everyday; It is very remarkable to recall that emotional journey that is today's joy and thanksgiving, what else is can a blessing more than this and seeing this day of miracle that God brought us more to hope for? To her is also why God's way is the best way and God made many more miracles as He answers us and made provisions. Faithfully, supplies all her needs, protection made for her and all that is how, God gave knowledge and wisdom with all His love and understanding mind to ignore them and move on with high a heart of hopes up and high spirit, love and joy; they couldn't imagine and Even though, there was no support for her from the Association; But our dear Lord-God was walking it out, always there and guiding steadily and, lovingly. Sure, guided and led and by His grace, lifted her up through His Spirit and grace. Heart-warming love is deeper joy and gratitude and that faith is currency increases as inspires!! More hopes up testifies, the Greatness of God and His miracles that alias's joy!

This is the testimony and very clear significant piece of evidence; critically shown is all, about power of God so good to us, "One memorable occurrence, though quite often ignored during Comfort's tenure, was her launching the Miss Akwa Ibom Beauty Pageant Scholarship Fund with her widow's mite as a student." Please, you read more, is in page 384, paragraph three of the below mentioned book for details and know how all of this journey of my inspiration just did not begin today and began, with hope in the beauty pageant being one of my great moments in life and well why grateful that 1994/1995 was day of joy and reflections of August 12-14 also as never before, is fresh in my mind, precious's memory will ever be that moment of praising God evermore believe more, He continues to do, marvelous greater things in our lives. Trust in God, for He will always be there for you and, be thankful for everything that comes your way/wait on Him and don't give up on hope, for God loves is unending, faithfulness endures for ever and more!!

Gratitude to all is joy remains good and loving Spirit is of joy and heart of hope is of our deepest gratitude! We are thankful, God is so faithful. Acknowledging Him always, as I stated in my other work, "The Joy of the Overcomers-Slavery from an African Perspective (2000), published by Dorrance. Stop to think when see or read about issues of human hearts and slavery of their hatred and mostly experiencing is how do you feel as a victim the million dollars question and what will you do as a mother and when your child is frustrated and helpless you are? Once again, and is true sure: "The dark days of slavery are not just something that happened in the distant past. Slavery legacy lives on today, and the people of the black race still suffer from racism, tribalism, discrimination, and a host of other ills". Is not something to take it lightly is not new for us; either for been from way back always challenges of life, something to work on eradicating. It is so sad that even among us, for it is not so nice among any of us be it black or white we shouldn't condone but condemn it! I am grateful for a blessing that emanates more, is to uphold is in knowledgeable wisdom and insightful the love of God and spiritual experience is of hope is individuality, and to each journey, brings more maturity, that we have experience, God knows how much to work it out and use to bless us more.

Experience, it is sure yes, in refining us to be more grateful for us there's hope, know, and spells confidence, resilience, courage, perseverance. Bravery, and makes it deep abiding love and joy, faith in God. That both is with His grace blesses us, God loves, it sure does, gives grace to us, be of joy, is about living a life that humility, and success and all of praying without ceasing, is in joy trusting and patiently waiting and action will surely result, and testimony always follows and there can be none without testing of your faith and blessings all. This, is it, it tells story of our very inspiring journey.

Though also one of an emotional journey, but our deepest gratitude, my daughter knows how far she has come, and how, been so blessed and to overcome obstacles in life. It is to give God the glory and the joy, there is no compares talk less of regret; if anything is more and more of hope, utmost joy and of everyday is thanksgiving to God always. He never disappointed of any us. Though also one of an emotional journey, and but our deepest gratitude, for every single day my daughter as much as she knows how far she has come and, incredibly how blessed she is truly blessed. Is joy to overcome of obstacles and is even given more blessings to write and launch her first book: I thank God for her and for grace for that her establishment, is of God's grace is more with thanksgiving and He has been a blessing in helping her to bless with this publication as in teaching more on the joy of being a self – employed and to write her own book. That is as name and titled: Vannes, C.C. "SELF EMPLOYED and PROFITABLE: LESSONS in BUSINESS." That is her God's gift, and is an excellent reading for those who want to know how to enhance their skills and on –hands on is to also able improve on their technical know how and the joy of believing in God's power and goodness that is by faith! (Please, see Bibliography, for more information on this and how you can get in contact and order your copy). Tutorial as well.

I highly recommend it for everyone is both the private and government sectors of our global economy will benefit.

My reasons for more thanksgiving are many; blessed to see her blessings are the joy all is power of God!! Testimonies; Always, is something to be grateful for, there can be none without the testing of our faith and as well blessings all. Blessings all blessings that is!! Always, grateful we are, and thankful to experience is a blessing. All is of strength and God's, loves us all as well! This is it, sure tells story of our very inspiring journey and is of joy and hope though through hardship, tears, pains and now, triumphant, is a day of marvelous celebrations of the love of God! Is amazing grace God, and you too can make it and today, is see you read, how it is a blessing turning all of it as obstacles to opportunities and as said all along having seen it all, and be victors; being of very thankful that is all that remains and happiness is exclusive blessings from the love of an unfailing Eternal Living Almighty God wins all! You better believe we are your friends/family as well so grateful; you will help patronize all the helpful books! What remains thanksgiving and nothing beats being victors/winners; and hearts of more devotions is too, is in trusting more that of abiding faith and courage to endure and launch out courageously and tell the story of love! I also want to thank God for Engr. Sebastian Ikpe/ Mrs. Grace Ikpe, for their love to me is (Prayer/ reviewing book).

It is where it all started 1994, in Cherry Hill Hyatt Regency Hotel and Resort, Philadelphia, something never to forget it was day of great joy as my daughter contested won and crown!! I am thankful as was crowned as winner; it shows God's glory works our favors, always miraculously! She was frustrated as winner, but deprived in the local chapter, Miami, Florida; the local chapter bitter and hurt to see your child is being mistreated by your own people. Could be painful and for same feeling any mother and you heard me mentioned earlier and thanking God for Mrs. Esther Ekong of California. That's very correct! God is good used her, to get me to where needed the blessings the victory, is all in the celebration and in Orlando, Fl. The Silver Jubilee as channel, for she is who God used to give me the blessing and the time for me to speak on behalf of not only for my daughter, for others and all of us. Well, that is the 25th Anniversary's celebration as, 1st queen's mother. Moreover, is Queen's mother; her daughter was not even mentioned in the program.

I say do you see what it is and what now can you say and can see why, it's very important to show her my love also return, is joy. Why sharing friendship is of this information, the joy of hope, what God does is in Testimony. It is all about immeasurable love of God that goes beyond human race and culture. is the boundless love, transcends obstacles, it gives the grace, joy of God is of the Lord and to be kind, is hope and expect to be blessed and experience the joy of the Lord, nothing like it. Peace of God for the heart, mind and spirit is healing touch, freedom, and peace with God, joy, peaceful living and abundance life that is amazing grace. And, so I pray God that, none of our children and/or any of us encounters anymore of what I and my child have experienced among our very own people in my community and May this instrument of healing (bless us all); this is through greater grace is of God's love that, we overcame victoriously victory is of God's power and, I am forever more grateful to Him and faith in Him matters and there is no other way that I could have made it alone and without that power life would be lonely. Hopeless and unproductive and what more is greater than thanksgiving on behalf of my family and friends and self!!!!

My daughter's case was so sad, to watch and, I recall how it impacted everyone lovely, Yoruba/Igbo Community in Miami, Florida, so much they protested on her behalf, and they were, sad to see how she was cheated and deprived of her privileged right. Most appropriate candidate the beauty contest as the winner but, politics played by her very people. And, so sad, she had earned every effort, put to work day/night. Blessing that this brings closure was deprived and ignored by some of our own people, even in the National. As you read, now is over, and can you please show your love, and always is do join us to thank God. I know you want to be there for each other, as is joy at the end of every journey that may have started to be as horrible as shared. Let's celebrate and "From everlasting to everlasting the Lord's love is with those who fear him, and his righteousness with their children's children"(psalm 103:17).

Yes, it is an awesome God, and that is, "Anyone who trust in (God) will never be put to shame" (Romans 10:11). Sums this by the grace of God, that was meant to be and, where God wanted it to be in supporting my points raised is proven and beyond every reasonable doubt, all must read as, His truth prevails over lies of the world and, August 12, 2012. Was another unforgettable day, as heaven came down, His glory did shine more and it was right there, happened in Orlando, Florida; venue again at the National Association and the 25th Silver Jubilee; God did something new for us. Again, and celebrated us again, during the National Convention Day. Greater is our God and Almighty is always in my journey as also in the making of nothing short of miracle's for our lives and, so what a blessing and how can you make it, a blissful; fails to be more than grateful to Creator? That will be down right hopeless, ungrateful heart; count my blessings all those supporting are also be acknowledging it may not be all of them this time but all are cherished!

God is marvelous and, I see God God's hand always doing mightier and greater things everyday in our lives. God's hand always at work is moving in miracles!! Never stops praying, for God listens and answers, miracles of God's love, as Dr. Philip Udo-Inyang, is the Associate Professor, Temple University, Philadelphia, PA. In (Department of Civil Engineering); kindly, came up nicely to the floor and very politely, sticks for us and is act of love, bravely and boldly took charge and with microphone only to let them know that is Comfort is and was the rightful Queen, first contested. As winner of Akwa Ibom National contested Beauty pageant contest, USA, Inc. Sadly, who they always believe to be, as their choice is not as they thought it is what it is; they were all thrown into confusion and some shocked to hear and asking me so your daughter was and not the other girl? Is that case is closed that's there was truth out that is all is God's work. Nothing more for me to say than being thankful and publicly testifying to His holy name and holiness!!

Is joy to share with you what it is and why I am being grateful; for power belongs to God and not to man. Shared is Love is demonstration words and actions, so I thank God from the bottom of my heart for His truth and for what He has done for us by using Dr. P Udo-Inyang, unblinkingly shows not just of boastful mouth is, all genuine love shows by: "action that speaks louder than by words", so true as often said. And is thank God!! For, "In God we trust," is of encouragement and inspiration is of joy that is how God works in mysterious way and as our Everlasting and Immortal Redeemer. And, is the Father of the all of the fatherless, voice of the voiceless and hope for the hopeless and the afflicted and of helpless mothers all those often oppressed by the system and denied of theirs right and privileges and is for the intimated by people who are ungrateful to God and unloving to their fellow human kind being drunken by power, pride of their hearts and ignorant arrogances.

But God is always there for us and steps in always for all those mentioned and never ever fails of them is taken care of by Him and what would life be without Him and the power of His love? Where else can we go for refuge but for His grace, love and compassion is greatness to us? How could we ever survive in a world of injustice and oppressions by the heartless and those wicked domineering people and believing it is all about them not knowing is all about Him and is Omnipotent and Omniscient, so take all your cares and bothering situations to the alter where boldly we can to and present our humble hearts.

You can read more: The Joy of the Overcomers: Slavery from an African Perspective (2000). Chapter 13: A Case Study of Nigeria and Why It Is Agonizing (Page 380-384) highlights more on this conversation as it features more on activities of Akwa Ibom State Association of Nigeria (USA) Inc. Pageants and other activities of members, mentioned here and others is joy to know God's doing mightier things His grace that is my other work in print (www. dorrance.com). I can't put it all in words and that is why others need to know that trust in Him is the best of love and to seek for inspiration from Him foremost!! Is joy and this has been fun to write as this is with you in mind because is from One who loves inspires my heart. And fills me with love and joy is with laughter His power inspiration in all that I do!! That overflows is, I am so thrill is to leave it there!

And it is friendship is for sharing and is fellowshipping together as well all for happiness and is of the Lord God. Remember this always that it is by togetherness is of friendship, love and faith, all matters and gives more to hope for in each life, it is of what makes life bearable as and is also what crowbar that is and the only way is with His grace as well faithfulness is the power of that faith. Faith in God that is awesome is all! This by God's grace is by faith, is how to be as well able to respond to any situation. Use God's word and that is for those situations described above is what makes me to come thus far in life. God's gives me joy in the midst of trials and of tribulation and, I learned the secret of contentment as well, it is in our humility before God that greatness is revealed, the joy is sure as well, "In my distress I called upon the Lord, and cried out to my God; my cry came before Him, even to His ears!" Thanks be to God is bless you.

Sharing, more that love is inspiration. Enjoy and, of hope!! Remember what happened to young David being always troubled by the Philistine, He used His God's given wisdom and that strategies armed with amour of God that is what Saul did for him and said to David, "Go and the LORD be with thee" (1st Sam. 17: 37). I have seen how, that was what people meant for evil turned to be of good in all kind of ways just by one's faith is in God. Is all in God's hand and not human! Is true, when you had thought negative about a nice person is a vain thing, for no matter how manipulative you are, and wants his or her downfall, it will be opposed by God's love and of the power of God, surely that says He calms the turbulent and all you need to say is, **"You come to me with sword and spear and javelin; but I come to you in the name of the Lord of hosts, the God of the armies of Israel" (1 Samuel 17:45).** I glorify and give my Father God all my heart, soul and mind and being, for victory belongs to Him, my heart wells up in praise to the Lord God Almighty as I am highly motivated inspired by His unfailing love, His power thrilling!

All those blessings are glory is also is to the Lord, for giving grace to endure to the end of my faith journey and being in my journey with me and mine making a way where there was none is God marvelous for me to see this day come to pass and mostly for this day is with high note of praise, "I will give thanks to You forever" is to God, for open doors and windows, I give all my love and thanks again connecting me as with the right supportive family and friends who is god-send, Love as well reach out and inspire. These are His children with huge hearts of love for my interest supporting me sums that part. Is all in their hearts as giving comes from the heart.

And, so does love and the power of love all is a blessing and inspiration that empowers. I treasure God being there and so happy and nothing beats me living a life of love and inspiring of hearts and participating in activities that is more of heavenly significant more as blessings of it is love for humanity work advocates for all those out there, in need of His blessings as well. Above and beyond, I am so grateful to God for rescuing me and being there and for me to love and joy is serve Him with all my heart and mind and soul and being all that is what makes this my day of rejoicing and this is my tribute is Hallelujah Party to God's work and this a dream come true and that is what will also be a topic of discussion in subsequent reading coming your way soon too!

All is all by the glorious grace of God, so: Greatness is in the Heart –A Tribute to Inspiration That Empowers, is reading that inspires and re-shaped our faith and makes us blessed God's gift for gives us all love that inspires; to empower is A heart that is blessed and mind renews. He also and Transformer made a way to me this won't be feasible. Had it not been for His grace and infinite mercies over my life and love and power of inspiration as all team up to bless me my life is a testimony and I can't thank Him enough. God is awesome! Is good to be highly praised by me, for loving me as much giving me this is blessing to have a part in this worldwide ministry of love and of showing mercy, is possible for me and His love have taught me how to do is great!

Many things and much fun are in experiencing the peace. It is just so much and much and He kept me alive is with His promises, loving-kindness and with mercy unfailing love is also His compassion is amazing and more is than human condemnation anoints me, His mercy is over me, is an incredible great God. Who anoints me with His grace and who offers me life loves with all of His and limitless blessings and gives opportunity all for me to overcome my life's challenges is from networking connecting me to the right people. Amazing Grace of God! There is no word and am so thrill that He brought me all that I ever needed just to be close to Him and feel His presence everyday of my life inspires! Many of them (my people and community) who received from me some books never thought at all of what it takes to publish and everything for them it is supposed to be free and no matter the work is it takes money to do it well is of God's power and that is blessing too. Through His greater Grace of God is everything that is a lot of love is efforts.

It is put to work too. And, I thank Him for it takes thoughts to be as well love standing up and sitting to type, sleepless nights, and is joy you also research, and my wilderness journey was clear eye-opener and reawakening call for me is and to see is joy to know more what God always requires is sure, God provides too always. He always makes a way where there is no way, more is that there is more to be thankful for in my life knowing Love, nothing that is impossible with God. He is means and methods are provisions that He also made readily available for us is joy!

His love is with deeper joy and that is the source of my strength and of that is Happiness. It is also is excitement and my finding that love is Scripture says the ultimate always is and that is, why love is the key truth and that, "His loving-kindness is better than life" Psalms 63: 3). And, that is so true finding love ultimate it is, and inspiration within offers my passion and I keep on saying, I don't know what my destiny life could have been, if I didn't call on Him trusting Him is as well and sure, "Everyone who calls on the name of the Lord will be saved" (Titus 3:6 and Acts 2:21). He is the eternal One and, is as said, Love. All those who need His help/ healing can get!

Lights shines on and, it illuminates and always at work waiting to bless and heal always. God is and shows us love and is manifestation of His love and brings His Majesty to us and heals us! I know that too well for this is my story of God's love. How He loves me so much manifests in my life and is first –hand! He brought both His love and Majesty to this child and daughter of His and through my faith it works is God is His glory shines through me and radiates His beauty and in human spirit shines my face. Is in me and brightens my day- to- day is everyday love and adventure and that is of my excitement of finding love in a moment when I least expect and joy.

Likewise, love is what matters most. I don't have to know you before I love you because God loves me and joy is for me to love all and He taught me how to love you as I love myself!!!! Regardless, of where we come from is irrelevant and my faith increased more everyday, I have seen the best and over years because He loves me so much and of God is overshadowing me and all parts of my life is transformed and blessed marvelously daily is by the love of God, His Holy Spirit refreshing and is my inmost being and He graces me with His love and taught my heart of beautiful lessons of life daily. Moreover, Peace of mind is priceless is grace and by faith, to come to pass is a Comforting and Healing Touch is divine Touch is divine health His Word, I needed it.

Is most need and in my life's challenges and this is the cure that also amazing grace Love and is testimony of love and joy always so though this journey began with so much of difficulties has very good ending with joy and power of faith, it is an excellent happy ending and God's Joy! God is as is being credited everything is all about Him, for without Him, I couldn't imagine how. I ask myself how could ever survived, let alone have all functioning and suddenly being healed? Able and, talk less this blessed to write another book on the journey of which power and miracles of God's love and inspiration with touching stories of heart that is blessed with love and laughter.

And of love that is the theme God and human kindness is as well is who God's for Love blessed my life with both. I see that manifestation of God's love in human heart on earth and that as and He uses both supernatural and natural well in my healing process. That is why everyday, I must start with love and thanks for my gratitude is also with thanks is joy and this is how much it is using God's words is preventive and curative Love. I am grateful for the Bible and thankful!!!

For God's is all that and loves is eternal peace and unconditional and the presence of God in my experience is as all along said, "Joy unspeakable". No word and am speechless, but only is God is Joy what my feeling is deep down is overwhelmed is joy and with excitement of growing in God's amazing grace is love gratitude that is indescribable and so desirable that is love of God is surpassing. It is also the answer that we are seeking to achieve peace and progress for our society. God is Love is marvelous and His love is moving me. That is the love answer and expressing and that we are giving back is has received. Soaring that is where I am, also have always wanted to be and, I do.

Thank God for that love been unfailing to any who trusts Until when that love is found is answer that I am thankful for and that love abides and in abounding God is love and what we are seeking in the world most love and inspiration of God is love, peace and to achieve too. He is the Love that warms and soothes. My life to be at peace with Him and also you, and so faithful is our Almighty God and Friend Love, is experiencing God's peace and progress in the world is blessed being contented in Life and whatever and wherever that you will be, is blessed able, to be is also by the love of God and is also is by faith through the power of His Holy Spirit, and you can cope.

Oh yes, in any weather, and wherever you are is same rain or shines, capable is so only by grace through God's guidance is source and we have it together; It is living triumphantly with it radiates God in ours and is His will for us to love is of God is the blessings. Is that Love is who makes life bearable and my Joy is He Knowing Him that is personally and is also of intimacy for me! I thank God who radiates a spirit of peace of His, Love God in my heart; I have found Jesus is with me! That is when and how to use those words and pray and claim and call on the name of our Lord is the weapon to use and mention the blood and plead and cover that is all that matters. Marvelous thing and only those who know the hidden power and believe it that is what matters.

It is by faith. Sure, if you let Him handle your situations. It is everything all, including anyone who does create bitter situation for your and yours and want also to cause your downfall and those of your family using malicious intent. They want your downfall, and is with intent to thwart your growth and/or child/children' physical and spiritual growth and progress but sure it God won't let it happens for that is not His plan is not going to be your portion so leave it all to Him; continue to pray, watch, trust in Him is to also give thanks, trust more and serve that is to be inspired is. So, I encourage instead of revenge give God the Highest is give Him all the glory and He will give you also all the victory. Give and love Him most too. And more is and serve as I have all along stressed is all about God's love and power is so: **"For the LORD most high is terrible; he is a great King over all the earth (Psalms 47:2).**

Is joy I must celebrate publicly though, I had made my vows in secret and promised God that, if He rescued me and my family and friends and also healed and fulfilled His promises for me and as it is in words, deeds and actions and intervened in my cases as it is always is for me to glorify His name publicly testify and uplift for joy evermore, He has done even more than, I had anticipated And is with spiritual favors is growth in my faith journey. Is joy to see that your love is amazing grace and fulfills, so I thank my dear heavenly Father and my Lord, God Almighty is only Him who understands all my plights and fought flights. And, so I say again, Thank You for loving, caring, carrying me through all meandering of my life's challenges of twisted and turns.

And of rivers that were also of ways blocking obstacles. And you parted the red seas the river Jordan as well the Egyptians are no more part of my life and many miracles you have done and one by one, I am also counting all of my blessings and naming them all is joy. As well one by one also everyday is a day of my testimony for all that is my blessings and what you've done and given is also, helped to write my testimonies and, joy to share is of your great Healing Power and continues to be a blessing. Is to those who need your divine healing and interventions and all is of your love and joy that is so they can benefit, is everlasting and never failing and thank You Lord for your great Love is peace of it am alive, and blessings me and mine and offers hope to us That never ever will not cease, nor fails to accomplish all what you promised is so shall it be and all is come to pass for all who believe and trust in your love and power evermore. I have seen all!

I have, is in my heart and <u>He is my wonderworking spiritual power</u> <u>and also directs my steps bring me to fullness of His presence and glory</u> <u>that shines on me with comfort</u> and sure God knows all of us as well of everything about me and cares. He is also always in my life/journey as is and in all that I do all is clear to Him and He is in the details of my life in our lives and that is whether or not others believe that is what I know and believe Him, for God is working evermore. He is real as He knows about me and lives in my heart and knows of my desires and making all things work together for my own good. As far as you rely on Him that is you know that you love Him. And relax and trust more joy. Yes, in His love everyday a great thing and proof that love is endures and conquers and that demonstrates that God's Love is an empowering love that for sure empowers and awakens me up and here is the chance God's power and nothing beats that Love.

<u>Love of God for me a sister, friend and mother</u> with a vision born out of sorrow and that shows the power of love God's greatness, and, is a great joy is in heart. His love, how it is much to offer, He is limitless. And, He can make something that is beautiful out of a broken heart that was and put the pieces together and wearied heart and that is peace is there for me is awesome. I say again God and hope that is one of the greatest of thing to seek. Seek for inspiration for there power and only God is who can as He is, gives eternal peace that is everlasting Love. It changed my life and for my happiness, joy fills my soul and heart with His love and joys that never ends- God's Awesome!!!! It's amazing is of heart of love and graces with love and blesses me with joy.

Love is a great gift is God has given to us and it works best hand- in-hand with grace and faith is of profound joy is enjoying today is because love is the greatest and power is within. He in me is that is of healing and curative thought. It lies within you is good for me is to know God personally better and more better is the best and He is greatest of love, is empowering and is strongest love He is who gives us all is the Peace and His kindness is all that moves and inspires that is also ways serving Him is more and love is the key, see the remedy also is everyday joy as it is and His love and is and believing and receive and live and love's access is the code love for He opens me up. Please, let's us be hopeful and it is joy to beware of the simple priceless love is treasures of life; they are much more are all powerful.

All are spiritual principles of God, not just mere as often said to be just saws, clichés and is more than that, are as Spiritual words of inspiration priceless. Treasures and all are divine joys our blessings are a gift of love. As are sure also life savers and, also this is the doing of the Lord is sure big time that is in my life and, love and power and miracles and as He is over generous to me and mine. And my special thanks to all the members of the Qua Iboe Church of Nigeria and mostly those of my faith family of my home town and Mary Slessor/Mbukpa road, Calabar. The Apostolic Church my dear maternal grandparents' where devoted members, they prayed for me!!

Powerful prayer warriors of faith Is for our victory and there are also as well miracles on your way, if we trust to obey and is God is marvelous and greater than you and I, is also as well more than able to deliver as our miracle working God of wonders! I found that if you allow God to have way in your heart it is awesome, for you. You will be very much happier and healthier as am finding that is fulfilling with love, and joy. Is there are all great things of the heart with hope and in His love and inspiration you will be healthier, and happier fulfillment is being happier it is more than and happiness is satisfied and much is more productive and His Word is never wasted. It is rather more fulfilling than I had ever dared anticipated in wilderness and so is encouraging is so fulfilling: "Bless—that's your job is to bless. You'll be a blessing and also get a blessing" (1 Peter 3:9: The Message). Today, being so blessed the passion is ignited motivated more passion.

And is also all the joys that life has to offer me are love in action and with God you will be surely be blessed and be delivered! And, is what this resulted is from that experiences of my faith and it is a gift so thrill that God is real. I see and alive He is an Action Power and this has also is so become a testimony and how God abides. An inspiring inspirational story that shaped our faith and all these, more spiritual blessings as well are added to my passing days. Happiness much has all is worth sharing; It makes me happiest as I see all that is find doors and windows for me from front, back and sideways, also is no more closing, more waiting to be revealed of mightier things. Are all sure more doors all are mansions. Happiness is life, joy, hope is of Love.

Is of God Priceless as more, I never seen someone who loves me so much and is forever and ever my Friend to be this awesomely closer and my joy as well no one can steal and/or dare to take is can't be taken from me either, rather, as read, being so awesomely daily is celebrated. Along joy with my happiness everyday is a day of greater cause for my gratitude and publicly to be proclaimed testimony. Thanksgiving, though my situation personal and request made as well was my personal issues to be that is well were my responsibility and, but what do friends do? It's is obvious: Friendship is for sharing which is the next chapter for us to read and is Friend shares their blessings with each other and celebrates thanksgiving as well together and that is what this occasion also it is about love is to be shared, celebrating God and enjoying ourselves as well too.

Togetherness and feasting is I thank God for all this miracles as well sharing friendship; I am thrill and for my blessings also, I celebrate the love of God and goodness and victory, happy survival and good works of His hands and have all been proven and beyond with uplifting spirit too. And, I can see how the psalmist wisely sums: "This is the day that the LORD has made. Let us rejoice and be glad today!" That psalm has literally is sung through my heart and that is also this! Friend, if you don't mind, let me ask us this is both for you and me and let's face the truth squarely, "Who among us can say that we made it solely on our own power and strength? Can you answer to that honestly? As for me, is by God's grace!! And without stories shared and love.

There will be no book of love and testimonies that says, **Greatness** lies within us is Joy of salvation is it is that through grace and by faith, we can always be an over-comers with joy. And if boldly, one takes a stand for is to ask from God is all and for any need and is also personally or collectively and, also will be given, for He says for us to ask for anything is in His name and His Words! It is confirmed in the Book (John 14:14/Math. 7:7). I am so glad, and my heart inspires is of great joy that says gratefulness is joy, for, am the healed also survivor, one being inspired and He sets me free. Absolutely He's whose miraculously is Savior and touches me by Him, rescued. He helped me and daily looks after me; what God has done for me all these are blessing Love and that sums the Greatest Greatness He has given me the joy of my heart evermore for my life, and hope and faith and love all comes and I depend totally upon Him for without, I'll be lost and wouldn't be alive.

Either to talk about Him; Talk less of write to inspire our hearts as He inspires! Given me generously to be received and that includes forgiveness of our sins also, no one loves as He does. And, disobedience is also sin, amazing grace love is keeping steadfast in trusting God that is part and parcel of enjoying life fully is living that hope and faith in God and wisdom is applying that words of that knowledge gained with insights. From His words, "Knowledge, is power, but, "The fear of the LORD is the beginning of wisdom: a good understanding have all they that do his commandments: his praise endureth for ever" ((Psalms 111:10). He is Spirit and Truth! We are connected face- to –face also yes, with our Lord and eternal living God and is with us and we are with Him through Scripture, Words of love and that is grace is sufficient to us through Scripture and through God himself, is by His Holy Spirit also. That's why a smile on me is He shines me!!

He lives in my heart and life-giving healing spiritual Word, and also life-giving Spirit of God first is who gets all of my glory that is Encourager leading and is encouraging me, inspiring my passion and heart and mindset is who gives me all to share and it is in nurturing the spirit and changing lives thorough creative expressions of love and faith that it is my All God is and Joy. I live by that faith. My divine favor is joy inspirational as it is intervention as and He is God was the only Anchor to hold on and thankfully the Lord, for He went above and beyond blessing me. The Lord helped me to hang in there! There was much to hope for me is who motivates, inspires.

All by faith and, He worked well for me and favored me and I received from God's grace, when with results from the oncologist came, there was no trace and whatever. That was there, the Dr, happily told me is good as well grace of God can heal and cure anything is Good news. Said, "Caroline, I am happy for you and I couldn't find anything whatever it was, but there is no trace; but there was something is all gone!" Hallelujah, God is so good I shouted glory and Hallelujah. To the Almighty God is Hallelujah-to God be the glory is my thanks eternal is for everyday life!!

This just goes to show us that with God, regardless of our circumstances with faith there will be our victory and good news, one with faith in Him can't ever be disappointed and that is in other words is that where there is faith is hope in God and, there can be victory because there is a God that has more than enough power and is, am evermore must believe in Healer-Creator!! I am grateful to Him and: <u>My children and I were so</u> happy, and we also jumped for joy and celebrated thankful that God is our Savior who watches over us; listens, and answers our fervent prayer of faith and I love the world to know and share in this joy. I love to add to that, even the Oncologist was happy that, God answered our prayers and as it is for He is Always, there is joy is a miracle for me and as told is good news always God is so good to me evermore is no more beloved like God!!!! That is why we testified at the Church and that is what makes me so happy.

He is worthy and deserving more always there, answered us and my family their fervent requests presented on my behalf and this is the testimonial and today is that day of joy to be and am thanking God is a must do and I thank God again and over and again too. This is for every answered prayer and for every miracle that I received and of His unconditional love, grace and infinite mercies and compassion all infinite and giving me of their love as well is blessings of the outpouring support of family and friends throughout the globe, for I have been privileged too. I am more than thankful to Him as I found favor before Him and man, and is for me am thanking God for friends and familial and all and working with all kind of people the believers and non-believers and I have come in contact with black and white and Jews and Muslim and Christians as much to know that the true children of God are believer in one God and worships by love not of their faith only! This is so awesome that God's Love is love and alive and His of compassion.

Too is unfailing love in actions, words and deeds! He made me stronger, more useful as am purposeful, courageous, bold, self-esteem, is high. He healed and blessings me is also am so proud of being His lovable child is Joy. He is worthy to be praised and adored more forever He is who rescued my life and then re-builds my life from setback to comeback-back, self esteem is confidently His love and blesses of my soul, He is who remedies life is one from the horrendous terrible nightmares and made me a victor always is as I am blessed is Scripture is as it says the ultimate, "We have also a more sure words of prophecy; whereunto ye do well that ye takes heed, as unto a life that shineth in a dark place, until the day dawn, and the day star arise in your hearts; then Knowing this first, that no prophecy of the scripture is of any private interpretation. For the prophecy came not in old times by the will of man; but holy man of God speaks as they were moved by the Holy Ghost.... "(2 Peter 1:19-21).

God doesn't withhold His Love from us and, does not lie or waste His words but loves us is much more than we know well is a treasure and His words are all is real and true and that is of inspiration that empowers and why the sub-title of this work is just that and simple is all His love and thanks to God is for all and thanks are for progress as it pleases Him, blesses me and as well you and that is what I am grateful for all His unfailing love and kindness to me and love for all is blessings for me to behold His beauty evermore. And beholding too to look up to Him, life is in His hands and unchanging love! Love is a gift of God and joy is must have to this proper thing give thanks and adoration to Him for His love that is Super, and gives creative ability, pure love.

With Him is hope for everything is possible, and assures us that everything will be okay. To me, oh yes, everything will be okay; trust that power and words is everlasting Father is okay!! He says and meant what He pleads cause, says, "I love them that love me; and those that seek me early (earnestly) shall find me" (Proverbs 8:17). The world needs more inspiration, it inspirers is and makes us lovers of progress of goodwill to us all and blessings and more of encouragers than discouragers and, I believe too as read and we all have seen what the Lord has done for me and I am blessed inspired. So excited and, invite us to rejoice as always have been empowered and can inspire, we are all created to inspire, business women and men and builders and, so it is always a thing of joy. Delight and humble pleasure as well, to find inspiration of myself the joy is to share as given the power of inspiration for all I do and, I am so grateful for that and for you to join me.

Please join with me and experience that excitement of my finding all this and see how it is possible for me to can be a blessing and offer hope. I pray this testimony will bring you many blessings in the Lord and your love for Him will also grow everyday in proportion and may you delight in sharing also with me that excitement of finding love and power in His love and enjoy every moment with joy. And is of joy with vision and of hope of sailing through your situations with joy is for a brighter future. That bad news as hell of pains and agony and struggles, I came back, and to be in heaven times without number and this is where I belong; where God loves for me to be and everlasting Home is in heart where God's abiding within!! He is leading us back to where there is hope for us, inner peace and strength to endure. He shares His love is He lives in both heaven and earth. And right in the heart as well and we can find Him when we cry and call on Him. He is there, listens and quietly to our hearts. Upon all those situations, I refused to give up on my faith is because He guides and directs me with heart of joy for my happiness is within.

In my inmost being and is to me all given, inspiration by the love of God and by the Holy Spirit His glorious grace; is immeasurable is **miraculously** reversed the cycle of that orthopedic, physical, emotional health and to provide me all of blessings, healing, spiritual strength, as well ability and capability and coping skills. Mostly, for my life, happiness is grace and strength to endure is relevant coping; is what am to be of most thankful for God He lets His Love and grace and power of anointing shine over me and joy to serve Him more and also is for success and it is this testimonies all evidently proven He is Almighty all is whatever is possible begins within us, is of hope, love potentials of God's love and power! I have received my healing and my miracles and is wonderful, as spiritually empowers me with His Love, power and anointing more spiritual and for God loves me so much, growth is maturing me is progress, happiness, self-improvement.

Resiliency and am stronger; I too must love and give with thanks that is what testimony is all is love is to give with love and thanks the over generous Giver and I have received, marvelous for God loves me is so much, growth and always progress, happiness, is of the Lord is my joy is self-improvement for development both personal and professional gave me all is my promotion. I received to higher level of understanding and during my faith journey too. Many times in my life and, He has been there for me in my times of crisis and so another bad news; I had a terrified one too was when I went to do my routine is annually blood work which you read in the introduction chapter and all is strings of victory upon all is joy. I am so thrilled and very humble by His love!

That is for now what I love you to celebrate with me and let's together rejoice as thanks is to God's love and continue to pray and walk by that faith and not by sight and be happy daily. I love to serve more am a woman who has been through all kind of situations and still God loves me more and that is, my reasons, I have never been disappointed by Him ever and He could meet every need for me, and just to be able to turn your eyes upon Him and is testifying also is always. Because He sets me free from the burdens. As you have read from the beginning of this book and how it works, more of everyday abundant is God's love and grace is more than is prosperous life.

Why should I kill myself because of the money and whether the culprit return or not my case I handed over to God, and answerable too. The culprit is answerable to Him, that is not my case to handle again and all I have rested the case with the right judge too. And that is all what I needed to do, and I wasn't given a chance by them to defend but, I move on and left it to who is more than knows about it all and all that was my part to do is what I am doing as assignment is to do be thankful, pray, watch, and, serve and trust God. As He is who says, "Call on me in the day of trouble; I will answer you, and you will honor me" (Psalm 50:15). That's what this is all about thanksgiving-testimony does. Honoring my heavenly Father He reigns Supreme Being. And, He answered, defeated them all for me enemies are all put to shames and **this was real wicked ones.**

I'm neither a judgmental moralist nor saint but I know one thing always is a truth stands out is as clear as a perfect picture and, "Honesty lives confident and carefree, but Shifty is sure to be exposed" (Proverbs 10:9: The Message). God rewards, He is a living God and His word only is what endures. Oh yes, like Him as His love and is one of these days going to question and visit us all, and that include everyone in the world. All of us as well one day and one- by-one moment, of truths is very soon coming and that of rewards and consequences all accounts will be rendered is sooner than later all is for us to stand, culprits, molesters, invaders and imposters those for who think for now, is their thinking that they are happy in doing havocs to harm and exploit people.

To hurt innocent people and everything is all about their boastful of self and pride as self-sufficiency that is their mindset not in tune with reality of what is living real life is, but the evils all is all theirs too. Wisdom is of God but their thinking is so badly screwed up with negatives as the dubious self-destroyers as their thoughts is weird all is about leaving off others, blind views, all eludes them. Living in denial also as their dark dirty cruel hearts is deceiving them and, sure eluded those as their time is coming shorter when they think are enjoying and that is the storyline that wicked people are also heartless as well the same is culprit, who so deceitfully lied to me.

And, theirs is deception all the evil doers are in big trouble and buying it for themselves and that is nothing to blame on God His Words clear on that, regardless of one's religion is the truth that matters most. Love is greatest as they are also traitors, terrorists all over the world of them, is damaging others. But, always that hunts them though thinking they are having fun, well fond manipulating and invading others wrongly but are also in a biggest trouble buying it too for them is a choice. Truth, "Honesty lives confident and carefree, but Shifty is sure to be exposed" (Proverbs 10:9: The Message). Again, Scripture is a noble thing and as always ultimate source is as written, and is plain we are to trust in God and His Words is for joy if you do really love Him.

God is He Knows all His friends and enemies those who wait on Him shall be blessed for they trust is in Him and do Love is God is by power of faith, grace through Scripture has this to say as always ultimate Truth and unquestionable validated. "Thou <u>hatest</u> those who pay regards to idols; but I trust in the Lord" (Psalms 31:6). This is what works love and works, cites a good examples of the good and also rewards of evil doers to show the power and greatness of God and is not something to think is clichés and take for granted as you have read but to be serious more is about God; He is a living real God. And His word endures like His love and one of these days going to question and visit us all, is obvious because is His words. It says "what we sow is what we reap" As, it is straight talk and does not mince words and that is God's word and the doctrine of love is for everybody be it any faith, believers and non-believers is everywhere worldwide is.

Christian's is in the Book of (Galatians 6:7) the culprit is who says is a Christian of those and as also who told me all lies that there was a property for sales, whereas there wasn't any and it is not there and not even was anything truth to it, and he did well craftily planned all and may have thought that was the end of everything and intentionally crafted wicked means and plans on how to get the money from me. Using tricks and deception and lies all to dupe as well scammed me, is what happened and was also to hurt and ruin my life and future to get my family hardship.

It is evil that culprit and obviously real wicked human being and that is just to show how this is a must return thanks for God is with me and mine and thwarted devilish efforts of all the culprits. Scripture is awesome: "The Lord has made known His salvation; His righteousness He has revealed in the sights of the nations" (Psalms 98:2). Awesome that is my reasons being thank God most But, for Good God Lord life would have been fearful and miserable but since God is on our side and hears me my cries as you see, read, my Father's Love is everlasting and himself my Joy is full of grace and glory; Ultimately, by His love greater grace, Victory is mine because there is a God who is looking out for His own children that trust and live that life of faith in Him and I ask God also for hope as I was hopeless, helpless at the initial moment of my despondency.

As read earlier all He worked it out and all the plans He's God for me manifested and the culprit plans all thwarted. What has been planed of the culprits But had failed themselves though may have hurt and causes pains to my family, frustrated and but, never defeated you are reading everything and is they never succeeded for my God never let it happened. He is Almighty Power, and the Lord God too and wonderful name above all others, none shares His glory!! I thank God! Is For my loving family, for the infant/youth and adulthood blessings and love is my family loves me so much, as when in my beloved mother's womb they all thought well of me they introduced me Him and that is am grateful and, as I was, identified, am sold out for they dedicated me to be His child solely is awesome. Is what made me happier that love inspires, empowers what makes me thrills is my inspiration first came from my beloved family shows God's Love, Joy is Good!!!

All is, so blessed is to know Him personally, thankfully, is a long time ago I made up my mind. Not to let how people see and think or judge me to bother me more than it should, and it is rather be all what they labeled and their verdicts is their situations and not mine, their problems. Better for me is to move on for that is not what I am after, so it's never to pay them any mind and I press on for forward for the goal! And, mostly more joy is to focus more and look to Him and is awesome. Looking up to God Not human is so gracious. Certainly, is my life being more on how God loves and sees of me and that is awesome and best that settles it for me. It is assures and so, rather than to be distracted, is for me look up more to Him and I rather have Him than what is all of life's challenges, barriers, as all complicating to life and their labels, is nothing to worry about, than serving the Lord, for none made me God who created me tells me that they can't intimidate.

Let alone, to make me scare. And, is when you are confused and is when we let them that is problem so also God is where to turn to first, else you are in danger zone Is look more to Him, else, is more than likely to be demoralized as well and you get lost in the waves of entanglement of pathology and all the cobwebs of this and that they of this world. Is sure is monsters much as it is too much baggage to carry also doing man's will than God's and is the weight is God doesn't want us at all to carry those much are too much and He simplifies my life, got me on board and so makes on His side is of great joy, for me. That is obvious for: "The LORD will give strength to His people, the LORD will bless His people with peace" (Psalm 29: 11: NASB).

Please, confirm and what a joy and what a blessing are for love having Him in my life first. I am blessed very much is awesome and intimate Friend and Father who loves me most and carries me that is His favorite most and certainly, that He is greatest love ever known to me. That is why, am unable to stop this conversation without testimonies and is compelling Love and is what it is all about greatest of all love and It is that is more than is what inspires am also away from complicated demand of this and that of this world is why. I believe in God for He lights my world up, makes me so happy is everyday!!! Yes, I strongly believe in Him and He solves all my problems of life's challenges and dispels the fears and doubt that stared on my face also as those were perplexities scary. Truly does scare all, and did frighten me to be honest! I was scared.

And that is with those mountains that you have read and are going to read all about what my life has faced as life's obstacles and were very scary too! Too much joy for to be all that God desires and designed for my life is heaven for me is as is already hirer and it is in my heart is joy. It was terrified life and how grateful that I'm today being healed and transformed by the love of God of my emotions, as all negatives are now passionate and all my life is beautiful also. From the inside out and, is so freeing and is to thank God being my Rescuer and Lover is joy is more than thankful that I have awesome Father who is one gives beyond generous and He gives me what makes freedom is never to be ungrateful about. I received freely is to freely give as my love and life also thanksgiving, is all of my heart and being to the One who loves me most. Scripture sums beautifully as, "Freely you have received, freely give" (Matthew 10:8(NIV). That's dainty.

Miraculously averaging does say is a Gift and a Treasure for a lifetime! Love of God is amazing and empowering, He is! Inspiring, empowering me is the strongest love ever known. I am blessed everyday is that there is enough love and grace is of sufficient for me and power and is grace is for me is power above all. From all indications is for my deepest gratitude. Victory is of God as is Love of God that carries me through those entire situations and spares me too. His is everlasting and His Love is inspiration that empowers and thing of beauty and joys the ultimate and magnificent that power. Of His inspiration and glorious love is Grace's power of hope, God's greatness is and spring well of fountain of life too. Is as freeing as nothing beats being grateful as being yourself and regaining your life back from setback too is something to be thankful for and, is now comeback and amazing is life to find joy and what you have been looking for and puts as well something positive in your heart. Look up more than down and, but watch out more is also.

And cautiously, you watch your steps. Oh yes, you, where you are going. To step in and that is the best is the joy and, Truth is it doesn't mean that freedom from facing hurdles of life as human, for we are always all going through the blues of life daily. Life is we all human and we as well do go through things, the good news is that, with the blessings of I am free, is from much weight, of demand of this world, I am blessed by God with peace of mind and that peace is what human being can never ever gives to you and me is truth that endures forever!! <u>Is all about love of God, and power of faith being myself and insightful understand more about my circumstances, endurance and rescue and I know more of how to use those tools and when and how that power is the knowledge is God. Is the best than being someone else's</u> too and, this is me, Caroline Arit Thompson blessed of God and healed, transformed by the love of God, and remolded, reshaped.

<u>Of my emotions</u> as well of His Love transforming my heart and life is never the same is evermore blessed I am and sanctified and filled full of the power of His Spirit and thank God is Yes, is all the mountains that beclouded of view is all being removed and, is a thrilling life and as journey, too is a happy ending and one that I have learned so much from the journey and I cut my coat according to my size always, is for me blessing it is peace of mind that is priceless. And that is my oldest daughter's motto and her name is Comfort! She has also seen the grace of God and is as you read has also her reasons for gratitude as well. Is of Everyday love is of God and that is the language and she said it as well loud and clear always to be the truth that is God's language.

Love is and peace of mind that is priceless. And, (sorry about that dear for I didn't mean to talk about you and your business); It is just that as it is nothing compares that is experiencing that peace of mind and have is eternal peace and priceless and I remember, where we come from. Is an emotional long journey, and one of my deepest; I rather have that peace is love than how do people see me. And want me to be and act and be everybody's pleasers is God's first! First how does He as God see me, He sees and He knows me and first is a better thing doing His will in my life and is question periodically. That is what I do pray, also I take time to evaluate myself, I am asking is for only God is to evaluate my life justifies with, so I "Caroline, how does God see, you mostly, my heart, life, attitude and behavior and, my not joining all kind of sorts of affiliations as just for me to belong and fit in? When there is, no love there and how do I force myself to fit in where you're not wanted? Identify and be with people who do not like to see me at all? No love!

How does that sound and is that of what God requires of us to be, and decimate is so how about that and is that love and makes of hope? Neither, do any wants me to be around them, talk less about of liking me, not to mention love to see my physical, let alone my spiritual progress as said and those are don't want to see me alive? Talk less about my being productive? Not of their interest to encourage me and show any support? I ask for support and none and, do they like me too to live my life happily and to the glory of God?

And, the taste of love too and happy And, I am so proud to be a living testimony to what God has done, blessed approved is living is of joy!! Hope with a brighter future my lifetime that is me and is all about love and fulfillment is as well and happiness is God's desires are for me to be a blessing to everyone and love humanity. I have a God who never fails is being blessed and is as He destined for me, love and growth and progress as is all divine blessings and sharing my joy also are gifts that is my happiness everyday is I am blessed to make others including them too to be happy, despite also the waves, and these are all the answers is love for my life is a great story.

He takes delight in our love calling on and asking from Him whatever need is faith must be there says in Scripture, "...but the just shall live by faith," works for us to walk, "But without faith it is impossible to please him: for he that cometh to God must believe that he is, and that he is a rewarder of them that diligently seek him." (Habakkuk 2: 4b & Hebrews 11: 6: KJV). Faith works and it matters as of the heart, it takes love and faith and wisdom of God results this is my story of inspiration that is there is joy in us to walk For God's Joy and Grace and Love will never ever change and He is changeless as Northern Star. He is everlasting and constant and true neither will evermore stops loving and being there for us and no matter His word is Love forever.

"God's with us" is with me and you and He is still with us and wherever we go is there. He is with me and still gives me more love and with abundance of grace and lifted me up by His grace and He lights me up with greater and deeper joy, everyday is for thanksgiving and He helps me to write. Blessed and experiencing the love and joy of the Lord, I feel like going on and on am and I couldn't just help, nor stop praising Him. Seems, if this is unbelievable fairy tales story of "wonderland

land Alice," but is not! God is real and is an incredible great God and marvelous is wonderworking spiritual Power. Yes, He is this is all about Him and blessings, of great joy and is as read and seen He adds daily happiness to my passing days and Brings out the best in me.

And with the gorgeous smile of mine and is why and of what a joy it is to be this blessed? Blessing to make a difference in life as well for my life, family and friends and beyond reaching out to touch others, for friendship is joy sharing and that is next too for us to read is continuity of what I have been blessed in my faith journey. God He Lives His words and people globally must be blessed. The world sure is now my classroom and the world needs more love and inspiration is best is of God, is awesome to be a part of this ministry of love is nothing like being in love. Also and counted among the living that's on His love and plan that mostly, I love Him more and mostly for my joy is full having part in this world wide ministry of love and being a steward too.

Oh, yes, so true more and more and for all these and more, I am more than grateful and I love Him so much everyday imagine among leaders, what a blessing has a loving humility? I'm thrill and couldn't be happier than received Love, power and entirely most wonderful Bountiful. Gift and of a loving Father, family is of the royalty! I always pray same prayer for my family is and friends, and also those who need healing to know that you are secured and look forward than backward do trust in Him and in His love Word (Isaiah 53:5). He has the final say, and never is He as God ever fails me yet. He will never and will not do to any of His own child/children and by grace, I, too, will never cease to love and praise Him evermore and, I say worship, adore and glorify Him and His holy name come what life will always be lifted up daily higher and higher.

He is Joy, for His grace lifted me up and fills my heart with love and joy too! I say it is well with my soul is as well so blessed and, whether the sky is blue or gray, and is sure as also is certainly is no matter the pain, there is a cure, for there is a God who loves me and you. I see the remedy and but for Him and who works it out for me and my family to survive the odds. Who is else but God that can work it out for me and my family and for my healing that is the point that is am basing my gratitude on past and present and in continuity all what I have received from Him. All His hands supplied and asking now are there any better exhibits indefinitely, than of His both love and sufficient grace? He is the best abiding Love, if you know what I feel inside of me!

Is so freeing and marvelous is like heaven is then, you'll that I have been through many meandering rivers will know how blessed I am to be healed and overcoming what will you feel, will you do? As well thankful for His amazing grace; Love grows and matures and empowers my life. Though is an emotional story and journey that is how much power of God is gratitude! More is so awesome is more capable as He changes not and more than is inspiring heart and then is story that is turned to glory and, now what makes, testimony. It is also is I can live a life of hope and love and faith triumphantly and success is through God's guidance and blessing is with grace and of faith and also is by prayer. Is very possible achieving our goals that is the richest blessings of reaching and living and loving and is relating also are divine health and power.

The blessing all is of God is healing and happiness and for our healthy life it can be said also is prosperous living. And, is quality living all is Quality life; God is relevant. Health is one crucial thing no one should take for granted. That is a healthy mind is a healthy body with radiant health and joy there is always a chance that something could change abundant living all puts a smile on us is of God who is the working all; is daily from above that is all love are expressions of truths that Love have ability to bring complete healing and everlasting spiritual transformation that Love is and is of lasting spiritual transformational power. In addition to knowledge, wisdom is of Him that is so awesome. Stimulating thoughts and that is the Love and Power in this great discussion what can offer purpose with life and meaning and fulfillment to live a life of love and insightful knowledge too with hope and inspiration that inspires faith, helps us to be is happiness.

Story of love and is everlasting joy for God made me happier, and healthier and the self- evaluation questions that I often pause. To think over things! And, I asked also are answered to me is thank God for all the ways, He has carried me through all the odds and the Jordan's rivers and meandering roads influenced is positively loves, God is Joy. I thank God is power positively influenced my life is positively with love and miracles I received, all are reasons for my deepest gratitude and is a must give my thanks first as is mandatory before anything else, is how grateful that I am there is a better and big difference in my life and God brought me back and I am alive.

That is why doing this is sheer joy the thanksgiving publicly as that is the best is the only way for God's love is greatest and my joy is full and God awesomely blesses my life with love and grace. And that is also why gratitude is my priority for; I have seen a great love most power of incredible is our great God. One who changes the situations of my life and that of my family and gave warmest is Love makes us inspired all what makes for hope and inspiration and power empowering cures!!!! I do not believe how anyone can live and survive without a blessing of that light within you and, is believe or not, the pain inside is worst of which only God can heal that is for sure too. I see as say only He has enough power to heal and helps me bear it all is endearing!!

I can, now walk though moving not as fast walking as I was used to and dance and, I can sing for joy. I can be of joy and do that for my God. My other testimony is as it changed to glory for I've joy is all received blessings, my miracles and is moving though slowly, but steadily it is amazing and also is awesome to see all exciting things God is awesome power and His miracles. All is for me and to be walking and joy also purposeful and is being grateful for God loves me so much and growth and progress, and so much joy and happiness, self-improvement and, there are many strings victory. He is God's love is His work, power for me to be here, I have come from a very long way thanks to Him and you for everyone is have together been there praying along too.

With Him for me and supporting that says Love Empowers and Inspiration that empowers is God who inspires the passion to love and to care for one another is everlasting Love awesome. And it is a thanksgiving. That summarily shares capability of God's love for me and mine and of His power of greatness for my life all are breakthroughs is the faith is the victory. Is what it is faith, love, and wisdom is inspiration is all about. Conquering power is faith in God as that is the power is of God is delightful to know Him and trust! He shows me really deal is well with those who place situations and have faith in Him as those is that dare to love and trust Him. And, is all those that duped and victimized us all are being put to shame also are disappointed all of them is evermore. It is instead of me is them as read God is so awesome. What they had done thought done a permanent damage eludes them is blessing to spread good news (Mathew 5:16).

That was all as bothering me and cures that is of joy. Is of certainty what makes me so eager to share testify of the good news, is by sharing, telling to all of us what love and friendship is all about. Is Love and Healing is given of God's and is joy for me is cooperate and also offer hope, reach out and touch someone that is God is awesome for America is a nation blessed with huge hearts of love; loves everyone, she is a reaches out touching us that is what I have seen and, learned as well admired is regardless of where we come from and God also blesses Africa, is also my home sweet of birth the joy place, where I was born and was bred with God's love and raised a child of faith. That faith is power of love within us and that is what inspires stimulates thought!

Don't forget please go to (**www.iuniverse.com/dorance.com**), comes from love above is more all are the real joy as testimonies and of the wonders of the blessings of God's love and His is power's healing Love, is joy, His inspiration, daily Empowers and Heals. Supporting and, here is for you to find the manner and the "Man who told everything too. About me healed and He's transformed my life, molding made me bear witness and trust to obey to do what He says, for He has demonstrated Power and also Love to me and showed to me how as He put all my enemies to shame. I do appreciate His love, acceptance of me and healing touch and straight away, I did my testimony." Yes, I did at the church is right away, sharing story of love and faith and inspiration is all is of that is of power of God, and is who works my miracles too? God is and but who else and also is what does it take better? Takes God? Nobody else! Also of Faith in God is the currency of life, it takes of that power is the victory is in the hand of eternal Living God who gives and loves.

He keeps me and is with me as refreshing faith and hope alive. He keeps my faith afresh and that is just why I can't stop, for Friendship is for sharing and blessing us together and being there for each other. This is of our God is awesome. Is too to feed those who yearn and thirst for that same living water to be refreshed and quench of theirs is for the thirty soul as each words is what can heal, and it/s soothes of troubling mind and wearied heart as well in receiving of their healing.

And faithfulness to keep my faith afresh is of joy is power of life. And sure and is; never ever let your faith fails you and don't give up hope in God. Please! It is so very essential and the remedy that's love the key and faith as grace of God proves effective is God's Word!!! Is love of God and that love is expressed in the human hearts here on earth is out of the abundance and care of mostly is of God is that is everlasting as well, power of His love as inspiration and victory.

He knew all about that as well me and, my family and was going through so much with us together and sure God is love knew all about me and my situations. God also was working for us from underneath, He is the arms as I say is what a marvelous God He blesses and helps me to shine on, and trade my heavy heart for heart of joy, moving spiritual experience today it becomes the moving experience living that dream and beating the odds of life that dream of mine is He is God and love and power for is Who is of most knowledgeable and power that and is only Love is Lord who is understanding more, He is who knows about our situations and knows how to rescue and keep us, no one else than God who shares in details of life are His grace, love and power has been awesome to me God is faithful and awesome to glorify Him and testify to power of His joy.

Joy is to carry out His instructions and obey orders and it is apparently, Bible says, to let our light shine and confirms "Let your light so shine before men, that they may see your good works, and glorify your Father which is in heaven"(Matthew 5:16). Everyone is to enjoy of His love, goodness to me and am so happy. Please, let's us be hopeful and that sense of gratitude and excitement with bond of love it is joy to beware of the simple and the priceless treasures of life; they are much more are all powerful. All are spiritual principles of His God, not just mere words as often said to be just saws, clichés, proverbs and mores is more than that, are as Spiritual words wisdom of inspiration, priceless and eternal and you can't put a price tag on those Treasures and all are divine blessings are a gift of love. As are sure also life savers and, also this is the doing of the Lord in my life and, love and power and miracles and as He is over generous to me and mine, I do also "Offered willingly … for the service of the house of God" (1 Chronicles 29:6-7).

It is not always with monetary value the only way to demonstrate genuine heart of love is by what you have been given and according to your ability and capability that is love in kind and is in knowledge sharing and your expertise, cash is just as good as kindness in thoughts and words. Creates profoundness as with confidence and thinking that much as is all are part and it is been given with warms true hearts is love. Power and spirituality all is awesome and receiving divinely is divine health and benefits. It is all about your heart and then it gets to the mind. And, is please receive of God's love, is for hope as there is as well and helps us to embrace others and the more you do that the more you are blessed yourself. He is the means is need. I will bless His holy name for ever more; joy is in my heart to be me a poor sinner well saved by grace! Inspires!

And, joy of finding love and joy absolutely that freedom and empowering me that is ever –present. Love is throughout this work and each page inspires is the power of His presence in my life! He prays for us and cheers us to be with hope. His Love transforms the Human Experience is talking, about me and is of joy to share more love how much God's Love and Power, the story is simple sharing love is my passion and likewise inspiration, is all a gift as transformation, is the truths to the power of the human spirit and miracles of God's love to me is the Love that endures. That Love opens more doors and limitless opportunities and a chance to grow more as He heals and helps me and my family and friends, we positively trusting in God's love and power is why! My gratitude is of deepest and of a greater cause for public thanksgiving for us to benefit also.

Please, refer to Books of (2nd Cor.13:14; Psalms 63:3; 68-69; 115; Is. 55; 1Jn.1:3; Rm.8: 1-17; Genesis 21:22; Phil 1:7). I must do this is to give my love with thanks and is what I live for, is of daily being His poem of praise and joy is And to serve and love, and never could I ever be satisfied or happy, if not shared the love of God and joy and grace also and testify always is of His goodness to me, I am to glory in Him and honor and bless Him publicly always, is to glorify Him for Friendship's sharing is next reading for us all to enjoy keep faith, hope and love alive!!!

END OF TESTIMONY MOVING TESTIMONIES, there are so much to talk about.

Caroline thanking God.

Chapter Eight

Friendship is for Sharing – Why I Am Grateful

"Behold, how good and how pleasant it is for brethren
to dwell together in unity…for there the Lord has
commanded the blessing, even life evermore."
– Psalm 133:1-3

Practical words of wisdom have helped me in tremendous ways, and its inspiration has ultimately turned this work into something similar to a friendship, resulting in significant is of deep **joy** is from the bottom of my heart. The best part of all is sharing my blessings with all of you, for you all are part of my prayers, which doubles the blessings for everyone else. To be very honest with you, I don't know how to describe the joy I feel, other than to say that it's a pleasure and an honor to write this book so that I can share my joy with all of you.

This work blesses and also enables me a rare opportunity to express the gratitude that I have felt for all of the blessings that I have received from childhood all the way to my adult life. Gratitude is the memory of the heart, inspiration its legacy and its love its power. Love must be always reciprocated with kindness and gratitude and share with family and friends always too!

These uncountable blessings achieved are not of my power, but I hope and believe that I have used them to their fullest. I am so grateful that these blessings have the ability to multiply, for when I share my blessings with others, they continue to flow indefinitely. My writing is of joy and with gratitude to God with love and thanks, reflects fact that throughout my life, quality time was well spent and devoted to practical words of wisdom, with dedication that focuses on common goal and interest is with passion to offer hope and reaching out to all with love always.

We must all realize that we cannot forget that our wonderful past helps to usher in the present day. We must also not forget the staunch supporters who have been there for us, alone we couldn't do it, so the mighty blessings from God, is to be properly acknowledged. I'm deeply grateful for gift of friends and especially, thankful and happy for all and of the joy that I have experienced, as well as the blessings that I have received from family and friends across globe. And that resulted to my inspiration in all kinds of ways and from people of diverse backgrounds.

I have learned as well to pray that God bless me to give back what has been given to me. I continue to thank God for my life and the benevolence of His grace, for without which, my life will be forgotten, it is by grace that I made it this far and, I thank God for encouragement that His words brought inspiration to my heart day after day to make me hopeful and happy, filled!

It is impossible to receive love and blessings of this magnitude without acknowledging the generous Giver from whom all blessings flow! God's love is amazing, and is always giving. He is beyond generous and marvelous to me and more deserving of my most heartfelt thanks. Is of joy of God's unfailing love that inspires and encourages my heart to keep living life and keep my faith despite the odds. The fact that He gives me all of His blessings graciously is awesome! There is no way to better express my joy than to share it with you through, "Greatness is in the Heart-A Tribute to Inspiration, and His love motivated my passion of emotion to keep going. Is the love that makes a difference is a book that keeps me aspiring, as I have more to testify to God's love!"

Ultimately, reaching out to others with love and support inspires our hearts tremendously. It motivates our hearts to bring more love and truth to the world, for peace of mind is a necessity along with unity and harmony. Greatness in the heart inspires hope for the expansion of God's kingdom, for "To whom much is given, much is expected." We all need His wisdom, because it is crucial to us leading fulfilling lives, and wisdom matters to the soul what life is to the body in my estimation, though, "Knowledge is power", wisdom is both power and wealth. I have more than enough reasons to be grateful, and what better way to celebrate my joy of inspiration but by writing this tribute. Sharing God's love together is heart-warming and fulfilling, and cherishing our brothers and sisters around the world is a good way to unite our hearts and inform our minds.

These words of wisdom as eloquently stated by a renowned Evangelist, Billy Graham is sure the truth that, "Knowledge is horizontal." Wisdom is vertical; it comes from above." Also, I have learned from my educational psychology class about the important of education is essential to a well-run society much as giving is good and love is the soul and giving comes from the heart is great to show my gratitude as grateful heart. You are a part of this blessing, and sharing these hopeful thoughts with everyone brings joy and happiness to my heart and how I derive my joy.

With every blessed day comes hope, and I am thankful for everyone who has shown love and care to others all over the world. This book is my chance to help build hearts and strengthen our communities. It is such a blessing to be able to give back something, so graciously received. Love offers hope and improves the heart, which leads to an overall healthier society and lifestyle. Even though they may seem like small gifts, hope and love are the best gifts to give, and I give it all to God and He shows me how to give them to you from the bottom of my heart is to multiply.

You all are among one of my joys and, there greatest of my blessings one is expression of love that is God's gift to me and inspiration that is awesome and sure joy is to keep it up more. There is a proverb in my Ibibio dialect of Nigeria that says "Owo Odo Inyene," which translates to love is progress and unity human resource is one of the most resourceful, love is for "united we stand, divided we fall." Is that there strength in number, as the human being as we may know; Is among resourceful elements of progress One of the greatest resources in any given society, is love is the most as single workable tool too, for unity is progress and that is the solution that we are seeking in the world for peace. Is love coming together as a people with love for one another and team up, for togetherness is crucial and together (each accomplishes much and team) efforts.

Human resources is crucial element and very vital an assets in every progressive society. Without love, human and material resources, there can be no real development in the world and its lacks causes limitations and many often don't realize that lack of love is a disability and what stunts their growth. In order to advance as a society, we need to be hard working with a heart full of genuine love, united in love and bond fronts as well endeavor to show support to one another. Is how we all can soar beyond and be able to better the world, not just "me, I and mine" progress.

It got to go beyond those and connect them we to ourselves and it is ultimate, "While three things reigns namely faith, love, and hope, love is supreme" (I Corinthians 13:13). Love is outlasting and most of lasting great of investments, for unity and growth and harmony and peace. Book of Proverbs eloquently states that as "Unity is progress and "There is strength in numbers." I am grateful that the various expressions of inspirers and great leaders of the world read herein are able to share their wisdom, with true love that portrays the role of love any relationship and is not crafted by man and corrupted by infatuation but compassionate purpose filled with pure heart of love and kindness. Former President of South Africa, Dr. Nelson Mandela, knows all too well what it took love to endure 27 years in prison and to emerge from that desolate place to a palace.

He did it and knew too well real love, and sees its value wealth that comes from love and lasting of resourceful, are people **to** work alongside diligently for their happiness as, much as joy and those of others for their happiness much as well, sure that is how and mobilization sacrificed. And led his people out of apartheid, because of the love of God that was in Him and it inspires. It is eloquently, as he believed so stated: "My country is rich in the minerals and gems that are beneath its soil, but I have always known that the greatest wealth is people, finer and truer than the purest diamond-" Nelson Mandela. The power of inspiration is the power of love and positive thinking, inspires us to have the motivation and empowerment to be successful and in reaching!

Please, realize that love is not measured, but is given to everyone equally, and the more you give is more you receive it works with strong faith and takes strong prayers and believers of progress. Give to the needy, your love will grow, let's also all enjoy God's perfect gift is grace; which is given to us free of charge, and please, double your joy by sharing it with others, to grow as it grows, germinates and multiply your love and friendships, because doing so will bring you great joy, in your heart and peace and the ability to have a prosperous life. Life you shared brings joy to you and others. The things that you can share with your friends are numerous, and you will read more about of what you can do with your love, time and resources and benefit more from them, including those great potentials and your gifts of talents and skills in the pages ahead.

Remember to relish and cherish the prosperous life that you have, because there is reward in being righteous and nothing like faith in God when understanding and cultivating friendships. It is for sharing and cultivating your God's given potentials and gift to glorify Him and bless of his humanity is awesome. I am very happy and thankful for the faith that my ancestors possessed and passed on to me, because it has helped me pass on hope and happiness to others. As these words of wisdom say, "The only preparation for tomorrow is the right use of today." As a child, I used to wonder why the elderly would love to say "there is no future like the present." Indeed, being your best in the present is crucial to seek and, prepare you for "D-day" before it happens.

Your goal should be to achieve greatness rather than trying to impress people, because you can never achieve true happiness by living just to impress someone else more than living the moment and aspiring to live your pursuit of happiness. Cultivate your gift and utilize your God given talent to glorify God and bless others to offer hope and make them happy as well to reach their optimum potential, and independently operate and successful and, sure we all can be great! It is of love that we grow and prosper as a people with a common goal and interest. Surely, with our love according to God's word, we can grow and build a community of authentic friendships. I have benefited from that kind of support system and this work speaks on that voluminously.

The greatness that we all possess can potentially be shared to help the poor, unemployed, and uneducated by training the untrained for employment. This would at least help them solve their immediate problems. Please, don't allow anyone to rob you of your self-worth. Let us all each be willing to stand up and be counted as one who has left a mark on others' happiness. Indeed, love that knows no boundaries can only come from the bottom of one's heart. Being kind-hearted and loving inspires others to be passionate, thankful, and proud. Making God even more proud of his children will fill you with love, joy, and inspiration. It is more of divine love!

I being a Nigerian, African-American woman living in the western world, I can tell you that it has not been an easy journey, but I am very thankful and I very much cherish my dual citizenship. His love is amazing and is beyond all physical and human boundaries. There this joy of a beautiful chorus of a song we love to sing says, "Heavenly race, I no dey tire, I no go tire." I often find myself jumping with praise during faith gatherings, trusting in God's grace to follow on the right path to living a happy, prosperous life. His love has given me the inspiration to write, is of great joy to share, even more inspirational thoughts, and I am more than happy to contribute to this world ministry of love, His Kingdom by building friendships and sharing love.

And kindness through these friendships of authentic love building with encouragement is of inspiration and that by itself is a blessing(s) when you give someone inspirational, kind words of love, it touches them very deeply and can renew their faith and improve their lives with hope. Ultimately, "you can give without loving, but you can't love without giving." That is so true, is word of wisdom and His everlasting love in my heart is a feeling of greatness that has no ending. I gladly receive this great joy and am more than happy to share it with you and others, for, as the immortal words of wisdom says, "There is no fear in love; but perfect love casteth out fear".

That is the truth is to speak the truth is love and not fear, "because fear hath torment. He that feareth is not made perfect in love. We love him, because he first loved us "(1 John 4:18-19) it says it all for He loves me, so what then shall I render, than to love Him back?" All my life, I have prayed-imagined being able to do this, so to actually be able to achieve it is a dream come true from above! What can be greater and more amazing than the following passage: "If a man say, I love God, and hateth his brother, he is a liar: for he that loveth not his brother whom he hath seen, how can he love God whom he hath not seen?"

That right there friend makes it the point of self –evaluation and you have to think of it as to how much love is inevitable and a need that is absolutely important to us to think love and act it by words and actions and is food for thought to make every effort to love and inspire with that power of God's love and inspiration that is what makes easy for life to be simplified and easier to make through the danger zones and proactive rather than reactive and settles for love than hatred. Friendship is for sharing and that is why am grateful and sure, "For with Him (God) nothing shall be impossible?" (Luke 1:37). Undoubtedly, all things are possible when we allow His love peace to rule our hearts. I cannot compare anything in this world to His love. It is a divine love!

That, I am proud to acknowledge, and I glorify His name by giving back to others what He has blessed me with my entire life and is in Him who gives me all that I lack. Certainly, His love it takes incredible strength to give, are all endowed with diverse gifts and talents, and these are blessings that we should enjoy and be happy about sharing and inspiring each other from all. Remember, happiness results from within and His joy, and He loves you and me, just as we are. He will help us to become what we are destined to be according to His plan. Have hope that His will is more of a secure plan than anything we could ever plan for ourselves, God purpose best!

Believe it or not, His purpose is far greater than what we imagine but by only relying on my own strength alone, I couldn't accomplish anything. Thankfully, it is of His will and not my will, and rather than claiming it to be mine, I must thank Him and acknowledge how good He is to me, has been to me by allowing me to share my thoughts of good will and words of hope with inspiration with all of you as my friends from the heart and to thank all for well being thoughtful. By doing this, I am able to glorify His sweet holy name more and thankful for educating hearts. Of love is and encouraging hearts on the greatness of His loving power and kindness, which is a blessing and power of inspiration. It is important to remember that words that inspire hearts with passion foster continuous growth. This is what I have found; God's Helper gives love and joy!

It warms my heart to be able to devote time each day to concentrate on my heart and the blessings that I have received revives and renews transforms of my mind as the greatest source of my inspiration with the courage to keep going and doing what He loves encourages of my life as He inspires heart and passion to love and bless that is fruitful life for my living and relating love. Cherishing the words of wisdom and knowledge that I have received fills me with even more of inspiration and it encourages me to share my friendship with you all through thoughtful, healing words. Love is the key – it is what is needed to build each other up, and once our love becomes supreme, in we are able to find happiness and peace. Love outlasts all of man's physical wealth!

And, it is this same love that makes this project feasible genuine hearts of love, like peace and harmony is blessings, is what we need in this world more than anything else. Hearts of love holding up and uplift each of us as we continuously pray thoughtful prayers. As we delightfully continue to do this, our hearts become filled with love and joy and are stronger than ever, and by being thankful and showing gratitude for all of the blessings that we have received from God it is what causes our blessings to multiply even more. Nothing beats receiving and divine guidance in love is. There is no doubt in my mind that love increases blessings, and the unity that it produces, results in all of us living a life of prosperity. Equally, when we share our positive attitudes bless.

And, is gratefulness, we feel even more joy and happiness. In addition to the growth in knowledge and an informed mind, we are also able to possess the power of love and inspiration to live an abundant life. We are blessed and empowered, and mostly, to be in harmony with one another. As stated in my other work, *A Daughter's Love:* "In effect we are admonished to learn how to love generously, serve faithfully, and live in peace with one another." I can't suppress my love than to share and appreciate who blessed my life and celebrating also with all. That counts!

I have benefitted from so many people and their loving hearts in such beautiful ways that my heart rejoices daily as I write to continuously promote the messages of positive thoughts as I am inspired motivated by all that love that I receive from great loving Lord's all, and hearts sent to me as well. This is beneficial to not just me, but to you all as well, because it enables us all to grow in and prosper as people who inspire others. That is what friends are for, and sharing your friendship with others is a wonderful thing to encourage others to do is cooperate with each too.

If I could make just one wish, it would be to make a difference in at least one life, and is especially if it is a child's life. I would be more than satisfied if I can enable a child to have a mind love loving and gentle heart that is sensitive to others' needs. I say all of this to reinforce the fact that we are never alone in this world, because we are dearly loved and cherished by our heavenly Father. With God's love, we are all connected by God and word of love and love we have in our hearts, is that same heartstring-love is of God and His love inspires of heart to love.

To have passion too as have stated throughout this book, the heart is where greatness lies. And, it is in our humility before God that greatness is revealed. And, with the knowledge of this love and power, we can make a huge difference in this world we live in. By returning kindness to others and love is encouraging hearts of gratitude, I am giving back what God has given to me, because I am more than happy to share my blessings with everyone and that is where my joy is. When you read my work and share it with a friend, I am blessed because my inspiration will be passed on to even more people. We are all uniquely capable of having caring hearts of love in more ways than one, and when you have a positive influence on your community is by sharing.

Is sharing your love and that begins with you and is my work, that wins my admiration even more. Think of the many hugs that we give and receive; the reassuring pats on the shoulder, a smile, or even when someone simply says "Hi!" The people you interact with on a daily basis, though they may speak a different language, one thing we all have in common (need), is ability to love and offer our friendship and encouragement. Don't forget that the tears we shed are often for a fallen friend, and the prayers that we offer give hope and even more encouragement inspire.

I would like to take the time to acknowledge and give a heartfelt thanks to our uniformed men and women who work so hard to serve and protect our countries and many others are doing. These individuals are amongst our best friends; we should all thank them and cherish them from the bottom of our hearts for ensuring our security and a better way of life commitment in service. We may cry tears for them, especially the ones we have lost, because as the saying goes, "tears are a language," and even though we shed tears due to sadness, we can also shed them because of pure joy and happiness, knowing that they left a legacy for us and that is love and inspiration too.

But, most our hearts need more hope and blessings from tears of happiness instead of too much tears from war. In school, when I was a teacher, for the first graders, I was always inspired and moved by their love of little tender hearts with love and helping hands. Inspiration works as it makes for us and was demonstrated by how my little friends (students) never lose their desires to play, have fun, and work as a team. I love and cherished them with respect and admired their effort and understanding to accept me as one of their friends as well, as a leader in the class and I also borrowed strength from them though they looked up to me as their role model, inspiration.

I wanted us all to understand that the best and most universal language is the language of love, and we all share that thought in words, actions and deeds. It was very rewarding to all as success and mutual benefits is love that is spoken from one to the other and that exchange power. It is what we all were reached, achievement of great success and happiness resulted more by us working for everyone had joy as no one was left behind in the class it was all about passing with great efforts love and, high accolades through hard work and cooperation. I daily marvel also at the wonders of God's works and joy, beauty of His love that comes in Majesty and beauty sure.

That is beauty boutique and small package, and I'm thankful that I discover the secret of inspirational wisdom. Yes, love by inspiration is hopeful. I was blessed by my students who were part of my blessings and source of joy and inspiration for hope, and happiness, for I saw in their bright, twinkling eyes and radiant smiles a hopeful future and that is what I always pray God to bless them all and our family and friends known and unknown and those who will always cross our path all from far and near and young and old that they will have love and trust in Him more.

Little did I know that God's love could be used to make such an impact in a lonely world and, I cherish it so much and thankful for all my friends, young and old, especially for a faithful and hardworking friends like Jennifer Davis and Dianne Lee both sent from above to be kind to me and my blessed editor, that is Jennifer that was in this book and making sure it is error –free before It is published and my encourager inspirer and a great blessing that is Dianne Lee, she is working day and night to make me happy. Even though they live many miles away, they have been of love and my inspiration and real friends from the heart, that is what friends do helping.

I feel like crying when I remember their love, and I said thank you for being there for me. We would not have come this far without their help, and thank God for grace and for friendship. We all are linked by the heartstrings, and that is so touching concerning that greatness is in the heart, and I am so happy that we could work together and show how much God loves and wants us to love and grow together, building each other up with love and support as a team player. The life you share doesn't bring only you joy and happiness, but to others as well, and that is all what I love about power of love and building a community of authentic friendships as well among us.

Speaking of friends, another friend of mine from a far distance too has become interested lately in the dialect of my mother tongue, as often as possible when time permits by grace as we chatting or sharing thought on friendship and love of God. As we were sharing thought, suddenly one day she pops up this request, "Caroline, please let me know how you say, 'Good morning' in African language?" I smiled and replied, "Thank you for asking and expressing interest dialect." Is however, since we have so many dialects in Nigeria, I could only share the one that I know. "I must inform you the honest truth in Nigeria we have more than 135 tribal groups and dialects!"

As soon as I said this, she looked frightened! "Whoa, well, can you tell me how to say it in your dialect?" I was expecting her to ask how do we communicate with so many dialects, and when she didn't, I proceeded to answer her question: "Well in Ibibio/Annang/ Efik language, 'good morning' is 'Emesiere', can follow up with a phrase such as friend, titles and all the pet names you could think of adorning 'Ete ye Ma', followed by any names. Example, (Ete) is Father/Mr./Sir and so (Ma) means Mother/Madam (Adult/grown ups ladies). "Ufan" is friend, could be to anyone and I am a friend as telling you this story not to scare you, but to illustrate that love is part of progress and, we all can love and also be loved and capable of loving and is of public/

human relations for is an effective source of communication, amiable, respectable what thrills my heart love above.

And likewise with respect, it could be reciprocated in meaningful ways, because, love is a blessing and respect for all is respecting God and that is love could be everything and that when love is reciprocated with gratitude or kindness are good manners and represents being a well-breed person and mature as well responsible it is great both for self and others. I strongly believe that morality is still in vogue, so good attitude and manners, always is highly appreciated and can be more of one's blessing than a curse, sure! Civility always is in vogue! And never old or stale and very much welcome in every society and like kindness it will never ever fails to be priceless.

Respect goes hand in hand with love. When you love someone, you are willing to show affection with respect. Isn't it so? Sure, it blesses and helps us to relate well, and that is what is a gift is inspiration(s) does well for us to open up. When there is love with understanding mind, and able to open our hearts and welcome everyone as friends. Life is peaceful and blesses each and all is happiness. Let's talk some more about true love, respect and effective communication and connecting with God's love, to be able to come together and to share peace, and love, and rejoice with everyone. That is the hope of the people and that is what love is all about inspiration's God.

It is a thing of joy beauty to make this world a better place. But, no matter how we look at things, any relationship that doesn't honor God first, is, one destined for some trouble and, is all the fault we have to bear the blame, as parents, and custodians without teaching the children early well. The time to do so, it will be a little difficult to manage them, when they are grown. We need to make every effort to train the young up and help to encourage them early in life is all for preparing them and aspiring for peace, love and faith in God, decency and greatness all helps.

We all need friends and reliable and responsible one with love and respect too, I love you and happy, and am grateful to share my friendship with you and perspective and thanks again for being my friends, that rallied around to support me. Mostly, blessings of God's love comes to us with joy and opens us up, we have to celebrate finding that happiness in our hearts, we have hope. We are blessed with a sense of vision and, successful, prosperous life and without thinking good thoughts and showing gratitude to show love to others, it makes it fruitless efforts and hopeless!

I must love and appreciate God to be able to love others and appreciate them, as much as that is the way to give God the glory, for my victory and all what He did for me, comes from His love and power. How can I forget, the Source and the one who got me out of bondage? His love teaches and encourages my heart of joy is being a blessing, loving everybody and reaching out to them in love as well. So, respect as with love for self and others matters, and is about God, we all are His and others-commonalities! When we bless others by our words and actions is same gift.

When our hearts are able to express love, we are able to pass our passion and blessings on to others, cherishing our spiritual/human connections, family and friends and tradition of faith all are blessings to me. Since, I have the blessing/honor to be an inspirer, I cannot help but to share with you all the knowledge that I have acquired throughout my life in hopes that it will make you and I even more blessed. As we are friends, as divine blessings are a gift of love and to multiply is joy and we are more of family than are friends as I have found a profound thrill in my life with the love of which, I have to give our friends same gift by words and actions all a gift of His too.

The sincere joy that I feel in my heart in being able to do this is blessing-unbelievable. The inspiration that started me on this journey reminds me, if anything, is to be thankful. Is why my heart rejoices is everyday as I proudly count my blessings. Thank you all for being a friend at heart and for having me as your friend and a blessing. Heart filled with joy and love, I thank God for the blessings that I couldn't give to myself. Please, remember to share the greatness in your heart with love and the words for others, as well to be blessed.

My passion can't be substituted, is just thrilling, not even my culture, and passion is identity the badge of love that I wear is love that God inspires to empower all is for inspiration. That is His love is surpassing and friendship is sharing. Thanks for sharing your love with me and that's what I am thankful for daily! "This is the day of the Lord has made; let us rejoice and be glad in it (Psalms 118: 2(NIV). Let's enjoy all what we have been so blessed in this day while we have it and trust God to be there for us as His love is with us evermore. Is an unchanging Love, and more that needs Joy is more gratitude and more is releasing blesses!!

CHAPTER NINE

Passion cannot be Substituted

"Write in your heart that every day is the best day of the year."
– Ralph Emerson

There are many wonderful things to be happy and thankful for in life, but you have to know exactly what those things are to you. What are you thankful for in life everyday? Why is it relevant? For example, writing this book in manuscript form is challenging, but it also encourages my heart and fills it with inspiration and love as rest of the chapters. Is the focus of this chapter will be on the idea that passion cannot be substituted and, if you were to ask my opinion on any number of topics, I can tell you that no matter what may be the subject, it would be a positive one and, my opinion that differs I love it to be also!

That way this may be totally different than what you may think, which is normal. And we are all diverse people who have different opinions and passion and times also the seasons and mood and sometimes that could be alike and well with that being said, let us pause for a minute and think of the things that make you happy and why is it your passion as well what is your purpose in life? Simply put, do you think that your passion matters; is something that makes your heart cheerful and thankful? Personally, I would definitely say yes! It is a marvelous thing to be cheerful and thankful, because the power of God is inspiration, makes me very passionate.

The power of inspiration reveals many beautiful things with important clues of what lies within us is supernatural and uses natural always. When we take the time to compare our blessings with situations that may not also appear to have given us what we believe blessings, we will realize that these blessings far outnumber any of our negative circumstances. Thinking about how I have been blessed over the years has also enabled me to use the talents that I possess to further spread joy and love from experience is an all blessings. We must be willing to be available to serve God, because His plan and will is to fill our lives with purpose by revealing to use our talents and skills for happiness and our successful living. This is the most important reason as to why my passion cannot be substituted. Love of God, I have had so many blessings in my life, all made me happy.

And it has made me to realize that everyone has the unique chance to grow in His love for gave us grace and joy is the privilege tap into the hope and inspiration that we all have deep inside of us and, I have always believed in my heart of hearts that, if we all strive for excellence rather than perfection, there is more and something we can all do in our small, unique ways to be blessings each blessed of us all. Self and others, that is if one can embrace the idea that "happiness is meant to be shared", I believe we each can also contribute a little and together make the world a better place to live. It is why I choose to be happy over being perfect any day! When we are able to find our passion, we are able to feel a joy and peace that man cannot offer. These blessings are special, are given to us by God is encouragement for hope and empowerment; enrichment, and there.

That is the opportunities that He gives to us enable us to find our potential from within and to have a meaning in life. When we reach our goals, we are filled with joy as well are happy to share of that happiness, which results in the happiness and the progress God offers us all to bless others. Remember, you don't have to be the best and/or look. Yes, you don't have to look **too** rich, is a choice! We are all blessed equally with these free treasures from the heavens above, so go ahead and enjoy your privileges is gift! Just be inspired, passionate, and, rejoice serving and benefit too from His gifts of grace to the fullest by helping yourself and others, because living is by giving and more you give is receive more as is more you grow. As these words of wisdom say, "It is not the man of great native talent who wins but the one who pushes his talent". However small, use to its utmost capacity it pays to try and use your passion to benefit yourself and others than to not try at all. Love is begins from our hearts, and power is with that comes the beauty of one's joy and inspiration. Inspiration comes from inside and exudes outward as pure joy.

Always, giving comes from the heart and there is the power too. I stated in one of my other work, <u>Priceless Love</u>, is shown more by actions, passion to care and bless not by boastful words, and giving our true part to play is investing in the lives of those who need most words of love and for encouragement to offer hope, and it could be in kind or cash is giving from the heart and all inclusive. More of out of the goodness of good heart and thoughtful ways, to be a blessing, is to be true, and your gift shared is love that you don't hold back but share and give cheerfully and thankful to be able to give by your word and action are gift of divine love extended to one and all and that is what loves is.

Keep in mind that inspirational blessings are always acknowledged more so by action is gift of love, than by "cheap talk." When we are filled with joy, worth reaching out to others to embrace them and share our joys with them. We should and ought to be always having appreciation for our blessings and remember that we would not be blessed if it were not for our King of Kings is the Lord God. Have you ever stopped to wonder what this world would be if there was no inspiration for passion and no love to share and also a God of love to appreciate ultimate power and one who loves us most and gives us is all the life that we enjoy? I'm sure many of you have been trying diligently to meet of your goals, but you are having a hard time understanding why you are not able to do so.

Thankfully, am sure by reading this book you now know that the ball is in your court, so there is no one else to blame and the need to show gratitude is vital. Please stop playing the blame game and put your heart and mind and God's words into action! Apply the word and it will work, when you believe and open up heart to accept and who you are in Him that will make a great difference too is to know that part of Your natural gifts and abilities are God-given blessings, and potential is you know He is a Creator, and you are His child and creature is that should encourage and inspire you to feel of your heart with thankfulness that is if you are a believer in His love blessing's Him empowering us to do.

Pure joy in doing what you are meant to do. Inspiration enhances and encourages and motivates us, to be even more passionate, which in turn helps us to let go of the past as negativity and embrace the endless possibilities. Consult with the Lord through prayer on a regular basis, for He has the answers to any questions or concerns that you may be having. Now that you know the rules of the game, when are you going to let go and let God? He is your greatest Source of encouragement for your inspiration.

Inspiration inspires you and blesses and helps you to shine through for everyone to enjoy.

So, when are you going to let that happens for us to celebrate with you and all of others to enjoy you as well as you enjoy the blessings of others? Please, always stay in love and hopeful and highly motivated that you can use your gifts of passion to find your purpose. If you don't tap into this passion, you cannot blame anyone but yourself. Don't forget that a gift such as passion is deep within all of us. We just need to pray and also to be happy vigorously pursue it so that our dreams can come to fruition, and keep it shines.

Well also take the necessary steps to find that power wisdom and inspiration! Put more effort into that finding what makes you passionate and what you can do to share this love is joy, passion with others. My passion inspires me to inspire all of you and to share with you all of my blessings, so take heart in the fact that passion cannot be substituted. It is a matter Believe it or not; work on what *you* are good at instead of trying to imitate others, because their passion may not be the same with your passion. Once you become blessed with happiness and joy, it is important to stay focused and on course, because it is what makes you happy is what keeps you stimulated and you can find inspiration

Please, do not steer off the path of your destiny, for it will bring you nothing but heartache. When something in your life causes you to be unhappy, your misery will be also resurface, but when you stay on course with what you are good at and what makes you truly happy, you will be satisfied, happy and triumphant. Everyone in this world is bound to be blessed, from family, friends, our neighbors, and co-workers to strangers that you see on the streets, for God has blessed us gifted, empowers with each our blessings.

He told us this much, "Do not let loyalty and faithfulness forsake you; bind them around your neck, write them on the tablet of your heart. So you will find favor and good repute in the sight of God and of people" (Proverb 3:3-4). Be happy and thankful for all of what you are blessed by God and using it wisely and His truths are sure and abiding.

Every little effort of ours He makes it to be of eternal worth and that is why I am so proud and very grateful and with uplifting heart and spirit being it is the passion given by God.

To me and I am so excited that I should love all and cherish and, I serve with joy, thankfulness fills my heart with joy everyday is blessings and cheerfulness and hopeful is of that within, happiness is the life that I live everyday is a blessing so much for that is a thing of beauty. Lately, I received evaluation from a long time co-worker by the name of Samuel Essien, and he and his family all lives in New York. He has been monitoring my work is with inspiration is helping me in the area of consultation. I had no idea had been posting my articles on the "Ibom Forum"(network website) until lately another watch-dog and a dear friend, more or less a brother, Tony Umana, informed me of what he had read of me, my work, and he was very impressed and I was filled with great joy with that.

The information I received is am grateful for everyone who supports me and in my journey to give of their time and talent beyond the call of duty and friendship blessing is always with thanks and is of joy in my heart gifts of God are always thrilling and all is inspiration! Out of all of my works as an inspirational writer, the work that has received the highest praise observed is evaluated is, "Priceless Love." This is the very book that was acknowledged by President Barack Obama and First Lady Michelle Obama, the ever beloved first African-American family to hold the Presidency of the United States. I was thrilled, realizing that my work makes it to the White House and confirms that whenever we do what we are blessed at doing and cultivate our gift is to the glory of God and joy is in sharing the blessings with others, we share our inspiration with them is love everyday.

I will never forget that blessing of my receiving such an honor from the President and it is what made me another history made in my life to be blessed by my great loving hearts Presidents who demonstrate compassion and the first was President Clinton and the Word of God is the joy to be of anointing, confirms that our work will not be in vain, or our efforts. And, I will always remain grateful to them and their family for acknowledging not only my work. They have done a great job and I always thank God for them and, all have great hearts for humanity, as it is in dedication page reaching out to me is beyond call of duty, I would have been deported, if not by the glorious grace of God that He used President Clinton to bless me as the vessel at the time.

Inspiration can help us to grow, and inspires of passion to be ignited. Sure, and ignited my passion more and motivates me and is you are inspired is stimulating of all of your thoughts and feeds you always of it your heart and mind and, strength and warmth is readable power of God manifest love in our human hearts here on earth and there is no question about that either is as we are capable of loving and reaching out to show a little bit and share of the love as given too. To be is and is loveable, inspiration does to me marvelous. Daily, is the words of God that feed nutrition to inspire are of joy and as well power all is nutritiously as are unfailing love daily.

His and feeds of heart and mind, even is more than that for, it satisfies you and you feel wellness and feeling is it awesome. Mostly for the soul; I say it is marvelous and for self-esteem, and courage spirituality as I see, says is for my self-improvement and empowerment is to taste and see! It is happiness and till it is you want no more others, and there is no other substitute for me ever. It is for as far as God Lives within you and as His Love is "joy unspeakable," abounds endlessly is so sweet to trust and God's love, does it all for me and mine grace more is sufficient an love abounds all is God's abundant love and everlasting joy is more than enough power and is abundant grace and love of God. It is and yes, it can carry you through all is for anything, covers till the eternity with His blood always and that is the truth it abides through eternal life's of hope.

It is the Eternal Word of life and ages past and is, "Bread of Life," and heavenly given. Being so sweet and gives me deeper joy. I am very satisfied and very much appreciative of what I have been given. Am so thankful for it, is everything, I will forever and evermore need for my fullness is that joy and we are given everlasting love and, that is you're not alone in your journey of life, and is never lacks! Indeed, He loves you as you never had it before, as have seen God's love both by actions and deeds as my strength. Is joy with encouraging voice leading me back home to His love and joy made me to be a lifter and not a leaner with His Powerful healing Love words and of His touched my life is with inner peace, and strength, it is how I found comfort and guidance in the Bible and through prayer, in my moment of acute and intense crisis, He rescued!!

I didn't think I could make it through the night let alone think about good things of the heart. My blessing that is all I can say and I was not sure of survival and look what God did and, still doing and life is will not be desperate the culprit(s) had thought that what they did was the end of my life but God did not let them triumph(s) over me. Wickedness does not thrives among His own children and this is what He did for me and healed and helped me to accomplish what was His purpose for my life and destined to be this is sharing ultimate truth it's unquestionable!!

It is without any iota of doubt God lives His Words and does not waste words He, is all of blessings as I have seen it worked it is with my naked eyes how that power is hope and joy of the Lord that have played out in my life and situations that the culprit had thought that it was the end of my life and, but what he didn't know that power of God in my life is working and underneath "are everlasting arms!" He is a living Father and Word of Life and Hope is what He says stands. I am sharing as He turned around things that were meant for evil to become good for my life and what He is lights to my life is for His Love is faith in action, words and deeds fulfilled evermore!

And, is the joy of my life, and I don't know what my life could have been for all as what I had been through those battles as intensive as mine, were wars as life's challenges being challenged and faced by the dirty crooked work and also cruelty of those heartless human beings who created burdens, for my life; but see how it is also God's blessing and I had no idea that God was going to use it to become my blessings at the end of which my journey is my testimony is blessed, and how blessed to see the power of God's love and outcomes of my believing in the miracles of His power that is unfolding beautifully too.

Yes, in my life and though many may not believe, more or less want to hear it as the truth. But, in every human life, is God is the Only Almighty and no one else can share His glory for all is power, dominion and glory and blessing is ascribe to Him and that when we pray, worship and believe is awesome miracles always happen and that is the only way to communicate effectively. Is joy with the heavens and find solutions at the heart singing and praising, I love all that is what makes life more lovable and living and relating with God and fellowship is awesome power of it.

And focusing is more on what is on good more than on the evil, I have found that in this work also is greater things are of the heart with hope and in His love and inspiration you will be healthier as well. Your heart is always blessed with love and laughter is the happiness, happier and satisfied and more purposeful as well and, has love and laughter than wasting time to attack the enemies with words of mouth. I am telling you as I have seen the glory most effective means and methods of approaching God in every situations is let Him as problem sovereign Solution.

Is God and power of His love and inspiration makes my life a blessing (s) and, words of His is the light as well makes miracle and sure that is God first, consult Him and that is leave it there. And, remember faith matters and also prayer is power and what makes life bearable and faith is also the crowbar also power. Faith is the currency as it works with grace and that is the only way to respond to those situations. Faith in God is the hope. He is of ages past and you will be all that He destined also as happy, thankful and excited as I am blessed and I did surrender all of my life.

And, of every situations too Let Him have all, as He wanted me to and that was the real done deal idealistic ideas is God's ideas, word-based is and powerful is you will be inspired and satisfied as well very thankful acknowledging as I am and celebrating; He is more than deserving and, I couldn't think of any other person for He blesses me that is you and yours all marvelously. And sure God is so awesome and you have been blessed by His goodness and in good company are love is that's God's power for you is celebrating life with joy, happiness, is growing in love!!

And, is soaring over those obstacles, I have no word and, can't is that all that, I can never pay God enough than to give Him my love and thanks and glorify His name is the greatest, that is let all of us know and benefit from all what He blessed, is given, to that is loves me is too much, as well answered. Scripture intimates us that when He has answered. I celebrate the victory with Hallelujah Party and give Him due honor and recognitions is always relevant to honor whom is due when you are blessed and reciprocate love is sure that is kindness begat kindness act of love is and had argued that Greatness is in the heart!

It is my joy, "….to thank him for His answers" (Philippians 4:6). The victory and is for me to give God the glory. The glory is His and honor due Him and that is the goodness of God's grace, in equipping me and I can overtake of the enemies and claim my blessings and all that are mine in the name of the Lord! I am thrill that there is power in the Name of the Lord and in the heart is Spirit of God divine is Powerful that is awesome and need is Him and together, "Sword of the Spirit" (Ephesians 6:17/5:1-20); It is really is thrilling and reading that marvelous Words.

Of love is voice of love and joy that is really is until we acknowledge Him can we really come to know, and fully also will understand am blessed, greatness is in the heart and love is the heart's power for there is the vast greatness of God and words that is healing and life giving to me is apparent that Greatness of God and power of inspiration, for there are much kind of great people in the world but none to be compared to the one this work discusses. Is that power whom we live, and breathe from is what am talking about Gift of God that "Man of Calvary" who gave me hope and life endures for me, also, love that is evermore and through eternity and for eternal life is all so secured and that is who is the Greatest of all in heaven and on earth here and Lord is.

God is the Master designer the ultimate and Greatest Power and Savior of my life. Those culprits need to understand that as well that none of us lives forever, nor is life in our hands and, it is as simple that is no one owns life and is sure without God there is no life and always He who inspires and empowers, so loving and kind He's watching us for be it in good or bad deed is only Him is the Lord who is lording and same He judges and rewards us always according to each of our work, be it good or bad also! It is also is best to let Him handle of your case is in God's care. And controls and I could still as well feel the pain of the horrible nightmares, but it is can't draw.

It can never stop me loving and caring or take me backward for that is, it doesn't thrive in my life and their wicked cruel minds too none is impacting, and is against them as is destructive exploiters of themselves and all that is good and such there is need to pray more for our revival. I can be thankful and God is our greatest Revivalist. And, let's pray for love more love well and is more education and enlightenment for that is what we all need. Most is praying for them also our revival and renewal of the minds to all of us and transforming of mind and heart and that also all is what God is capable of doing for and also in re-shaping of faith that inspires our hearts to love.

When all else fails, keep praying, stay focused and on course, and remain faithful, for in God's your time will come to shine through even in your moment of challenges, God still loves you and empowers you with His love in heart and treasure passion. Above all, know that your passion cannot be substituted! That, is why I show enthusiasm and gratitude and appreciation to all, and thankful for all the gifts and blessing, including of those in words of encouragement and much as with financial aspects, because this is self-published endeavors and people do support.

But, more than thankful is for the spiritual gift that is intimacy with God knowing Him for myself as He has helped me grow in grace, revealed Himself and to be transformed by His love that is amazing truly developing me and maturing spiritually that fortitude personally and as is professionally is enrichment. Why, it is that passion cannot be substituted, you may ask? That is a good question, but a tough one to answer. But, I do know that when your actions glorify the One who is your heavenly Father, you're made to become blessed and are able to bless others. Once you continue to be obedient to Him and do is for your unique purpose in life, you will feel great peace and joy is within and comes outside practically my heart deeply wants to share with you that you need not be afraid use yours all is blessed with spiritual gifts and we must be also enjoy being faithful and use that passion sparingly always.

Your passion to its fullest. It is a beautiful feeling of joy to reach out with love to a dear friend who needs you too known and unknown for you never know where your blessings will come as well from. God has for all is to do great things with what God has provided us, talents and skills, knowledge and wisdom. You must remember that in order to help your friends, you must first be pray diligently, sought too. I want to give all of you the blessings of a great heart, but you also need to appreciate inspiration. It is a true blessing is the gift, from above and only God can give these blessings. Please, pray as you do work hard at improving your talents, and most of all, joy work hard on being happy and giving! It is how God makes our day to count more and more too.

The grace and sufficiency is already yours God has provided – take action and read the words" (2nd Corinthians 13:14). Inspiration and gratitude should be used appropriately to benefit all of us, and nothing is as rewarding as being thankful for all that we are blessed with. Think of the depth of God's love, and it is to understand that this same love is given to our hearts and that is His love enables us to continue to be inspired and blessed. For me, the passion for the work of the Lord that I do there is no replacement cannot be substituted. There is no turning back, for the gear is already on forward, and I let the Owner steer me in the direction that I need to go, knows it. He is the Most High Supreme Power, and I can't accomplish anything on my wisdom alone.

But, because He lives, I can continue to have hope and the joy of inspiration is uplifting of hearts as each day brings me new joys and experiences, and I have been able to discover even more hidden joys, which makes me even more blessed, have been taught and trained properly by Him in my journey to know that not all storms of life are as bad as we may think, neither only for us to see as the cross but grace is, His discipline, as it is all and more than that, gives us meaning. Is to live with a purpose and the means and methods, to achieve wonderworking spiritual power is that will win for you more than you ever dare in your wildest dream, I never though could do!

I am talking about it from life's experience, as it has won for my health, security, peace of mind, contented life as it is with adjustment to any condition and there are time that I can't imagine me being happy in some situations that no one else could endure, let alone to laugh too. I thank God for that sense of humor and even in wilderness God gives the ability to maintain the spirit of joy in our hour of trial joy and love and sense of humor to laugh at times at yourself and marvels has God has blessed me empowering with love and joy within and the faith to endure is as l witnessed is working wonders in me. With that ability and often I laugh at myself too as God is who so incredible. He also has a sense of humor, sure He bless my heart with love/laughter.

I have discussed this conversation with that power of inspiration is love. In all that I do inspiration spurs has given to me in all that I do, God assumes responsibility of transformation. I am grateful that He alone assumes the responsibility of transforming life with joy in heart as our characters. Once we open our hearts to inspiration and passion, we realize that we have reason to be hopeful, more thankful, and faithful, as something good can come out from our hopeless and helpless situation. This word of wisdom has says it so beautifully for my inspiration, "Let reason hold the reins of passion." No matter how one's situation appears to be murky is a blessing's that is, there are always things for us that we can rejoice over. God is still God and He is great; He is the source of our joy and faith and happiness is also, why we can have the best of testimonies in our hour of trials He teaches, disciplines us and prepares us to a higher level of understanding.

So, I am to be rejoicing in the love of God, this work, like many of my previous projects, is structured primarily on practical wisdom. The only difference with this work is that it is part of a series of volumes five and this is the first one as stated in also in the preface, stressed in the special and general introduction and chapter one. This is a chapter of series four is first, so be on the look out and please pray for me and remember to support and thank you for gives a future. It is always fun and an adventure to inspire and motivate hearts. I'm to sing Hallelujahs song, for what only God can give, and celebrate sharing faith, laughter; Friendship with people who shares in my journey, such huge hearts of love and thoughtful prayers for me daily is faith community.

Believing that God is able to turn obstacles to opportunities is growing in God's grace to be, living in the freedom that comes from being confident of God's love inspires me everyday. It is awesome to find myself blessed to do something and relate to Him and those who cheer me on fostering my love of being able to overcome loneliness, rejection and fear too. Instead of looking down, I response to life's challenges in a way befitting for the daughter of a King. Being able to fill hearts with joy with more readings of inspirational wisdom can definitely inspire one's heart.

It enhances one's quality of living. I have found that one cannot open a book without one finding something interesting and/or something to learn from. No matter what your passion is or what types of books you may read, you will always gain some sort of knowledge by reading it. Often, people judge books by their covers (or authors), and that's fine. But I will tell you that whatever you read, you will more than likely learn something that you didn't know previously, which will nourish your heart with healing thoughts, especially that which comes from above!

These healing thoughts that I speak of will result if you read books systematically and as well prayerfully and systematically. Can appreciate and benefit from every page, cover to cover, such as this book you are reading now. I hope that this particular book is able to give you all of blessings and inspiration. But, I would be remiss if I don't thank each and every one of you for your prayers and support and sharing your lives and hearts with me and allowing me to write of our relationship based on the grace of God bestowed upon my life and now we have another book. I am much appreciative of everyone who takes the time to read my work and support me and so am grateful, is about love and our relationships and fellowship with our loving Father is joy too.

What I have previously discussed in this chapter (as well as the entire book) sums up one of the main messages I hope this book conveys: passion for humanity! Each day holds endless possibilities, and we should all be thankful for the strength and passion that we receive through the joy of inspiration. No one knows matters of the heart more than the one who created us, and He is the mind fixer of all of us. God is good and so gracious to us, as the Author of wisdom, and Inspirer too who writes the Best of books, Author/ Finisher, who constantly promotes this work!

Is a loving Treasure, my very best Friend at heart, lives and watches over me and I am so very happy, to have Him all for me is One of the best things about Him is that He never fails and, is always He will always have everlasting compassion for His children! I should be passionate as well towards He who faithfully created me and the world that we live in and who has encouraged us to be happy, filled with hope. I do not want to disappoint Him, so I carefully do everything as He wishes, and it is best for me if I do not rely on others, because I only need to rely on Him.

Is by faith, I surrender my heart to Him and allow Him to guide me; for He is my Father is also far more capable than I am to do so.

Please, always believe and trust by faith, because the Creator is able to do miraculous things for the human hearts and remember where you came from ultimately, finding joy and celebrating that joy is celebrating God Himself. By stepping forward on faith, He doubles every blessing we receive. My passion for Him cannot be substituted, for I look no further than Him for hope and inspiration. Friend, there can't be any story without you as well being the readers and so it is all about love, friendship, sharing and fellowshipping together.

The Grace that God has given me is such an excellent gift and it proves that *He* is the Joy love of my life. Behold, for He has two dwellings! I know that many of you are wondering what those two dwellings are. Can you guess? Isaak Walton sums it up succinctly by saying this: "God has two dwellings: One in heaven, and the other in a meek and grateful heart." What a joy wonderful realization! I hope that Walton's statement fills your heart with love to stimulate too.

It is heart-warming to know that once we realize and have the knowledge of the greatness of the heart, our faith will increase and our hearts will rejoice even more. I implore all of you to let Him have His way with your heart. He says that if we give Him our heart; you will be able to find Him and treasure Him. That is why I did not hesitate in surrendering my heart to Him, for me is, because I did not want to disappoint Him. How about you? Do you still have a hardened heart? If you do, please realize how much He loves you, and just let go, and let Him abide, you!

Give God your all, and do not try to take matters into your own hands. He is in charge, so much allow Him to give your heart the love, passion, and wisdom that it needs. He is able to miraculously restore your joy and give you hope. Once you are blessed with a loving heart, it is others will then become blessed by feeding off of your wisdom and inspiration. Don't you want Him to reveal His secrets and show you His covenant? Please read The Book of Psalms 25:14 and that will tell you what you need to know and be of a great impact and effect for all reader.

See to it that you understand that your passion for Him cannot be substituted. Above all else, "your heart shall live forever" (Psalms 22:26). It is a blessing to be His public steward and to take this journey in faith with you all through thoughtful prayers and encouragement. My joy is my passion is to pursue love, peace and happiness with wonderful, healing words and I read to study. More I read and learn and grow more I understand and more I can do more is of rejoicing. You may be asking yourself how I ensure that my passion is realized. Just keep reading and it is giving words of encouragement to those around you, because this makes us all happy in the long run. God never says "Forward march to his people without Him leading the way!"

Please, make sure that you are on board the love boat of world-wide evangelism and, give love that is of eternal significant, and investment that is never regrettable. Most importantly, get on something that offers hope and, be happy too by motivation to others, for He is appreciative of His children; we are all His children, and blessed of His heritage, though human race. It is a great pleasure and joy is my working with Him and shinning light of my faith journey inspiring.

By conducting the business of our heavenly Father and living our lives to the fullest, is of an empowerment and moreover, we are in a movement of love and expanding His kingdom and making Him a proud Father. When we are all able to care, follow the rules, and obey Him, He is more than happy to bless us more and rewards with life-transforming story of loving hearts. My goal in life is to make sure that my work makes my heavenly Father proud and inspires us all too. I have made my mind up to go forward, no matter what the surrounding circumstances are, and it is for me never look back. My passion cannot be substituted, and thankfully, the inspiration that we receive enables us to make our dreams come true.

It is so amazing when inspiration enables our hearts to dream big dreams and to serve God in all capacities. Hopefully, it inspires us to educate our hearts and transform our minds. Above all, inspiration should get us ready to take action, as each of us can be the very tool for change that we want to see in the world. This is the best part of having an inspired heart – the passion is there. As you continue reading, you will notice that at one point, I considered taking a step backward, thinking it was all over, but thankfully I did not go back regressing that is so bad.

When it comes to matters of the heart, it is comforting to know that no matter what the odds of life as circumstances or shortcomings you may be facing, that with God all things are possible. Sometimes, if you feel that you cannot go forward, it is best to take a break and re-evaluate things from a different perspective. Actually, the best way to help others is being able to take care of your mind and help yourself first, and that is the very position that I found myself in to be able to help others, He blessed me first with the training and equipped me ready and that is as shared, I was helpless, powerless, and hopeless. I thought my world was crumbling around me, and then when the power of inspiration was given to me, my cup overflowed! It felt as if all of a sudden, I was uplifted by faith and hope moving more of joy. That's anointing grace of God.

Words of encouragement from those near and dear to me helped me to embrace the past and to look forward to the future. The support that I received from numerous family members and friends, including "Inspire Women Ministry," were among the best of the many words of encouragement I received. Encouragement, like many of life's adventures, can change one's life and heal the heart. I thank God that He was teaching and preparing to call me for this service, but I had no idea. Certainty is that God works in a mysterious way.

Unexpectedly, I received a call from Ms. Tatiana Fox, who specializes in public relations. My life changed after the conversation that we had. At that moment, she was blessed in that she was an angel in disguise sent to me to restore my hope and faith. Once my hope resurfaced, I was able to regain the confidence that I needed to move forward. I was blessed at that moment because God knew that I needed the power of inspiration to continue to make my dreams be a reality. Today, I have been blessed again by my God who never gave up on me, to add another credential in my inspiration field. I successfully completed a one year certificate program with the Inspire Women Leadership Institute, Houston, Texas. That story coming in next series also.

It is awesome; to obey and wait upon the Lord in patient trust for God's perfect time in deliverance is the best yes, of God's loves time too. Certificate to my writing Ministry as, I was blessed, says don't give upon hope. Realizing that my heart is full of the manifestation of God's love and power is amazing, and is a marvelous feeling as well as an incredible experience. It is a reminder of what a close friend recently reminded me of that I already knew that: "Coincidence is when God works a miracle and chooses to remain anonymous." The need to find expression in life for the joy you feel cannot be expressed in simple words. It definitely is worthy of more than a single volume of work! Keep in mind that you can overcome any situation and be also as well become who you were destined to be, not what other people want you to be, grace of God!

I decided to write a series of volumes on the topic of this book because I want to show all of you that there are many blessings that come from inspiration. I never thought in my lifetime that I would ever be this blessed. All I knew at the time was that I was going through a severe health crisis that impaired my ability to perform to the best of my abilities. It was such a burden to bear, and I realized that turning everything over to God was the only way I was to receive the joy that I so much wanted. "All power belongs to God," and knowing Him is to know joy and is happiness. Beyond my wildest dreams, I could never have imagined the blessings that I would receive on my faith journey and one that was so tough and hard hurdles and insurmountable!!

Joy helps in that it strengthens the heart for action, adding quality to one's life. If you don't already know where to look for happiness, please be encouraged to know that if you look within yourselves, you will see that you have had happiness all along. Happiness does not come from an external source, but from peace within, which is a gift and a blessing in and of itself. It is up to you to be able to release it to enjoy and to share it with others. As this word of wisdom states, "Find expression for joy and you will intensify its ecstasy." Look within your soul is there.

It is such an amazing feeling when we can have the peace of mind that we all deserve. I believe that my peace of mind is priceless. Sometimes, we unfortunately come into contact with people, who, for reasons known only to them, try to rob us of our peace of mind. Thankfully, joy is not something that can be "stolen" from us because it is within us. This work is not entirely about greatness in our hearts, but it is also about seeing clearer with both our eyes and our hearts, because "a happy young person will be a happy old person."

One learns that through the heart, knowledge is gained more so by faith than by anything tangible. You may want to think about that for a moment. Keep your friendship with hope and faith alive, and keep in perspective how important love is. Joy will manifest in your heart and will give you the greatness of the heart that you so truly deserve. There is joy that comes from seeing some things physically, but we all need to see joy spiritually. Unquestionably, seeing things with an open heart and mind are a blessing. We can all enjoy a prosperous life if we have willing minds and hopeful, kind hearts. All of the marvelous blessings that we have received have come from none other than our lavish Giver, and I am indebted and most thankful to Him.

God has done so much for me throughout my life, beginning in my childhood. How can one be forgetful and not be thankful for all of His blessings? I cannot be ungrateful, whether it be by failing to celebrate joy or failing to ignite my passion to write and encourage hearts, for it by the grace and power of God, not my own, and that is why I cannot substitute such is blessings. When there is hope, there is life and inspiration that results in faith, is a powerful force and gift's of that is the currency of life from above, should never be substituted for lesser and /or fake gifts.

Faith in God is a powerful force to be reckoned with, and I am thankful that happiness and wisdom are among my dearest of friends! Faith links joy with inspiration and helps to bring about the greatness in one's heart; for it is in our humility before God that our greatness is there always revealed. Remember, inspiration launches dreams, and what man thought was impossible is always possible because faith and passion in God empowers us, and God's love is an open gift is the access is by grace as well an empowering love. All of us should have a reason to be able to seek for inspiration that directs and always enjoy ever celebrate as our passion is of inspirations.

I definitely have joy in my heart today and every day blessing of the power of inspiration. And the celebration that comes with it gift of hope and love from above, that has opened me up with all the joys that life has to offer. That for me is very importantly blessings are of happiness, it is include the joy of having you all as my family and friends worldwide that is something for is I must be thankful for the fact that you are my friends just by having an open heart and by reading this book. What makes this experience so incredible is that once you finish reading, you can go out and spread the joy that you have received to others, multiplying these blessings continuously. Writing this book has given me pure joy to be able to share my experiences with you, and I love you all! Obviously, God gives harvest when we plant seed of love, so it grows!!

Truly, life's real essence becomes even more of a blessing when we see the prospects that are in front of us. Indeed, prosperous living should be a "household name," we should always be giving glory to God and be thankful to Him. Remember, He reigns forever, continuously is ever –present and showers us with His blessings, so we must realize that friendship is for sharing, and what is better than loving even your enemy? Bottom line is that love and friendship we'll need it is to share the most, because they are both lasting. Certainly, without love, there can be no such thing as friendship, let alone sharing that friendship is love in our hearts that need is to share as it is given to us as freely as love, which is from above, needs to be freely given to others to grow as something we are blessed with, must not hoard or hide love from any, because we all will suffer.

Governor Godswill Akpabio (of Akwa Ibom State of Nigeria), while once touring, visited United States back in 2011 with his family, more specifically, visited the Akwa Ibom community in Houston, Texas. His eloquent speech inspired many hearts, for they were happy to hear, and it showed support by clapping and cheering him as well nodding their heads in approval, I believe it shows people were enjoying the moment, having fun spirit and sharing friendship ambience of the community across board. What moved me was the familiar phrase that he spoke of that says, "Charity begins at home" and that is so true in his case invested in his community very well too.

He continued by saying "We are building today for tomorrow", and what I really admired about the speech is the fact that addressed us as Nigerians – and not only by our individual tribes. We were addressed as a unit, not as a division of groups. I was inspired, and when you are one inspired, you are bound to become even more hopeful. This hope, in turn, brings about love, for change, begins peace, and progress for us all. I pray that in due time, we are all are able to be all embracing love by opening our hearts. Transformed as informed minds and transparency crucial is oneness of hearts and purpose, productivity as united community that stands for what is Love!

It makes for hope, brotherhood and sisterhood in the past; we had our brother's keepers! And, still I sense such a warm, caring spirit, and I thank God everyday passion can be healthy if it is being positive as it is can't be substituted, for nothing passes God's love and His power also. As these words of wisdom state, "Learning to live is learning to let go." That is the truth, for an open mind and an educated heart bring about unity, harmony, and happiness. If we can let go of all the bitterness, hatred, and racial bias, we can all thrive as a people with one love and common interest to build more progress, more than. Just think of the joy that promoting progress amongst all of us will bring to you hope! Hope of a better today and promising tomorrow is the progress.

And legacy to us and our youths and the need to love and care is what is why the need to share in fostering unity among us makes a huge difference in the world. As the following states, "The object and purpose of our instruction and charge is love, which spring from a pure heart and a good clear conscience and sincere (unfeigned) faith" (1st Timothy 1: 5) right there is the ultimate. Please, let's continue to keep the spirit of love and friendship in our hearts, and let's cherish each other with love in our hearts, for it is in our humility before Almighty makes it joy!

Please remember to share the greatness in your heart with others, as its passion cannot be substituted, not even my culture, and identity! Above all, keep faith and hope alive, for your happiness in this world and the hereafter relies on both. Don't forget the passion to care and to love! As I've said before and will say again, passion cannot be substituted, for it is this passion that gives us inspiration, brings about our progress, and unites us in love and peace. We need to cherish and not abandon our passion. Please remember to share the greatness in your heart with others, as its passion cannot be substituted, for me it is not even my culture can stops me from its as it is my identity badge and, for my experiencing the love of God in my heart is everything.

Love is what transcends my human race/culture. It welcomes all kind of people and love as well is of God and we are cherish and values just same and precious too. Substituting passion is like driving a car without brakes, in that we would be wandering around aimlessly with no real final destination. I have been so much blessed as He welcomes me to His love and anointing and the way that I am so much blessed expecting the joy of the Lord, is amazing experiencing peace.

His love can never be compared to other things of the world. It is all the blessings I have and all the joys that life offers to me that I daily enjoy I am grateful for all that is in His heart for and graced my life with His love, True thanks just can't be fully expressed, for I have no words. It is undeniable word, losses in transition, not adequate enough, but my feeling God alone does understand, is all love for me to experience God peace, is love beyond measures and passion in wonders and miracles. Is good to know you through Him and is love! Am to be sharing about what the Lord has done for me and my family is over and again. Over and again as am so blessed is, I am grateful and I too like the woman in the well, a stunt believer of faith in the Messiah and, I don't want to see people suffer and/or be lost hopeless and ignorant either!!! About, what can be also be good, and is not right to hide it what is vital information and to share helps us out that it is for us to be happy and love can be a double blessings that is for our healing, hope, encouragement, joy sharing the words of love can alleviate suffering too much in life and either from the hands of all wicked those who are victimizers, abusive and/or due to one being ignorant of the good news!!

I believe is great to share vital information. It is to keep us abreast and that makes life as is more. Bearable, hopeful, healthy and freeing and happy is so refreshing to be aware of what is going on around you, your community and in the world. So it is so good to be always blessed about knowledgeable insight, is wisdom of God! Is awesome to add quality to life; that Healthy thoughts and wisdom and experiencing peace of God is and I don't know what else better in life than generosity of love sharing when we learn more about it is love to and know about power of the inspiration that empowers! Power of love is wisdom sharing our blessings and friendship too.

Efficacious power God is Lord Eternally our greatest greatness God our Savior He shall never ever fails us. His joy is Word to accomplish is all its purpose. It can't lose its power. And, there is no other proper Way other than His that is all. Passion much like His love and inspiration is what drives us to accomplish great things. Indeed, emotion of positive heavenly blessing is of His passion, as great of a gift as it is, cannot be substituted!

CHAPTER TEN

Let Knowledge Grab You

"Once you learn to read you will be free forever."
– Frederick Douglass

I am very appreciative of God much as those that He blessed and sent my way as angels as well also have been a blessing in my life contributed their wisdom and power of inspiration to me by being positive influence in my life and that is love of God extended to me in an incredible ways. I have come to realize that when you obtain knowledge and share it with others, everyone profits in the end. Living a rewarding life and taking an interest into others' happiness will bring us all together so that we can further ourselves along in life. In any place, time, or distance far or near God is with us and in all that we do and Inspiration of God has no limits is all around us too.

Is when His wisdom spurs happiness, joy and the celebration finding your inspiration will ensue. If we all make a continuous effort to be of service to God and to obey Him, we will all as well find inspiration all surely captures greatness in the heart, for wisdom is of God's Inspiration. It is His love and will find you if you start doing things that are positive and placing those words in heart, I can attest to fact, because in the wake of being diagnosed with a disability, my life was changed, and only one choice left and resorted to reading God's love letters like I had never read.

I always would mostly read inspirational readings, and I found that the more I read, more empowered I felt that inspiration as moving and, my disability was definitely a wake-up call and awakening for my revival and never did I know that my body was my business to take good care. Of course I know that sound as should and cherish all of what God has given me to use and apply words of His wisdom. I must confess that I never did pay too much to my health and I did pray to know and accept God's will for all I knew was more to work from can to cannot making a living.

But, let be clear that being a devoted steward is not a bad thing is good but is over doing it and at the detriment of your health and neglecting important thing as your life is not being so wise as it is not smart or something to do and wind up paying a higher price than earnings and at end of the day is you suffering that is the bottom line. I almost did lose it and I was scare as in a near death condition and all I had worked gone overnight. And, you have heard how it happened and then the worst of my nightmares also what triggered of my emotional health and worsen up all is matters for me as my world came crumbling and shattered all of my dreams and aspiration and hopes that I had with security and future that is all narrated too, that worsen up matters too.

I never knew how true these words were until I became ill myself and surely true to note of word of wisdom says truth is fact of life that, "Health is never an issue until someone is sick." Health, though it is one of life's greatest blessings, is rarely ever thought of until one becomes sick that is when it dawns. That was when I started appreciating my health more than my job. I learned with my heart, for as the days went on, I found myself waking up earlier each and every day, thirsting for the true Love and power of inspiration, knowledge that had begun to fill heart with more gratitude than ever knowing how blessed that I am to be alive and have this day too!!

As I continued to read, I realized that being thankful was what mostly mattered in my life is heart of inspiration that power. I learned more than what I had ever learned in school from the inspired words of wisdom that filled me with joy. I noticed that as the days went by, something inside my heart was of joy. Bubbling, yes with deeper joy, and that joy was inspiration to me. It was a blessing that I was so grateful for, because it enabled me to open my heart to the joy that I so needed the time for, "ye shall seek me, and find me, when ye shall search for me with all your heart" (Jeremiah 29:13). Time well spent on a one-on-one with my heavenly Father was real!

I must admit that to embrace this new lifestyle was tough to get used to. But in the end, I realized that it was one of the most beautiful blessings I had received and my inspiration and the passion. It confirmed to me the fact that the power of an informed mind and a dedicated heart all come from inspiration of God before those of others. As I continued to read and learn, my heart became even more filled with wisdom and gratefulness and that is how I am being able and I am so much thrill excited that this work highlights how great the heart can be, and how blessed we should all feel that it is within our reach. Life's essence begins with divine's guidance prosperous living is as my health began to improve, I was thankful that I was exposed to inspirational words.

That I had been reading, which included teachings from Scriptures. I noticed that as I live is everlasting words of life; I read these teachings and other words of wisdom, I became even more empowered. Additionally, my heart was not the only thing getting stronger – my mind was as well healthier and blessed more of what this proverb says is true, "The key to freedom is in your mind". He blessed to exercise my mind that's what I really would want to encourage, mostly by reading more every day of the words of His what helps educate enlightening the mind with awareness, which adds quality to life.

Reading good books allows us a space for our emotion to breathe as we do so; hope and healing are resulting with knowledge especially that is so true of spiritual words of wisdom is of God is most. If I had not taken those words of faith and believed in them and applied them to my life, I would not know the joy that I continue to feel today. My health could have, in fact, taken a turn for the worse, but I believe that by exposing myself to the knowledge and inspiration that I gained while I was sick helped me get better and progress. We all should be so thankful that we have the ability to be blessed and to keep those blessings flowing and showing gratitude is more.

There is joy of, "Gratitude is not only the greatest of virtues, but the parents of all others" (Cicero). Undoubtedly, it is harder for some than it is for others to come to the realization that we should be more thankful for everything and good or bad at times can forget to be thankful for our blessings. I have observed that many people actually find it easier to be generous to others rather than taking the time to pay more pray and be thankful. Many of my close friends have stated that they prefer to offer people a gift because praying and being thankful to God takes too much time! Is not too much to be thankful even when you offer pay someone to pray on your behalf, be thankful for that as well.

I must admit that we are not as generous with being thankful as we should and or are with other things that we enjoy doing. However, we must realize that everything that we have today as well with life is from the Divine blessing is Source for all resourceful blessings and, whether it is material or not, is a blessing to us and we need to be thankful and show gratitude to God. I don't think that I can thank God enough for the lavish blessings that He has bestowed upon me and my family throughout my life. Although our ability to serve others is very important, it is not good enough to help others without being thankful for what you have and the abilities you are given is to be acknowledged and, certainly, one needs to be more thankful rather than being forgetful too!

Ultimately, instead of brooding over our situation, it is best that we let our hearts handle it and learn from our mistakes. As the proverb says, "wisdom spurs happiness." As your heart molds, you will become more inspired with hope and awareness, even in those unfortunate times and situations you may find yourself in is still to be thankful. Be grateful, even in the moment of agony, for life can help us grow and teach us lessons. We need knowledge more now than ever!

As the saying goes, "The world you live in is created by your mind." I say Amen to that! Sometimes, life may throw unexpected obstacles your way, but please keep in mind that your life is what YOU make of it. Even though I went through a rough time when I was ill, am so grateful that my heart and eyes were opened with the knowledge and inspiration I was exposed to. I can now see so much better now that the "smoke screen" of ignorance mind neglecting importance of taking good care of myself caused more than what I had worked and saved for my failing health is not worth and imagine all that compounded by being scammed both experiences is lessons too.

Very tough to imagine is very costly a price to pay still learned a love lesson of the heart with powerful inspiration God has brought to my heart with attention also that being <u>ignorance is not fun at all being well taught by His guidance I have learned has been more educated about the need to take care of one's health; that is very important for you need</u>

to have life before you can enjoy what you have struggled and work comes secondary, as we need wisdom to be even able. I have more to be thankful for my life and journey and now I have a better understanding of how knowledge can give us all the power of inspiration and I felt that now was a better time than any other to write and share the plain and honest truth: There is greatness in my heart to bless others.

Faithfulness is the joy and knowing God and His words plus fervency in prayers that faith helps, many in the present and past. They were of perseverance, and such trusted as including the psalmists and all the women and men of the Bible who were of devout hearts of integrity faith in God brothers and sisters all of which endured, yesterday is also today is knowledgeable insights. The Book of Psalms 115:5 says the most: "Gracious is the Lord, and righteous; yea, our God is merciful." There is no time for despair, when you look and focus on God is always more to hope.

The good thing about Him, "never closes one door without opening another." That is why I look no where than paying closer attention to Him for He is more than dependable for me that is why, I searched and found Him, and He "delivered my soul," (Psalms. 116:4b). And, what that is awesome power and guidance a blessing for our triumphant living. Please, let's be encouraged more to pay close attention to God and take good care of you first to be able taking care of others spiritually, physically and emotionally is very good and mentally that is what matters all can be of best to do health need. Once you sense the marvelous blessings, having beautiful and caring heart, you will be filled with gratitude and you will have an empowered, informed mind. Your life will become a thing of joy and a thing of beauty and happiness will be for there is that inner peace and so, for me and I am so grateful that I learned to the will of God for my life daily is joy.

And, can now be useful to myself, family and friends known and unknown across board is the world that He brought to my path of life's journey of faith and mostly I am blessed by Him to use my circumstances to glorify Him as well blessing of His people. Please, friend, remember that in order to be the best that you can be you must be the master of your mind, instead of being mastered by your mind take care of yourself to be able to take care of others well. Surrendering my heart more joy in the aftermath of my ugly situation is best thing as I could have done stupid thing, hurt myself more and others, if I didn't pay close attention to His leading by Holy Spirit!!

One needs to be very careful and cheer up in every situation, and I have seen first-hand that once you are able to do that, miracles can happen. It is apparent that people with inspired hearts naturally are able to inspire others, and when others are inspired, they will return the favor to others, and the gift goes so on, thankfulness is to God for healing and comforting touch and of divine intervention and favor of grace and inspiring my passion, and building me from that faith journey to testify. Everyone should celebrate the joy of inspiration just as one would celebrate of his/her birthday. It is a thing of beauty when you can also acknowledge the fact that the power of inspiration has enabled you to become and more empowered and more knowledgeable also on matters of the heart and that is of God's love and power and that is awesome His is ideal idea, is the best tenet for my successful living, nothing else is better than that inspirational words of His.

One of God's greatest gifts to man is to be blessed with inner joy and that peace of mind. Is a great gift of God, and good health is of hearty healthy heart for that is aloes of God's grace. I can honestly say that it has brought hope to me and has increased my faith. Dramatically much as my life is transformed. I am changed too for good to be a stronger and I am a better person and it is that of joy. There is deeper joy within me not only empowering made me come to higher level of understanding, making me to realize of what it is and, that we can overcome of any anything. Please, let this knowledge take a hold of you and realize that you can gain so much, by reading and learning from spiritual words of wisdom more than in the classroom is of wisdom of God.

You will have the skill-set to be able to go out into the world and be the best that you can be. We should all make sure that in the event of life's journey we are to be ready well equipped. Be in the now and stay current and ready embrace change as God's love guides also is preparing. It is for promotion always to help us become more responsible and eager to share love and give it to feeding the mind good thoughts. Because the knowledge that you acquire will inspire you and give you the peace of mind that you need to change you and the world, but that power to change is not yours but begins with you first and faith to believe Him and then you can if you believe.

I am so very appreciative and grateful for my experiences of faith that believing makes it miracles of God's love, is your empowerment. Scriptures teaches us that "without faith you can't please God," and that is so very true ultimate truth (Hebrews 11:6; Habakkuk 4: b and this is the vision God has given me and had dealt with me graciously and told me to share the goodness.

When in doubt, or time of crisis, dare to trust God's love and power it lessens despair and there's glimpse of hope for you, and I am speaking based on my experience. And throughout the reading, I have used examples to show the key points to encourage your heart, well evidently my own testimony. As this is my defining moment too, to be more than grateful, as the very situation that caused me to be overwhelmed and on the "brink," with the help of God through the power of love and inspiration, I was able to transform it into a message of hope, courage and healing also.

You can be sure that there is a loving God, who never fails and nearer you more than you may know, is best to more think love, believe, receive and live it, for His words offers life more. And hope and joy that helps us to live every moment and laugh more everyday and love beyond words even in the hour of trial, there is spirit of joy and the secret of contentment is as well what my experiences of life and a force to reckon with as a motivational and learning tool is of His is love that there is always a good reason to be of hope and courage to endure to the end also good.

Is a reason to be thankful for, "God is good and great and greatly to be praised." Imagine your life blessed and spared, and you are able to do what you couldn't and never thought that it will ever was possible and suddenly and unexpectedly, you are blessed, healed and given another chance in life. How will you feel to see your health improved than what you had thought, that is also even reversed of the cycle? I am talking about circumstances that you had no idea how to handle. Your doctor's are very concerned as the problem they couldn't handle and then see how the Lord takes control of it all and easily the situation fixes? He is the one who heals and gives.

God gives us love with amazing grace and His grace can cure it all and I am sharing my joy and proudly talking about how to live with inspiration and reversed and healed you is what I know God is a wonderworking spiritual power in my own life and is why this is my testimonial. Is how today is a beautiful day and how both of my journey and miracles always in my life He is there is always something to love and be thankful for as well, hope for and I am always to thank God for my supportive family and friends, for all and that all makes for happiness, I am thankful; There is joy at the end of every journey is of happiness for I am a believer, and also when we dig deeply into truth that is of above, there is a way to soar past of any storm of life, and then you'll.

You will believe more then being a heart of appreciation and thankful more than doubting the wonder of God's love and power of inspiration as it can't be overstated or fully expressed in any word better and I am speechless and I can only be more than grateful and I am thankful of it and also on the influence and impact on my life, how His grace is for radiant health, for hope and faith that inspires my passion and more of hope and the victory that Hope in God, trust more than fainting, is devote more time to love, to obey, and pray more for the will of God to be done heals.

God is real and than your will is to be done is why I am more than grateful for my healing and prosperous living that is solely based on the blessings of God love and power that empowers. I see how He is blessing me inspiring my passion and mentoring to fulfill this dream is the Love. Is to be thankful for all that is amazing grace and love that abides within and is loving kindness! I was blessed to let that knowledge grabbed me and when you have tasted of that Love and know the joy and peace that brings your life more love is peace that calms you more perfectly and your mind is steady and concentrating only on the love of God more than your troubling situation that is human condition, is what slays scared but God surprised us with inspiration that makes strong.

You will be surprised and don't know what to say than to believe that God loves you so much as I am the one who's blessed and what a joy to have my miracles and received all of His divine blessings and are many uncountable blessings in the Lord, including spiritual strength that is of even more and growth in my relationship with God is the greatest of my faith journey. Had it not been for grace and favor God's love, I will not make through the stormy turbulent of life's threatening, dampening moment let alone to soar past the past and live this vibrant life of victory.

Is of storms of life and the impact upon our spirit is just so real. It is in that moment when the day is midnight of which, you will the loneliness of life's challenges more and, it takes favor and mercy of God's love. In time of my crisis what could I have done? Hidden within you friend is the dearest of all your loved ones and a friend in life that cares for you more than them is Him. I have a Friend in Him all aspect of your life as well will be transformed healthier emotionally as well physical and spiritually of development and capable with His love enabling you to move on from one level to the other and this is how He helped me wrote my own story changed me too.

Glory, I love to encourage and share with you how much trust and counting on Him, and waiting upon to give you joy and revealed more through the Scripture and through himself what I found is marvelous you need, is His love, in action and deed, has been my blessings at all times. I have seen the wonders of God's love and power of inspiration benefits my life tremendously. I couldn't be happier than to find myself being a woman with a vision born out of sorry and that is awesome and moving a experience when God touched me and made me wholesome of hope and wholeness in every dimension and that is powerful. Definitely, if you trust and believe to turn over all of your circumstances open your heart to Him, receive of His love, give and grow in Him you can rise above and push past circumstances that limit you and God shines you through.

Your most difficult moment can become best simplified of your difficulties to be so easy. As you become who that God destined, and be the person that you always love to be. God's love both heart and mindset and His inspiration. His inspiration surrounds us and, is like the air that we breathe and, His Love prevents panic, and helps us to defeat those, is those stumbling blocks (giants/Egyptians) and anything rising up against His children He controls. All that, you will find them no more, when you allow God controls of your life and strength your life of burdens is over is now blessings and that is have hope and keep faith alive and reflect more on Him as well of the beauty of Love with more positive thing in your heart is than all the mind boggling' best.

He will lead you by the Spirit where the living water overflows. Please, be alert and, let Him to take over your life and make residence in your heart. He loves broken and contrite heart, forgives our not so trust hearts, blessed your heart and tender and meek is home where God loves mostly to abide, bless your heart abides with love and laughter and able to grow in His love more teaches you practical steps by steps on how to conquer the odds of life and overcome them also!!

He communicates and takes you by your hand and walks with you to teach more words of love, and of His wisdom, encourages and inspires courage, nurturance, nourishes, refreshes your life with his love to renew, sustain, and satisfies. And more blessings in His heart for us and to be blessed and have satisfaction and enjoy and live life to its blessings and hope as one with a bright future. Please, pray with me and for all to have spiritual awakening and great revival and offer of more hope. We can all love and understand the meaning of true love and may our love to Him be in greater proportion to His love daily in our lives. Grateful for the good things, God doesn't lie.

As, I have always said, faith is the currency of life, though often said, "Money talks." But doesn't buy life and, not with intimate supernatural faith and you have to have wisdom to be able to keep money. Do you know who heals, interceding, intervening and, why I give thanks? It is all because of what God did and continue to do for me and, my family, and friends I have reasons to give thanks and that is what faith in God does and, I am acknowledging that God, who is faithful. He has all the power and authority every impossible, is possible with God and, I am a winner and justified by faith because not by work or what I do, by faith that God did for me (Rm. 3:28).

By love and grace, He is more than capable and is who conquers, wins for me achieving my freedom from imprisonment of my life (medical/emotional health), adds spiritual strength, reversed the cycle of my situations and transforms my life, helped me be healed, happy, resilient and purposeful, and don't forget faith matters and your doing your part is important just do your best and a little goes a long way, so pray as prayer is great and that is part of your work and, trust and dream big do your part to have a plan to succeed in life as well be a visionary leader too.

Mostly, don't let what overwhelms you to scare you, and you know it ranges from those created by people, pains, hurts and wrong priorities and psychological prisons and well what we cannot control as natural unexpected illness, death of loved ones, any disaster, of those stressors dampening impact is real and always brings traumas and impact emotionally more and it is what makes mental health more severe than physical. Because, lasts longer depending on cause and the intensity of one's pain differs and will always vary, but the dampening impact you're, our spirit is.

Whatsoever bothers you bothers Him, and our battles in life is not a fist fighting battle, either! Spiritual warfare, needs more than money, this world is not our own and since we are in a borrowed land as travelers and faced by bumping there is nothing greater than who is the greatest transformational power. You need inspiration and love of Supreme Being, and that is the key and divine's guidance is number one for prosperous living. Simple love God's affectionate and above all follow what He says for you to do, and that is all that you have and, neither is it by might and power of the prestigious this and that, except living righteously, is all about what is in your heart and, how you acknowledge that power also, and know how and when, to apply words wisely!

What one worships are heart's matters, motivation impacts life always. It is also what you think, do and are that affects and controls your mind most. Inspirational words wisdom are more than clichés, as experiencing God's peace affected my passion that is what it takes for me to be. Position where I am blessed to be today is never of my own power, but by grace and, through the love of God. Almighty God and power of His inspiration, comes from words of His mouth, and power of prayer, as much my faith, determination and dedication. Almighty power surrounds and within us as well, lies what heals your body, mind and soul, which is by God's abundant grace!

Friend, please dare to love and keep knowledge, wisdom and understanding mind and are from above and helps you keep your chin up while others are losing theirs and their joy as well as all His heart is all blessings and is love of God, Him in the program to help me reach my goal as a steward and not just as a lovable child of God but is I am ambassador representing Him as my beloved Father. Please, Support them as Inspire Women did inspire my heart for me in this work and His. Inspiration of God that offers us all hope and inspires all is an empowerment, too educates hearts to inspire, is to stimulate both the mind and thought is positively it inspires and encourages us in our hearts and helps us to think wisely. And positively that is what helps heart it helps us, youths much more for hope is what they need most with our support and love. We are all in need hope with words of empowerment, as much as the true love that have blessed us with more of encouragement, to think love, happiness, rejoice, enjoy every moment know that is with wisdom of God always, let knowledge of God grab your heart is with passion and inspiration!!!!

His will best and His plan and so dear friend pray for His will to be done not yours! Is it supernatural, great faith, little faith or no faith, which one is yours, to be thankful for more? Even if you don't have any, what you have is to be thankful for your life, you still have a chance to ask God for your need, and appreciate His love and hope for the best including faith that endures and inspires hope to sing through your heart. Inspiringly Confucius says this truth, "Wherever you go, go with all your heart." Faith is currency of life. It is awesome knowledgeable insights is to learn more about the will of God for your life and, pray for a discerning spirit, and understanding mind, power, wisdom, and divine guidance, nothing beats that capacity to love, and acceptance.

This book is given for our inspiration by God's grace, will be so inspiring, educational all inspirational, is entertaining us all is on faith, hope, love and that power is spirituality, is for hope and success all powerful and, please friend, don't ever buy trouble for yourself, is don't pay back with revenge, when you and yours are hurt, but pray more is best for you to keep loving more joy is forward than to fret, you keep moving on up. Praise is more to press on is the prayer more and trusting in God is best character and Joy to be loved and you love back, give and receive is serve.

Chapter Eleven

Happiness comes from A Person's Character

"All inspiration meliorates the heart and
launches dreams to come true."
– Caroline Arit Thompson

We can achieve pure happiness, is ultimately in the hands of the Lord and also, whether or not we are willing to open our hearts to Him. Absolutely, God is in details and each of us is as usually as happy as we want to be, is also amount of happiness experience depends more on what comes within. Is reminding myself who is the most Inspirer and Transformer of my life and love also highest power and greatest only God is my own choice is Joy! One, whose love is amazing and unfailing is for my heart which is my blessing, He is greatest source of my inspiration for my happiness comes from within and relies very little if any on the exterior things.

That is why I am overwhelmed with excitement for my joy comes from within as well. I should always be grateful with Him to have Him for my happiness and what comes from above, inspires my passion ignited more. His love is joy and that settles for me. Happiness is God gives grace is by that anointing to do what I had thought can't and that is for sure was impossible and I had lost hope down there in the trail. And to come this far after a great calamity and imagine all that I went through in life to navigate all and God is marvelous to me, for He made me soaring.

For He led me and had proven Himself and time and over again of His love and power that is greatness and, I often pause and asked myself in quiet contemplation of self and is that is also is joy with an excitement of finding all of this and more spiritual and greater blessings.

I am puzzled too also is this me rejected by my people? (Thank God is just a few) of them who went about scandalizing my name and trying to tarnish my image and reputation after they scammed me fraudulently). Took all of my life's savings, ganged up against themselves thinking was me, but were totally wrong, were all against themselves. Because, God loves me so much that He is who kept me alive, He covers me up in His precious hands and blood that never any ever fails.

And love that is. His love the "banner over me;" He shows me of His divine favors with interventions. His love this is me that was unlovable by those who do not want to see me alive; neither do they like me, let alone love me, talk less of my spiritual and physical progress than for them to judge and shun, tease, to gossip about me and pointing accusing fingers and am like each day is a little more happiness added to spice, is this me many talked so badly about like nobody? But, God says, I love you too much more and more? Everyday, is joy and excitement am blessed of His love is of hope, joy, adventure me to be about His love and hope? He told me He loves me more than all of them and, to keep focusing on Him and move forward. Move on and pay them no mind, but just to do what He says to follow Him and do what His will is for me and, gladly.

He did caution me to be about His love and business of loving as, is best caring, praying, watching and serving Him more and trusting most. I see how much God loves me wraps His love over me and all around me everyday is Love refreshes is for eternity and happiness is everyday as I see, is the remedy for me. He helps me do something beautiful and aspiring more and that is the attitude to be in place. He refreshes my heart with His love, sustains, renews and satisfies me with good and perfect gifts. I can't believe this is me and but it is real, for is all about God's love and grace is the mercy upon me. I thank God for my life and miracle of believing in His love and power and that inspiration, what my faith in Him does is Love Empowers as, I can always testify.

To that, love is makes these true testimonies. To the power of the human spirit read in the preface. Much, as I am the one transformed. This is my story and journey of faith is also by grace and faith that I found a profound thrill all is as God has brought me aboard and safely home that is happiness. I have the blessings of His love, power of inspiration; I have my transformation and unwrapping more love and joys and love and I unwrap daily of many more blessings everyday is testimonial, that is I have a gift for each and all of you as part of my blessings and love is a great gift at any time is true and pure is of joy moving is an amazing experience and journey that Love.

Blessing me is eternal love and for me living and seeing is believes and it is awesome, is an incredible great God who in times is. He is wonderworking spiritual power. And being healed by His love and transformed also by the love of God and by the Holy Spirit to eventually become that love for others and that is growing and showing that happiness is of the Lord God Almighty. I am dialing Him everyday and every seconds, minute and growing in God's amazing grace love and is power that is what highly has as read inspired my heart, it is true God is who transforms us is by Love, our greatness is in the heart. I have and Love is the heart's power and in our humility.

Only possible before God that greatness is always revealed. I am so thankful for God has been awesome as amazing is my experience, experiencing the love of God and peace of mind is a blessing that no one should ever missed, is for courage and happiness a miracle that takes comes from God. It is by grace the love of God and by leadership of His Holy Spirit to become that love for others. Awesome, is our incredible eternal living God and in my life is my Father, my Friend and Mentor and Inspiration, and I see happiness is a form of courage for without being happy is no joy and peace and harmony and that I am so grateful that He is the Source and source of my strength through faith and most of all I am most thankful gave His greatest Son to save my soul.

I receive from Him most awesome Gift His Love everlasting is which thanking God for all things and that finally, I am me Caroline Arit Okon Thompson, not someone else. I am being myself, is the person I have always love and sense hidden inside of me! This is marvelous great thing, to have Him for my happiness and what comes from above, inspires my passion ignited more passion and what a joy to find the courage to look for inspiration and for finding Joy in me.

As I write this very chapter my heart is filled with praise, for God who has thought well of my life. Truly blessed I with a new heart, which is pure, and my greatest joy and wisdom am more of self- esteem, confidence powerful than before calamity strikes. I now see why the wisest man as a King Solomon wanted nothing from God more than wisdom and that was given also to him. How did he know what was best and, I see why he gets to be so wise? How did I come to be this close with God in my life, you may wish to ask? I confessed it changes your life forever, is what I have now repented of my shortfalls and ignorance. I confessed my short sightedness.

Of my ignorance, mostly was of people allowing people's attitudes influenced with their own self-made and that company will get you off track. Bad philosophies of what they think and speculate about me to impact my living, my joy and that is a not for me today is to the fullest and standing on my Father's promises! Oh, sometimes believe or not, the evil minded will tempt to see, if your faith will fail as you get distracted. So, you will quit being inspired please keep faith deep and abiding with love. Is very crucial and that is source of strength is and God's love lasts.

And makes hope alive that grace. Indeed, so many were not happy of my walking with God and, they tempted to test my faith in so many ways, but God helped me always is by greater grace and faith that power is inspiration to do what I destined have stated previously, happiness cannot be bought and neither like love with any amount of money! No amount of money can buy it is within more. And first impression matters always too. Think about this: "Who really wants to be bothered with mean unhappy folks? Often, many this days, are about happiness being just engaged only talking politics of more of it is all money and power, sex, drug, alcohol and getting high with it and get drown is all with drugs performance or enhancing and illegal it substances.

It thrills and kills and it is money only buys temporary happiness, but it will not give you the true happiness that you need and desires that is fulfilling and deserving for that type of peace is within. Happiness is not of this world and has nothing to do with anything that is of man-made, is not based solely on materialism either, corruption, bribery is defrauding and illegal means is not substances and all those cracks is not that type cocaine's and is drugs that is not what it is simple, wisdom is what I am talking about that is the pills of wisdom is "word-based".

Is talking about good instructions when you receive from above is priceless and pure only given from God and will help you is word-based peace of mind and that is what I am happy to receive and pleased for it makes me sleep peacefully and mind is cleared and cleansed to "wait on the LORD"(Psalm 27:14), instructs me daily to do so and there is a miracle always in my life and so, there is a reason for my choosing happiness over amassing so much riches of this world. So many want to get rich quick by fraud and cheat the Book is (1 Thessalonians 4: 6-9). We must remember that we can only do what is possible, as limited human beings; so it is best to adhere!

To the instructions, do those things to the best of our abilities and leave the impossible up to God. He wants you and me to maintain joy within, to have love and inspiration from Him and maintain unity of spirit of love as well as to "maintain the unity in the bond of peace" is all about power of love is togetherness of hope, peace of mind, believe in Him and there is joy in service. I know and brotherly love Scripture sums it, "That they may all be one." That is not my word let's be very clear on that as it is in God's Word and I did not write it either is in the Book of (John 17:21). I know that it is all inspiration to love one another, therefore, becomes both as I see Joy.

He is Means! Wisdom than mental knowledge and it is of God, inspiration that power is all love of God and is joy is a legacy to cherish heavenly treasures are greater by far than of all the earthly accolades and wisdom of man! It is a thing of joy, beauty of joy to see God moving. Yes in my life and heart is filled with love and laughter to me is apparently, as is we all do also need a little inspiration and What really helps us to be of hope is as well and on the right track to be able as well and overcome is always is Joy and is my time for my testimony that is as His providence is awesome and is without Him we would all be gone, lost, I was and I can't imagine what my life could have been but for Him! God is over generous always watches over us and all with His kindness as I see is His goodness and His infinite mercies and that faith in us is what I thank God for He's a Loving Father/Friend! Is He Always surrounding us and with love power is that His Love it is also inspiration through grace and inspiration is like the air that we breathe!

Is a remedy for it, a solution and is awesome, speaking truth in love and is from collective responsibility as well as our obligation. Individually and you can be all that God wants you to be. To be work hard daily to be of your best and smartly, all of it for God loves you and He always wants you to have a smile on your face. So, please keep joy and happiness in your heart, and let celebrate with family and friends when you find it within and remember love is of God and this is the spark that God placed in my heart also, I have a message from God in my heart for you as a friend is, and I am not a saint as all along said is just a poor sinner saved by His love and grace.

His and mercy upon my life and lifted by His grace that is it! Ephesians 4:15 is there and says, I should speak the truth in love and that is exactly what I am doing and the passage is all as about all of which we need to do it with love. Please, don't forget that all of them are they are essential ingredients for good character, to be cheerful and smile, for you are all loved! I find it interesting and so fascinating that of all the things that we wear, our facial expression matters the most and is the first place most people look when examining one's overall expression as well is. Please, change your mood from a bad to one in which you are constantly smiling is as good as it keeps you happy, rather than frowning of love and inspiration. You will find it more favorable.

It is pleasurable and likewise knowledge and wisdom that both comes is by grace doing this by love is you will constantly smile and exude a cheerful confidence is that is contagious is of joy and blessings of God's love and power! Happiness results in hope, which can give us all the most beautiful of smiles. Even though Charles Darwin said "survival is based on the fittest!" I respect his views is opinion and, but I believe that survival is based on the joy in my heart more and I know this for myself which what thrills me most is on inside. It is that the Holy Spirit shall increase in us true knowledge of God and so happy that His will is being done in my life all too!

Is a charming quality to have obedience to God's words and that is true essence of life and what a joy and indeed, it is the moral challenge of one's faith that strength is the making of my charm. Although, we may not always feel God's presence but it is there and is the strength in many is of a man's power and that and charm is the strength of a woman. I have found that happiness, like gentleness and greatness is in the heart, and matters too and works miracles for my life saves me and bless with the wisdom to harness my potential to the fullest, even in the midst of trial and, I have seen the glory of the salvation of God and that means salvation is not just always of eternal reward only but more than that are other spiritual blessings and excellence.

Of integrity is being myself and not someone else and that is hope right there for me and faith is also an incredible gift of God's love for my divine health is wholeness in all parts of my life from inside to the outside am truly blessed, and I am justifying by faith and not of my good works or righteousness being myself is of that divine intervention the favor of God to lead me. It is an undeserved favor and by definition an "act of grace" that I have been this blessed and given inspiration in all that I do and God saw it all of me. He saw my tears and saw it all and saw it fit to come to my rescue and bail me out of rage and anger that I felt toward my abusers everyday.

I hated their and exploiters of others who took my humility to be my weakness and what a day of rejoicing and celebrating that power of God's love in miracle of my transformation was a day of jubilee. I believe in true obedience to God's words. I believe strongly in that indwelling healing word and life giving Spirit of God's love for it helps. It can also works miracles for all of us, because whenever I am faced with an unpleasant situations God's takes me to what makes me become better person, stronger and able to see things in a whole new way and think differently.

I know that God will take the sadness away and gives me joy and that revealing power of His inspiration that I needed to cope in my life's journey and certainly, inner direction gives me strength, and what a blessing is more lasting and most liberating transformational power that is God is who helps me with power of inspiration that transforms emotions in my heart and through Scripture and His leading is soaring me over my impeding obstacles and growing more in His amazing grace love inspiration that is a gift of hope and how much Love is power is happiness.

God's love helps me take off my envies and rage and bitterness, jealousies, doubts, fears and unforgiving spirit and dispelled them all of perplexities turned to become my prosperities as is also burdens becomes blessings, discouragement is courage and sorrow joy and what more can one asks for in life? When God can solve all of our problems?

I have so God blesses me and that being blessed, and thankful that He healed and transformed and to help me come this far in life is of knowledge of His wisdom that happiness when you have suffered and blessed healed and with despair is hope. And, I always love to show my eternal gratitude, am happy to receive of all His joy and, I recite the following prayer to Him and is to thank Him you are more than welcome to join me: I just want to thank Him God's love nothing beats transforming my life with His love:

Thank you dear Lord, heavenly Father, for my soul blesses your Holy name. Thank You for saving me and loving surrounding me daily with your infinite love, mercy and grace with all of your power and in presence every blessed day. Father, I desire to become more grateful as a humble, child and always mindful of each blessing that I receive of your unfailing Love. I thank you for including me on your loving kindness and faithfulness. I thank you my dear Lord God for your kindness, and your peace of mind priceless gift for my peaceful living and daily blessings.

Please, continue refresh, revive, and warm our hearts with your love, and bless everyone the world over. Help us to cherish more of your unfailing love of grace, provisions, sustenance, protection, for which I am forever grateful! Please, guide our families and guard us from all the harms and dangers. Please, continue to keep me from anything that may take focus off of my joy and of your essence! May I continue to humbly please you more than anyone else in my life and thank You Lord for ordering my feet in your word my light and Father in heaven, as I desire to serve You, grants me Your precious grace to be able to handle others with love in my heart also. I want you to teach me more of your wisdom, thankful for every situation that is my daily prayer.

I thank you my dear Father for your Love and making me that love for others. You are highly lifted up and appreciated most of all, for happiness and peace with your love and Majesty you brought to my life, and so much love and I will forever cherish and adore you! I thank you for your love, forgiveness my Father and Lord Almighty, yours is the kingdom, glory and honor is all in dear Jesus name -Amen!

I am so glad and thankful that God is God and not man and this is how He has been my Joy is marvelous, holy, greatest, faithful using my tears and that of my children as well relatives as orphans too and prayers and love of friends the world worldwide to bless us and it is to know Him more and more is wonderful His is alive. Practically, my life has been a struggling life those are, shared that is what testimony is blessings and how is what was so very unfortunate and hard in my life, impacting both body and mind to overcome all is inspiration that is God is more than powerful and what makes the story of inspiration that empowers is God made it easier for me as it motivates, is faith for me also it is possible to navigate becomes passionate purpose is to love.

It works, blessed with strings of victories and, what a joy and what a blessing as well all of this is His the glorious triumphant stories of joy; His good work and victory; I am thrill of this is hopeful, for far exceeds my expectation in wilderness, indeed. And, am committed and He has been there for me, is everyday has been a blessing for me in my moment of crisis, when all being a tumbling and saw me through He was there for me and endures with me when to be my whole world crumbled was and every step of the way there. And told me how to keep steadfast and trust in Him for He will see me through and He did keep to it His promises all! But for His grace and of love and His teaching me how to keep steadfast in my trust of Him, for I could have long gone and forgotten been gone, but, thank God for He is the remedy of all my soul and only One who is my everlasting Healer and Comforting Touch is also as well the precious and most Gracious too!

"Rapha," my Life, Healer and my Salvation! Evermore God is and awesome Power He is my delight is the only problem Solver of all of impossible things and that is you will read more. In in-depth of details under other chapters, all is of testimony each chapter more in the next series second is there is absolutely, deeper joy is for me is living life of hope is by faith in God and that His grace is blessing to cherish Him more as His love is for joy, which is the grace for my life; is also what was for my escape is Route during the unbearable moment is that cures, all was terrible and so it was a horrified; my life and a moment, which I was so lost in thought, and battling with unexpected, failing health and both physical and emotional as so of all acute crises and suddenly.

Was also plus that terrified which was the other human created agony as emotionally was not a great life, and God forbids them and Not my portion! But, be that as may have happened, I have been truly blessed and this is how. How much God loves and shows up for me more to me is His Love that empowers. That love is expressed and is a divine favor, blessing that is what it is and more of what makes me alive is to continue to be most of thankful heart and celebration too. Is thanking God. And am being grateful for His love, and living by that power is the faith that is to live fruitful life and His Gift is peace of mind, grace is the gateway is His love is marvelous and through the Lord God. And He alone has power, and the answer is the Almighty and capable.

Oh yes, more He is of power blessing and keeping us alive and safe from harms/dangers. He is the greatest and is definitely what will completely transform your life in all areas of life is God is miracle Worker; also am grateful of walking today likewise for Power of His Words all is everlasting spiritual transformer and happiness of the believer and miracles of God's love Is His For it is not up to man rather is up to God. Him, is whose love conquers that is, so it pays to trust and believe in the promises of God's love and power for He is who lives His Words and this is how much that love is empowering and changes things from negative to positive. It comes from the Lord, is joy of that also power of God, took place in my life and all blessings are divine, also.

All are fervors, as all are divine interventions what a joy and what a blessing of finding love that inspires and empowers and is so amazing and it is healing with it cures, also for us the Solution and Answer what we all need it is for hope and our encouragement too. Is so hard to fail to share, as I can't keep it just to myself as hiding those blessings than sharing is food for us and are life is words of love, hope, and comfort with all, it is best to share for us all to have a little bit gift something that quenches thirst and yearning and enlightens us all about power of inspiration.

We must all keep in mind that we have to put in some hard work to be able to build the character needed to achieve true happiness. If you want to be happy, you have to have that joy is within is in you and is a kind and loving heart, which sets the foundation for good character and it is what makes you. Kindness is a blessing, and we must also remember that we should rejoice in being cheerful and giving our service to Him. As I said earlier, of all the things we wear, our expression is the most important and always first spot. Your facial expressions matters and says much about what kind of mood that you are in always, being happy is with contentment in God.

I am impressed and I could see the advantages of wilderness journey more than crosses is that the grace I feel happy and that is literature evangelism and beauty of it all is that, though we are all different in our diverse ways, still no matter what, human we are and need more love and of joy. Is in helping each other and I find is awesome to help us in finding inspiration in our daily lives. And, give of what I have been given. I am so grateful is well with me and that I can afford as blessed to do the work that I am called this and is from the love of God and amazing grace. He is my Supreme Being and He is and has given me power to be that love for others, is inspiration.

Finding inspiration is living in the freedom that comes from being confident of God's love and that inspires me is soul-fulfilling is most the True Love. I love the fact that, I am one of His joyful servants and students for I am still learning and leaning a life-long more to re-learn as well on Him more I lean and more and I grow and never have enough of Him and greedy more I am for more happier and am greedy of His love and more I lean more sweeter than ever; and from where should I find my refuge and salvation and beautiful smile and all these is supreme blissful. Luxurious blessing and all is always, Greatness is in the heart- A Tribute to inspiration His Love.

For, I am sure that many people I come in contact with on a daily basis with are so very appreciative of my smile and cheerful disposition and, I am thankful that we are all unique in our own ways, blessed and gifted with something unique that we can express in our own way as well show love that is to express ourselves and what we feel inside and is the glory of God that we are enjoying the benevolence of His grace daily. True love isn't always about expressing Romeo and Juliet kind of love. Love is our real happiness measured by true love of God and am blessed that is deep joy within and couldn't be fully expressed of its magnitude but be defined in happiness.

In many varied ways, so what we need is more inspiration that is love of God exposes us to better uplifting of spirit of joy and love is of us need His kind of love most, and is dating Him first is of what matters most in life and empowering my passion, for I am compelled by His Love. Please, remember is just my view and though human we all are but differs in many ways. This is how I am privilege of looking at life and don't forget everything in life is good and all has also of its places and differ in different ways and opinion as well and taste and choice and decision make influences us as well it could be positive and negative and judgment is same way for what I have.

My biggest hope is in God and my faith makes it so and may not be a big deal to you but big deal to me is God's love. Right now of critical is more enlightenment in educating the heart is empowering is spirituality. To be transformed by the love of God and by the Holy spirit for me to gradually become that love for others is a breaking news is matter of the heart and mind power for awareness always is life and happiness and adds more value to my life; Scripture teaches that "While these three virtues, namely faith, love and hope, love is excelling (1 Corinthians 13:13). Love is supreme and, as pilgrims, we are just travelling along the way, living from day to day.

Is all about love of God and living, loving and I am relating with love both with God and fellow kind in fellowships in this borrowed land makes life more worthwhile living with hope of His love more because we as human we are just in borrowed land and in transit as we transition. Makes us vulnerable, our love needs to be stronger and, I believe strongly in the word of God. I sense the need to express of my emptiness and limitation and glorify the God Almighty for His greatness, holiness and faithfulness to me and sure, of God's mouth come full of grace and truth and in the world, there are many beggars. And whose human nature makes souls thirst and need.

Faithfully; Joy will come, and good things will happen, because you will be constantly learning and growing from His knowledge and inspiration inspiring your passion is Greatness in the heart does matter and; it is not man's journey alone, so we should all find comfort in the fact that God is always by our side. He blesses spiritually, physically, emotionally, mentally, and also psychologically well is mentally and of course financially and otherwise, all are cares to nurture and satisfy. He knows us and all our needs and desires and is a Friend indeed, helps in our time of need and plenty, especially through trying times and cheers us on with inspiration.

Once, I was asked, why I don't talk politics much more than what I have been inspiring though my writing is always love more with counseling education with focus on molding youth and family unity. I said I do it all and first is being right with God in order to be right with each other and answer very simple. We are all, but love empowers me is more for me to do with it and that is the language. I am more familiar to express myself better too and truth is that as for me, I cannot stress enough that there is no other friend like the Lord. He is the best friend that anyone could have that can make us truly happy and fills your heart with love and joy in an hour of trial and you can still be contented and still find contentment with spirit of joy. I know for me, for He always walks and holding my hand tight to His unchanging hand of grace and love but we are all political minded. But there's something more to life than what is seen physically, that inspires.

Spiritual words of life is what they need simple but priceless truth and when inspiration is not part of not part of one's life is so sad, spiritually, words of inspiration are not part of their life and vocabulary, which furthers the disconnection. It ends up being a never-ending cycle. Once, it is a missing link from where wisdom is always from the right Source (God) is a blessing and the Giver of all blessings. Truth is this, there for they lack inspiration that radiates the beauty of life. Is always best when life is ruled from within is the inside unfolds one's life beautifully spiritually impacts is a positive and that refreshing love is from inside to the outside inspiration is of God.

He is the Almighty God who helps us with power of perseverance is a blessing be it in all seasons. Spiritual of socially, and you can successfully battle and overcome with it and combined with love it gives you the strength to start things over again and even straighten up your life how the love of God and power of inspiration work in my life and how it is possible for me to be able. Beaming, bringing sunshine to the lives of others, and I can't keep it away from myself either as it is of the life that I live and share and joy does not only comes to me, but to all of us as well and both in words and actions is a direct correlations both are indispensable. I have seen the salvation of the glory of God and absolutely, there is hope and joy and peace from Him is I am contented.

I am more than grateful with what I have life and, have learned the secret of contentment as well from Him and that is how much I am able to cope and growing in His grace is awesome. I couldn't be happier is the blessings that keeps you going and without which you may wind up attacking yourself and hating it for nothing because you lack the tact and no real self-image, no confidence, no passion, and no fear of God. There is the problem, no love for others, is no hope. It is a just devotion to selfishness is all around their hearts, and they lack knowledge of insights, vision and wisdom to know difference. The difference that inspiration is all surround us and joy is for strength and comes from the Lord! Spiritually, word inspirations are to some not a part of their vocabulary that furthers their disconnection. It ends up being a never-ending cycle. Living in isolation of what is relevant that adds quality to your life, but you are not aware that is so sad!

The world seems to be lacking in crisis-management skills as well as the skills to cherish the wisdom of things from above. There also seems to be a lack of meaningful fellowship – the building of hope and faith that makes for a prosperous life, which of brotherhood, once enjoyed. Character does matter in one's happiness, and it is indeed so true in my own case, so that is one primary reason, why am sharing my joy. Allowing God to use my trials and build my character. He re-makes me His vessel of honor is awesome, so others can be blessed to bless others and it is paid off. Initially, I was all worked up with bitterness and, focusing in the past, hurts and thought of a revenge but God said to me no way, you are my lovable daughter and you are fine, building.

What a joy to reflect on that moment when I saw the Lord and my salvation that made me a living testimony to what God has done for me and can do for you and all of us to be victorious.

He told me, "I love you so much doesn't pay to waste your time thinking negative thoughts of it negative;" and that were it, I wanted to revenge of more raged of being abused and victimized and robbed of my money, yes, I had a reason to say, my fellow kind did it and you have read that was monsters and wicked cruel heartless all.

I realized how they made me a victim of this and that and was hurting and just because of being used and capitalized on my kindness as being weakness. I was in pains and hurt to be taken for a long ride and how can people be so selfish motives and heart with evil intent and wrongful ambition and manipulative lifestyles and addictive to exploiting and hurting fellow human kind? Imagine and I became sick. I was very sick and in addition to my physical conditions that already wearied me out, it was a crumbling world. I almost lost it all, for I didn't think there was hope, is now clear to me that God was in the details anyway more hope left for me and He had bigger and everlasting plan and was working in and through me brought to a higher level of understanding.

I remembered that, my doctor told me, "Please, Caroline promised me that you don't go out there and do something stupid. Please that will hurt you, family and friends." Gratefulness, I thank God that I didn't get out of control and God forbid for; He helped and took over my life. I am blessed and kept me and thanking God in my journey, for friends and family and support of all and, for all those who positively influenced my life too. Thomas Edison says, "What a man's mind can create, a man's character can control." Positively and, friend what kind of mindset do you have? After reading – a positive mindset or a negative one and that is a personal thing too!

Your life to love and do the good for one's attitude is just as powerful as one's character. And, as Booker T. Washington so eloquently stated, "Character is power." I'm grateful. Am, so thankful God was with me in the midst of my trials and He used the very circumstance that also greatly caused me to be upset and overwhelmed and lost in deep thoughts, to become bless me! Overwhelmed and on the "brink," blessed me more added happiness to my passing days! I saw God's love and power and, we can find guidance for our lives from Him and His positive words.

Is a blessing by our first seeking inspiration, is first from God and divine guidance is the number one source powerful principles for one's successful living. I allow God's will to be done for my life, not my will. That is the Biblical way of approach and is very much in place and most effective is in always vogue everlasting. Truth is all about Him and you can find your way back to home also is to the place where you first did belong with an identity and integrity and growth. More without hurting yourself and others is His will for our lives. When we allow Him and let go of our lives than going after revenge is the greatness and most favorable thing in one's heart.

I also thank God for my physical doctors as blessings true Christian and reasoning along with love, joy, Godly people. Life is sunshine's delight and the attitude to be in place and that is the life of happiness, when I say God has surprised me with the right people at the right time am talking all based from that experience. Of moving, building forward and not backward because is of the grace as I found salvation from God's hand, being good to me and what works for me are all miraculously for me the love of God and His glorious sufficient grace. It is for me and I have been truly blessed to move on because of Him and His lifting up my spirit there is hope for me as is always who and what is helping me summarizes that is feeling of joy that fills my heart daily!

We should be seeking more after power of God in prayer. Through Bible study and the leadership of Holy Spirit, is helping us, supports, and lead us to be where He loves us to be and makes a understanding of the words of God made a great difference in my life, importantly awareness is a profound thrill that I have found and how much God's timing is different from mine and how He loves me and good placing people always in my path. And, I cherish more what I found God's graciousness is everlasting and more spiritual blessings and I am so grateful to God for reaching out to touch and to show me more of His love and meeting me at the point of my need just at the nick of time. He is my joy as was salvation and will forever be my Source, Power and Lover of my soul. He is my only Salvation. Deliverer of my soul in His mercy saw releases me from the burdens too to be becomes, blessing and that says, There is hope is joy is also most importantly taught my heart great things of the heart and He releases me from the past to fulfill His purpose and destiny all according to His biggest plans for me in life that is super exciting, how His hand guides and takes care too.

He takes care of me and my family that abides and finishes with good ending that makes it thrilling experiences. In my journey and whatever I do and say in wherever I am and situation He abides within me in my inmost being and revealing love is God and so I say inspiration is a need. Please, refer to (Genesis to 21:22 and 28:15-22). Continuing on with character, we must keep in mind that one's character can be becomes one's destiny as well as how content our lives are. Yes, we all have different opinions on what makes each of us happy. Is there a correlation between needs including character and of happiness? Do you mind, if not let me say this, it is as I believe the real essence of positive

302 | Carol Arit Thompson

character is one basic need, which is of inner needs love to care and of compassion, that is noble is Scripture!

What it says is this: "Love the Lord your God with all your heart, and love your neighbor as you love yourself" (Matthew 22:37-40). One may say that happiness comes from a variety of things, indeed you are right. Based on how you define happiness. What makes you happy it is; some may come in so many different moods and modes all ways of lifestyles, but still for real to possess heart real true love and His kindness, and compassion, like transformation, it is only God who gives, transforms human heart, for real true happiness comes from Him, and inspiration. I have also noticed that people are generally as happy as they make their minds up to be which is as all well based on THEIR definition of happiness. I am proud of the fact that, being raised by faith, is made mind up early to be happy in the Lord as it is a choice and love is a choice and what you make of it which is my passion, lifestyle' choice.

Thankfully, wasn't a bad decision, and excellently way of God's path, ever since always turns out well, as a very good is of joy and decision with greatness in my heart. My heart enjoys of God's love, compassion for me humanity, as it turns every blessed day blessing to be thankful of love that flourishes cherish from my childhood to adulthood. Still keeps flowing with joy and is never-ending and awesomely blessed is the Bible contains what makes for hope and happiness. Never fails than inspires to compel me and mine, is this passion to be a steward of God. His love so sweet and compelling, for I couldn't be happier than living in His vineyard, all the days of my life, else would have been retaliating and drifting away from what is true, real and just to live on.

Absolutely, He gave me the blessings of a happy childhood that have carried onto my life in adulthood. He is the source and center of my life/ hope, resulting my happiness and inspiration. Soaring with God, makes me powerful, is freedom, more love and more power. Importantly, His love is surpassing peace of mind that, I needed, and liberty. For me to share is that, marvelous is the Lord, best thing that I ever needed and love received by faith. My family prayed and thanked the Lord for His love and how He loves them was same way then as now daily and loves dearly.

They were first in my life to be instrumental and worked together in my progress along with my community. That is how the kids grew up, developing interest for a privilege, that I am enjoying today because, we talked and opened our hearts to be relating first with God and same makes us of love relating to each other. That was freedom right there, as quality education made it, good communication is freedom. It establishes confidence, sense of dignity and self worth for any child to know how to love others and not just themselves. But, to be quite honest, always of beauty, but always good education is empowering but, that freedom, is always secondary to none the liberty that I received for my salvation is from God and that is beacon of hope, is always life.

Quality living is not just about having money but genuine love that is of inspiration opens many doors for success, diverse opportunities knocking too, is of character that is what makes it a blessings and that is power right there by itself speaks voluminously that is what money can't buy and nothing can make me happier than what comes from above and that is within me always. Apparently, it was them (my family inspiration to motivate with love of God) that made my life. Beautiful, is all by of teaching me the knowledge and showed me the way of successful living at childhood. In other words, my parentage, gave me both root established, and wings all to fly too.

Soaring with a good education is having the wisdom. Love is training a child early in life is enhancing and promising has given me victory with His power and God's guidance is the way. To train up a child and Love of God's inspiration inspires and, I have come to take this phrase to heart: "Train up a child in the way he (she) should go: and when he (she) is old, he (she) will not depart from it." And, that is the ultimate truth (Proverbs 22:6). And, unless the child doesn't know the values of being loved and appreciative of being capable of loving and that is so sad and is an ungrateful and unhappy child is in the heart. I am so blessed and so much very grateful that what was taught to my tender heart faith and word of love are of everlasting values and that faith sang through my tender heart's joy. There really is such a thing as enough except that peace and hope.

Hope in God that helps most is what teaches and guides on to be able to make important decisions and when you are in a good mood that is even the best time to reason along and good for character is life and power and rightly observed "Happiness is the Lord," so memorably sang by Ira F. Stanphill. Greatness in the heart is legacy and real happiness that is totally, dependent on God's love, as my special sufficiency is of Him, yes, divine is God. Of same grace is source of my knowledge and wisdom, glorious victory and power. God is love and endures for one's success; He is one that is expert in character building and, even building family and community.

All of His grace feasible and that is happiness is life and that makes me to know the joy is God's love hopes and, makes everything unlimited to me, all because His love like Him forever. His is an unfailing and unconditional and sustainable love and, living His love is assured cheerful thoughts. Behold, His love is joy and brings always positive outcome, which ignites a loving and happy heart, and you can't have either without the right mindset. Pure heart of love involves one being of a willing mind and is being risk in commitment, and faithfulness as a responsible child of the living God. In my case, my happiness is to be devoted and obedience to the living God and as well of His is Word of God's wisdom, which is what results this inspiration for my happiness.

I have love for you to relax, and because with God all things are possible, there is joy is also is within us. And, I don't want to scare you more than bless, because we are in this journey together. But, truth is this, don't let anyone fool you that you can't be a better person, for you can be if you choose to become and that is in the hand of God is a choice between you and Him and happiness is a commitment to make that choice. So, try to take a deep breathe and relax is of joy! Remember, do not be afraid seek from God His kindness and inspiration and remember, He is all of love, wisdom, joy, peace, happiness, success, knowledge, understanding mind, power to heal and carry you. Oh yes, that is so true carries through anything humanly imaginable and beyond.

God can through anything, and grow you mature is grace is growth and confidence to do anything all is possible. Remember, never be afraid more than trusting more for happiness comes from within and is not the absence of conflict, and is not measured by the wealth of this world. It is not nor is all by the amount of money you have that makes you happy but by God's love and is grace that is a sufficient power to heal and help you cope is that ability to cope, do your little part yours is more to pray, is do it to work is serve, watch trust and your little effort every bit put into works and is joy and that will add up and before you know greatness is in the heart and inspires!!

I have to do what is the love that is ultimate and happiness is not the absence of conflict either. Is not what defines you, nor does the limitation for your life measures is love of God is for you. That is why I want you to relax and, Scripture teaches, us to be thankful, "whatever your hand finds to do it with all your might" (Eccl. 9:10). It sounds to me to be hopeful and be glad to serve and work for God. No matter what you do is something, even sweet prayer to others helps. Because one can be happy as one decides to be, even with all the limitations, flaws; isn't it so much wonderful that even when one's life's full of turmoil's you can still smile and be happy in knowing God is with you? I'm thrill in what, am blessed to do and not what limits. It is possible to live a happy life because that is a gift of God and you don't wander for is what fills you most!!

That is Joy is and so happiness is neither until for you to have all the wealth of this world or to have billions of dollars, naira, sterling pounds and all the greener pastures of green world. Is purely love of a choice to make but be contented with what you have and do it rightful way is be happy and cherry and more is happiness is of the Lord. Put your little effort to do well and that is for me what a privilege to be able to contribute and give my love and work on reflection. Giving from what I have been given and that shows the passion to bless is a gift of God and not based on my giving just money when I can afford, is good to do, but I can give of my time and effort and is to joy to give encouragement and offer hope to anyone. So, be happy as you want and give of what you have mostly to those who are most as needy and impacting the world is great love too.

A needy and broken heart and I am very happy from deep within is my joy and attitude to be in place is being happy and not always unhappy and sad and, self-pity party going always. Is of joy and we can endure as much as we have faith and hope and love going on for us with also, a little gift of love. You don't have to be a billionaire to qualify you before have happiness, it is the good news and even though most of us are not millionaires, and despite that fact, we can still be happy and have ability to cope with our situation and still be effective person and contributing your little part. To change you and the world, you have to first change your negative attitude and views is not all about money, how you look at life and things could affect your thoughts heart is.

Happiness comes inside not on things but God's Inspiration leads, loves and guides us to be inspirers. Happiness is to love life and, be helpful to others proverb says it all, "Happy people love life most of the time." I am happy most of the time and is given that love and happiness with joy that comes all from inside and Proverb three also confirms, "Happy is the man that findeth wisdom, and the man that getteth understanding." That simple the answer to the above question, I posed, it comes from above more and it is tough part to swallow by many of us as many don't have the gut to stand up for the truth and to search and seek. Seek for inspiration and for it to be found is from God's wisdom and any person with a lucrative hobby is you have to put your heart and mind and every little effort results a good amount of joy and happiness for comes as success.

What keeps you happy inspires of your passion and motivates that's what you love to do. Singing and writing and dancing, motivating people and reaching to give lifting hand and for me all of uplifting hearts and inspiring are among some of my hobbies. I also do love to read a lot as well, many activities with arts and crafts. Do you have creative mind? Is a good hobby that takes heart of love for people is a must have inspiration for the passion who love life all the time is the love of God in your heart that is by words and action of His is happiness and creative you can be.

They love God and God loves them back and living life of love is of God is good all the time, not most of the time. I find it fascinating and that is so true! Happy is the person with love and a hobby, if you utilize your skills, using your talent to do something productive, it keeps you busy and engages your mind and thoughts wisely and creatively. What is your hobby? Is it good or bad? Do you care about others or are you just living for "you, me, mine and I"? Happiness is of God and also comes from good character as is what God requires of us and of good training is a discipline of mental and behavior and that too is another work as a book that will help to bless us also is living a dream that power is of God and manifestation that love is awesome inspiration.

Do you invest your time and energy wisely? Do you know how and when to apply your God's given potentials and gifts and skills to make most of your life and happiness? From my childhood, I learned a good character education, and having education is different from using education. And unity and character and success and money in life also revival and quality living all are important and not just money. My young and old friend-money as a medium of exchange matters a lot, but as this word of wisdom state, "money and class do not go hand-in-hand." We need to grow up with the intelligence to think positively, for quality thought comes from wisdom and likewise to keep money. There is power and prospect more with wisdom and that happiness and character as it is what makes for joy and in soundly raising our children-that is hope for all of us! You can't find happiness, unless you ask from God and that means you have to seek for it.

You have to search for it and it is inevitable and Proverbs three verse thirteen confirms, "Happy is the man that finds wisdom, and the man that getteth understanding." That part is the simple answer, but often many find that truth a hard to swallow. If you don't search with all your heart and believe that anything positive can happen, then is problem for it probably won't. When you have the wisdom, skills and have the confidence and know what happens and how it is done and when and who does how then you can work to achieve the desire goal with your God's given potential. Power is inspiration is words of wisdom that makes a difference in human life mostly.

As always believe we can gain from both formal and informal education (word-based). I also believe strongly in the healing Word of life just as in the life-giving power of prayer all of them and academic/character education matters, especially for our children they need both and a solid quality education is foundation and this work has also emphatically emphasized on the need and, focus on molding the youth and family unity because I cherish my family and friends and I also believe in my tradition of faith and as always; this also features tips on using unconditional love and wisdom in raising and accepting and encouraging today's youth to give them a positive life and better outlook in life with a brighter future and that is why this is work of God's love is also an ideal gift for every family believer or not, all inspiration meliorates the heart and blesses.

The Book of James says, All perfect gifts come from the very Source (1:17); ultimately, all of our true wealth comes from the riches of faith, wisdom, knowledge, love, and happiness. As God always gives us the best and to those who love and live for Him, happiness is waiting for us also to take it blessing of the believers and to take it by the reigns and soar with it as God is in the detail. Absolutely, in all aspects of life that is the truth and all circumstances too. The simple fact is that happiness is offered as a free gift of love that is found within us not all about exterior.

Though we received this happiness not of our own power, but from the power of our dear Lord and Savior from above, who speaks love to every heart. Everyone who understands knows "God is love" that desires universally. We still need to put the effort to find out what our goals in life are and that is when. The Lord's hand is in control of everything, and He has blessed us all with this precious gift of happiness. We must remember, how well we can utilize this happiness depends on how much effort we put into. Believe it or not, our responsibility matters in every situation and it makes a huge difference. If we focus, and look in the right places and have the right attitude. And commit heart also to positive things, we can be contented and that is what we need as well to do, it brings happiness, will not elude us. In essence, we are blessed to pursue all.

Authority is given for the pursuit of happiness we are given just as in the case of joy and love, happiness comes from the heart and from a person's attitude much as God gives grace and is a blessing. There are no conditions set for it one's happiness; what matters is what is in your heart and mindset how you want to make it work for you. So happiness is of the Lord God is joy. This is knowledge, along with an undying faith, and love will help you to decide what makes you happy. Sincerity, wisdom, gratitude, hope and peace, joy, faith, love, patience, trust, obedience, "honesty is the best policy," proverbs and it works..... the list could go on and on. These are just some of the qualities that result in happiness and that is power of the hidden treasure of integrity.

Sometimes, when we are not in the best of moods, we realize that true happiness can only be felt when we are in the right frame of mind. Please remember to make sure your character is what makes enough room in your heart for your happiness, is the attitude and manner that we see things at times that character determines your passion, and everyone has a different passion from within. That is what makes us unique individuals and ultimately, I have noticed greatness is only achieved with help of God's love, passion from within and nothing makes me happy than comes from within me, finding inspiration and love of God that is what motivates most the joy within.

For those of you who already love to research and to gain knowledge and wisdom, you may have observed the Joseph Addison quote that "three grand essentials to happiness in life are something to do, something to love, and something to hope for." Definitely, he raised very valid points, because I found them to be essential in my quest for happiness and that is where I derive joy. Ultimately, the heart holds everything that is good or bad in our lives, but just how effective we embrace the good matters. Sometimes we can be in the best of moods, while at other times we may be frustrated and unhappy, which affects one's ability to function at one's full potential.

We must all remember that during the bad times to keep faith and hope alive, because we will get through the storm. Ultimately, happiness is not the absence of storm or anything that is bothering us be it anxiety or fear God had the cure and how to overcome them for us but trust in Him is what prevents. We must remember to pray fervently and when things go wrong, don't go wrong with them there is always conflict in life and happiness is not from outside than outside is from within more and is interior than exterior things. Situation will always be there in life and it is of concerns but God gives us the ability to cope with any situation that challenges us and that is why the need to seek inspiration from Him is crucial to help us more is not revenge but pray.

I am grateful I learned that secret from my parents as a child. It is important that we continue to get on bended knees and pray to our Lord and Savior so that we can maintain (inner) our strength and remain on the right path. No matter what anyone else says, you cannot do it on your own power to get through life without love and guidance of God, because no man can do it, comprehend the magnitude of love and blessings that God gives to us to ensure a prosperous life. Finding right direction and guidance for the future life that ends in leadership, is by seeking it is from the inspiration of God's love. He is the wonderworking spiritual power, positive influence.

For us is sure is Right there is how to live a triumphant life of hope and victory.

Luckily, there isn't anything that ever passes God's power, grace, mercy, and unfailing love, which unconditional the everlasting. He has the power to restore joy to no end, and we will always need the joyous gift of grace from above to use as a guiding light. As the following says, "But ye beloved, building up yourself on your most holy faith, praying in the Holy Ghost, keep yourself in the love of God" (Jude 20). Ultimately, greatness in the heart is achieved when we look for mercy and happiness is from the Lord! Have you ever heard of the proverb that says, "A person's value is that which he sets upon himself"? I couldn't agree more with this. I know that there are some of you out there who are still skeptical, but I am here to share that, which I know in my heart, is truths it makes perfect sense. Do you believe or not? You are chosen vessel and capable than you know for we can all learn to our potential and thank God for that I am daily being thankful, in all circumstances, and in His being wonderworking spiritual power who offers.

That gives me the ability and capability to achieve for me my blessings. I can make it for as my strength is not of my own, but of my heavenly Father, and, "He gives power to the weak, and to those who have no might He increases strength" (Isaiah 40:29); strength to endure to end! And for that, I thank my Father in heaven for the release of that peace, joy, and happiness that He makes all available for me. I stand on those promised words claiming all of them daily so all by His grace and faith. I know you will enjoy this work especially, is for us and for evangelism also. "Evangelism is one beggar telling another beggar where to find bread." Are you hungry and/or, unhealthy, doubting about your situation? I encourage you don't be frightened but, pray more is to watch, serve and trust more than being fearful. We should all keep in mind that we need to be keep focused and continue to look up to God more and is to look ahead instead of dwelling over what had already been done, for you can't undo is not like the computer that is all true but is Joy.

Taste for your heavenly Father's love, for your happiness and success, every blessings, is in His care and wealth is of abundance of grace as in all facets of life fulfilling and enrichment is divine blessings all His favors for His is interventions for us spiritually, physically, emotionally, mentally including finance, if you believed in miracle of His love and power, you can't be poor! And, even if you were there is no problem, even bad character once all is surrendered could be a thing of the past and, anything is possible with Him and also is why a big change is possible for you by Him, provided you are willing to let Him have His love in your heart will work it out for you all. I am so grateful that I have learned much wisdom guided by His gentle hand in my life.

Think twice and live by faith and always remember: "Hath not God chosen the poor of this world rich in faith, and heirs of the kingdom, which he hath promised to them that love him (James 2:5). But, you mustn't just sit and folds your hand to be happy and happier, a little effort is better than doing nothing. Inspiring word of wisdom, not a question but statement of fact as it is possible with God, uses our circumstances of life and turn things around for us and we can be who He had intended for us to be and we can run isn't it? Yes it is and could be either way also; if you don't make yourself available for Him to bless you and be all that you can be and it helps.

I thank God for the privilege of knowing Him personally and for enjoying Him and great thing to experience His peace and ability to forgive and forget is true test of greatness I keep in mind best is yet to come, for God is good and just as such, encourages we need to keep focused and continue to look ahead. Instead of dwelling over what has already been done. God is Joy is who gives us grace to endure and focus more on positive thoughts than negatives and helps place positive things that is, I have found that praying on a consistent basis can give us the inspiration to empower and love ourselves and others. Our hearts become more educated, and we begin to open our hearts with love, rather than having a hateful heart, which is part of the problem in the world today as seen!!!

It is why so many people can't add quality to their life and miss their blessings, including real happiness and inner peace. Is which with joy can brighten their lives with hope, and they are not living their full potentials is because they are not receptive to receiving the blessings that are priceless and simple best treasures, the Lord has available to them because they are disconnected are missing. Many are crying of real living eternal "bread of heaven." That is not being poor, but is to be richer by faith and willing more to be humble and receive what is best of life given from their heavenly Father above sure; I am one of those beggars, but am of a greater gratitude there is hope is joy being a sojourner and finding what I was looking for in life that has blessed me much and even makes evangelism highly of my passion and that is what I am thankful for it as God is who anoints and calls me is so good to me and it has come to pass and that is one primary reason why I am more grateful for the power of inspiration that God's grace has extended and bestowed.

Is with wisdom and enables one's life to be happy and from the mind to be screwed up is what inspires and as well no one can ever stops you from using what you have to bless you and others. You can be as happy as you want to be, if you make up your mind to be and trust in God more and use what you are given and tap from it, is limitless potentials and now, this is my big question, "Between you and me, where can real happiness be found? This is an intelligent question to ask, correct? Words of wisdom tell us the answer fairly simple though some you may think it is a tough truth to believe and are still searching the whole wide world daily for it and in all the wrong places and, Scriptures tells us the ultimate truth that, "Godliness with contentment is great gain" (1st Timothy 6:6). Proverbs three and verse thirteen summarizes: "Happy is the man that findth wisdom and the man that gettteh understanding!" That is the simple answer, but also a very hard to swallow truth and if you don't believe you can't appreciate knowledge and love, let alone the wisdom that only God Almighty gives and that is where it first begins and blessed!

Perhaps, many don't even want to hear that part, but hey I can't help but to tell you the whole and truth just plain priceless truth as is and I am so sorry for that is all that I know. Indeed, having only money does not mean you are happy. However, in today's world, we are after mere money for our physical need rather than growing up spiritually with the goal to be wise and bless maturely. That aspect being wise with maturity speaks voluminously about this subject matter of love and wisdom, inspiration, faith, family, leadership, ministry, happiness and education matter.

This is education inspired of God's wisdom and hopefully, can satisfy ourselves and bless all our families and communities, making this world a better place to live and leaving it better. It is all about finding and living live of love inspiration my philosophy, All inspiration meliorates the heart and launches dreams to come true-Caroline Thompson (2013). Is with God's letters we can read and understanding as it is very informative and direct to its core values is in achieving. Excellence through spirituality to become a better person and more informed, educating the heart and transformed and that is what is renewed mind with a huge heart of love and compassion and able to handle tough things of life as well and cope with that changes excepted and some abrupt!

Many things of life are sudden and unexpected and take God's grace to adjust and that is why inspiration is a necessity. A heart that can inspire others; It makes others happy and you can make a difference as a responsible leader and follower either way it doesn't make you less and/or more and a lot of difference for you are blessed and can look to the need of one and all and make others happy and offer full services as well to them as much as you do to yourself and family. It is apparent to love and inspire. Life goes beyond mutual friends and your love can even reach out more and to bless others and positively even to influence those touched in your life to aspire too.

Is how and when, you use it wisely is that wisdom appreciated and use to glorify God and bless His people. Believe or not, from childhood, I learned the lessons from family about love of God and happiness that it comes from above and inspires to encourage our hearts and, inspires also you and me, and countless others and is all about love that is of wisdom and power of God's word makes miracles and that is based on exercising your faith and that takes you to higher level.

Do you believe or not, and do you know how much love can give you confidence to be able and to be a blessing to others and not just for yourself and family only? Education achieves as well as in school but is very different from that gained from knowledgeable insights of God's love and wisdom is for living every moment with hope and love and joy. But, when you combine the two you have an excellent education also on which to build upon and the building block with His education is the solid foundation that is unshakable and please, "Let us not become weary in doing good, for at the proper time we will reap a harvest if we do not give up."(Galatians 6:9: NIV). Praying that this will bless and strengthen us and our community and beyond to better all.

I pray that we can offer also get love and encouragement, gives limitless blessings and of opportunity too. I am blessed by God and others and so thankful that from their inspiration God has blessed me to be able blessing them and others as well by inspiring hearts. What a joy to be one among those being given opportunity to participate in this wide world ministry of love and showing mercy sharing words of love and inspiration much to grow in God amazing grace love. I am thrill as well that anything positive can happen as your wishes is and, yourself and family too is believing that as well is all about making positive change and the world will be much better.

Oh sure, as well than we met as well love is the foundation. A gift God loves us all love us to soar and love is the key for us all to soar beyond our numerous situations expected and the unexpected, that our greatness is in the heart and it is in our humility before Him is revealing too. And, we need to all remember that we must be honest with ourselves when assessing our life as well our character also; remember love is all we need and inspiration that offers hope and joy. It is love in the heart that measures the true colors and giving comes from pure heart and always is a gift of love that we can offer more encouragement in words and actions, not so much in terms of always of monetary value, for amount of happiness experienced depends on what comes from within more is that me. Happiness comes not from outside is more from within and not on things.

That is massed. It is not all about so much wealth in terms of dollar and naira and sterling pounds in the bank, but is love, and it depends on what you make of your life and what is in your heart and mind and what you believe and worship. From childhood, I learned that, "Happiness is of the Lord", from His words of wisdom to my heart and, I heard times without number and Joy sings as well, which was song sang by Ira StanPhil and now is one of my favorites among many others; as I love to sing and be happy and rejoice in the Lord's love everyday that happiness is vital, is also it is what it is results from inside is the joy and the Joy inside of you is the feeling am saying this based on what obtained in my situation and also is for counting my blessings are more than uncountable it is and inexhaustible God is Joy! He puts a smile on me my badge too!

Continuing on words of wisdom, it is very important, just as we need healthy food to give us of energy, stamina and to keep our bodies in a peak form, we also need healthy hearty loving words and knowledge that keeps not only body strong but to enrich body and mind and spirit is of love is inspiration and also spiritual and physical matters as both all is for personal growth and professional development and God is awesome for my heart, mind and spirit and results self-help work and improvement of my life which, I thank God for inspiration and love and His Joy alive!

Words of wisdom are always encouraging, and it is best that we take these words and tailor them to our own situation, for each of us defines happiness differently. I know that there are many people out there who don't want to follow words of wisdom – all they want is to find something that's a quick fix or to make a quick buck. What these people will learn in the long run is that the skills and abilities that they possess deep down can only be realized by living an honest, wholesome life. Sadly, in this day and age, "People know more that is false than is true."

Continuing on with words of wisdom, it is very important that, just as we need healthy food to keep our bodies in peak form, we also need healthy words and knowledge to keep our heart, mind and spirit of hope and is a healthy way of life for finding peace of mind is success to me is being at peace and so freeing and relaxing. Be careful of what you read in your quest for a heart of greatness. Have you ever stopped to wonder what this world is all about, who matters? Who and what matter most? Have you ever asked yourself why you are here and where you are and/ or will you be going? Have you taken thought as to when your lease on life runs out, where will you and your heart be going? Think of life as a matter of the heart, and focus more on God!

We all need to do a thorough search of our hearts as well as a thorough self-evaluation of each and know more about ourselves, and greatness is by living an honest wholesome life. If you have not been happy lately, you should know that something is missing. We must be honest with ourselves and realize that we cannot blame anyone but ourselves for our own happiness more or less it is that we are searching from the wrong Source and places, placing thoughts on such as I have stated earlier, God always gives the best to those who leave their choice for Him to decide.

And is all within reach, for we are responsible for finding that happiness from within. No matter what age you may be, you can still achieve happiness, but you must start realizing that is a choice for you to make how you want your life to be and for me, now is the time – not tomorrow, not next week – but now. The choice is completely up to you regarding the kind of heart that you possess, and remember that life is a choice and there is also the difference between good/bad and its consequences and reward all are something that follows you and your character is all along is a choice and will determine as what direction your heart will go, and if your character is of good quality, then you will be able to have an open heart ready to embrace love and change with love.

Awesome is to be able to write and inspire each other to live life fully through creative of expression of my faith in His love is greatest gift of all is that grace and faith with peace of mind. That I am so privilege among those given the blessings and all the priceless treasures that life has brings my way makes me so happy to be among inspirers and blessings from above, and I don't underestimate the power of His touch and love for Jesus is Lord and ever shall be that is priceless Gift of God of all greatness is His Love. Never underestimate power of God's love and miracles.

Neither love please for God is Love and Inspiration and, important of love and inspiration cannot be overstated in one's life. He gives you life and hope with real happiness and inspiration. Is what happens to me, when we allow Him and opens us up with all the joys life has to offer and meliorates the heart and also encourages and inspires to help us dream and also helps launching! Often, many of us limit to be so alienated from Him and themselves from being blessed as they are so afraid of embracing God's love and refuse to accept and give and wonder why what makes people happier is to become so sad. I often wonder why not be of joy and rejoice to reactive also.

Open up and receive and with warm heartfelt of love and give and that is the capacity to soar, when you are blessed with all both Source and resourceful resources all of His provisions. I see the remedy as made for my healing, He has the means and methods to achieve all that too are of the love from God for you and joy to think love and positively live your life to its fullest truly. Life and meaningful is living happily that love and power of inspiration, wonderworking power. Is what I have with His love been empowered and is always to me solely very romantic love with God's love letters I romance and found real thrill being in His presence is fullness of joy always.

Do you rely on God or others to give you a loving heart or solely rely on your hope too? Is do not rely good for you must start by thinking your own positive thoughts and following your own path but it is best being yourself and relying totally on God for God's guidance only is best. Assurance that is blessed Hope and blessings matters. It matters most and that is the number one principles for successful living and victorious life too. Sadly, in this day and age as I observed in the introduction of this work we are a part of society that is in eminent danger of destroying itself and all the good things that are gloriously given. His love gives grace and life with hope and joy and peace of mind. And, is what is joy that says hope exists in all of us when we trust and obey to follow and do God's will is the best for me to align, progress and is moving on up and is hope.

Forward than accepting limitations to be my stumbling blocks I choose happiness over all that and nothing can limits me as my happiness comes from within and likewise joy that sustains. As the following phrase says, "take heart and deal with care of the possible and God will handle your impossible." We all just need to understand that a positive attitude with an open mind is so crucial to being happy, but it all begins from the heart and of your being willing mind as well is a willing heart and mind can be interchangeable when it comes to matters of the heart is God first.

I can think positively for myself because my heart is blessed with His love and laughter by God's leading me daily in His grace words and through himself, and so I am thankful for the privilege of knowing Him and fellowshipping with Him and have the good time of life for we pray, laugh, talk, walk and the more I read the Bible. It is more I study more commutations and more happiness and more laughter with Him is daily and inseparable through eternity is my life.

There is no-ending and fellowship with God helps me to be more conscious of love and of His presence in my life and I love Him so much and, I do not want to act badly and do what displeases Him either. It is so freeing and I feel the power of His presence is ever-present in all that I do and say and, if we are not happy with our character, we can take the knowledge that we learn from Him and improve our character and overall outlook on life. Once we have done this, we can realize that it is possible to have the joy and happiness in our lives that we all need to do.

Since serving humanity offers me more joy for my happiness and passionate purpose is of more hope. One of all the things I had prayed is the manifestation of Hs glory in my life that is joy a dazzling glory of God is the perfume that I wear and badge that identifies who and whose I am. I am, when we wear, is our expression is the most important. I love to the fact that I am one of His joyful servants and students, and I am learning more and everyday living, I am always on adventure. Yes, adventurous and courageous and inspirational to be of God's redeeming purpose and it is for our faith journey that is never in vain and the grace outweighs the cross is for joy for me is to smile. It is in our humility that I have found my true strength and laid aside the garments and rending is of my heart, and I thank God that this day has come to pass in my life.

I know, as I am always happy. It is when I make others happy, I feel great and it makes me feel so good inside. I derive my joy. From loving and making people happy mutual benefits as I see and that is the support is of Him and He leads me to the right path of life, and people too. When was the last time you thought of love and inspiration being part of your happiness and that you can be happy if you want to be though it depends mostly on God and the amount you need? The amount of happiness that I experienced always comes from within and a bubble is that deep joy within me and I asked earlier between you and me, where can happiness be found?

Here is the deal and words of wisdom tell us the answer fairly simply, know though many will think it is tough truth and I am so sorry for I don't know what else to do than to tell it truth is reality of life. We neither must nor forget that is happiness how well we can utilize any of our God's given potential is a blessing there is awesome way of appreciating and making the most of our efforts with what we are blessed with and treasure too. Daily when also utilizes for the glory of God and utilize it happiness depends on how much effort you put into it, this work shares how God supports and leads me through my dilemmas, demonstrates that power of His Love's works!

Please, friend let's take all to God in prayer and also believe in the power of inspiration. For it blesses and is mostly, infinite redemptive love of God and wisdom, is for inspiration and offers nourishment to those who hunger and thirst for it and is sacred way of living, loving and relating with God and as well your family and friends and others world-wide in a friendly way. And manner and from His words of love and inspiration; Friend, till our second series of this in another edition that says God is good and there are more to chat on the power of love and faith and power of inspiration. Love As, it is the only adequate Way is more than enough is the banner over us is power for me and I am truly blessed truly loved and am more than overjoyed all love.

I have is to render love and thanks I am lost of words in transition to describe the right words there properly, there is no word for me at all to thank Him enough, is not even close as for all that am given is way too much and All, I can do best is to thank God adequately, but even with that there is not enough words for me to it as is beyond marvelous and super generous to me Is for me all is and what I know is to give back of all my heart, love and life daily and serve Him love lifetime. I see, Love heals, blesses, empowers. Love is of God and one another, is to share it. Trust to serve and understand His order; watch and be thankful and give heart is for all that what brings more love there are blessings of obedience to God as well as lots of love with marvelous blessings, as you always think of others, love, make friends with them and cooperate and share of your heart of joy to obey God's Words of Life is all that matters and I have a greater cause for my gratitude, much love Him as well my new assignment-inspiring all hearts. As we go through life, even though we may feel alone, especially through trying times, He is always with us.

Working and walking with us, side-by-side, cheering us on and ensuring our peace and is of mind and it is a great gift that is and works best your faith, security, sustenance, and happiness all He offers. Solutions to our problems and blesses us no matter what, and He only wants all the best of life for you and me. No matter how the world changes, God never changes, but stays the same and consistent, and God is the only constant love through eternity that I know of and that is what says all that there is all about Him. I must return thanks and wear my badge of love. I am so grateful for what God requires, provides is joy for me to practice it daily and Ultimately, love is deeper is joy with enough effort, we can achieve whatever we put our minds to, and we can be comforted in the fact that we can leave the impossible up to God and do just the possible!

That is all we are capable doing and gives all our very best is with fervent love is prayers! God puts a smile on me aglow my face and this is how it unfolds beautifully is from inside. Also on the outside shining for His glory shines through my face and radiates. Filled full of abundant and radiant of God's love, joy is sure of my "chief wine." Surely, God is a Blessing, Joy is Light who lights my life and fills of my heart so thankful that we are all blessed, gifted with something unique joy to me more a lot that always we are working in the business be it at home, at office in a glass building and in the hut is of His grace. Love sends this message of empowerment is love heals us from the soul it is, when we are faced with adversity in our lives, I can attest to the fact that He can calm of our hearts and anxiety and fears and lessens and prevents from further panic. And brokenness speak from what I do know and did prevent(s) mine and through leadership of the Holy Spirit as I have this evidently speaks voluminously and is self explanatory.

I am blessed and glad to say that His only by His grace is what can carry us and heals, leads us to salvation, mends broken heart shows you true love is unconditional, everlasting when the whole world has gone wrong, He is the only one you can look up to. No man can stop and help you with your broken heart because that is a job that only God can do for you. Awesome, is to trust and by faith listening to Him, His words, trusting Him is all healing; can do miraculously every deep rooted problem in my life was uprooted! Love much loves me inspiration is of God is power as every counsel, plan, desire, expectation and every activity of the enemy you read them rendered null and void, unchained my blessings that were chained very incredible and adorable. Spiritual experience is Am so excited, ultimate Power, He is a Friend. It is a blessing and so take this knowledge to heart, for it rewards us as it is empowered, educates heart and mind is renewed and for heart, and gives us all is peace of mind that is priceless in the process, thank you!

Chapter Twelve

Knowledge is the Power needed for Success and Happiness

"…Power belongeth unto God."
– KJV: Psalms 62:11

Practical words of wisdom are part of a good education that makes for a good future and for greatness in the heart. It's a quality education that inspires the heart to achieve this greatness and it is capable of molding and transforming your life. We need to stand up and take action with the inspiration that we have. When we teach our children to love with spiritual inspirational words of wisdom, we are solidifying a prosperous future for them and that is hope with a brighter life.

Think in terms of how one's overall life is improved with knowledge. A healthy, well-lived life brings about peace of mind, which is priceless. Unquestionably, there is no doubt in my mind that the greatest of all blessings in the world are good health and character. Certainly, these words of wisdom support that so well, for "good health requires that you have your body, mind, and soul balanced." In my quest for trying to live a better life, I realized that I must also surrender my heart with sincere love and thankfulness to our Creator on an hourly basis praying.

I also realized that His inspirational words of wisdom are imperative for me to keep my faith in Him. I am sustained by my faith, and it allows me to overcome hurdles in life with joy and gratefulness. Faith creates an atmosphere where one can pray confidently, because "with prayer, we can move mountains and that is so through for me that is life-giving power of God's word and I strongly believe and effective is the sustaining life-wire and hopefully friend this will bring many blessings to you as you read and savor this chapter and benefit your life always.

And I pray for those of you who still don't know, anyone can communicate directly with our Lord. We can all speak our heart to God and He can hear you and will respond to you. The beauty lies in the fact that once we humble ourselves to ask for His help, He will always make sure that we are taken care of in His time. Behold, His love is reachable, immeasurable, that is gracious. The joy of inspiration is based on the foundation of our faith our hearts are capable of anything as long as we have hope in God and faith not on just ourselves or other things of life is always God's way best. His love gives us grace and hopes with vision to be at liberty and is joy.

It is always refreshing to share the fact that once the heart is inspired to flourish and to excel, one's success and happiness can definitely be achieved. Thank God for His love and of vision, for He has given you the knowledge of wisdom, which in turn gives you hope. Words of wisdom are more than inspirational words of proverbs – they are the foundation for a successful life filled with a joy, happiness, and love like no other. Once one's heart is open and ready to be empowered, we realize that we are capable of great thoughts because we have an informed mind. Words of wisdom are uplifting and give us hope for a pure, healthy life and it means so much!

When you hear words of wisdom, do not treat these words casually or carelessly, because if you do this you will not gain the understanding that is embedding in these words. Use them to benefit your life and to give you love in your heart; for you can't love others without first loving God and yourself, by succeeding in taking words of wisdom to heart, you will always live life of hopeful, blessed life. We must remember that in our quest for greatness, we should not focus on amassing estates of wealth, but rather focus on pursuing goodness. Knowledge is power, and all that matters is doing what is in our hearts' best interest and for others as well. Once you tap into the passion that you possess, your heart will become thoughtful and appreciative, and you will.

You will know the joy and succeed in life. As a Hallmark Connections Card summed up so succinctly, "Success is not in how well-known you are but how well-respected…not in your power to take but your willingness to give. Success is the small voice you hear when you know you have done your best – Wishing you happiness and all the happiness in the world." It is true and was this card, a graduation card given to me years ago, that helped open doors for me also as its inspiration took me to places that I never knew and in the light of the words of wisdom joy in my heart. I ponder over the words of that card; they still move and inspire me to this day.

I have been through a lot in my lifetime, whether they be challenges or triumphs, but as I think back over those times, the one thing that was consistent was my constant prayers day in and day out, and I watch and keep serving and trusting God and miracle of believing in His Love is inspirational words of wisdom and that is awesome wonderworking spiritual power that wins it all for me and my health and security with peace of mind and contented adjustment to cope daily. No one knew how to motivate me except the Lord, for He alone understands the heart of a lonely and wounded child. As I think back to all of the monetary gifts I received upon graduation, is I realized that the money is all gone, but that card and the words included in it have stayed within.

It stayed with me to this day. Those moving words will continue to inspire my heart for the rest of my life. It actually turned out to be the best graduation gift I received. A life of real happiness always revolves around inspiration and how a quality education inspires the heart and opens many doors. Greatness is in the heart, and the heart needs love and wisdom to nourish it so that it can grow is with grace and faith for that to happen and that is the knowledge needed always for success is from God and likewise love, joy and power of inspiration can't be ignored.

We all need this, because without love, which is the foundation for a great heart, we will not succeed. Love and happiness is not just feeling good about yourself, but feeling good about others as well, for "love is the cornerstone and the foundation of life." Words of knowledge and wisdom can cure practically any anxieties you may have as well as well boosting your memory. They also help improve your sleep, because you are thinking happy, positive thoughts on a daily consistent basis. They can cure a number of ailments both physical and spiritual, and they play a part in creating a loving heart and is therapeutic as it offer hope more to a lonely heart and heals.

But unfortunately, many people have failed to realize that this is even possible. In the previous chapter, it was cited that "Happiness is the Lord," which was memorably stated by this songwriter Ira F. Stanphill. Happiness results in success, and important fact to know is that love is of God and because we all need to live by the power of love and inspiration ad living life to the fullest Love in one's heart constitutes happiness, and when there is no love in your heart and when your efforts do not bring you satisfaction, your happiness will be limited and constantly I am reminded that all knowledge and inspiration emanated wisdom comes from God is Author.

It is the mind that makes the body to think wisely you have to put the thought to work. It takes heart power before the mind to think positive thoughts and you will come to the realization that words of wisdom not only inform our minds, but they also educate the heart with love daily. It is that which in turn inspires heart to be of glimpses of more hope. Above all, it enlightens and empowers us to realize this: We all need the mindset that "knowledge is power" and that is how also how happiness comes from above and inspire you and me and countless others. It is thought is free and what controls the heart controls the mind is of dedicated heart and mindset **is wisdom.**

I have learned and benefitted from the fact that knowledge continues to help me to grow as someone with a loving, inspirational heart. We must remember that "For as he thinketh in his heart, so is he: Eat and drink, said he to thee; but his heart is not with thee" (Proverbs 23:7). Hopefully, we can all appreciate sharing the inspirational words of wisdom for it is a pleasure. It is always a pure joy and my humble pleasure to be able to work with you because I am a friend of all, as you are part of my blessings. Do you invest your life wisely and relying in God also? I am constantly reminding myself that He is the most Highest, whose love amazing and unfailing.

I have found a profound thrill that happiness is of the Lord, inspiration, love and power. I have to be grateful to God that this work has challenged my life in so many ways. Definitely, it has opened my heart and my whole life and not just my eyes to new perspective and vision. But word cannot express my thanks to all of you using these healing words that give us hope. And in turn enable us to heal from inside. It helps me to heal from my illness as well. When there is life, there is hope for us to keep on moving ahead and inspire each other because there is God with us.

Which is a blessing we should always be grateful to have, for He has been a blessing in my life in so many times of needs and, I have gained so much wisdom guided by His gentle hand and the words of inspiration and that has helped in my thinking better than I was before, because inspiration encourages us to think wisely and there is joy and peace of mind that comfort me too. I am thankful that I allowed God to use me for His glory and honor. I have found many blessings in my life through these inspirational words of wisdom, and I pray that He continues to guide and direct me, administer to use people faithfully.

I am hopeful that inspiration we share together would encourage hearts and inspire them, so be hopeful and trust more in God, because in God we find protection, healing, recovery, and the passion to live our dreams to the fullest. It is of hope and joy, "Glory to God in the highest, and on earth peace among men with whom he is pleased" (Luke 2:14). I encourage you to live your life with inspiration and love and create a life you love to live. But please do not forget God. You may not get what you want but He will satisfy you in due time and season, that is if you continue to believe and trust God confidently and faithfully. He will satisfy and give your heart's desire. God is good, and that's the mind to be in place, for I have seen His manifestation.

I am committed to ensure that I love and serve and glorify His name and more and I pray commit your lifestyle to quality, not just living in a daily rut; seek wisdom for the good of your heart and mind. Live the life you imagined, but do not forget to serve unto God by loving others. Please, understand why I feel that this inspiration is meant to be shared. I'm not pressuring you, but I will say that I believe that you and I and, all should chase real happiness, beholding Love.

Behold, proverb inspires, "Wisdom is of God" and every moment is sharing happiness is twice as good as other gift of kindness for a life shared through happiness brings joy not only to you but also to others which is good for encouragement and inspiration. The following words of wisdom are so true: "Examine what is said more than who said it;" And, "When all else fails, read the instruction manual." Do you please mind friend, (young/old), we need to believe that love is a magnet that draws us together by heartstrings and, listening may be the most loving thing you and I can do today, each of us is a blessing from God and He cherishes us the same, regardless of who you are and of the situation that faces you and that is don't give up your love for Him ever.

It is a blessing and cherishing love and each other more will enable us to cherish family and friends and tradition of faith in God and the proverb says, "He who saves another life adds years to his (her) own." What is in your mind right now regarding inspirational words of God as well wisdom? What do you think of knowledgeable insight, and gaining of wisdom to walk in light? Please, dare to use your head wisely and productively, and remember; knowledge is the power needed for success and happiness, but love is the magnet that draws us together as friends and family and that changes everything!

CHAPTER THIRTEEN
Being in Love Changes Everything

"The greatest pleasure in life is doing what
people say you can't do."
– Walter Bagehot

I am certain that the power of inspiration is alive and well, and being in love with that sustaining power is what is important to achieve greatness in the heart. The Supreme Being brings the heart hope and joy in abundance, and the inspiration that results is what can launch everyone's dreams into reality. As our hearts are inspired, we become filled with passion, motivation, and enthusiasm more so than ever, being transformed by the love of God to grow!

As has been highlighted throughout this book, reciprocating love with kindness can be a wonderful feeling. This can be achieved simply by uplifting someone's heart when they are feeling down. One can easily reach out in love with a big hug, a smile, a friendly handshake, a prayer, a visit, or a number of other ways that are simple, and it works wonders to make the other person feel so much better. Offering love to share to someone who needs it is encouraging to them because it gives them healing thoughts, nothing like being of gratitude to every gift given.

Blessing, I am immensely grateful that our heavenly Father included me in His plan to spread love and happiness, namely by writing this book. He lives within our hearts, and of His miracles can touch everyone's lives. His greatness is in the heart, and He makes sure that His children are taken care of. He loves it when we are happy and in a good mood, and He wants us to have both balanced minds and hearts, so that we may live a healthy lifestyle. He capitalizes in changing our burdens to blessings, and He is the greatest of all doctors, for He is capable of His miraculously easing us of all of our doubts and troubling thoughts. I love the fact that He works around the clock for whatever emergency we may need Him to tend to. He is available to inspire and direct our hearts unto the path of wisdom. Please, reciprocate your love and kindness and is always of more blessings to be thankful for your gift and that is the joy of receiving with love.

The greatest thing in life is the ability to be able to love one another, so cherish your love and respect the love of others. He gives us life, so the least we could do is take to heart the ability we are given to love others. I've always known in my heart that God truly loves all of us, and in His loving kindness, He does not shrink from His love. He tells us daily that greatness is in each of our hearts, and that the love that we have in our hearts should be used for good things. As these words of wisdom encourage, "Use your power for good." Thankfully, I have always cherished being blessed with His undying love, which makes my heart so happy. I am always amazed at the depths of His love and His ability to love us so deeply.

Once you have been touched with His love, you will see that it changes everything. His love is the greatest gift and is a marvelous blessing. Yes, He promises us that we will have an abundantly satisfying life, and He offers that life to us freely, so it is our duty to give that love back, not only to Him, but to everyone around us. I am very happy that my heart is highly motivated and inspired by the words of love that God gives to us. Words cannot express fully or describe the overwhelming feeling that I get thinking about how encouraging words of love have been able to mend my broken heart when it has been broken and wearied and wounded all here I am as a blessing and over the years, He grants me life's richest blessings and love's richest joys.

Words of God's love have been my greatest source of inspiration sure has been amazing grace, "The law of the LORD is perfect, converting the soul: the testimony of the LORD is sure, making wise the simple. The statues of the LORD are right, rejoicing the heart: the commandment of the LORD is pure, enlightening the eyes" (Psalms 19:7-8). Bear in mind that whether or not you follow God's word is your heart's choice, and none of us are forced to follow Him, but if you do, is good for your life and can help you and will bless and change remarkably it inspired and transformed and empowers and, by the Holy Spirit to become that love for others is as all along highlighted, love empowers was shared how earlier in our discussion, introduction. Is if you may as that was a special way getting started on inspiring our hearts and He prepares us. Slowly, by becoming that love for others changes story to glory. It makes me feels better. It rejoices my heart to be able to be receptive and open to receiving God's love and is sharing my love with others. I have been blessed to give and receive love from family and friends alike and throughout the world. Together as friends, I have no other words to express but to say that I am so thankful for His helping me through them. The power of inspiration tells my heart that I must be forever faithful to God and to remain in His favor, be always abiding, live by that faith and as is His love refreshes, renews, sustains, satisfies, is what gives freely, liberated my life to share!!!

I am so grateful that God's love is plentiful enough to touch us all with His divine favors. And, I am also grateful that He has given me the tools and the strength to be able to write this in a book so that I can serve humanity in a positive way. As I reflect on the many people who have read my works and have said "Praise for the author," it touches my heart deeply as I cry with a feeling tears of joy and more than blessings for my thankfulness. Nothing ever becomes real until you experience to express it and that shows love that is within offers us the peace that is "joy unspeakable," power to do what we never thought that we could in wonderworking, is spiritual!

Yes, I do break down at times and cry – both with tears of joy and sadness. It is natural that sometimes we may feel great, but then there are other times when we may feel sad and it is okay. Discouraged? No! Whatever we are feeling, it is important to remember that this is part of what makes your heart the great vessel that it is. Yes, you can be sad, but please continue to let a little laughter into your heart. Love changes everything when you are able to keep faith and the hope and dreams alive, for today and for the future. Love reaches far and beyond and can touch everyone in such meaningful ways, and I always count my blessings for this. The joy that a heart can contain is an amazing and powerful force, it energizes us the more give love more received.

It makes me happy to be a part of this inspiration, "for the Lord, has done great things for us" (Psalms 126:13). I am filled with joy and,

330 | Carol Arit Thompson

"we are all have reason to rejoice, and I want to rejoice with you all, and even though we may be of different races, tribes, or tongues, we can always come together and share our love with one another, and that will be success story, and for that, "and we filled with joy". We may have never met or will never meet face-to-face, but we are still friends that can cherish and love one another. We can share our stories with one another. In the hopes that we can uplift each other to live prosperous lives together and also be able to do.

I have been blessed enough to watch and listen to some of you spreading your love on television, on the radio, in books and newspapers, on the internet, and in social media, which all are great available resources in reaching out and touching and inspiring each other with messages of love and information that are vital and some may not be all that palatable but a choice of love. I have also been able to share love at various engagements and conferences and is best expressed from one heart to the other, and both hearts can be blessed to benefit from the joy and power of it when we come together to support one another's appearances and speeches, are communicating.

Practically, we are showing our love and support to each other through your presence is a gift of love and that changes everything through effective listening benefits us all in the long run. And, when we pay close attention to motivational speakers in any forum, it shows we care and to respect ourselves and others to love and coming that by itself being there even better than money is supporting and is a form of encouragement and making us feel less alone and more accepted is very much being understood and the people we love and cared for are always our source of love.

When we are blessed with love, we can do so many things with kindness, to show and/or offer encouragement and compassion by words and actions and, it doesn't matter where we are; wherever it is we can send a word or two, of kind words of thoughts and celebrate love always. Whether it is at home, conference, at school, or at park love is in the heart and, we must take the time to listen to what is being said so that we can grow. Show that you care, are available, and can give your full support to one another. Love can come in many forms, and can extend from private to public forums, to churches, travelling missionaries, hospltals, hospital, and a number of other places; love teaches us obedience and effective listening and study skills is so minute is the little things that matters most too. But to me love is a passion and so huge and important also.

One of the many blessings that I am grateful for is the fact that it can honor God through socializing with many people the world over, and is hopeful that love works miracles I was able to be inspired to launch my dream of writing this book. Inspiration can give us hope, love, and can increase our faith and energy. I always believe more love creates more blessings, if we care to show a heart of dedication to serve, love and obey God. From my experience, is uncountable surprises have resulted. He blesses and daily helps us to do His will, by making people that come across our paths blessings and, I have been challenged for He sends angels working on my behalf Much as we bless them, also much many do cherish and appreciate little efforts we put to work.

They are kind people that sometimes reciprocate and surprise us with their blessings. Just by our being dedicated stewards. Dedicating efforts faithfully for the services we do. Much kind of ways are you never may know that, your dedication to service is love. Touching those served for hope and your blessings to them God's rewards. Many with thoughtful hearts need hope too; Your love shown are rewarding, it may even create more love and definitely, you don't know is how far what does with love can, it results much more than you offered. Love can go so far; just with a little touch of kindness to the needy heart can results marvelous blessing that comes your way.

You can do a little for someone, but it went far and created an impact. Mine resulted more than what was offered, of hope and productivity to be thankful. There is more joy that inspires the heart, realizing that can results with many gifts; makes love a heart's power. Love in more than given away even, brings you more blessings for happiness than ever, which you may never, thought of in your widest dreams, is and hopeful and fulfilling and bluing is divine power.

Of hope, I have always come across and worked happily with great loving cooperative people.

A striking example of this is a poem entitled "Energetic Madam" by a youth corps member, Israel Chinyo Uhuegbu (NYSC 1984/1985

Service Year), which is an unbelievable poem, and was dedicated to this author's honor. Honestly, to surprise with such poem, astonished and overwhelmed at the same time with so much inspiration. I couldn't even imagine that from someone and I have no word the right word to express how I felt when I read it, let alone able to be thanking him enough. He served his National Youth Service in 1984/1985 Service Year, in Calabar, Cross River State of Nigeria, and was of the editorial suite. What I learned from him is that any person, who cares, client's world over, can work with us and cooperate in love as well to show gratitude and appreciate the way and manner that we treat and welcome them is well helps.

Obviously, is true when we care, and treat them well with love and respect is love that is blessings too, we are respecting ourselves, and blessing to each and others for we are all human. Are always loved and value same by God's love, precious with just the right mixed of good heart worldwide. I cherish your inspiring spirit, and **I see love of God through words of love is of joy it becomes heart's source of my inspiration as it is love words inspiring me travels with me!**

And travels the world spreading love along as well for others; is another inspiring way of looking at life, speaks to my heart is love in poem my joy is to acknowledge your kindness. Your kind thoughts have inspired me, may you be richly blessed and I pray that you continue loving and May God prospers you with more love and wisdom! What a happy occasion to celebrate the love of God's goodness in varieties of ways and hearts to enjoy it all together as all the blessings are in His heart for us to enjoy and benefits for happiness. I am happy have to celebrate His good works in my life and the blessings of knowing you as all are my friends from the heart for always God has blessed me and places great people in my path of life and is of great joy blessing all.

Including those others waiting to receive His love from me as well as I have received of others throughout my lifetime from God and from those graciously sent by Him to be my dear and beloved family and friends across the four corners of the universe. Love is all that I have to give, and strive to my best for good, and success from that love. This is what makes a difference. Is there something else great so good that we all can do? Yes! It is to be the blessings for hope that the world is waiting to receive and that can make a difference in the life of the lives of those who are discouraged to be of courage and find strength. Your love can go a long way even in a handshake of love is refreshing thought by action and word we care. I have noted that being in love changes everything to both the giver and receiver is mutual for be benefit from the exchange of that power too.

What I have learned from my experience is that blessing to properly communicate both ways, respect is to be reciprocating love with gratitude. Much, as care for their needs and show appreciation when someone is kind; you, reciprocate love with gratitude. The poem lifetime's a gift of hope that, I can never forget, for that experience opened my heart up to be even more passionate and dedicated of service of love with fun spirit, being more dedicated to discharge.

All the joys life has to offer is there and, everywhere you go, it follows you. Oh yes, that is so true, when you dedicate your life faithfully to serve others well, the joy you share is not just for you alone, also others enjoy as well. It humbled me to be so honored by an inspired youth Corps member. Just the thought alone, is so refreshing, amazing and took me beyond my wildest dreams, as I didn't think I could have made such an impact on another's life to be so appreciated. It creates joy in my heart forever, as I never thought I could be so remembered in an impressive way. I felt loved by someone and cherished enough to show my appreciation is the work of God.

How much God loves us, is what reveals the beauty of love in our hearts. He didn't have to do it, but decided to appreciate me in such inspired blessed manner, and that encouragement results an inspiration in my heart to speak about him, and the gospel truth is this: Thou shalt love thy neighbor as thy self (Mathew 19:19). Love must be reciprocated, and kindness inspires.

I will always love to selflessly dedicate my services to my country diligently. Whether it relates or not to my regular job; it was my responsibility to serve the Youth Corps members. My heart even more is more dedicated, whole heartedly, for their satisfaction was uppermost and it is appreciated by as it pleases him when we reach out I love to serve His humanity honors us also. Remember, it's always customer, first. When you read, you will know why it is described as an unbelievable poem, sure is a great keepsake that captured my heart with inspiration and, always it reminded me of my time as an Information Officer/ head of Information Unit, National Youth Service Corps (NYSC), Secretariat, Calabar from 1981-1989. Thankful together with my study leave and sick leave (together 1999); Grateful for all years, my experience, blessings, I enjoyed those I have been blessed to work with. It speaks for the glory of God too.

Daily, I read more I become even more inspired with encouragement. It warms my heart to see that others are blessed in their lives and can acknowledge my heartfelt love and that is fact. When others are able to benefit from my words and my message of love, makes me feel so happy appreciated and needed and being a happy steward is hopeful, makes me realize I am to do more. It is more for me to offer more hope unique creature created by God in His incredible image, and that all of us are molded in His image, is inspiration and that matters and should be cherished and embraced by every heart. My life has never been more fulfilling, and I have no words to qualify.

Inspiration matters and is something for one to thank God more being sweet Holy Lord, and loving and so kind for He is my marvelous and greatest Inspirer of joy inspiring my passion. He is the greatest motivator that my heart has ever known, and He motivates us to have loving and caring hearts that can use words of wisdom to benefit ourselves and others. I am so grateful. And, even for yet another rare opportunity offered to me by Him this time again to be able to be useful and capable as He constantly inspires my passion for helping people be happy, resilient and purposely and appreciative of His wonder of love and miracles changing lives to live fully.

What many people fail to realize is that even the little things that we do for one another can be a blessing in and of itself, even encourages your passion of more inspiration. Instance, as typical example is in Nigeria and, including my home town too, I saw it practiced is in childhood days. We were inspired as children to observe how many loving hearts were happy to show each other do it, though were not able because of our age. It can be something as simple as going to the market for an elderly person, fetching water from a stream, or even help to carry bags of the grocery and is done also what in America, other advanced developed have done too. People, sure people have been working in a grocery store as a bagger for someone who is not capable and is in need of bagging groceries themselves. Love inspires our hearts to do all that we can to help our fellow man, when we are able to do this; it fills our hearts with passion, happiness, and joy.

My dear inspired friend, please focus on God's love and remember, if you can't afford to show love by way of a monetary investment, there are many other ways, try expressing your love simply by sharing in kind words and thoughtful prayers too. Compassion is love that inspires to move the heart, and changes things around, especially for another friend to be strengthened in the heart enables more and able and to overcome. It can even be your encouraging words of wisdom with others too; how amazing could that be. It is a rewarding endeavor, and you will not only be helping others, but you will feel wonderful. Nothing beats one's capacity to help improve the life of another kind. Just knowing you have blessed and strengthened another's heart with inspiration for uplifting spirit, inspire us and stimulating thoughts and offers hope as encouragement heals.

And, who knows who that person will pay it forward to and bless next. Your words of wisdom will cause blessings to be multiplied throughout the world, which is more valuable than any amount of money. I am always inspired by this familiar word of wisdom, for it encourages our hearts to, "Begin all actions with a thought, and not to throw up words like you have learned nothing." I think that's so beautiful! We must keep in mind to always be a good student with self respect is good thought. And, instead of trying to be like the, "big and bad" boys and girls (or even men and women) that live around the block, are in schools, and/or everywhere else, you can be different. I believe, by maintaining our good character, helps a lot, we don't have to worry about how to regain its image back after. So, don't mess it up to begin with, if you have it!

Be thankful that you made the right choice, to choose happiness over being sad, and be happy to make yourself useful to others. Our unity with one another, enables our blessings too to grow and progress, creating a harmonious and peaceful community. That is more important than trying to copy someone else so that we can fit in with the "in" crowd. And please, show respect to your parents and to those who have authority over you, for your attitude matters and can help determine your present as well as your future and progress is peace of mind and that is from the power of love that comes from above and is in you always and the greatest of all is the presence.

Please, take the thought and time to care for your friends around the world and yourself. Do not forsake your elderly and handicapped friends, including their families, for they are among the millions who pray for your safety day in and day out. Above all, is joy to show respect and of due honor to God, yourself you will be so happy and is with love and inspiration to others, and most importantly, to our Supreme Being, is all for His love mostly is unconditional when you are able to show yourself respect and extend that courtesy and good manners is how we are blessed.

The thing I love most about Him is that, there is no other love more beloved than His own love! Nobody loves like God, and no wonder that when you get to know Him, the sweeter, you want to love and serve Him more and just to be closer and gazing at His beauty mesmerizes. Memorizes my heart! Definitely, you will want others more to know and have the same privilege and a chance to make it and overcome of their burdens with joy as you testify of God's love to others and share the blessings... That is my greatest goal and, mostly for youth and generations.

Generation after, all this what is worth, for sake's of making you and I both happy, I'll do of my best and to utmost best to God's glory. God's love is contagious. Saying goes, "Love is a two way street." Obviously, "love it creates more love and goodness begets goodness" awesome. Is love reciprocating love with kindness is realizing the willingness of the heart to surrender and invest your life, be there for each other and humbling. Remember, to not only respect everyone, but ignore of yourself and is also very good to also listen to what is being said that is everyone is expecting the best of higher standard from love and leadership by exemplary behavior you show.

They need a blessing to see says, for we can all benefit from each other's knowledge also. This knowledge can come from family, friends, neighbors, especially from words, individuals in a position of authority, such as parental priceless love after God is next in order and grandparents all are and including those others like our presidents, governors, ministers, teachers, mentors, and countless others, don't forget sibling and peers are also human like you and me and we love them all and our friends, do believe in us and what we can do to make them happy and proud of us too. You will be rewarded by heeding their advice, and they will always cherish and respect you, well and, "goodness begat goodness," the wise proverb says. Please, pay close attention and become.

Dedicated to show more love, more prayer, and more respect, more discipline and for, as the saying goes, "Love is a two way street," and that is so true for love is best expressed from one heart to another and both benefits from the joy and happiness and power of that love as it is exchanged then you show love and respect to others, that same respect and love will be returned to you. Certainly, love changes those whom we love and appreciate will not forget the love you and I show them. And they will reciprocate, from the power and joy of that exchange is a force.

I must take the time and say that I am highly appreciative of those of you who have so much shown me their love in friendship. Words cannot express how inspired and encouraged I am by your love and encouragement that is also hope. All my friends, I love for you to know that it is a blessing you have a special place in my heart that is filled with love, and all those who make me proud by being loving or, passionate, and enthusiastic to feel good and blessed to write more. This and other books for us to enjoy reading for inspiration have resulted from the love of God!

So to my little friends, I challenge you. In addition to making me and your parents proud, you should strive to make everyone proud of you by having good character and by observing the rules of life that makes for your happiness, and most and above God surely bless too and increase you and yours always. Please don't forget to heed the advice that is taught by words of wisdom. For, these words contribute to your knowledge and growth. It is a unique privilege that has been shared with you, so please appreciate it.

I must remind everyone that our heavenly Father always watches over us, always loves us always for us, He is a real true friend, whose friendship is the most intimate and ultimate that is to say, words cannot begin to describe. He loves us at all times, and He saves us and shares with us at all times, including our moments of adversity, and keeps us company as we walk the road of life's challenges and never ever dare to keep any who loves Him away from Him. That is why I am so proud of having the friendship of our God Almighty and, Jesus His only begotten Son is my traveling Partner that He gave me and that makes me happiest. As my heart continues to be obedient to Him, I know that I am making Him prouder and prouder of me. He has granted me!

Favor, and has made me so much more confident and full of joy, for His love is amazing. His love proves that He is the best in regards to unconditional love, and He is most a loving, dear Father and Friend. Who else can give such an unfailing love along with infinite wisdom? God is real, and His powerful words of infinite wisdom do wonders to hearts and minds to be around the world. We need His friendship more than anything and that is who transformed my life and love is love for eternity and that love is what is inseparable and is through eternal life is everlasting!

Please, do not forget to share the blessings of the greatness in your hearts with others. Be honest and rejoice over the happiness and love that you feel in your heart! Make no mistake about it, "God is love," and He loves you and I so much. He watches us wherever we are, and be there too. Whether it is at home, school, or work, and He watches over us in whatever mode we are travelling in, whether be it by car, airplane, or even walking on foot, all the same. He goes along with love and, bestows blessings of marvelous favor upon us as a reward for being loyal followers. His perfect love gives us all the peace we need to excel in our lives with it peaceful.

I am blessed by the fact that I am able to communicate and share my love with all of you. As the following says, "There are many devices in a man's heart; nevertheless the counsel of the Lord, that shall stand" (Proverbs 19:21). The bottom line is that as blessed as I'm, my heart has one aim, and if you ask me what it is? I only aim to write and inspire everyone, to glorify God, our heavenly Father, who has given me power and, made miracles out of my life everyday it is.

He guides those that diligently seek to serve Him and all of humanity, and that is why I will never cease to thank Him and worship continuously with all of heart, mind, soul, and whole being. My heart rejoices with praises and thanksgiving, for His love manifested all gifts on earth blessing upon blessings and short of words all what He has done for me excellent believe that it is best that we all show love in return to God for blessing us with His undying love has inspired. My heart follows footsteps of my Savior, who sacrificed His heart first, for "He first loved me."

In giving thanks for His love and for the sake of making the world a better place, I made up my mind to follow after His love. I am aware that as humans, we cannot love with a love like Him as He is the Savior of the world, but at least we can love the best that we are capable of too. I can thankfully and proudly say that His love lives in my heart by the inspiration of His living word. I can rejoice as I say, "Lord, thank you for your love." Eternally, I am grateful, because is surpassing love than human and understanding level that as love is my passion centers on caring.

I have passion for inspiring others, and especially the youth as our vanguards today and our leaders of tomorrow and, for am striving to achieve part of my biggest dream of becoming an advocate for these youth and, needy and the elderly and abused also in any help and support that I can get, I must give thanks to God, for every little bit helps and is joy for love is compassion is divine blessing and a gift and so, on that note, I would personally like to thank God for, "Inspire Women Ministry," Houston, Texas. Mostly, to thank Founder Anita Carman and board and staff for all their support extended to me and awarded a grant and scholarship the love is of joy to me.

I did not know that my ministry for token of appreciation for the passion that I have for spreading love and inspiration to others, to find inspiration in their daily lives could inspire them to extend their sweetness of fellowship to a needy heart and, broke as I was in my despondency. Gratefully, by that same grace of love all by divine favor, I successfully completed the one year ministerial program and Inspire Women's Leadership Certificate. I thank God for Anita to be a blessing and, "Investing in Women Who Change the World." They have encouraged my mission to write and inspire hearts and to reach the youth worldwide/in Africa; especially the youth in Nigeria is joy.

Is a challenging endeavor and love creates love and often said, kindness begat kindness is this chapter dedicated to all the women and young and old and all who inspires our hearts and is to say great men and women, boys and girls let's arise and shine our love world wide and show it and women of God worldwide to find inspiration and hope as well empowerment, I thank God always. Remember, "Greatness is in the Heart-A Tribute to Inspiration," which is also the title of this work advocates love, happiness, joy, empowerment, and achieving excellence throughout!

Please, let's be very happy and sensitive enough to love with hearts of greatness, because a heart with these qualities makes for happiness and mostly purposeful meaningful living, joy is as with hope with a vision as well as a brighter future. It is one that creates a peaceful and loving environment for us to live. That is love and for self and others can work together peacefully. And respect with love and treat humanity as a means to make goodwill for the gaining of all as well. I see as one that has an end hope is for the best in doing great significant human investment, with peaceful heart will have happiness and growth, and our children will benefit from such actions.

Hopefully, you will join me to celebrate this tribute to inspiration with love and passion to care. This is one of the rare chances that you and I have to do something unique together by showing our love and blessings with each other. When love unites heart(s) rejoices and creates a peaceful environment, for us to live, work, and to be happy in. Doing good deeds always is act of love and is a thing of beauty is of joy and comes from the heart as divine blessings too, is love. It is a blessing because it shows that we care enough to love and to make the world a better place than it was before, and we can share these words of love to inspire each other and that will make it even better because of you and me sharing and making a greater impact and positive influence!

As this work shares, inspiration is a legacy for our encouragement giving comes from the heart and love is the heart's power. That is an indisputable truth, by our words and actions we are giving same happiness that we obtained with divine gift of love is to help and bless another too. I have received to give away to multiply is about the seed to sow and reap more harvest. Always, "Love makes the world go round," and it is also capable of changing everything from a negative to positive. Let's promote more love and kindness to others, and dare to support anyone as much as a charitable endeavor that will make the world a better place for us to treasure God's beauty is in the making more of expansion of our horizons and enlarging our coasts vision for our young.

Let me close this chapter with the inspired words of Oscar Hammerstein: "A bell is not a bell until you ring it, a song is not a song until you sing it, love in your heart is not put there to stay, and love is not love till you give it away." Ultimately, being in love with greatness in the heart changed everything for me and achieving excellence through spirituality is just awesome. How about your life? Hopefully, yours has changed as well; "Goodness is the only investment that never fails," and so when your joy comes celebrate and share the blessings with everyone!

Chapter Fourteen

When Joy comes, Celebrate It!

"I bring you good news of great joy that will be for all people."
– Luke 2:10 (NIV)

When joy has touched your life and your heart, please take the time to celebrate it, with family and friends, not just yourself. Nothing can replace one of the most precious of gifts of life than to be blessed with joy, sharing with others. It is an amazing blessing, and we need joy to make our lives more abundant, for the life you share not only brings joy to you but to others as well. That is one of the primary reasons that this chapter is so unique, and as you read it, you will know why I named this book "Greatness is in the Heart." Joy without measure is one of God's greatest gifts, and in heart that is blessed, love overflows and joy never ends with family/friends.

As the Book of John states, "The thief (Satan) comes only to steal, kill and destroy. I come that you might have life and have it abundantly" (10:10). That is so true and so relevant, especially in the world that we live in, this day and age. As you may know, is mere journey on narrow pathways of life. Sure, roads that we travel are sometimes jammed, for there may be many travelers on that same road and, able to walk those mountains and valleys needs strength.

Not just physical food for stamina, but a full dose of pills of wisdom on our bosom, that brings hope, nurturance's and inspire strength of faith. Mostly, something powerful and better than cracking cocaine and other illegal substances that knocks your head off. Worst, much as it makes you feel high for a seconds of a minute almost always likely sends you to your grave. Is bigger than the problems that you anticipated and that means buying trouble for yourself there. Sometimes if not dead and you are also living-dead, in the big house more time to spend and rot.

So, instead of all that mess, isn't it better then this cracking of the words of Hope? It is by far better and more rewarding and lucrative eternal investment to celebrate and dance and toss up with family and friends across the globe? That is exactly what this chapter wants us more cherish and, please join with me and together, come one and, just as you are. My joy wants to celebrate with you, so please come all (young/old) are happily all invited. Please, I hope you don't mind!

And, please just give me that your support and, my earnest plead, I know your life will be enriched and benefitted. Come celebrate and, I hope as pray that this joy receives your attention. It is worth called an inspirational party- time and, is the real thing, and speaks to our hearts. Let it sparkle as well and heal your heart of whatever your need was, make it a living legacy -in-beauty party with words Creator's favorite, because is the real spark plug, and lubricant for your shock absorber. Inspires not only your daily inspiration, but make residence in your heart and lingers as the aspirator of passion. As an everlasting God who is the Love indwelling power, as your ever-constant Presence, you can never lack nor taste for any other alternative motivator or of wisdom.

He is God and life's journey the only one that gives and helps us to perform and enhances and everyone needs love and joy and a good travelling Partner that can feeds, guide and direct as well encourage you and definitely, especially of faith-family of God that top most of the tedious journey, so as to stroll on these roads as far and as happily as you can, takes something precious. To be successful and succeed in our walk of faith, for it may cave in any time as life is uncertain, and at any time an unexpected obstacle can be placed in our path. But, what a joy knowing that, there is always, "an anchor to hold on, even in darkest time of pressures, the Spirit's in-dwelling, ever –faithful and is of constant continuously presence helps with sustaining joy (John 16:7) testified. Many of these obstacles can cause adversity in one's life and they can impede us from meeting our goals, but please have joy.

The inner strength to continue in your travels and that is how to survive and spirit of love and that is why I am sharing this passion given to me with the love and power of inspiration that is reality of life and valuable blessings when we are threatened with the possibility of not being able to move the leadership of the Holy Spirit of God progress, it can have the ability to hinder a traitor and is there for our effectiveness there is connection and the benefits of love and power of God blooms everywhere planted. As someone whose career has spanned over twelve years as a senior vocational rehabilitation counselor, I can testify along others that, "Experience educates." As the old wise Proverb says, "The taste of the pudding is in the eating," that is statement of fact of life. Suffice it to say that in today's world, there are many harboring pains that exist, and so many individuals suffering in silence and often find it difficult to express what is bothering them.

Some of these individuals that are plagued by this pain that I speak of do have physical, psychological, and/or emotional impairments. Still, there are others who are not blessed with the hope for a better and brighter future, merely because they feel that they cannot open their hearts. They have become disappointed and sullen, and if they are unemployed, they feel even more as are stranded in this world, all risks with implications and roots limitations, is called handicap too. The lack of financial ability and scholarships along with other negative life-altering changes are factors, more such as divorce, wars, loss of loved ones, loneliness, and a list of other difficulties. Can mess up people, big time, including a lack of opportunity to have quality education matters.

It can be very devastating, and tempers with one's mental and, keep people from getting the proper education needed to enlighten their hearts. Emotional needs, like physical needs, can have a severe impact if ignored. There are many people out there that need our help. There are many factors that contribute to the need for that help, such as low self-esteem and ignorance. All of the factors that I have mentioned can cause many troubling moments, depression and the mind is one of them, especially when it comes to the heart.

I say this, as one who has been there and, I'm sure you will agree with me, there are great gifted and sophisticated doctors in the world and passionate to their calling too and loving most of them. Wonderful to experts and blessings with modern technology and can treat many kinds of diseases, but only the Almighty God fixes the unfixable. The mind is a serious matter and, it is mental wounds only God can cure, it takes longer to heal a broken heart, but He is than capable of fixing both physical and spiritual with His healing words, much as warm comforting touching with everlasting arms. However, there is a global need for more than just man's wisdom, for this is these individuals need to realize that they must be capable of opening their hearts to the Love. Love and Joy can give them the spiritual fortitude to be empowered changes any sorrow to joy.

Their lives purpose and we can only encourage them until they can open their hearts, they will be blessed and nothing can work like God blessings us with the power and no one can limit us and why the need for praying and asking God's divine love and wisdom and help to be all that He loves us to do and be, sure everyone starts small and showing interest for what makes for joy. I am one of those who know that God helps me and to get to where I am is because of the vision He gives and is His favor and knowledge and wisdom comes from Him and given inspiration to do open my eyes to see how God gives the ability and the confidence prevented from wayward.

Presentation and quality and being creative and how to package and appealing to the joy of functioning and performing at their maximum potential if we know the quality and positive; I Know there is joy of simplicity. Sometimes, even when you are given the tools needed to excel, such as getting a new job, you may feel that something is still missing, and this is because you have failed to open your heart, One can successfully battle and overcome difficulties physically, but if your heart and mind are not capable of handling life's battles, you will never get ahead is so. But thankfully, once we can feel the joy that comes from above and is to open up is a loving.

Heart and, we can obtain the strength to heal from the inside out. I am always looking out for a chance to explore more beating the odd and, discovering new things. Writing is an art also which is what communication is inspires. God is interested in the art of humanities, so let's rally around support is to network His business, and promote a good cause, collectivity's there is joy.

It is joy within us every human soul and that light is what inspires. When we have been blessed with the feeling of joy, we must celebrate it in whatever way we can. I like to be and to be is reminded of the saying "Where there's life there is hope." I must admit, however, that this isn't always easy to believe. At one point in my life, I almost lost hope and faith. It was a silly thought of ignorance coming from a once uneducated heart. Thankfully, I have not felt that way since, for joy has guided my steps and has directed me to my comfort zone. There is nothing like joy and peace of mind, and that joy is within us! Good light it up lit and keeps it to be burning!!!!

I discovered that the most successful tools and the key to a practical, successful life are to take refuge is in joy. God is Joy, and, He is the one who holds the key to all our needs. Once we release our heart, surrenders it we can be filled with overflows of joy. Joy is about what inspires, so celebrate overcoming the tempting moments of life and keeping on the correct path, this joy. As these wise words say, "Man does not live by bread alone, but by every word that proceeds out of the mouth of the Lord" (Matthew 4:4). Again, life is not always about politics, but more it is of spiritual matters too, which brings salvation with joy and, joy is within all of us, not within the all world material things, and this joy is the result of the inspiration that we receive from HIS is Hallelujah joy as love is kindness of God's grace the Word of God is Love to bless all wowed.

We are not alone in this world, and we must remember that our strength is "the joy of the Lord" (Neh. 8:10b). I found my joy and happiness, and it gave me the peace of mind that I had sought after for years. I want you all to know that you are loved, and as you rejoice in hope and wait on our great Physician and Provider of sustenance and power, you too will come to find it and celebrate Joy. Remember, "… neither be ye sorry; for the joy of the Lord is your strength."

If you are reading the right books, it is just like eating the right food for the soul, and if you ever get hungry for more knowledge, taste more and continue to take the pills of wisdom to fill your heart and mind with even more knowledge. One of the greatest things that you have going for you in your life is that it doesn't matter so much where you are now, but the direction in which you want to move. I would suggest to keep moving, because the heart needs healing thoughts for it to flourish. Greatness is from the heart, and leads to a sound mind, body, spirit, and soul of both young and old. Direct you heart inward, explore, your dream and, I bet, will be amazed, as God will help you to discover unbelievable unlimited possibilities beneath your heart.

When we are able to celebrate the joy in our lives, it gives our hearts great joy and love is of most encouragement and inspiration. Desiring in life's fulfillment, happiness and meaningful existence, which is worth eternal life guaranteed, is that which is of satisfaction and offers hope with peace of mind, it comes from above and of God's wisdom and knowledge, of all wisdom, is best. Of all said and done, please, hold on to that thought, because today could be the day that you have that miraculous "breakthrough."

Indeed, you don't know what God plan is for you, so wait on Him and don't give upon hope, no matter what, trust and place of your faith in God's love. One of my favorite words of wisdom, "Nothing passes God," earlier shared and, the tide of life is sometimes very rough but, I have found that, each storm ridden through makes us take authority over the constant memories of fear and abuse and limitations and we become better people. Better educated and how God stands by you through thick and thins, makes your heart melted in the wonder of His power?

He is always standing to show Himself strong in your battles and wining them all proofs He is the man, and center of your joy and captain of our souls. What is your take on these words that deals with the soul? Indeed, from my perspective it is a good question, but honestly it can be answered only by you personally. So, because this work is not about faith but love, it is not my place, to tell you, but the difference is there. I cannot advise you on what to do. My job is to offer information and what you do with it is yours. I rather talk more about God's love for us and my love for you is to share words of inspiration that transforms, what makes for my healing. I believe in the company of good hearts and loving caring people who can encourage each other.

This too, which says, another beautiful one is words of graduation card, it was from my dear friend as well, Mrs. Shirley Corn and family (owner of little Giant super market stores) of Rock Hill, S.C. She sent years ago with priceless love at my graduation from Spelman College. It is something to share and maybe you are already familiar with it wordings, but let's together read reflect upon, memorable keepsakes! To me is never enough, I read again and see what it says, "I shall pass through this world but once, if therefore there be any kindness I can show, or any good thing I can do, let me do it now…for I shall not pass this way again."(Etienne de Crellet).

What is your take on inspirational words of wisdom? Do you think it helps or not? It is so beautiful to me to be inspired by those words is everyday blessing and that is what the Book of words of (John 9: 4-7 shares). Personally, I believe in its power of inspirations and, wholesome and reflect upon it's strength-heartedly, healings are there, and with good humors too. I am sure that all of us have been praying and waiting for miracles. But, have you pray also for us to have more showers of blessings with love and laughter as well? There is nothing wrong with that, and, never give up for hope, for your joy never ends, so smile and be happy, and thankful everyday!

I want you to be aware of the fact that, your life may be at times sad and discouraging, but please always do yourself this one favor, to remember that when joy comes your way, do not hesitate to celebrate it. I have been in the same place that you may be now in, and just as you are reading this, so was my heart filled with pain and sorrow, but thankfully there is always victory in sight when we have hope, works!

I have found that it bothers me to see someone being labeled as limited or disabled and/or even the poor children; particularly a person with impairment who has no control or power over that situation. That is what inspired my heart that it is good to take the message of hope and love is all awareness, as part of my mission as, this proverb says, "An offense against your neighbor builds a fence between you and God." They also need words of encouragement more than that of aggravations. Scriptures says, "Let us consider one another in other to stir up love and good works" (Hebrews 10:24). "Disability," is one word one may not want to include in vocabularies. Let alone allow ourselves to identify with it, as is one of the worst of nightmares that impact us.

Saddest situation! Just imagine: One minute, you are a capable and able-bodied human being, and then the next minute, you unexpectedly become a different person with an unusual identity (the "disability"). You feel bad because of how others have labeled you, and continue to laugh at you, instead of helping by uplifting spirit for hope, and pray for a time to laugh and, to rejoice with you, rather tease you! Many may aggravate and laugh at you instead of showing, empathy and support to help you with hope and encouragement and that is so sad of such hearts.

Severity of significant limitations, much in slow learning too, handicaps with low self-esteem. But, I am here to cheer you up, encourage and motive inspire your heart. Perhaps you did not know everybody in this world has some type of disability, and need, so majority of are victims as well of one thing, at one point or another. Cheer up, and remember with that in mind, also that, you are loved by your Creator. What is more than His unconditional love and, joy to be everyday, you need to realize simply being there for you as someone who understands your need is more than blessed. That right there is all you need is an unfailing Love and everlasting always.

Don't give up and use your little talent, it could help, with love, praise and thanksgiving everyday. You will be surprised at what you can do, for nothing diminishes your value despite so much suffering! I tell you that based on my life's experience, we all have the potential to have greatness in the heart, and no labels of any kind should keep us from achieving that greatness to the glory of God. Remember, my friend (young/old), no matter what our situation is, be hopeful and remember that we are ALL blessed, send your praises and thanks to the Lord in prayers, he will listen and answers and wipes of your tears, encourages your heart!!!!

I can attest to the fact that things can be going so well for you right now in (our) lives, but before you know it, you are faced with disaster and heartache in the blink of an eye. Life can be unpredictable, and so can your health. Indeed, you cannot say that nothing bad will ever happen to you, for we cannot predict the future. Nevertheless, we have no choice but to reach for God, who is in charge of everything. He is the ultimate voice and power that we need to guide us too.

When we reach out to God, His joy will fill our hearts as we continue to obey Him and live an honorable life. Your life will be at its best when you can contribute meaningfully to the development and progress of society, especially within your own community. I know how you feel, and might even want to ask, how can I continue to contribute, when I can do this or that, and can't even help myself, let alone another person? All great questions, and wonderful to ask and know, but never can you get all the answers, but God understands and answers to your need.

The same question that you asked I've also asked and this is my rehabilitation time, as I believe, is the answer God has put together in His plan for me, and I see perfection in everything that He does. An old wise proverb does not lie when echoed, "What God requires, provides." Ultimately, He gives all strength and courage God, will make a way and provide what is required in your life to make it better for you too. Joy to be full is a matter of time, stay strong and keep heart and also an open mind and heart to believe, with thoughtful fervent prayers trust and obey!

There is this little reminder also that is of my inspiration as word of wisdom, "A society is only as good as its people," so does it apply to our hearts in loving the unloved and unwanted. Do you still remember this familiar old proverb says, "Charity begins at home?" Definitely, it is talking to all of us, things will be better, if we come together to rebuild and make our community beautiful and society will benefit from our looking out for the interest of one another. Living a hopeful, productive life with the mind of a visionary is important because it inspires the heart to reach far and beyond to touch others so that they can celebrate their joy. As Vince Lombardi said, "It's not whether you get knocked down; it's whether you get up."

We all can have happy lives with the knowledge that we can leave a legacy behind that will not only benefit our closest friends and family, but everyone the world over. When we are not being useful in significant ways, we may tend to view life as burdensome because we are handicapped and deprived of doing something that we love. It is important to remember that when a significant part of you is gone, your mind will be at war – at war with being worrisome about your health, family, children, etc. Though living life itself is something to be grateful for, we must strive to live the best life we possibly can. Even when we are at our lowest point in our lives, we must be thankful that we still have life, and that things could always be better though is worse. We must still maintain our gratitude and be open to receiving joy, while at the same time remaining hopeful that God will alleviate our worries.

We all have the capacity to have loving and caring hearts, but we must be willing to open our hearts up so that we can be educated in how to find our true heart. A heart of greatness is continuously fed with the power of inspiration, resulting in joy and happiness. Be grateful when you are able to feel unbridled joy, because you are blessed to have it in your possession. At any moment, we can potentially lose that joy if we allow ourselves to, so we have to cherish and covet it when we do possess it. Keep in mind that "a thankful heart is always a (joyful) grateful heart. And, it is a beautiful heart that does not delight in doing things to hurt people, which is the best of life's philosophy and successful living" (A Daughter's Love, p. 34).

In life, there is always a time for everything, so regardless of any unfortunate circumstances that you may be facing, it will only last for a moment, and then it shall come to pass. It is encouraging to have hope in your heart, because "sadness only endures for a night, but joy comes in the morning" (Psalms 30:5b). Think of what these immortal words of wisdom say, and seek after "a heart of wisdom." Let the joy that you possess overcome you, and allow God to have His way in your heart. As these words of wisdom say, "The great calamity is not to have failed but to have failed to try." Please, refer also to the words of Psalm 81:1-16 is for us to read.

God is the guide that we all need to inspire and empower us, for He is at the center of all of our hearts. He dearly loves us and His greatest interest in us is a heart of greatness is supplier. Ultimately, He is responsible for transforming man and his character. I know for a fact that He wants us all to give more love from our hearts. He wants all of us to model our lives after Him, for we are His legacy. One of the greatest gifts we can receive is the joy of knowing Him and loving Him with all of our hearts embracing His love through the words of life and living it also.

We must all give Him the glory that He deserves, and He in return will abundantly return glory to us. Walk with Him closely, and give unto Him, for we will be rewarded by His drawing us closer to Him. Again, be encouraged to "exercise your faith to pursue this joy, for it is worth the effort." Always ask for an understanding mind and devote the time to read His word.

Devote the time to pray and work hard to maintain that prayer because "faith without work is dead" (James 2:26). Hopefully, with the message of inspiration that I have shared with you throughout this book, you will learn to be strong. You need to hold on to your faith and do not let it fail your heart. If faith fails you, your joy will not be fulfilled. As I have said earlier, faith, along with love, hope, and joy are all blessings that are given to us free of charge, so be thankful and count all of your blessings.

Do not forget to be appreciative and happy to be alive. Trust in God and believe that you are in good hands, because "God is so good," and "Those who walk with God always find Him close at hand." If you have not received your miracle of the power of inspiration, do not worry, because it is on its way. He will demonstrate His love sooner than anticipated, so instead of wondering when it will happen, spend your time being thankful. As the proverb says, "He, who gives you teeth, will surely give you something to use them on." This is what I have learned as a child as I observed my family. As I watched them continue to be happy no matter what situation they may have encountered, I was filled with inspiration is knowledge I could make a difference.

Those lessons that I learned as a child have helped mold me into the person that I am today. As these words in the Book of Proverbs say, The just man walketh in his integrity and his children are blessed after him (KJV: 20:7). If God had not blessed my ancestors with the love and ingenuity that they possessed, I would not possess the information and knowledge that I have today, which has been imperative in preparation for writing this book.

All of our dreams as children are to be happy, but you have to know how to achieve this happiness, and I am grateful that my ancestors were great historians and great men and women of faith who cherished knowledge and wisdom. Do you remember when you were a kid and wanted to grow up so fast so that you could become something unique? I too, as a child who grew up in Nigeria, wanted to grow up fast to become something special. I would always say "When I grow up, I will be great!"

I dreamed of being in an influential profession when I grew up, such as a doctor, editor, writer, teacher was my father's favorite and I thought about that but I was mostly craving for the engineer, or a lawyer, among other professions that people admired. Likewise, as an adult, I find myself dreaming again, but now I dream that my heart is great, and that I will be guided by God in the right direction. Amazingly, my heart mostly wants to fulfill my childhood dream of living a purpose-driven life. Fulfilling our childhood goals and dreams can make us very happy and to content with the life that we have created for ourselves.

I hold many beloved and cherished values from my ancestors' teachings. Those great teachers' teachings were treasures to my heart that added even more blessings to my life. As I write to the embassy today, I am inspired by the traditions that I learned from my ancestors. They were spiritual paupers and empty vessels, and God loved them and filled their hearts with wisdom to better their lives. This just goes to show that we all need each other's support and prayers, because we never know how much we can impact another person's life for the better.

I am so thankful that my inspiration gave me passion and made my dreams possible. Even though it was not possible to be in all of the professions that I dreamed of being in, I knew that they were reachable goals. Above all, I am thankful that there were other people around me who also wanted to demonstrate their skills and talents to the fullest. As the saying goes, "the sky's the limit." Achieve your dreams no matter what, because it is simply a matter of the heart!

I am very happy for those of you out there who are working hard and are blessed to be in the profession of your dreams. When I witness this, I am always inspired and optimistic that everyone can be who they want to be. I count my blessings every day to be able to witness such greatness, and I relish in the fact that you all will be able to teach me something, which in turn will double my blessings. The teachings that I received from my ancestors, along with the teachings that you all supply me with today, add value to my writing.

Children all over the world need encouragement, so pay close attention to family values and traditions. I learned from childhood that, as I stated previously, spiritual paupers are the empty vessels God loves to fill. My ancestors have shown me that love is not love until it is given to others and multiplied, and more than anything else, it has inspired me to be hopeful and filled with joy. Sharing this story of love and inspiration with you was one of my most pressing needs and one of my deepest heart's desires. It is remarkably rewarding and refreshing when we are blessed with God's grace, for nothing heals like thoughtful, loving words used to encourage.

When, I reflect on all of the blessings that my heart has been opened up to, I feel warmth, beauty, and joy, and my heart feels even more fulfilled. Therefore, I resolved to use this channel to sincerely thank you for supporting me and for reading my words of encouragement. Much of my joy and happiness results from the wisdom that I have obtained, and I am blessed with the grace that is allowing me the chance to reach out to you.

Though I am far from my native home of Nigeria, I am still so grateful that I am able to use my writing to reach out to my fellow Nigerians as well as everyone else in the world. Please, challenge yourself, be inspired, and make sure that you fulfill your childhood dreams, whatever they may be blooms. It is very important that if you are blessed to become the age to do so, that you encourage your heart to do all things enthusiastically, diligently, and with dignity. I am one of your friends; I am a youth advocate by choice. I chose proudly to identify with your situation. And, I write as to help you find solutions to your problems. I will do my best to be there for you.

This is my passion and, I am thankful and there is no iota of doubt in my mind this is also where God planted me to bloom and support you in all of your endeavors! Even though we may be of different tribes, races, or cultures, that does not matter, because the universal language of love binds us all together as one. It is true what Sir Winston Churchill said: "It's not enough we do our best; sometimes we have to do what is required." A life shared happily with others brings joy not only to you but to others as well.

A kind heart matters and kind hearts work better together as a unit celebrating joy. Greatness is in the heart, and I am grateful that my joy came, and now it is time for me to share it with all of you. Will you be ready with an open heart when your joy comes? Please, open your heart and you will see just how happy you can be. Celebrating joy is amazing, and everyone should be able to experience it!

Joy is the greatest of our hearts' happiness, for it comes with inspiration, bringing with it peace, hope, power, and passion that results in the willingness to allow your heart to open up to all of the blessings that are in front of you. But, this motivating thought comes with a question: Again, will you be there to celebrate your joy with others? Will you let your heart be hopeful, kind, and great? If you are willing to do these things, I can assure you that your life will change for the better and that is why of grace that is given to me, am happy to share all the joy with you.

Please, take these words to heart: Celebrate your joy when it comes your way, for you will never be the same again. You will aspire to want to be the best person you can be, not just for yourself, but for everyone around you and around the world. My job is to encourage you and to share what knowledge I have with you, so that you can make your own mind up and decide. Take courage and know happiness does not come from exterior situations, and that it is not from the pocketbook, but from the peace within you. Joy is in all of us, so when it comes, celebrate it!

CHAPTER FIFTEEN

Wisdom Spurs Happiness

"I stopped believing in Santa Claus when I was six.
Mother took me to see him in a department store
and he asked for my autograph."
– Shirley Temple

Once I was able to find words of wisdom and embrace them, I became highly motivated and inspired as I found happiness. Please be wise and cherish the inspired words of wisdom that you come across in your life for it spurs happiness. It feels so much more rewarding when you are amongst friends who learn the truths from God's words that speaks to our situations, right is there by itself can be a blessing, as His wisdom spurs happiness and, you can count on His love. Inspired your heart by their hope and their dialogue and joy, is vice versa, and a good practice.

As the proverb says, "Practice makes perfect and experience is the best teacher." That too true and, the truth always raises eyebrows, for many don't believe in the real transforming truths. Truth is that the wisdom that matters most, is only that of God, and spurs real happiness. Please, if you have time read the Book of Philippians (2:12-16), confirms this more. When my joy came, I soaked in every little bit of it, and took pleasure in the peace of mind that followed and all over me were joy and happiness like never before and where, and at what point did I make my choice to embrace joy? As soon as joy filled my heart, I was inspired and highly motivated to realize it.

My passion of serving humanity, once I became have an intimate relationship with words of wisdom, for they have given my heart a much-needed feeling of serenity, and is a relationship closeness with God and having quiet time more and my heart and mind and harmony with Him. A happy journey almost always depends on choosing the right companions, and wisdom that is He been my best companion from childhood to adulthood. However, I needed more knowledge to understand other things that were equally as rewarding and as great of an investment, wisdom.

When I was struggling in my life with my illness, I realized after all was said and done that there is life after suffering through a disability, and the need for me to inquire was even greater and more appropriate then than ever. I repeatedly asked myself: Was there such a thing as a positive quality of life? My determination is to live a prosperous life and it is God's will for He kept me going for is God who guides and leads me. However, relying on physicians to give me their expert opinions on my physical health was doing nothing for my spiritual needs at all.

I thank God for His wisdom that spurs happiness that words that is one of most powerful and truth ever known and reliable and to read daily it, sure makes wiser, wealthier and better. As words of wisdom state, "Good health and good sense are two of life's greatest blessings" Life is relative to the circumstances that surround you. There is beauty of words of wisdom for me too. Mostly, those from God's mouth and I realized, after some time, that my heart needed more the spiritual food, I needed to live a complete, satisfying life. While, I was severely ill, at times I felt that life was hopeless, but thankfully, I was not faithless. I quietly told my heart that I needed a doctor of that is beyond this physical world. My heart needed the comforting touch of our Father above. And that is what I found was the ultimate of my need and for my treatment everyday Joy!

I sought after my Lord and Savior to "grant me the serenity to accept the things I cannot change, the courage to change the things I can and the wisdom to know the difference" (Prayer of Serenity). I consulted continuously with the Lord to help guide me and my doctors in the right direction to give me the best treatment plan available, but though I trusted those doctors, still and quitting was not an option, but my being incapacitated beyond the physical was something that I knew they could not help me with the emotional scars and wound that was troubling my mind. I was suffering from unbearable inner pain which needed stronger medication: Spiritual healing.

Wisdom is of God and not a man thing and in the Bible God says, "But you will receive power when the Holy Spirit comes on you" (Acts

1:8). That is what gives me the strength and the ability and power and anoints me to take a bold step of courage and, once I realized this, I knew deep down in my heart that though I was embarking on a journey, I wasn't quite sure how it was going to turn out, but I maintained my faith with joy and contentment is of God. I have no problem admitting that I could not handle my problems alone on my own power. Wisdom really does matter, and as these words of wisdom say, "Wisdom is about learning how to live a better life." For that reason alone, I was convinced that my survival was dependent on me searching for my true happiness is from God and thankful for relevancy of the Bible. Those are words of love is all that God sends me and those comforting touch, hearing from Him, happiness too and food!!

True faith and courage were the blessings that I received that enabled me to embrace the joy of inspiration that I so needed at the time more things of the heart that matters most and God was faithful to give me the willpower as the ultimate power. That power is from within, and not without the grace and power of our Almighty God. I am nothing without grace and faith in Him. As I stated earlier, the end of a journey is what matters the most, for where we stand now is not as important as the direction we go and where we will end up. Whether we will go in the right or wrong direction, we don't know and cannot predict, either. But, if we live our lives with faith in God and constant prayer, we can be assured that we are going in the best direction for us is joy.

In my heart love lingers and that is because wisdom of God spurs my heart and makes me a believer of miracle of God's power and at that moment. I believe that one can gain knowledge from anyone, but trust that power is everlasting and the best knowledge to get and gain insights it comes from above. No one can compete with God's love and power that is knowledge; talk less, "infinite wisdom!" Calling on Him is all and, I was ready to accept His perfect words wisdom, my life changed miraculously. I had more energy and was happy because I allowed Him to take over the wheel and guide me through life and injecting vials of true medicines that healing touch.

It warms my heart to think of the blessings that I received once I gave everything to Him, but I must let you know that in order for you to receive these blessings, you must have faith and, it takes patience, because those blessings may not come as quickly as you would like, but hope. I say is rest assured, that with prayer and patiently watching and serving faithfully believing. The result will come. It may not be instantly as you may want right there and then and that is as well what the blessings of living life with open heart and mind does is that power of willingness.

Is joy to live one's life wide open to embrace life and accept change and take life as the blessings and gift of love that God brings our way anything that be it known or unknown is all of His will and, I have realized that in being human, we at times have no clue as to the progress of our own lives. For example, when I became sick and visited a doctor, I asked him, "What is the prognosis?" He replied, "That is a tough question to answer, based on our earlier discussions. It is too early to say, so let's wait and see." I wasn't quite sure what to make of his response. For I need to hear the sooner. Little did I know that I was going to receive blessings that would relieve me of my burdens of illness, and heals me and as I learned to grow and blessed to be a blessing.

My spiritual growth is mature, spiritually also physical responsibility, turned out that the words of wisdom which I received were just what I needed at the right time inspires and support. Nonetheless, not being able to return to my job in counseling still hurts, but life is worth so much more than making my big money, and reaching people in my big office and nice glass window of a view overlooking oceanfront's and highways but more than that now I have more am grateful. God shows me His unfailing love and power that is a blessing and has a plan bigger and is better.

He has purpose far beyond what I had imagine and given me victory and that love and the power and more strength and blessings of joys and vision of hope and a brighter today and of the brightest tomorrow. A Medicine Of heart and mind power were all given to me in overdoses and is that meditating and medicates of my heart with incredible amount of love and inspiration that is so much more that moving power of finding inspiration and wonderworking spiritual power. I wouldn't trade it for anything in the world. Yes, my employment was the primary source of my physical bread, and due to limitations that I could not change, what has been done that it was a heart-wrenching realization that I could not.

Impacted with significant impediments with limitation to my functional capabilities and I couldn't perform and can't go back to my work and enjoy what I love doing job, but now God is showing me that gaining knowledge of His love and wisdom with it has given me life and more. Certainly, no one knows what the future holds, but I know who holds the future and now I have work to do and something to love more and to hope for everyday is an adventure in my life. This is awesome something to be thankful for, because life is, as one often says, "a long lesson in humility." I realized this more than ever as I humbly surrendered my heart to Him, pleasurable.

Claiming my joy and happiness and I have learned a lot from the good education that I have been blessed to receive and the truth is, "one line of wisdom can change your life more than a volume of books." When I surrendered everything to God, it resulted in an increase in my faith, knowledge, growth, and wisdom, creativity and He gives me everything that I ever needed words of love and I trusted in Him and though, I was in excruciating pains, and hurting from not able to walk and move and return to do. I made sure that I kept my heart open encouraged and I used my time productively and wisely and meditating on those words and studying religiously blessed me.

Than worrying more about pains and my limitations and prognosis was a roller coaster as for me, and the resulting rehabilitation was not easy, especially with the severity of impediments. And on top of all of that, I was financially incapacitated as well as you read in introduction all of it were, I am sure that you all have stories somewhat similar to what I have experienced, for we all have faced some sort of adversity of our own. Hopefully, you all will be interested enough to follow-up on my story by reading all volumes of my work. My tribute to inspiration is included in each volume, they tell the story from my heart and how I was determined to be happy instead of being sad. I choose to explore the best options for my life is a gift for love from God not right.

Indeed, it was incredible to be inspired with hope after being hopeless is a rare privilege to learn more about my circumstances and endurance and rescue. My heart was severely hurting bruised, and my life had many limitations and restrictions, for I had personal and medical issues. I with my bones problems, affecting all part of my life these bone problems were very painful as physically, but the emotional ones also caused me great sadness. It took a lot for me to realize that dwelling on the negative would not enable me any good thing let alone to grow, soar above.

Those obstacles overcoming them am so thankful that, inspiring spiritual words of wisdom can change your life forever and, not knowing whether this pain would follow me in the future hurts.

It was a stressful realization, fear of the unknown but my inspiration for hope enabled me to realize that any situation is bearable, if you follow your heart, and let God steer and take over them. I would say that my heart was overwhelmed and on the brink of collapse, for my mind as shared was very devastated, when I was duped and scammed of last dime that I had for rainy day I was tempted to think that my burdens outweighed my blessings, but once, I let go and God took over my life inspiration helped transform my life! It became a story of greatness that is in heart is where that power lies. I began to find joy and pleasure with my life. I began to see things from a different perspective and love took over my heart and rules all over me and that is God is love!

As I chose wisdom, which spurred my happiness, I found that all of the negatives in my life became positives. Being angry was not in my best interest, and thankfully I refused to let it take residency in my life. The truth is, jealousy and anger can shorten one's life, and it is best to conduct oneself with grace and dignity, even in adversity. Gratefully, by continuing to listen to powerful, inspired words, my attitude was always positive. Inspiration changed the course of my destiny, for which I am forever blessed. Yes, inspiring wisdom can change your life forever, and encouragement from can make you very happy and best is sharing that happiness and joy within.

That grace of God's life and happiness and you will find power and wisdom that of God is based on this testimonial, I can tell you that thinking that any of your burdens outweighs your blessings is not the right frame of mind to have. Though our minds may deceive us into thinking and/or believing that way this is true, please do not believe it. Many people think that there is no hope after a devastating loss or a devastating series of experiences, such as death of a loved one. Divorce, sickness, and unemployment, among others, disappointments and hurts created by man, and natural but we must remember that there is always hope in God and faith that is what it takes to be strong. You'll find even greater spiritual blessings wonderworking spiritual power is of joy.

This wisdom says "People are lonely because they build walls instead of bridges." I was one of those and how blessed to realize that no matter what was wrong with me, God loves me just the way I am and am His special child with a unique and special personality. Blessed me in planning my destiny of being one who cares for others' and happiness was my life to live fully. And, happily and, I was thankful that this was what my Father's will for me, and as I cherished. This blessing, I would read the Book of 1st Thessalonians, which crowned the joy of my heart of happiness as it comforted me. Follow your heart, and doing something you love is your life will become filled with joy and happiness, power to be claimed as you read the words and call Him.

Believe or not, God has purpose far greater than we imagine and helps us to embrace life with adversity and it tests us to see also whether we are what you and I thought we were in faith. We must be reminded of the Biblical story of Job, who endured so much and still came out more blessed and also is as pure as gold. I do not write this to scare you or to tell you how to live your life, but just being happy to share thoughts with you how your thoughts of what make for hope are possible and perhaps you can bless others as well. As the proverb says, "Never deprive someone of hope", what is greater than inspirational wisdom and hope? Never underestimate God power of inspirational words of wisdom, for nothing is better and permanent except change that makes me a better person and His love as read in previous chapter what changes everything.

He is the power that make us become happier and better and more useful and changes us of negative emotion to positive and empowers as He fuels us with love that is emotion of passion certainly, there is always hope in life after facing adversity, and in many instances, we come out of the adversity better than when we went in far more healthier and more prosperous and blessed. Listen to these words of wisdom: "Things turn out the best for people who make the best of the way things turn out." This gives hope and enables us to grow, prosper, and be happier, stronger. Please, let's educate the heart, and "rejoice in Him" (Philippians

3:1 KJV). Wisdom does indeed spur happiness. I remember a morning in particular when I was touched by power of inspiration.

It was, when reading the words of wisdom and, was a beautiful morning, and during my devotion time, I came across a portion of the Book of Joel that caught my attention immediately. I thought deeper and deeper as I repeatedly read those words of wisdom, became overwhelmed, with great joy and that as those words penetrated deeper and deeper into my heart. Miraculously, it captured my inspiration. It said, "And rend your heart, not your garment" (Joel 2:13). God was who gave that to me and it was liberating, and I have shared that as well in chapter introduction.

I've mentioned this passage previously, but it's worth mentioning again. It was a gift to me a moment of serious reflection and was very thought provoking. The Book of Joel taught my heart not to get attached to materialism more so than heavenly things. I realized that it was more important than ever to undertake this project of writing, because faith began setting my heart in a motion in my journey to share my love and blessings with all of you. The joy of realizing love is the heart's power and within depths of a heart of greatness was inspiring to me spurs happiness.

Not only did I have a better spiritual understanding of my heart being uplifted, but I also understood more about my situation as God's words inspires of heart passion and inspires me to do more soul searching to physically. I learned the medical definition of a heart being a reservoir for blood, that it has right and left ventricles as well as an aorta. Emotionally, is I learned that if I don't comply and also something to be aware we should take it easy, relax, and do not eat foods that are junky, is too high in cholesterol, or other fattening foods for that matter. When I learned this information, I was inspired relieved of stress, as it encouraged and enhanced my motivation.

I had, for it broadened my scope of knowledge about my physical and emotional health. It taught heart and how it works and also emotionally to know how fear can be something that keeps us in bondage from lack of knowledge we are made to be slaves, depressed and frightened. But and God says, "Abide in my love, if ye abide in me, ye shall ask me what ye will, and it shall be done unto you" (John 14:15). I did ask Him for blessings of knowledge and wisdom and love spirit of discernment and most for me to love and serve Him and know more about Him. How to be all He wants and with a zeal just for Him and my passion never to be substituted is happiness.

That spirit of joy, me to be a blessing and inspirer too and take every opportunity to reach out was challenging to get a grip on my condition, including appropriately managing life as well. To know my right medications and eating the proper foods all are part and parcel of my journey. Thankfully, my adventurous nature for the joy of God's helping me with love to guide and lead me blessed me more to know about unknown. Of which I got excited, for I wanted to search and learn more about Him and understand my condition to satisfy curiosities, to learn and grow is joy

To understand things know more is nothing, like the moment you discover new things on your own. I have the knowledge that, the condition relating to bones (osteoarthritis) has no cure. Be that as it may but you can manage it by eating right and have become more familiar on those foods. I have since stayed away from those that are not so great and agreeable too. I was blessed that, instead of witnessing how "curiosity killed the cat," it did just the opposite for me, because I was able to use my curiosity to give glory God for inspiring my passion and giving me the power of inspiration, to be happy and joyful with education by awareness. Greatness in the heart means having the joy of knowing how Love in your heart gives you the strength to love Him most daily.

He is more than all others as Creator and, "All- knowing and All-wise and all powerful is all about Him and He so wonderful as Greatest Greatness and He taught my heart how to be that person I had prayed and entire He loves and pleasing to Him most. And, He told me how to love others and yourself is for whom you believe you are not what others want you to! Is God before people, and God loves you most want of you to be what being yourself as destined by Him and is doing what makes Him your God, wants of you first and serve Him also most, take good care of your body and balanced yourself and be wise and you be strong and organized and steadily stand firm in what you believe and on the solid Rock not shaky ground, so I release myself from caged.

Let people talk about you, and is okay if they do not want to believe you are, blessed and He is in your inmost being but, they don't know it, thankfully He directs and empowers you. You cannot please everyone in this world. So, don't try to do what makes you sick and sorrowful for the rest of your lifetime with you a lifetime of stagnation too, when you let people becomes your stumbling blocks and caged your life in a box with that is setback rather than forward moving. I know obviously, what happens around us is largely outside of our control, but how we choose to react to these situations is up to us and what makes. In my situation, I learned one of many great lessons, which was, that wisdom spurs happiness and I did choose happiness over being popular. And by loving, witnessing how the simplest treasures of life can inspire greatness in one's heart, I became moved by inspiration and found my own passion and that is why everyday is being joy.

Doing what God loves, unique way to express my love for Him and be about business of living and loving and relating with Him and others and show-case Him more everyday adventure is joy and happiness and, who says that there's no power of inspiration? I'm here to tell you that there is indeed is, love and it is what helped opens my heart to all of my blessings is knowledge. Is pleasurable, faith in action and victory and power and strength and inner touch and wonderful. I have come to realize over the years that there is always something new you can learn regarding our journey through life, for there is always uncertainty, but mostly, there is more to be grateful!

I have learned that the more we spend time on our worries, the more that they will worry us. It has been proven that constant tears and agony does more harm than good. The blessing of discovering the joy that brings hope is peace to one's heart is amazing grace love of God and that I have enjoyed blessings for quite some time, and I know that lacking joy inside and lacking love and inspiration can stunt one growth at the long run, your life become stagnated and confusions. Is the odds and frustrations is all that you get and all because no outlet to share your love and joy with others and releasing emotion. If negative no smile so let your face relax a while some more.

And we need the emotional power to engage thought that it should be stimulated and that is what inspiration does it encourages the heart to think positively and transformed emotion to be of passionate purpose from negative to positive using God's words and building a community of authentic friendship is only possible when that happens and that is why we need wisdom above. Is the best for happiness comes from God and likewise wisdom and this is how He enables me to be become person He created me to be. I sure rejected limitations and failures and choose love.

In particular, if we are not able to feel the joy of inspiration, it does damage to our heart's power and takes away the heart's strength. I have come to the understanding that there is more is being in love is joy is nothing for me to do but to be happy and to measure life by what I can do for others, rather than by what others can do for me. Dependency on man is fruitless, and it does bring nothing but despair and heartache, based on my experiences. I learned that it is best to love and, leave everything in God's capable hands than to rely on man, else you will be disappointed!

The goal that we should all strive for is to genuinely show love for one another, because is all that matters that what greatness is all about, and the love that we hold in our hearts gives us hope, patience, perseverance, and happiness. The natural law that says you never get something without giving something also applies in this case, for only God's power can transform human as your heart. No human can make you surrender your heart to love and is not by duress either you to do what you don't want to! I can't force or convince anyone that is up to you as a person to do Your best though it is a wonderful thing to have a heart filled with love and joy, is best to taste.

It is better to show your love with words and actions that is the best of what it is all about. What I mean is that you have to use your power, passion, and persuasion to make a difference in someone else's life influence positively much as you want happiness for yourself, wish others as well the best as you are wishing yourself. Positive impact that encourages someone to be inspired and motivated and is purposeful that is when you will feel the most joy and happy is true love is happiness sharing your joy and happiness as is a gift and grace with love is awesome to the heart. Is all it inspires and inspired people always loved to show love and inspiring others they know it.

The value of wisdom and inspiration from above is worth more than clichés and blessed. And we are all encouraged to surrender our hearts peacefully to our heavenly Father, for He said, to us, "My son, give me your heart" (Proverbs 23:26). Greatness in the heart is all about seeking the kingdom for wisdom, and once you have searched with all of your heart, you will find peace with happiness and a good conscience along with that is awesome inspirational power all are real happiness, favor, joy, and grace all are other countless blessings think positive thoughts, because they enhance the joy that you feel and will give you a more productive life. I am among the first to also admit that life can sometimes be miserable, but know within your heart lives that life will go on and you will weather the storm. We all need a blessing and knowledge that is of Wisdom!

Always, knowing the value of how love enhances life and increases our productivity is a blessing from above. A life of happiness enables us to count our blessings endlessly, and even, if you are sick. Plagued with an illness or disability, be thankful that you are still alive. Always be encouraged that is there is Hope, will give you the blessings you need and deserve. If you find it that your sickness will keep you from that plush job that made you a lot of money, do not worry. Is better because that does not mean that your life has ended and with life you are blessed for it is what money can't buy and wisdom is better to have it takes wisdom for you to manage money as well as life and, please, do not let that stop you from thinking positive thoughts and being happy.

It helps us to be what God destines our lives bless is to be alive and witness that power of God's wisdom what matters most is a life with peace of mind. Do not dwell so much on what you have lost, but thank God that you are alive. When I started reading deeply into words of life it wisdom, it helped to resolve my inner turmoil. I struggled initially with my negative attitudes, and it wasn't easy until I decided that it is up to me to choose wisdom and happiness over all the things of the biggest obstacle was developing a new, positive attitude to accept these words of a love for my culture and wisdom that I was absorbing. Instead of going into a deep depression, I developed my skills in spiritual awareness to improve my life more than about what people say.

I can admit that as a Nigerian African-American woman, I have become set in my new lifestyle is more passionate from my old lifestyle, is more on spiritual than worldly perspective. Sure, my joy thinking thoughts that would transform and liberate my soul was not easy initially. Thankfully, inspiration directed my heart to the Book of Romans 12:2 and Ephesians 4:23. I'm grateful, realized that freedom is a true blessing is liberation of the mind good for the body much soul, and the peace of mind that you gain is priceless and experiencing God's peace so exciting!

Please, "keep and guard your heart with all vigilance and above all that you guard, for out of it flows the spring of life" (Proverbs 4:23). Sow the seeds of love in your heart, for soul needs it a good attitude with a positive, open mind will follow. Indeed, your life is always blessed, but you need the wisdom and understanding to overcome your hurdles, and provided you have faith. With hope that inspires joy, you will be just fine, knowing that hidden with us the greatest of all of us. Brother Paul knows it too well and said it all, "For we know in part and we prophesy in part .... But when that which is in part will be done away....For now we see in mirror, dimly, but then face to face" (1Corinthains 13: 10-12a). What more can I say than God is with us, you/me!

We can all be rest assured that if we have the courage to give our hearts to our Supreme Being, He will always be there for us and are you afraid? Make time to invest your energy into your relationship with Him, for He is the greatest of all providers and protectors. Be hopeful that He can turn our impossibilities into possibilities. God will always be there for us, and with Him, we should never fear, for He can change all things around you for the better and bigger than ever. Nothing is ever beyond His scope of provision, and nothing is ever beyond His power to do all is of proficiency. Friend, if we believe, His grace is more than sufficient unto you, and I. He is the self-sufficient gracious One. Book of second Corinthians confirms this,"...but our sufficiency is of God" (3:5b) – Everlasting love! He is who healed me and I know what is to be blessed always.

Behold, for He loves us all unconditionally, and with undivided mind. Glorious are the love of God and, that unfailing love always shines through the words of His mouth, as blessed to be of hope. The assurance is this word of wisdom says all beautifully, "As one whom his mother comforted, so will I comfort you" (KJV: Isaiah 66:13). Choose happiness rather than sadness, and cherish the wisdom of encouraging words, for God's love is unfailing, and soundly secured always to trust! Let that love of God, along with power of his presence inspire your heart and, you will find hope that makes you happy. You can never be alone, nor stranded, you are with a good companion and an everlasting compassionate traveling partner whose wisdom spurs us on.

The encouragement, and together with those of your supportive family and friends' love, is of inspiration. Powerful inspiration can make you a champion and a star for God's glory! Yes, you can be a star for Jesus, even in the midst of crisis, and find real happiness with success, when your heart believes! Learn to believe that everything happens in your life for a good reason, and aspire to inspire others and, it will help you more to be able to live every moment, and do more. You can laugh more everyday and love beyond words, which are the blessings of hope in God.

It comes with real happiness and sure when you have that you have it all. That is ever-constant power of God's Word! It works miracles in your thought and, gets you inspire and all you want is to be busy loving others and helping, you are doing good both to self and others, too. The benefits are mutual, blessing of wisdom from above, is the ultimate truth. Aren't the words of God more secured in your heart than all the world offers to you? Yes, it is! Sure, at least now you know, there is our secret wisdom, friend. What are you waiting for friend? Get on the boat, and rock and row, let's paddle along together and learn how to lean more on God than on the world. Knowledge is power, yes of course that we know, says Hobbs! Wisdom is more power!

Of course that is so true, because there is knowledge that is wisdom and power, life and hope and love and light, joy and happiness, and eternal peace and all that, and more than that! And that is all you need in life to be more secured and successful! Did you know that you don't need any other performance enhancing drug to mess your life up? Yes, there is no need for more than the goodness of blessed love of God inspiration in your heart is the best and good stuffs than relying more on junks in your body, let alone your mind. Applying something that messed your mind up, is what makes your more helpless and, additionally, besides torturing yourself mentally and psychological, and emotionally wind up in jail and, often times it results in your being dead.

Let your passion and your friendship with God grow and become more developed day-by-day. Indeed, nurturing this relationship is very important, and in the same way that you grow is nurture your family, is same way is you should nurture God's love, for "all things work for the good of those who love God" (Romans 8:28). By listening to His soft, whispering voice and can be singing His praises, we are able to become blessed with the empowerment needed to deepen. Our love for this unique relationship we have with Him, it can bring a dramatic positive change.

As my relationship with Him deepened, and as I spent day and night meditating, I fell in love over and over again with Him, for His words of wisdom continued to blanket me in warmth and peace and more that saturates my thought with love for Him and I have been anointed to be. It is very important that we praise Him even when we are at odds with our lives, that love will be the access for us to be at peace with God and fellow kind. Life does get better, and it is best to be Am a believer of God's goodness and favor, for His love is glorious and priceless and unending.

Love is the greatest pleasure of life that love and relationship and my growth in the Lord! Peace of mind. Please think of your blessings instead of your burdens, for you are never alone in this world, so cheer up and as you open your heart, smile and share loving words with a heart of love is with deeper joy and is with gratitude, for happiness will find you. Remember, not some things, but "all things work", for those who love God and I am honored to share my thoughts of hope with you so that you can have a prosperous, fulfilling life is practical words of wisdom are the essence of the knowledge needed. To further your life for the better; wisdom definitely spurs.

It spurs happiness when you open up and let it be with warm thoughts and love of God's deserving of my humble and deepest gratitude and who, else will heal me and shows up for me and Who else would have been faithful to do this? I have always thought of all, of where should I ever begin my thanks with love and thankful more than to share that joy is love that I am the one who's truly blessed and so greatly indebted and He answers to me? Answers to all my needs, and this is for every miracle and all the answers to each and my entire requests all I have asked Him. I presented and He made me happiest. God never fails me and never does His promises. I am His child always standing on the Rock. He has been my strength and Rock on which never fails me.

And I will forever trust Him and the Power and Blessing of His POWER and WISDOM. That's what spurs of my happiness and that Love and is enduring forever and ever more and is as wherever you go He goes with you and carries your heart along and mind saturates more love for Him, and more the joy and spirit of love and contentment in hour of trial and everyday blessings. I have seen enough power of God and miracles that happens to me and others and enough to talk about the goodness and power of inspiration that gives direction to bless my life and educates all.

He fills me of my heart with love and joy, and transforming my negative emotions and re- shaped and renewed and into passionate purpose and such is of joy and if I could be a blessing to help any of us by sharing about the things we really enjoy, the things that brings us hope and that inspiration and empowers to make life worthwhile, then brings us together all worthy cause and I am grateful to God who loves us, love unity and encourages us to share with one another to build and is apparent that sharing friendship and joy and helping to re-build each other is all good, joy!

I thought of what makes Benjamin Franklin shares the ultimate truth; its doors are never shut. Is so true, the door of wisdom of God is wonderful and marvelous in His infinite. And, it is the love and mercy for my survival kits. The door is new and even wider now, with it brought me brand new-confidence and brand-new joy and more love and His Majesty. I have lots of good fun and laughter, for He added too more spiritual blessings and strength. And inner healing and peace all is possible, for me to do the real designated work that I am called-inspiring hearts to find that love and joy with inspiration and find empowerment to live life fully. This makes for happiness!

Is doing, this is by Him inspiring and teaching me how and when and what to do and why and where and whose glory and I have shared in the introduction. I am not supposed to be here and alive but for Him is the Lord God of love and joy and the everlasting Savior of my life and is the remedy of soul and remedy I found, He has been with me and been doing marvelous things in my life and now shown me how to love you, helps me also write and nurture the spirit daily and-inspiring our hearts and nurturing the spirit by changing lives through creative expression. All of faith and joy sharing is credited to Him its credits are due Him. For, I have been truly blessed!!!

And, this is for His glory and honor and it goes to show greatness and power, goodness as I am so grateful about and happy that I praise the Lord, for He is good and His goodness endures forever. His grace is upon me and anointing to share and serve gratitude and how am promoted to have the spiritual fortitude, learn, discipline and cultivate all these and more thrills my heart with joy. Heart of love is given with inspiration and is for strengthening me and also each other and is a blessing all is a thing of joy and beauty and better understanding of God's purpose is amazing.

Evidently, that God is everlasting Love, for there is joy and hope for me and nothing that is hard and/or impossible for Him to do for us, and that is so true and, when one door closes do not panic, He opens another. Wider one and it is inspiring my heart to do the work I am called to do –inspiring hearts to live life fully and happily as well think thought of love! Joy that is in that helping people now worldwide in finding inspiration in their daily lives and globally testimonies are all over, there is hope for us, and both for me and you, trust in God's love more for He gives.

And, power is what is all, helps us to live joy blissful and it is triumphant life before and after a great calamity in life you can still find joy and happiness and enjoy and can still serve and offer hope also for family and friends and others to know when it comes. This is of my aftermath of many bump shells; as He continuously blesses shields me under His wonderworking spiritual power. He prevents panic and as well makes a way for us where it seems to be no way, same with hope and, this is it in black and white. I say this as you all have read of my story of faith and seen that what was helpless is hopeful. Have seemed very difficult way in beginning hopeless initially, changed to be hope and healthy happy life of more hope and happiness, when we depend to rely.

On Him solely, dependent on God's love is need to realize that His love and power can do the undoable. There are other ways to be a blessing, always is a life of joy and happiness that the world is waiting for us to bring them and hope and it is scholarship, the blessings of the LORD are always upon you and me and generations after us are also as we are all branches of the Lord. Scripturally, stated, "In that day shall the branch of the LORD be beautiful and glorious" (Isaiah 4:2). We alone with the Father, Son and the Holy Spirit and Godhead as Holy Trinity that believe or not, "One with God is a Majority"- Evangelist Billy Graham rightly observed.

And, better yet is more than for He is capable to deliver those trusting in Him, so let go and rejoice let God to handle it. He is the best being the One; and in handling all your situations, for it is the best for you will be satisfied is as well happier and healthier and I don't want to see people suffer and/or be ignorant either is joy what can be also be good, and is not right to hide it what is vital information and share that's all what love is all about!! Is as well, your situation for marvelous is; if you are hurt by anyone, when you do allow Him, you will be more than happier! Finding, His divine favors also are why friendship is for sharing love, joy of an incredible power of God! The gospel truth has this to say and adds to our awareness, proving more of the power is of the Lord God Almighty the Savior of the world; the presence of God in human being is real!!

He says loud and clears very precisely: "Believe me that I am in the Father, and the Father in me: or else believe me for the very work's sake. Verily, Verily I say unto you, he that believeth on me, the works that I do shall he do also; and greater works than these shall he do; because I go unto my Father. Ask whatsoever ye shall ask in my name, that I will do, that my Father may be glorified in the Son. If ye shall ask anything in my name I will do it. If ye love me, keep my commandments. And I will pray the Father, and he shall give you another Comforter, that he may abide with you forever." (John 14: 11-16). I am quite certain we have all been doing some soul searching trying to figure out how we can make a better living/decision. Is the message of hope, courage and healing, is the voice within and speaks love to my heart and yours whispering softly!

Chapter Sixteen

A Good Education makes for a Good Future

"A wise person hears one word and understands two."
– Yiddish proverb

Life requires as much knowledge and wisdom as possible, more so than any amount of money. As these wise words of wisdom so eloquently state, "Knowledge is more valuable than money." Be careful how you live your life, because "life is learning to put principles into practice," It is important that we ask for grace to turn the words of wisdom that we absorb into action. Incredibly, the quest for wisdom and education is for us to become a better person who matures and responsible, else it makes no sense, if not well utilized of what we learned to bless. A wise person seeks for the good of self and others, much as well, cultivating a heart of love.

It is that blessed positive attitude, which promotes, helps us to establish community and authentic friendship among us and others, will admire that spirit of love and ones and be inspired as well to think of quality education and good education for a good future and our society is what people make it to be! Good or bad, choices and quality of people in that community affects too. It is also what impacts on both the individual and collective consciousnesses as well. Certainty is that, to a world that feels empty inside and hopeless outside, which is in imminent danger many as a part of terrible society are destroying themselves and all that is good as well as all treasures.

I often do take a good look around, if you do around your community and neighborhood, you could probably the once great and as beautiful, harmonious lovely beautiful hearts and sight is fast disappearing. And, change though inevitable is undertone, but supposed to be hope and not for it replaced ugliness, mean and dangerous heartless people acting ruthlessly causing risks both to self and others, that is not showing a good education, let alone good future for generation coming after. The generation after will have nothing to show, if we don't change manners, and/or behave well and do things right in consideration of others, to show genuine love with sensitivity.

Instead of ridiculous and heartless the havocs as so many cruelty, that are uselessly going on, love and harmonious, will be better action and, I do observed my community and, I have to say vexed and pain me too much, to see actions that will not help of hope for much future is not there, unless we must do something now. Drastic measures with positive and productive is what we need and, many in our midst today are missing out a lot and sadly, won't have the kind of good education that my generation had the blessing and peaceful and progressive community as it was all loving and caring hearts people and prompted of a good community and comrades and hearts of gold and goodness that I enjoyed those experiences were of hopeful and inspires hearts.

Many in our midst today have difficulty to reach their full potential, due to lack of love. They have the academic qualification but lack love in heart, understanding mind, which posses another severe problem in our society. Lately, a young friend of mine, keep on asking after she loves the inspirational reading shared in one of my books, *"The Joy of the Overcomers: Slavery from an African Perspective-The story of Enslavement and joy of overcoming from an African Perspective"* (Published by Dorrance. com 2000, Pittsburg, USA-1-800-788-7654). Please, check it out and you will love it too and, what she learned inspired her to ask me. "Aunty, how come in Nigeria are academies, with great talents and skills and this and that big titles, but only few have wisdom to apply what they learned? I said could it be that they have intelligent, but not wisdom.

Are limited in the way we use and how and when is the actual application of that wisdom. It could be in a number of things and personal reasons for everyone's situation differs and we see things differently and is in knowing how and when to apply but, I can't really answer as I am just as limited as well inadequate human. But, thankful that with grace of God and help, I can do this and joy is to bless you and others, is not of my own power, for me to brag/boast either, for is not me doing and, if anything I must glorify God inspiring my passion and helping me to contribute.

To the progress of my life and our society and help boost the economy for growth of one and all, it can be of hope to learn to read and inspiring hearts is my gift is by literally work that is all of God's grace and, I am so grateful that I can use my gifts and skills to glorify Him and bless His people to be happy and resilient also educates hearts offering hope through nursing the spirit.

And as well purposeful is a blessing being an honor and privilege God whom honor is due, has it all and that is what I am thankful for a good education but not to let it get on my head only but mostly my heart being inspired for I know God's will is done for my life be glorified by His love and grace, hearts will be blessed. Is all I pray for Him through this work that it will be a contact point. Sadly, many well educated, can't use it, growing in love of God makes difference. Beyond frustration and weaknesses growing in God's love and power is amazing grace it soars!

She said that is truth!" I was happy that, she was hopeful to note that even our good academic qualifications, that from my standpoint that good education with a future takes more than the piece of paper, other relevant qualities that includes love to God and a fellow kind and faith, following and meekness all are applicable. The will power to make it and show by words, actions and deeds is only what come from the disciplines of divine's guidance is crucial wisdom.

Wisdom of God is what matters more than man's wisdom, else you can't utilize and that is what will help us of more hope and economic independent society, is apparent a good sign of what a good education that makes a good future. Now, many are so reliable on the government. We cannot do something without telling stories about the Government. We need support, need is to reach out too, and mostly, "seek to read from the book of God" as Isaiah encourages our hearts (34:16). And, the Book of Hosea (4:6); says precisely and concisely, "My people are destroyed for lack of knowledge: because thou hast rejected knowledge, I will also reject thee, that thou shall be no priest to me: seeing thou hast forgotten the law of thy God...." (4:6: KJV).

God inspires hearts all inspirations and have the answers and solutions to our everyday needs and happiness and quality education is the answer and is all what matters in rising up all. Incredibly, and is the quest for wisdom ensures survival, and based on my life's experiences, is a spiritual principles should be appreciated a great deal, for awareness, is very important is a Need! I always believe is a good education, need is most truth that endures eternity is what comes with inspirational words of wisdom for knowledge that is essential more than human knowledge that is what matters most and mental knowledge alone doesn't do it all as you will be unable to do it.

Nothing beats reading something that educates heart and encourages the mind with heart educated inspiration. I am aware that many of us have made many mistakes throughout our lives. Even, if you are still young, look for inspiration, and open up your heart and mind to be healed is and also is delivered as saved a soul who can come to see the truth and that is what makes us free and liberates is the transformational power and most lasting and spiritual. That is what shapes of our faith and encourages and inspires all of us as are human who can be educated and can evolve through many human situations and adapt to changes that are vital and workable solutions to life.

Definitely, we can adapt to various conditions, if we have right people support, tools and resources to work with government too, need to help us. Those willing to move forward, while as individuals we are trying our very best as well, but everyone needs some type of root and wing to fly. That is why God's love is relevant and words do empower power of works so wisdom works for us and inspiration that is sure. Many terrible things happen in the day and age in the world we live because so many of us are lacking the wisdom and faith that is needed to make things right. I have always believed in God that it is safer to have faith in action wisdom because it is healthy and rewarding and will make us better to fulfill our hopes dreams and the world a better place to live and, we work together as a team in love and progress. Peace of mind is priceless and indeed, wisdom of God is priceless and power of His inspiration all are of divine blessings is powerful.

And can enhance your mind with enablement of knowing what to overlook, it is of good education. People today in our midst are suffering many among us is all due to lack of quality as education and that is love and education one of the most important qualities to possess is a good heart of love and quality education. I have personally witnessed throughout my childhood and adulthood that a good gift. Education makes for a good future. A good education is like a good friendship, is a gift is blessings and joy is too and seeks for wisdom from truths that endures, and knowledge that is of God is something to crave and finding is worth all the prayers, so thankful. I am blessed, like I said in the introduction and know for sure, God's love and He inspires passion.

His Love and His words are marvelous from it, is inspiration and love both brings me joy, happiness, knowledgeable insights wisdom all is pleasurable to have are treasures but priceless as divine blessings is of God. This wise proverb says the fact and so true, "You are born a genius or not; what you do with that genius is a sign of character and talent." A curious mind may want to ask this can your character speaks for you-consequential? It may be question begging question is that what you think? What do you think? If you want my Opinion, yes! Your character speaks for you, we may differ for sure! I will be the first to admit. Definitely, our lives/society on a global all will be of happiness, peace and tranquility and successful still, is if, and when we can truly learn from God.

One of the many things that has stuck in my mind are words these words that my parents and other family members used to say to me, "Take good care of yourself, and try as much as it's possible to make education a priority after God's love and family and friends His wisdom matter also to seek is joy, very much and But don't forget to pray and ask God everyday for wisdom and take advantage of reading good books, mostly Scriptures." That is what I will never ever forget. I learned from theirs. It takes love and parental unconditional love for my education and studying words of love and wisdom praying over it. At the time, I didn't pay thought to think reading was that much of a big deal, and though I knew about God's love and His power to love Him, and He loves them as well our friends and neighbors and me very much, for they shared Him with me.

As our family's best of Friend, Jesus was His name and that Friend still is with me and is through eternal life and they told me about how

He came for us and me, I was excited about Him. When, I remember the goodness of the Lord and jumped for joy and still I was naive. Also they shared the words I was naïve about. What was I naïve about the power of its words that it could have the ability to heal and make blessed. I had no idea what they meant about spiritual transforming power: The truth honest truth, when I would read as a child, I was mainly reading just for it the fun and I had inspiration of it, did not make too much impact understand quite well!

But as time passed, I grew up some more and mature, I discovered on my own that joy. Inspiration, is stimulating the reading a great book like, mostly the Bible, both systematically and prayerfully daily, could be all that I need and is all can be such a powerful tool and of a dynamite inspiration, the words and, is equally a creative experience and timeless resourceful of all others. Resources of all the others! True, I love to read books for inspiration as much now as I did then as a child, but now more blessed is power of passion, God is so serene and, coupled with writing, I am able to feel pure joy, for which I am so thankful for God, in His infinite mercy, knows what is best for each of us, transforming!

For only He knows our frame of mind and transforms us of our hearts and diagnosed us it so much more than clichés. Maxims and saws and axioms and proverbs is life-giving power is all is the wonderworking spiritual power. I have not yet reached the heights of a world-renowned as writer, nor have I made the best-sellers list. But I have hope and I know God helps me write all is in my heart and that is how search for meaning, there is nothing that can compare to my spiritual is that power and personal relationship with God makes life worth. Is development and a process and, so I don't doubt that one of this days trusting by grace will be it all that He wants me to be!

Oprah Winfrey said these words that should inspire all of us: "I know what it means to be poor, and not have your possibilities revealed to you…but I also believe that you tend to create your own blessings. You have to prepare yourself so that when opportunity comes, you're ready." I can identify with these words because I have been preparing ahead of the game slowly and very grateful for all I have been given and, thankfully, my upbringing paved the way for me. From childhood, and today I look back at my family's faith and strength. Their words of wisdom based on wisdom of above educated my heart to keep an open heart and mind, and gratitude also.

I must be thankful, embrace enthusiasm, every blessing of possibilities for opportunities. I am and happiness is gaining knowledge and wisdom and acknowledging the Giver foremost and is also put to use time wisely and praying and hoping and holding on trusting and pursuing it faithfully and that is for any of my dreams that will come to pass and the joy is fulfillment and I don't have to be perfect. But, just keep on moving do my best and trusting God for making us be educated hearts and hopefully, this straight talk from the heart of a concerned sister from Africa who also inspiringly is an America by being adopted, can bless your heart based on what I have been blessed by God. To me, it is a proud declaration to claim responsibility to add value to life.

Awareness all is a good education and to both countries. I love Nigeria much as America and, I cherish people as God's heritage from every racial background as His beloved human race. His glory and honor, supersedes, and by exalting His glory, we can serve humanity all around the world. Whether we are black or white, married or single straight or gay, young or old, this book speaks to you, and you must take this opportunity to shine the light and promote Godly education and wisdom of it. This is your book, and I am writing to inspire your heart as much as mine, for I have been blessed and transformed by the love of God and by the Holy Spirit leading me of love.

My heart is educated and mind, "A mind is a terrible thing to waste." If you recall, that is the United Negro College Fund's famous slogan. While I hope to inspire all of your hearts, I am also writing this book for my own personal joy is for my self-improvement and development as much also, As, I've stressed all along, there is no substitute for the glory of God's intervention is that power. Divine guidance from above matters in our quest for inspiration; for divine guidance is the first principle of prosperity of which blesses powerful inspiration and trust in God's love of power, God has enough power and what He says we are to prosper with peace in us our hearts as well and peace minds, happiness throughout our lives, which is a blessing we should all cherish!

The following words from God resonate within me: "For I know the thoughts that I think toward you, saith the LORD, thoughts of peace, not of evil, to give you an expected end" That is not my word (Jeremiah 29:11). This book talks solely about positive expectations and how to as well put an end to your (our) misery, and it is so encouraging to know that there could be an end to misery! It is of infinite Hope, for whatever comes out of God's mouth stands unchangeable. Is apparent that for sure makes life wholesome. Oh yes, His inspiration surrounds us and transforms lives is inspiration inspires every hearts and all can use it too and we all can learn to our potential and that good education is all blessing is worldwide and love is language of God's love to us all!

It doesn't matter where you come from or what your race, background, creed, gender, or sexual orientation. Be you a boy or girl young or old hopeful and know that each of us is unique. In God's eyes in our own ways is precious and dream big and go after your passions, for that is all what is what will help you to accomplish greatness. I have been blessed, and these words of inspiration from Sir Winston Churchill say it all: It's not enough we do our best; sometimes we have to do what is required." God is so good to me and my family as well and friends around the globe, for He is "great in, counsel and mighty in works" (Jeremiah 32:19). I am always thankful that God has surprised me with the right people in my life to love and at right time to support me.

I have cited many instances throughout this work and others writing I have been blessed. A colleague in writing as well as a good friend of mine has encouraged and challenged me to write at least six books in my lifetime. He said to me, "Arit, I know very soon you're going to make it and become famous like other world-acclaimed inspirational writers" (Dr. Ema Etuk). Is Amen, Dr. Etuk himself is an author of sixteen books and he never relents on his effort more is to encourage me as much as writing is as possible. I always appreciate his best wishes blessings, wishing me well definitely as it inspired and will come to pass in appropriate season and time. As far as I go about doing well my part is trying everyday and praying and serving is a task as work that, I trust God in mysterious ways, for has promised and He will never fail to fulfill His purpose in my life too!

And blessing his children across the globe, immediate gratuity is doing what God inspires of my passion most is to continue believing and by faith that is what is to the keep and everyday is for me to live it and keep hope alive with patience love and strong prayer. I have to look up to God and be faithful in doing. So, it is great being passionate about this and, reaping good harvest meantime is the inspiration that continues and fills my heart with joy and that also makes me feel so good about myself believing that power and love of God and inspiration and love of family as well and friends that believe in what God can do for me and faith in what I can do as am guided.

By Him, immediately, I am benefiting, just marvelous, of how God's love is guiding and directing me of passion to love Kindness, care and bless, is accordingly to deliver those services. All to His glory; I couldn't be happier living life in Him, is awesome when you understand from a personal perspective, it is a great investment, what love is doing. His love has directed me to do my heavenly Father's business, believe or not ultimate goal is to please God as a vessel used for God's glory, and the big breakthrough are apparent that the sunshine is this and, save the best for the last! How? By reaching out to touch hearts and encourage is of edification of His people.

I know He is blessing me, and my success include not only spiritual rewards, but all of areas of my life is enlightened and light shines both physical too, including financial blessings. He knows too to keep this ministry of love and mercy wants for me to succeed, so success comes from His power, and makes for my joy and happiness, for His love always providing, sufficient by his grace, making provision for the sustain of this ministry is that of His will not my will. He makes a way and makes wealth, and wants us to enjoy. I am always happy to be encouraged, and that has been my inspiration forging ahead, for come rain or sunshine it doesn't matter because it takes going through both to finally see the rainbow; if you want to find hope search for His love.

And joy is a blessing that is insightful, you have to read the word of hope and secure the word in y(our) heart(s) and keep it with you (us) at all times. Just like the American Express commercial says, "Don't leave home without it!" We must all remember all truths are easy to understand and is so simple and once they are discovered you will know what makes life worth more than rubies. I am grateful for those who recognize the value of quality education and appreciative of wisdom. That comes from above as truths and, "All truths are easy to understand. The point is to discover them." The man who said this particular word, Galileo Gallilei, was a great man of wisdom, and was absolutely correct and many are still searching for the truths but can't find and are not there!

It is not enough for me to say, God loves me passionately and does everything for me, as and yet I show no passion toward Him as the only Way for me to be alive is through His love! And presence in my life has been the only way of my happy survival and happiness in life and is relevant. If you do not do what He requires of you, how are you going to receive hope and live it in your heart, mind and spirit? We are here to serve, and give. To give freely of love is to receive as more in abounding from God, and He has been supporting and encouraging and educating all of us with His Inspiration. All are what encourages my heart, and regardless of how people look at life. God the Light that shines my life and my everlasting and only Way that I have come here this, I have come far too. Scripture sums this beautifully and eloquently that is the Lord of Love.

God Almighty says with His mouth, and "I am the Way, the Truth and the Life: no one cometh unto the Father but by me" (John 14:6). That is why I have Him my best of Friend, Jesus. That's who died for me and loves me, reverses the cycle of my life's challenges. Always, sums, my life without Him and living new life with Him daily by faith won't be alive and no salvation. And remedy to my soul and I wouldn't be here and there is no way I could have made it without Him. My growth will not be feasible either and talk less of my physical and emotional healing!

Spiritual strength and of inner peace and joy the benevolence of His grace education that I am blessed all of inspiration is given. Scripture confirms that in the Books of Isaiah 53: 5b says precisely as it relates to me and you, if you are a believer, sage and trusting, "the chastisement of our peace was upon Him; and with his stripes we are healed." Friend, I don't know about you but I know and can only speak for myself my God is not a death God and is alive an incredible great God that is who am serving and is in my inmost being me lives and I can feel all over my body!

It takes prayer and love and wisdom, and faith that power of inspiration to flow in a heart. "We must accept finite disappointment, but we must never lose infinite hope." Well said as well re-collecting back over the work of Dr. Martin Luther King, Jr. is all words of love and wisdom. I respect and cherish and I admire and what spurred me to cry to the Lord and ask Him to think of me more. I needed most His love and power of inspiration and words of His wisdom to teach me some more. I admire and appreciate men and women of wisdom, because I also want to be as blessed as inspirers such as Dr. King were and many others and sharing you may not realize this. But all have visions, makes contribution great inspirers world over who want to make difference.

You have to have a plan and a goal, or else you are working toward your failure. Oprah Winfrey said these words, and considering her background, which is similar to yours and mine, is joy that they should fill us all with hope: "The big secret in life is there is no secret. Whatever your goal you can get there if you're willing to work." Please remember, all we can learn to our potential but we have must be willing to work love, appreciate what we have, and work on finding the beauty of God's love and power is in us and within our reach; for we all are blessed and given inspiration is God's love and words of wisdom and spirituality given potentials that all we need.

Many of those who find themselves in a state of constant dilemma don't understand that their situation has to do with a lack of will and settling for ignorance, is not what God wants for us. Indeed, a great number of people in the world, though blessed, are ignorant of the fact that they need to be willing to work to be the best they can be, and focus their heart on God's love as well ad power and hope ad faith all. This wise adage says well, "Life is not a matter of holding good cards but of playing a poor hand well." Many years ago, I shared in my book, "Parental Influence Matters", that.... "Love and wisdom are inseparable spouses. A wise person loves all that contributes to the social good. He revels in showing love, respect and kindness to himself and others, delights in meditating day and night and abides by rules of wisdom"(C. Thompson 2007: xxii).

Playing with your heart and conscience can be an added deterrent to one's personal development and the fulfillment of one's responsibilities. Willing minds don't forget that, God's a great Provider and always gives the best to those who leave the choice to Him to handle. If, you surrender to do Him, He will do your life best with His will, bound to be surprised. Certainly as I always believe, everyone needs the benefits and power of wisdom to help us function well in our personal dealings, including our governmental sectors. Please, let's think and pray be inspire and alert to wake up, understand how blessed you are. Also, please keep in mind these words of wisdom: "He hath showeth thee, O man, what is good; and what the LORD requires of thee, but to do justly, and to love mercy, and to walk humbly with your God?" (Micah 6:8).

I have found much of my healing through worshiping and praising God, I know that everyone thinks their God is the best, but 'am thankful to be inspired more by reading, writing, and reaching out to touch and comfort the many people in the world who feel hurt. Good hearts of encouragements is to say that, inspiration is amazing of joy. I can certainly say that we all are not alone and that the Lord is always with us and will never leave our sides and must remember. I must thankful where we have come from and where we have been in order to progress forward.

I have hope in the Lord, so I do not have to doubt what I have been assured but to believe more and trust Him, all is well. So, many great things have been promised I must stand by those promises and claimed all my blessings, rather than duel on estimating the suffering. I have made up my mind to move forward and cherish God's love for myself on what my Creator inspires of my heart. I know God who created me has a purpose and redeemed my life for that and tells me: "I am your Creator; you were in my care even before you were born;" (Isaiah 44:2). Education is to be of obedience as a faithful steward, because from an early age, that is what I was taught.

My mother used to share with me that, all God wants from us, our love and that is heart's am being obedience too. I want to see the glory of the Lord, and have blessing of fulfilled dream have been portion destined unto me, including those of a financial nature, to have breakthroughs. I take every opportunity to do my best and to do what is required of me, knowing that I will also be rewarded to be of eventually reach my goals by focusing more on God. Believe it or not, it is healing to me to be able to share my stories with all of you and to encourage you all in your life quest for inspiration. From all indications, writing has a way of healing as much as reading does.

Both can inspire the heart, and motivates even more passion by stimulating the thought is process in amazing and refreshing ways. Over the years, as you have read, I personally have so been hurt by so many people in the world, consciously and unconsciously in such a way that it so crushed my spirit and soul, but I found my healing through reading and writing (Bibliotheraphy). This type of therapy has enabled me to heal and give me more hope and inspiration. According to Francis Bacon, he says "Reading makes a full man and writing an exact man" and it is true and amazing to have been so blessed an educated mind, for it sets you free. Moreover, it enables me to make a contribution to the world by writing to you all about the joy of inspiration sharing.

To those that need hope, I will not hesitate to say that both reading and writing can be a source of fulfillment and joy, as it helps me to appreciate more the simple priceless treasures of life significantly. Mostly, helps me to be able to move forward and keep my life busy and helps me with healing and also, I have fun that is doing what often said, "Every word has a meaning." And, apparently that is true, for my love of reading. And knowledge has helped me to become a creative writer and that is a better person after all calamities, my passion to look for inspiration.

In other words, reading increases our vocabulary, and in turn improves our grammar and ability to express our true thoughts and feelings. I keep thanking God for helping me to write my story, glorifying Him and being proud of all He is and all that He does and wonders of His works Love is the heart's power of all treasure. Indeed, parents matter and they know what is best for us as their children and; they know better, and more mature and wiser and are good advisers.

They also encourage their children to be successful and love to pray and intercede on their behalf.

When I was young, my parents were my teachers, confidantes, and protectors is why I call them earthly rocks God-send them to me and for my guidance and counseling as well is they were prime examples. They knew that the joy that I would receive in reading would be of great importance in my life, so they encouraged me to read a lot at a tender age even though they were not well-educated themselves. They were wise enough and blessed enough to guide me as my amazing inspirers, too. My parents inspired to live life to the fullest and helped me to find it.

My place in the world full of love, joys and inspiration, and I'm grateful for them and I will never forget their love and care. Although proverb says, "Influence begins with parents and ends with peers." but I don't think that's always true because I don't have to be like my peers. As I have stated in one of my previous book, "Regardless of one's faith, a child's proper upbringing is always, to some extent, proportional to that of the parent's moral living (Parental Influence Matters, p. 35)". As we may know, Proverbs 22:6 stresses the gaining of wisdom and knowledge in the proper home training of children. It was that kind of inspiration that helped me to realize my childhood dreams. Children/students need encouragement, and it is very important inspiring.

Also, that they pay close attention to their families' traditions and cultural heritage. They should observe every teaching that gives them wisdom. In other words, a good sense of history matters in one's life, don't you agree? It takes a lot of love and a good sense of inspiring wisdom imparting and strength to teach comes from faith in God and of prayer and the hope of God for it. I truly believe that if we live our lives as productively as possible, we will acquire a heart of love is greatness that can serve all of humanity cultivating certain values to pass along that Godly love takes faith and patience, strength and deep integrity is all about unconditional love. I embrace the following words of wisdom: "There are many devices in a man's heart; nevertheless the counsel of the Lord that shall stand" (Proverbs 19:21). The rewards that you will receive are far greater.

Than the risk of being ignorant and faith brother Hosea encourages our hearts to choose knowledge, rather than ignorance. Please keep in mind that when your joy comes from acquiring the knowledge needed to live a prosperous life, celebrate it! Your happiness is and of itself can be an inspiration to others. Words of inspiration have brought understanding to my mind and it also transforming all have filled my heart with joy. They have enabled me to communicate my healing love is thoughts with you as dear friends of mine. I definitely am writing this book with you in mind, so that your hearts can be uplifted and inspire you of yours. Hopefully, this helps you great men, women, and children of all racial backgrounds to have hope, because you can be and achieve whatever you put your mind to and placing positive things in your heart that matters.

When we are blessed with the knowledge of the true meaning of a quality life, education we are blessed beyond measure. It enables us to impart knowledge and words of encouragement. To bless others as well we do and our blessings must be shared and that is to be the thought also is love to give. Friendship creates joy, especially when hearts come together to rejoice and exalt one another. These words of inspiration always move my heart: "We must learn to live together like brothers and sisters, or we will perish together like fools" (Martin Luther King, Jr.).

I admire, love him and all his speeches, especially the "I have a dream speech." I would suggest all of you take the time to read it and absorb all of the knowledge that it offers. It will definitely be worth it is inspirational and transformational words of love and hope and spiritual words of it! As I think back to the words included in this speech, it was truly a speech of hope, and to this day, it still helps me to keep an open mind with love in my heart. I always keep in mind that I must strive to be more kind-hearted, and improve society but that determination has first to begin with me as that begins like our patriotic heroes of the past and present who inspires.

They inspire us with inspirational words like Dr. King's speech helped and when you do understand what that means It is healthy and gain knowledge in my head and love in my heart, as well as how to love beyond boundaries and fight to do my part and change the world for the best and inspire hearts. I have come to the understanding that in my quest for knowledge and wisdom, I need to tolerate all of those that for some apparent reason may dislike the fact that I am friendly with everyone. I cannot help them, but because all that I know is to be loving, kind, and joyful towards my fellow man, I can only pray for them. I cannot forget where I came from and how far I have gotten, for inspiration has made a great difference in the quality of my life and thank God transforming me.

The heart is the temple of greatness and certainty, and with inspiration, I am fulfilled with love of God in my life and that is the heart's power and can't apologize than all I want to share it. Share the joy and with others. I realized that if I can be a source of inspiration and motivation to others, I too, would be inspired even more. I am so blessed that my sorrow turned to joy, and that is due in large part to the grace of a higher power from heaven above. God's glorious grace gave me the faith and hope that I needed to receive my joy and inspiration in all that I do everyday.

He gave me the grace and encourages willpower by His words of inspiration. Though, I didn't know He would honor me this much; my joy is knowing Him in person and loving Him is who I mostly treasured and most loving and also legacy, "Word of life" powerful that enables us to realize that we are capable our potential is greater than we could ever imagine same with grace is lighter than the cross that the Savior of the world bore on our behalf, and paid of ultimate cost.

He paid it all, I was thinking about this all the time that I was living in tedious struggling moments, then it dawn on me that there's no worries than being happier and to be happy and not to worry about what obtained in the past more than what lies ahead secured all by grace for me to enjoy and that is how much love. His words have helped me to think more positive and to not be so narrow-minded, thankfully, I read it daily and continue to pray on a consistent basis; Listening to His voice of love and received breathtaking encouragement. Above all else, He has helped me gets rid of my anger, bitterness, fears, and doubts and all those perplexities that overwhelmed.

Have a testimony is today. I am so happy and joy is being highly educated brand new and have the privilege of sharing my inspirational story of God love as well testifies all to be blessed: A

Nigerian African-American woman once in anguish that God has completely turned her life around. I have been transformed by the anointing power of God's love, joy, and wisdom that all renewed mind is of divine blessing and to be happier as a transformed heart of negative emotions to positive and passionate purpose and that shows the joy of a heart that is filled of vacuum all is of purpose driven and problems becomes prospects and prosperities as an indeed, I was a woman in distress, overwhelmed, and on the brink of collapse and marvelous is to see things differently.

Now and my view(s) are enlarged and all grace of God's love and power. Inspiration gives directions and that is how the Lord came and lifted me up at exact time I needed Him most, and I am so blessed through His grace, glorious love, I have been blessed. I have been truly blessed by powerful words of wisdom and, am along with His good education that I learned, life-changing is the entire story, of how, He transformed my life and story to glory and from disaster and turmoil is disciple and triumphantly is to love and power. Glory, I didn't know hidden within my heart in brokenness was liberty-the librating power God's glory was waiting to be revealed to me in my faith journey. His inspiration's legacy it meliorates the heart and full of power and glory.

His is Joy to me. God is awesome the love and joy that both inspires my heart educated more and heart of joy, and happiness, which reads glory hallelujah, but to who else is the glory? But for The Lord Almighty of glory, whose love endures and emphasizes positive things of the heart's encouragement and gives us life with hope and a mind full of hope and faith is far more? Fulfilling than one of hopelessness and despair and grieve that I had. In moments of despair, He is hope and faith always makes me laughs at impossibilities, for there is no room for such a word in my vocabulary of a child of God is power and joy of inspiration, and is because "For with God – (my ultimate Inspirer), nothing shall ever be impossible." (Luke 1:37).

All things are possible when you trust and believe in Him nothing is loss with Him and is all about Him and, there is no inadequacy or limitation and, is why this is possible and miracle of God's love and in Him, believe, and a dedicated heart and mindset are needed to understand this. Takes discipline, enthusiasm and consistent perseverance with prayers, faith, love and wisdom of God are all of joy to have and, life begins when you start to understand we are just helpless and a broken small part of nature as humankind are in my one of my classes of education psychology, I studied about John Dewey and one of as lesson that I learned was inspiring me most, "Education is not a preparation for life; education is life itself". Life is a learning process is education and is a journey, not a destination, and often many of us failed to realize power is of God's love only.

But for grace of God that all said and done is all what it boils down to is all about Him. Is "If you lack knowledge, go to school. If you lack wisdom, get on your knees"-Vance Havner. Yes, that is all so eloquently well said and Thank you Lord for who knows you and your power of your wisdom, guidance and blessing. Wisdom is of God's power inspiration that is it matters. Is love and indeed, is you who has to do something about your situation, and God completes that impossible part for is a process is power of being faithfully acknowledging your helplessness and weakness as human each of us are and no matter the status and position is we are still human.

Being, we are inadequate and, I always like to be reminded of this inspired word of Ralph Waldo Emerson, "Though we travel the world over to find the beautiful, we must carry it with us or we would find it not." To me it pretty much says, you follow your heart and do what God says and have dreams, and trust God to help you forge ahead, for your determinations are what define and refines of the effort you put into any work, for your success being the person you want to be. I know is the choice and decision you take and, an obstacle that you can overcome is a success is of God's love is. And, is success measures by bank accounts and all the wealth that one mass in this world or fame?

No, I don't think so and I know so because is what we carry along with us being the seed, what we sowed and good harvest is all what comes from the grace of God as we are blessed to be happily reaped with joy what we sowed and that is love of God and power that matters most and is happiness of the believer. Heart of a happy person, that delights to prosper with wisdom, offers hope, which is like a good friendship, warms the heart both friends has mutual love is given each is to appreciate and compliments each other for their happiness comes from the joy of the Lord.

The willpower to march along with the passion in your heart that will inspire you of joy to inspire others is a gift from blessing that should be shared, for great things are accomplished with the blessings passion is of God and shouldn't be substituted. I think back to the times in my life that were like nightmares, and it was only then I realize that getting through those was all a miracle and circumstances made me the person I am today. The truth is that, "I love the Lord, because he hath heard my voice and supplication," (Psalms 116:1). He is an unquestionable God.

I cherish His words of comfort to smile, and yes, I've received my blessings, like other brothers and sisters of household of faith, who sought after God's heart and, were happy to rely upon His unfailing love and wisdom too. They were blessed of testimony to share, so was I too. I read about, when someone was anointed, dramatic positive changes took place in that person's life. Likewise, prayed and said, "Dear Lord, even though you have blessed my family and I, but more of you is what I desire most. It is time with you for my personal relationship and, is that of specific desire is to be your intimate friend and a woman after your heart. Please, show me your love and fervor, I learned from your words, you did for David and Abraham. I too, have suffered.

Many agonies like them, including Sarah, Noami, Hannah, Lydia, Jacob, and other faith ancestors, and even my family too all were blessed. Behold all, were people who hoped in their time of desperation upon you, and leaned though as human, equally thought, there was no hope for them, or a second chance. But you visited them all and put laughter in their mouths, thankful. Guess what? The Bible is full of inspired stories more than histories, literatures and tales, fable. It is a life's changing healing tonics to drink and balm, dine and dance, and be thankful for they were surprised to be inspired of the Lord and marveled of what He did. I too, this is what He did.

God showed up for me and happened upon all my tests and what I went through, I found that same blessings and grateful for the God of my ancestors and that faith that has never left me. I can share that, there's less nagging, complaining, and talking, as I was more inspired, for being the same reason, my joy is full, more love, power, freedom and peace of mind as I recall as I read of the word of God that they suffered many pains and cried as I did, that gave me strength. And, of all great encouragement with joy to do something more positive, I said to myself, if He gave them such amount of unmeasured blessings of bounty and abundant joy, including knowledge and wisdom, all that comes from above, when we remain faithful to Him. I will do my very best.

I was passionately determined and so confident that, I will do whatever it takes or costs me to give of my heart totally and surrender to the Lord, for I want to love Him more and be just closer like they did. We can't play being of wisdom and power, for we have none of our power. And, our strength is weak and that is can't endure either, like His power and what we can do most is to rely on Him. But, we can love more and share of the knowledge, bless of what we've all gained from the truths. I learned that benefits us more from my lessons as, I read daily the Bible, and is one of my most cherished possessions, valued that I treasured possess that is what gives me joy.

Why, why do I believe Him and totally dependent upon? You may want to know God is all that and more ever has been my Rock on which I stand. The Bible is lifesaver, contains God's word. It is anointed words that not only inspires, but transforms one's life with the power of the Spirit of God. The more I explore it, the better I enjoy and even fall in love with it over and again and am eternally grateful, especially for Hope and that by itself is an appreciation for what I'm! It is inspiringly sensational that, I romance with, as "My beloved is mine, and I am his: He feedeth among the lilies" (Song of Solomon 2:16). There was a time not long ago, was hopeless!

I want to tell you that at times as we know life is uncertain, it will get tough, but you will be fine, and the end result will be worth it all for there is Hope. After, all it exists in all of us and is all joy to know that we are all blessed with God's Love and that fire is in us and Let's rise and shine for His marvelous glory! A good education is a solid foundation and gives us all a unique perspective on life and the Greatness of God and His Great Healing Power. I have shared and am still enjoying the benevolence of His grace with us all the world over there is no place we all are.

The world is a country which nobody ever yet knew by description; one must travel through it one's self to be acquainted with it." There's beauty and strength from inspired word of wisdom, especially from above it carries my heart along the memory lane and is within great is the love educational too. Sadly, many of us never learn, let alone know as shared by Havelock Ellis, "Travelers never thinks they are foreigners." Indeed, education is the most important aspect of society, and like the air that we breathe it is inspiration and inspires hearts important aspect of humanity to explore and it makes dream(s) becomes reality and discover more about life and enjoy unquestionably can change our lives for the better, especially the biblical education only that can transform one's emotions and heart, is awesome of wealth, and truth is assured to be, more than.

Truth that has lasting spiritual transformation and that says it is more than clichés. There is nothing like growing in God's precepts. Sure, is mind of God, and who else can deal with a state of man, way of salvation, the doom of sinners, and happiness of believers? All are of the power of God: Impossible to man is possible with God. The doctrines are holy, its precepts are binding, histories are true and, much its decisions are immutable, and also that helps anyone to rise above. All and every, human limitations than all others and "infinite" wisdom is only of God nothing to be compared. Think of how He heals us, iniquities and deceases are also possible with His protective words, power, if we pray and believe to claim them by faith as praying His words.

Is His will for us and will do what He says and, John 14: 13-15 is there for us to check it. Education is all of love and power that makes for hope and health and understanding the means is of all, is methods matters, and "knowledge is power" because it helps free your mind from the shackles of oppression and gives you the freedom of hope and love that inspiration only God can give. Is there someone or something that needs healing, call upon His Name, and trust in that His Word and power of His blood? Read, or do you need protection and happiness, change character, only as God refines you some more, you will be a chisel for His glory and honor. Call on Him as the name is all you need and that is one of the messages that I was to give as given to me, for us.

Is simple that instead of looking for so much ourselves look to God, I have to admit, even though, I was blessed and inspired when my problems were so acute, there were days, I felt sad and so much saddled with weight and burdens and though we can call others for help and support when need be and nothing to be shameful and I was finding it so uneasy to people, I couldn't tell them about all my struggles, but I was telling it all to Jesus! I was not ashamed then, neither 'am I now, and that is just me. "Teachers open the door, but you must enter yourself." He gives me as the best of Teachers and my Therapist, all the diagnosis and prescribed workable solutions is Answer with practical, applicable, Biblical Words-"Pills of wisdom," and all we need wisdom and it makes life beautiful and blossoms.

I have to take it daily and meditate upon them each just as passage, given builds my confidence more on Him and increasing my faith and healing is inspired, for I have benefitted of His love/teachings. God is my bosom Friend and traveling compassionate Partner then and as now of which indeed is today exceedingly blessed. Mostly as it resulted this inspiration of love is my joy, amazement. I am more devoted more dedicated and having a great time and even more passion in listening. I told Him all my burdens and He gave me all good instructions and is inspiration. I am so blessed.

And, He wants me to share as well and encourage our hearts to daily be so serene to find inspiration and so, dear friend look for inspiration. This is so comforting to take a step of faith as well launching into the deep, and do something that we need to help us overcome our limitations. It takes them off shoulders and heads troubling minds and moves on and you give thought more room and emotion to breathe and smile and give your face more relaxation therapy a while and it will rest by reading good books makes the mind learning simply and mostly reading the "Biggest of Book ever and is of books. We need to trust more on Him and His words for our needs, is that simple, God's love is joy that love is dignity dignifies, and He loves love and is of simplicity and there are all of priceless treasures.

Gift shares all is blessing. Mostly, this is the secret to successful lifestyles, and peace of mind and contentment is all priceless simple are treasures of life and pleasurable are all a gift of love. Why I'm so thrill is I take pride and, happy to make friendship with my Jesus, the humble Savior of the world's Hope. He is wonderworking and spiritual power that Scriptures confirms, "Though He were a Son, yet learned He obedience, by the things He suffered" (Hebrews 5:8 (KJV). If that is about Savoir of the world and Redeemer that humbled to overcome then what do you think humility can do for human being that were rescued? What humility does to me means a world this word of wisdom says, "Honesty is the best policy". That is what love of God does!

Is true, "The world is a country which nobody ever yet knew by description; one must travel through it one's self to be acquainted with it"-Lord Chesterfield. Myself, I found this to be the truth, evidently inspiration is joy. When you experience something, you will learn more and look for inspiration to learn even more about life's circumstance and endurance and rescue then you will appreciate every little bit of any kindness and only those who suffered to be healed and despair and found hope can better be appreciative. Yes, they have witnessed that power and love of God and know how marvelous His love and words are wonderworking and all deals truthfully.

Is to be, is being alive and well able and far from what it used to be is what it is and how. Blessed thrilled to be adaptable and adjusting to life and from setback to comeback that is quite a journey to share is all through it may have started with much agony I learned also, big time from what, I have learned and humbled through life lessons that first hand experience is moving and is of joy to know and first to be acquainted more with appreciative heart. I appreciate inspirational words of wisdom. I love them enough to be more captivated inspired and find contentment, with myself. Is all with love of God with being a lover of wisdom too; it goes without this saying, "It is with a good book as it is with a good company"-Ralph Waldo Emerson.

I learned from a great Book, not just a good "A good book is the best of friends, the same today and for ever," (Martin Tupper). If that could be said about a good book how much more the Book of books? "Teachers open the door, but you must enter yourself." Absolutely, it pays to abide by rules of love that all comes from wisdom. God has bestowed with His mercy upon us. And has a way of showing us all His love and mercy and grace and then anoints us with power. The Book of Daniel shares as well on wisdom and what he learns of God's perspective of both from experiencing Him sums with Word of God's actions: "He changes times and the seasons; …He gives wisdom to the wise and knowledge to those who have understanding,"(2:21).

Daniel loves God and wisdom and prays always for His people and asks God for them to be forgiven and that is apparent for us also today we can do the little acts of kindness that makes life bearable and better for us and others also! I thank God for all wise, loving people of all racial backgrounds who have devoted their hearts and mindset dedicated to a good cause and education of witness their inspiration and love of God and power of wonderworking spiritual inspiring us is through sharing their words of wisdom; I cherish them for contributing their wealth of worth that knowledge, is and with all of which combined, we can add true meaning and enlightenment also.

Is a gift of love from wish each other's all our lives reading good books gives us all an education that warms hearts. And inspires as it encourages us to learn about different people and different ways of living with love is joy other part is of exposure to people in other places world-wide and how they live their lives and relates as well in different ways and we all can think wisely and pray for all to be too.

This in turn gives us hope that if they survived their journey, then we can as well. Indeed, everyone deserves to shine! As I think back to those who have educated me with their words of wisdom besides the love of God and my loving family, one of the first names that come to mind, readily as I've mentioned previously, is Dr. Martin Luther King, Jr. I have been blessed to hear his words and make them part of my inspiration and education. His words, along with countless others, have enabled me to have a full, blessed life and knowledge. I can't even begin to tell the story of my life's journey without acknowledging the many blessings that God have given come into my life in many ways and from of love of family and from of friends. No money equals the wealth of wisdom, knowledge, and great friends who give encouragement warm my heart daily.

The joy of inspiration is what made my heart grows and flourish, and I can testify boldly and proudly that inspired words of wisdom make for a good education and a good future to me. I encourage everyone, especially children, to take advantage of the history of our leaders that have come before us and know more about life. Dr. King, who had a great mind, also had a great and loving heart. I have always admired his great character and the fact that he lived by example in both his words and actions. He loved everyone despite their racial and ethnic backgrounds and had a passion to promote love, peace, and progress. During Black History Month in February of 2012, I was pleased to have a conversation with a young friend of mine by the name of Jonathan Essien. And so impressed to hear him speaks good words of love and kindness about Dr. King.

I was speaking to his lovely mother named Elizabeth (who I lovingly call Eli), and she had no idea how well-versed her son was in the history of Dr. King and how he contributed and continues to contribute to society today. When I mentioned Dr. King's name to him, felt all of joy and excitement and passion as he sung Dr. King's praises. I was very intrigued by this young man, and I wanted to learn more from him, as I was filled with inspiration listening to him more.

Excitement, I asked, "Jonathan, what do you think you know about him? "He told me that he has studied him in his social studies classes, and that he was a pastor and a rebel against segregation and racism. Jonathan also added that Dr. Martin Luther King Jr. created a successful civil rights movement, and his famous "I Have a Dream" speech, which was given at the Lincoln Memorial, and he fought for human rights for everyone"(Caroline Arit Thompson: The Christian Herald, Feb. 2012, p. 32). This reminds me of the fact that our imagination needs exercise more.

And that exercise of the heart and mind and nourishment, for life is a balancing act of love and that is of grace. Learning is fun, and we all can learn for the sake of learning, and even children can be inspired by learning and we all can learn to our potential and make the out of it! I was so inspired by his eloquent remarks, for they were such challenging and thoughtful words of wisdom for an eighth grader, is a student of River Heights Intermediate School in Corona, CA. In participating contributing part of our future, and students such as he makes me realize that we have prosperous future and with our children there is hope but education is very crucial for them.

More to have a chance and opportunity to display their blessings in skills and talents and harness all of it to its maximum potential as God's given blessing and none should be left behind. Black or white, we all are precious and can shine be all that God destines, for He is good and His love and goodness endures forever for each of us and that blessing is ultimately confirmed for us. Is joy Knowing Psalm(138:8) please refer and see how much God has already planted us as well secured and has a purpose far beyond what we imagine is bigger and better and the best is a well. Meaningful life, with that being said, I pray that children the world over will pay close attention.

To their parental unconditional love and words of wisdom and to their cultural heritage as nothing beats Godly parental unconditional love by teaching a child God's word of love early in life and role modeling after them by examples is witness the power of love and inspiration and it is motivational tool is the learning. May, they be blessed to excel in everything they aspire to do as successful vanguards of today as today's youth and, our hope and great leaders of tomorrow. That will make God proudest, us to be proud of them as well and themselves prouder and faithful followers and leaders, loving all the same and inspiring. Dr. King deserves every tribute that had.

As he still receives, for he sacrificed his life all in the same way and loves, to see all kind of people be blessed and so, left a legacy of hope in the attempt to bridge the racial gap. He built a community that left a legacy that contributed immensely to the progress of humanity, life is all about love and being kind to one another and sharing truth in love and serving God that sums the purpose of life and each other sharing with one another and that is what he did and, especially in the United States. He left a blueprint for people to emulate, and from the lifestyle he lived worth.

Created many of positive influence, caring and cherished hearts and this is why the story of Jonathan Essien and the teaching of history in schools are so important and that is the visions. Is blessings and hope with a future that God has given us we are a part of His blessings because we can gain knowledge and of insight from His words of wisdom as love for us to want everyone to be happy and, be of hope, remember that we are connected, whether it is by heritage or by our loving hearts bonding together in love with love matters to us all and, when we think love better, for, we are not just friends – we are brothers and sisters, and promoting this crusade of love and greatness in the heart is crucial for us to have a world of peace, love, and joy to aspire for also as ambassadors of greatness and I am inspired for, "Blessed is the man that feareth the Lord, which delights greatly in Him" and that is why I always have my deepest gratitude and special thanks!

There and happiness as love is all we have left for us God Love is the heart's power and, faith is to me its greatness is blessing, when genuine love comes from within, our hearts always will fill with love and joy and unity in strength and progress, harmony, and happiness so results. From His, I am thrilled with His love and power and education that love has brought to me and has taught me of, "A new commandment I give unto you, That ye love ye love one another; as I have loved you, that ye also love one another" (John 13:34: NKJV). That is a good education that once able apply the wisdom attained from the books you read all is we can secure such treasures from within, ability to live a more prosperous life will be possible and all is enhancing as well is.

Is hope with a future for our children and they can as well have dreams to live and better than all will be capable of loving and dreaming and whether big and small all shinning and that is everyone can shine as there our light as well to help others see their ways as well. Again, certain it is of most importantly, your heart will rejoice as you realize that no one can take your joy away from you, nothing as John 16:22 and Acts 20: 19-24 states the need to serve and move on sharing of your life and sharing with one and all that joy will become more meaningful when you invest. Both your time and effort into being more productive and as well propagating the good news is of joy building not only yourself up but all others blessing, that is each other up and encouraging.

And, inspiring hearts and growing as well responsibly wisely utilizing love as goodwill is the best of investment. Beware, "he who has a slack hand becomes poor, but a hand of diligence makes riches" (Proverbs 10:4), and similarly, is a heart that lacks inspiration has no joy for there is nothing that motives the heart and inspires of passion to cultivate of your gift and use as well to be glorify God and bless each other. When you become lazy in living your life to the fullest, sad, you will eventually be suffering from despair and heartache, but if you stay dedicated to any good cause finding hope, joy, and happiness, your life will be filled with joy, blessings is of God.

I believe strongly in thinking positive thoughts of love and joy and of progress is a good thing education that offers opportunity for everyone in living meaningful life is assurance that is a fulfilling life will result in the growth and progress of everyone, and is the word of God that is another thing to reason, that I am writing this book with you in mind, for greatness is in the heart. And, is therein of inside lies inspiration with the passion that launches every dream is all given is inspiration that is a marvelous blessing to be able to give to a child in need and to live a fruitful, life fulfilled is life of happiness and success as you expose the child to know what the Lord God teaches about love and power of inspiration and sharing love awesome to use that unconditional.

Love and grace both when success is achieved, we must share it with others so that they can feel the same joy and contentment that we feel and be as happy as we are this is what living a life of love is good life entails – sharing your happiness with others, for the life we share not only brings you joy, but to others as well and that is living your life prosperously and in heart is fully! It gives my heart great joy to be able to take this long- range home learning of contented life and is of joy and is spiritual project assignment that God and many others inspired of wisdom also.

Were my mentors and pray for me day and night. Each and every one of you out there, all are my brothers and sisters, again and over thank you for supporting me and contributing as from your own pockets it support me is out of love, and donating a gift to others is greatly appreciated. In the past you did not let me down, and I know with this work more book, you will be a blessing reading and makes me even more to keep publishing, now that you know it is self-published and is a ministry of love and for us all and mostly to inspire the youth and women to live life fully, is of joy promoting a good cause that will help. Remember, love is the heart's power and greatness is its blessings, and inspiration its legacy and gratitude is its memory that kindness offered freely.

Without demanding anything in your heart but just loving and sharing return is kindness of which begat kindness as love creates love and love must be reciprocates with kindness is love. Love creates love and it's a characteristic of this greatness observed throughout this book, you may wonder some, why this author acknowledged so many people? You are right about it that! I love people, and all of you are unique in your own ways, so I'm a people person, blessed to be a blessing and bloom wherever planted and there are a so many of you who have over the years, been so nice individuals, time you have put and how much you cherished me, that I have to show my appreciation this time for their love, along with countless others. This book will not be a real complete one without my mentioning that as part of word of thanks and that is power of love and inspiration, a good education and manner is in expressing love by words and actions and thanks!

Majority of those have been blessings to me as well as my family, to the extent of being more than friends, from all ethnicity. I have watched with admiration of how loving their hearts have been when it comes to my need, especially of help with my love ministry publications. It comes from their support and, people like you. Mostly, they love to rally around to raise funds to help build and inspire their communities as well and make this world a better place for us all as it is by inspiration of love, and emotion of passion, gift results our abilities to do so. In other words can we inspire and promote a good cause, contributing to our communities with love of God that is what comes, and passion is our progress, and indeed, yes! The group that has love inspired my heart to admire and acknowledge of their love as beautiful hearts that are filled with love and joy.

Cherishing to admire my work and is there is no such thing to them as tribal and/or racial discrimination. There are no tribal borders in their eyes, only love is a faithful group and money is not hoard that is not power but willingness to help others with any of their gift is love in their hearts; it is the heart's power and they cooperate and share friendship also by sharing with me in words and actions and so determined to chip in and make sure that they do something nice for me to write more as classical is reading is in vogue inspirational, educative and informative also is entertaining and family friendly always we need what inspires to motivate us and encourages.

Love is what I am so thankful that they are not selfish, because selfishness diminishes all things and true love from our hearts and as the Apostle Paul said, "The love of money is the root of all evil." Bear in mind that he did not say that "money is the root of all evil," but that the love of that money is where evil comes into play too much love of it than God, yourself and family and neighbors all will be impacted negatively for you are thinking of insignificant more than what is most significant- love is a learning tool much as motivations. Please, continue to pray in spite of the difficult times that the world faces today trust that the love of God does not change.

Its values and remains ever faithful for all and makes us strong and courageous and is always. Although we are plagued with numerous situations including physical, emotional and of spiritual and global economic challenges, we must bear in mind and remember to stay inspired and to have loving hearts, for selfishness diminishes that love and poses troubles for society your life and all of the society and not just you but loves one and all over. There is always joy in one's life when we can help others develop a heart of love is good thing for inspiration that educates us is a blessing and one word of wisdom changes life and encourages a broken heart and fills of the vacuum. Hopefully, these words of wisdom will inspire your hearts, because "love is the heart's power that educates hearts and encourages the heart and motivates to stimulate of our thoughts.

That is in part why I continue to thank those who have contributed immensely to giving me love and of their blessings that is of inspiration. I thank God for giving inspirational words of wisdom, which made it possible for me to thrive from a quality education learning from Him and examples that He shows me how to love you. I am sincerely thankful to all those who supported me as well as their kind gifts, which enabled me to publish my previous works, as well this one. I know there is more for me to be thankful for this current book I thank God for family and friends always. I have such gratitude in my heart towards the Inspire Women Ministry for their support.

God has blessed me through their awarding me both grant to write more books as well as the scholarship for my training and my Inspire Women's Leadership Certificate means a joy that God's love from His power of inspiration and always surprising me with people who loves me as He put good people in my part, nothing beats accomplishing God's mission for my life through Him possible for my education in the Leadership Institute training influenced life is in inspiring hearts. I am so grateful being blessed able. Reaching out to all of you, even those I have never met, I thank God for the blessings and all of your friendship. Fulfillment of a lifetime, and is for contributing to the literary world is is wonderful to be blessed, having a part in this world ministry of love.

Because I can share of the love and joy as is to encourage the hearts of today nurturing the spirit and changing lives through creative expression of faith and changing lives is actually is done by only God who transforms our lives but God can use this work be blessed to be a positive influence today for tomorrow, and a lifetime of impact and it enables me to enjoy even more of happiness is the spiritual fortitude for my divine calling is a great appointment and blessings all of my personal and professional development is blessings in my own life! Family unity, tradition and heritage of faith in God make for love and power of inspiration for sure is of heart of joy.

It is happiness sharing faith and laugher and having a great moment together to celebrate love of God and His good work and friendship sharing all of the blessings and is good education. Equally, knowledgeable insights and similar to those who give of their love inspiration by song, I give inspiration through my writing, and for this I give sincere gratitude to our Lord and Savior. Indeed, I have been destined to be able to help people solve their problems and to be happy, have fun learning inspirational words of His wisdom joy is awesome and that education is ultimately, reading good inspiring books engages one's mind with words of wisdom and so serene to pause.

As well your mind is at peace that with God and grace to grow can be an amazing source of inspiration, which can nurture and nourish your heart as well as your mind to think positively. I am grateful for that thought that makes life more meaningful and resourceful of motivation that inspires most stimulating thoughts to be. As Frederick Douglass noted, "Once you learn to read you will be forever free." I have found that by reading good books, and following God's valuable principles mostly, I have been able to intelligently demonstrate of my passion for helping others.

Frankly, reading is learning, and growing so good to study the words of wisdom, mostly get my inspiration from reading to grow, and as happens, makes me happier, wiser, with wisdom. So, is a motivational tool and, as read I love and learn more and grow from studying the different words and that also helps build my vocabularies. I gained from information I gathered builds my mind, and heart enhancing of knowledge. I get informed mind and educated, valuable awareness. Most importantly, I gained more from reading words of wisdom from Scripture, and I am always reminded when reading that there is always something to strive for, to live for, and to hope for.

Above, and someone and something love and be always thankful for the greatest love of all and great achievements all of which God's. Is in an effort to improve my life and higher level of understanding and that more about Him and my situations and is how rescue is in training and discipline and obedience and positive encouragement that gives me something to look up to God. Every minute, day and night, I can hear the voice of inspiration, calling tenderly to my heart than anything else that makes me feel well from within and makes me happy, for an informed mind is an inspired heart and mindset that is drawn to enabling others to feel the same way and be happy.

You too, by reading, can have the same experiences I have had and enjoy the Spirit of God's love and power always! Though reading enables you to expand your knowledge and is to have an educated heart, and of informed mind, the passion that will result comes from the heart, saturates your thought and love for Him is this enables you to open your heart to faith, wisdom, hope, perseverance, patience, and courage, among other positive qualities is all given by God is what can help you embrace change and transforming the emotion in your heart and re-shaped.

When that happens, that means you have achieved true happiness, which has resulted from Him is great for your passion to learn more and to help others makes for hope right there for you is to sow and reap good harvest and soaring beyond your obstacles that is amazing grace love is growth right there. So, what do I suggest to all of us please, let the inspiration within you flourish so that you will see the glory of God and it is a blessing to learn and grow, prosper, and happily serve Him by serving others, sharing your blessings with them to enjoy life to the fullest.

That is fun to be for God has given you His inspiration in all that you do and education as Love, is so that you can actively pursue a rewarding, fulfilling life and when you live a fulfilled life of hope and love and joy and can share your happiness with others, you are multiplying that. Is joy is happiness and prosperity that you have received and passing that along to others, it takes strong faith. Don't forget that the heart is the inspiration for joy, and it can bring a radiant smile to your face shining every day of your life, but you must do good work for faith works is to help.

Helping others is as much as well to derive more joy for yourself our happiness is not the result of our own effort alone and is God's glory that enables us the strength and offers power to do, enhance is therefore responsibility for us to inspire others to be happy and help them in living life fully and sure is while making your life even more rewarding, much as you work to achieve. Finding inspiration is God's love and joy that is giving us the grace with capability and ability to do all and joy to share in His love and fellowship is sure that Love matters and comes from heart.

And love is meant to be shared with each other to multiply. As family and community of love that, is to, care and bless is "in walk in love" that is filled with love is a communal blessing. The Book of Ephesians 4: 15-25-32 teaches us many things of love and life with joy and visions and hope of mutual understanding, harmony, peace of mind, and a legacy worth being passed all down from generation to generation is the best gift. My intense desire is to use the passion in my heart as blessed to write inspirational words to inspire us encourage others to build up each, their hearts inspired and the little acts of kindness in love that educates hearts and own communities.

By using words of love to help you all deal with passionate purpose, informed education your heartaches, it can be bless and inspired hopefully work on changing that heartache into love and understanding mind that is of inspiration finding love and joy and empowerment everyday in my life and this is how God blesses and makes me strong and courageous is building my self-esteem and giving me the courage to take a bold step of faith daily all of His love is examples. Is of good education to follow and abide by its rules and that is why the need to look for that love.

Inspiration from above surrounds and gives us power and transformational liberation that is wonderworking and what I love want to inspire all of you to learn from our own examples, and to help you all understand the true meaning of love and kindness with inspiration can inspires us to think love and live and use the power and strength to sharing faith and laughter and friendship. Many of us are dealing with a wide variety of heartaches that are caused by numerous situations, such as lack of love, health issues can be complicated and financial issues, lack of spirituality as I have stated all is lack of love is lacking knowledge and wisdom, and faith and the joy is of God is by power of His and the truths that is the light of all of us. As such matters most and guides us.

Obviously, in today's unfriendly world, educating the heart and the mind so that they are educated and both well-informed make a lot of sense. Most importantly, it helps to make sense of what is going on around us. You can be able to know and to make quality, informed decisions. Choice that helps you to live a better and healthy successful life and healthy living a blessing in other words, find out what you do best and stick with it and that is of great Love and Greatness of God that is in the heart inspiring passion to think love and hopeful thought and rewarding life.

Overall, thinking wisely is a blessing of God's grace and that spells love is power and all is part and parcel of our wellbeing knowledge of insightful is for great achievements is all good for us and, is a good education that makes for a good future. Please do not forget that this is book that you are reading is part of that good education, so please help by patronizing and promoting. Is a self-publish and all is on reaching and touching each heart inspires around the world to offer us hope. Greatness in the heart is the ability to open your heart, embrace a good education, and to be more appreciate what you have achieved by acknowledging the Giver of all gifts and thankful.

I am more than thankful for education that He taught my heart more words of wisdom to Him be all glory and honor and for yet offering me another opportunity to be healthy and useful as well helpful be and all of our friends to be happy and resilient and purposeful and that is more reasons to be grateful. Why emphasizing the tips and need and importance of both academic and character education to shape youth for He keeps the heart from breaking and that is what God's love does. I am sure you will be happy to read and keep faith alive with words of love educating the heart for it motivates and same with faith and inspiration for love is of Him and likewise joy.

We must also show respect and serve others passionately and diligently. Additionally, is so good to love your country as a patriotic citizen, and do your best to trust, and obey the rules of Supreme Being and that of the land will be easy to follow because you have the willing power of heart and mind and family unity, tradition, and heritage along with unconditional love and is joy. All is vital to the healthy development of us, mostly of our children and young adults gaining the blessings of being guided in the right part of life early that is the basic foundation of quality also!

To close this chapter, I would love to encourage us and remind everyone to protect your family and your community, respects others and their property, treasure yourself and others, be cheerful, and reach out in love to show kindness and empathy the world over. Be studious and stay focused in your studies, my young friend and strive to be an individual of dignity, integrity. These qualities will make for an educated mind and a dedicated heart, and always, as your life shines on in full bloom, remember that "a gift with kind words is double the gift." Please, take good care of your health is the greatest of our human blessings and take time to read more love letters and take more advantage of any quality with what gives good education, most from above.

Giving comes from the heart is by making use of your talents and gifts; you are uplifting. Best is that not only your spirit with it is joy is for of everyone around you to a better life! It is a gift, when you are filled with joy and happiness; you are inspired with a mind of creativity. That many people that I come into contact with are very appreciative of my smile am blessed with that joy, cheerful disposition to be all because of God's grace. He is the one who is in control as loves me most, whose love graces my life with His love and it refreshes sure does with His love is my joy, renews and satisfies, He sustains and preserves is with divine love and security is His. I have found love and the banner over me blesses. He opens my heart blessing me with it is joy, love and laughter as God puts as smile in me. It pays to seek Him out and put your worries into His hands, for He is the basic foundation for our lives He has the solutions to the problems.

We have to remember also what God requires of us and me inclusive justice, mercy and humility and no matter where I am and live I must carry along with me in soul, in the heart, mind and spirit always is. Uplifting and we can express in our own ways, live to our potential and live life to enjoy to its fullest and find empowerment and thankful daily. Friend, with that being said, we all need to be of hope, able to express our love is gratefulness for receiving these gifts, and a cheerful disposition is an excellent start. It definitely does not help us if we have an ugly attitude. Is not reaching out, so best is be loving and kind express love more for if we have an unpleasant facial expression, that may rob our joy, and chance of opportunity, let's keep faith and hope alive and not at bay and, sure to cheer up is better than rub off on others ugliness and, bad attitude that impact negatively from realizing our true potential with beautiful us and lovely hearts always and a smile is an added impetus at all times is a gift of God's love and use it well is all of divine love.

Blessing to your advantage, why always being so sad and frowning and showing negative more than positive when we have been all so blessed receiving our daily blessings from above?

Be cheery cherish all what you are blessed and given freely without bargaining for is of joy to have positive outlook on life depends on how we see life, and a negative attitude will give us a negative outlook and is Thankfully, we have our Lord and Savior, who will make sure that we are on the right track. We should all endeavor to have a positive attitude, for this is the direct path to life being empowered with an informed mind and educate your heart let it inspire you and let Love to have His way in your heart as fill with love and joy to experience peace with God is so awesome. Please, as God speaks to your heart, listen to everything He says and follow Him so attitude matters and one's character is important and that is why this conversation will continue in the next work of this caliber by grace of God friend keep that in mind and that you can find love and joy Is Your imagination can take you to places you never ever imagined, and you can realize those dreams that once upon a time eluded you. In my estimation, a happy person is a healthy person and also successful person who knows the value of quality living and loves others with a kind heart, is to strengthen yourself and others and that is just my own opinion. Yes, with that power use that gift of grace to better self, family, community that is a thrilling journey of my faith and how much God loves me is how much He also surprises me daily it is my time to shine and proclaim much His love abides and blesses me every step all the ways and His goodness and this is how those experiences of my faith as well prompted strength, resilience and opens me up with all the joys that life has to offer.

And, I had no idea that wilderness journey can be so amazing with it is experience and I can be used to be the love that I can make a difference in the world to become a better place. He gives me grace to endure and power to help us and influence others positively. "The generous soul will be made rich" (Pro.11:25). Is very beneficial to love and to serve God by serving others is beneficiaries to it as God's love and joy has no ending true what this wise adage says so well, "Happiness is a by-product of an effort to make someone else happy" and Happiness is a gift of love of God and if you love Him you and God loves is more for it is sowing for yourself, not just others and being a compassionate heart, makes your life awesome and less complicated, happier more blessings are activated from above, giving is good for us unity, self-esteem, best is for soul.

For it makes for a good education is future and these are tips for using unconditional love and acceptance to shape our faith as well our youth of today will also benefit themselves as well all need. As William Blake said, "See the world in a grain of sand, and heaven in a wild flower."

CHAPTER SEVENTEEN

Never Give Up!

"Gratitude is the memory of the heart,
love its power and inspiration its legacy."
– Caroline Arit Thompson

Greatness lies within us, and it shows in our moods, our actions, and our attitudes, which can change with our lifestyles. When our hearts are full of joy, then we feel more hope than despair and are able to be freely inspired. It boosts our motivation so that we are blessed with the ability to do more than we ever imagined we could do in our lives. These are all the joys of having greatness in the heart. In order to reap the benefits of greatness in the heart, one must examine one's attitude daily, for our attitudes help guide us on the correct path to inspirational love and spiritual words of wisdom. I am hopeful that this book has helped you understand how important it is to have a great heart of love and find love and joy and happiness with inspiration.

And hope and faith that is unwavering to us is a matter of the heart and the gift of grace is for a lifetime. It gives me pure joy to be in a position to write this book and share my words of love as it is encouragement with you all as my friends from the heart as my passion is inspired by the love of God daily too! His love is always with me and power as well inspiring my passion as is through His grace also builds my character and renews and refreshes my heart with His love as such giving me priceless love, healing of both my physical and emotional health is of happiness!

Friendship is for sharing, and it inspires me and warms my heart. Gratefully, in spite of the hurdles that I have faced throughout my life-rejection, criticism, and countless and more of other obstacles, God's grace gotten me through the turbulent and times, and I didn't give up on my journey, and I am so pleased that I have made it this far, for my life is blessed is blessed. Is to thank God from the bottom of my heart, mind and soul for helping me complete this particular project and that is for this day and what He has given me is love for a lifetime and happiness as well as joy and empowerment. Evidently inspiration is a legacy from God and love is from Him.

Sure, I am happy because I am blessed to be sharing the very joys that come from love and His inspiration. I was able to discover the secrets of a successful life, which includes peace of mind and love in my heart. What you worship determines your destiny, what you think and are all. Apparently, our greatness is in our heart, only. And only in our humility Only God can fill us with His Spirit and leads us daily. Blessing that we need to walk by faith and hope for best though life's challenges, but mostly is in our humility before God can only greatness revealed!

It is absolutely a blessing with opportunity to be given liberty and you know you are free always. This is the joy of power of inspiration as a legacy and heart that is empowers with God's love is. We can benefit from formal education and informal school of wisdom (word-based), both works. This knowledge that I acquired overwhelms me, and words alone cannot fully dare to describe express my joy and heartfelt gratitude. The best that I can do is sharing my happiness and wisdom with all of you, to inspire for it liberates my soul and offers my life more to hope for and, I want to further encourage your heart to never give up on the joy of inspiration! Persevere with determination and hard work and you will fulfill your passion and your dreams unfold too.

Rely on faith, in God because without it, you will not succeed without an anchor in tough times and, rough; is joy when you know how and when to successfully apply your efforts to right goals. You will be blessed with happiness and joy and success comes with happiness is of above. And, it calls for celebrating with family and friends and all; first to glorify the Great Giver of all as He is all is what makes life more prosperous and keeps you going. Day in and day out, as you are inspired with passion that is of fulfilling of your dreams and live your life's purpose is hope.

You will find new meaning in life through prayer and even stand tall is God's abundance grace and my reading the Bible and being is learning more from a good education for life itself is a challenge and only can be faced by faith in God's love and wisdom that is the best path of life. As, I see the remedy for my successful journey and, so never give up and seek for inspiration too from Him. Spending quality time to pray and ask God's wisdom is healthy and healing to life as well heart and mind and great to the soul is being blessed and your self-esteem and courage also.

Is asking God for guidance in His wisdom and knowledge, with strength and discipline is received, from Him, you will make it, the attitude to be in place, to prosper and have abundance always of radiant health and living your life to the fullest. Like salvation it is by faith, to believe is through grace and that God is able and, by your praying and ask from Him to be of hope and cheery, with perseverance. Encouragement is to believe and being courageous and consistent read more for that is where to get inspiration from God is the way out and that love offers hope.

It is best to follow the words of love, and thank God for everything and remember it is always best reading those words and inspire of your heart. That is what creates faith for salvation and eternal life, and is for peace of mind and success in life is to acknowledge that power of God first. So celebrate joy when it comes, for your efforts should be rightfully acknowledged Him. It is and your sacrifice never in vain, as God hears and answers prayers. Certainly, we all know by now that happiness is what comes from within and of the Lord and the lover of God, receives, all the blessings that is in His heart for to enjoy is inevitable, if you know how to utilize your time.

Here on earth productively. I was born with happiness and I am thankful for that, and so am thankfully with that power of God to make happy, always gratitude is the memory of heart is why heart wells up in praise to the Lord God for giving me the grace and strength to endure to do and be all that I never thought was possible. And, sticking to His love and inspirational word of wisdom are marvelously beneficial to hope for. Sticking to it helps me to hold on to faith in God, and never to give up. I have learned to embrace happiness and the joy that inspired motivated of my heart to move forward, not to ever relenting in my efforts in helping others to be happy even when faced with fear and broken heart. And, challenges in much kind of ways, it does not affect.

My happiness is from God and helping another to be as happy, that is even adding to my happiness, resilient, helping others to make them happy is being actually happier yourself. What we must remember is that happiness is inevitable, to us is and reinforces by love of which only God gives and that is deeper joy and harmony with peace of mind and that peace is from above. Is not what you struggle for is given free is by faith and grace and garrisons. If you know how to control yourself and don't let your situation to overwhelm you, and is comforting to know that, is happiness though a result of hard work, would not be feasible without the power of God and, the passion of feeling of emotion of positive and not negative thoughts is always what fuels passion.

Positively, your emotion of passion to keep you going; It is all about what is within more than outside. Happiness is more of what you do, love and hope for, so don't let fear and doubt of your overwhelming limitations or disability, or anyone to deceive or scare to stop enjoying life. I say, don't let them mastermind you for this and that little talk can scare you and, so set a goal to pursue in life for God had given you the blessings with authority for your pursuit of happiness; Is all you need and pray for wisdom, guidance to have focus, direction, self-control and discipline.

And spirit of discernment and, to find your own purpose in life is all with Him. So don't let them scare you that are when doubts and fears will run your life and ruin, stunt your growth and shut all of the God's given blessings away from you. Once you are blessed and transformed is out the doors emotions of negative thoughts and passionate purpose comes open your heart too embrace new insights with confidence to taste more of God's love, you will be amazed yourself!

I mean flying high and come to the realization that your are capable more than your know about yourself. Do you know that lack of love and inspiration can contribute more to your lack of vision and weakness and frustrations can come also from harboring bitterness, envy and jealousy and all those worthless thoughts of malice and gossips and slander and hatred all those are heavy. Baggage and something to do away from there is hope for your life is great when you aligned it with God's love and perspective of faith and wisdom comes from His inspiration and is of hope.

When you apply yourself and hope for the best always to the love of life and words of life, though may be faced with seemingly what seems to be hopeless and worthless, "give thanks always for all things- unto the Father in the name of our Lord Jesus" (Ephesians 4:19-20). Faith in God is the currency of life and love and wisdom, all makes us to arrive at power of inspiration. Hold them tight and, be thankful that you are dearly treasured by the love of God and you don't need to worry about what gives you more panic and heartbrokenness. Perseverance is great and it is what I am as thankful about God's love as it empowers even in the critical moment of tougher situation, helps you to persevere to keep positive mindset, for your growth and inspiration helps.

Did you know that love that endures, grows more in love and is the heart's power? Sure, your growth is with love in your heart and happiness. Life is easy when you walk in the light of hope and in knowing God's amazing love, is always with you, are blessed and will overcome. He is able to help you overcome too, if you believe and it is that believing His **Love is** life and love is by faith and hope and more healthy living. Living the life of love in God is to know joy and is contentment, to grow and soars above your hurdles! Well, practice makes perfect skills! Indeed, "our help is in the name of God is of hope nothing beats capacity to love and be loved, your joy!"

Applying those spiritual principles of words of God added happiness too. Ultimately, for successful living, nearer approaching God the easier for me to navigate life's twist and turns and, I don't know about you, but even as I write this still puzzle about the way God love us so much. And mostly, His love is so infectious and empowering strong love that will not let you down and, won't. I am here to affirm that truth favorite of my sayings is, "Love is supreme." I am a survivor and one who have been blessed and cured of my long standing physical and emotional health and among others, include orthopedic, conflicts in private and business world, I was swamped over.

Head and shoulder and, I didn't know how to handle any of it and that is for sure because it was too much. Also, as if that was not enough, another bump shield that shattered my life total being scammed of the last dime and nothing left for me to take care of my family, talk less of my bills and roof over head. I was homeless and thank God for Rita Smith who housed me for two weeks. She is a blessed as Rev. (Dr). Francis Ekene niece and Mr. Steve Bassey is her cousin who made arrangement and all of them have blessed my life in ways I always treasure and did work hand-in- hand together with me till I was able to find me a place through connections of heaven and is earth we linked by the heartstrings. I was blessed by God else would have died, is right there's hope for God always make a way and brings us people who can also be of blessings!

I know God used Dr. (Rev) Ekene and Helen Okop to bless me and in my moment of trial with my acute health situation and Mr. Willie Udofia in finding accommodation for me to rent and God always is my shoulder to lean on, was love of God is His of my favorite words of wisdom shares. He invites me thus, "Abide in my love!" And thou shalt love the LORD thy God with all thine heart, with all thy soul, and, and with all thy might…. "Thou shalt fear the LORD thy GOD, and serve him, and shalt swear by his name."(1 Corinthians 13:13, John 15:9 & Deut 6: 13). His is love and happiness, both contagious!!!!

We are connected by God through His words of wisdom and by heartstrings always, you will be also rewarded through eternity when you let Him make the right choice and guide you to the end of your faith journey. There is always joy and, what He wants for us is to draw near to Him and He will draw near to us and any who draws near to Him (James 4:8), sees divine favors. What we must remember is that happiness, though it is the result of hard work, would not be all possible, if it weren't for our Lord and Savior. All of the joy and passion, inspiration, of God is your happiness, and success all are matters of the heart, which have been freely given to all of us.

And is possible to achieve by His grace as well the by-product of your efforts to bless is for bless another brother, or sister (young/old), regardless of color and tongue and background is doing to God's work. And, if you are doing good will to the person that is you are doing as it is to Him than to the person is you're blessed, are blessings, and watch how much you will be love of His prosperously rewarded. If you apply the wisdom from above to your daily life, inspiration will emerge, and find we must not ignore it. If you start doing something positive for the good of all, goodwill it can inspire the heart to spur it is for greatness. Believe it or not, you can be great.

At any age and surely, everyday we are blessed. And every deed you are sowing is a seed of love and that too is a gift of wisdom and Scripture says, "Enjoy serving the LORD, and he will give you what you want" (psalm 37: 4: NIV). Psalms 119: 165 here sums, "Great peace have they which love thy law: and nothing shall offend them." Experiencing God's peace eternal life beyond human imagination and is the eternal Love blessing and power of WISDOM. Above all, wisdom spurs happiness, and this book you have in your hands should be used to acquire of it more of inspirational words of wisdom as all is a gift of God's love, knowledge you can gain and is for evangelism as all along stressed is the will of God for us to encourage each other to inspire.

Reach out to others and we all are in need of help for hope and inspiration for strength to move on, don't give up on hope in God. And neither to fear and doubt what God can do for you. For, His purpose is far beyond our human imagination. Please, don't let your faith in Him either to fail you and words of wisdom hold them tightly all are divine blessings and a gift of love and is through words and actions is from Scripture and God himself that we all finds grace, the joy is the strength to endure, praying God uses this to bless us and teach us to love everyone same also.

It will raise your awareness on the importance of finding inspiration, and it also reflects on its power and joy, including how love empowers to overcome. Hoping, you will not give up and praying that the days ahead will bring you more hope as well as all blessings and happiness that you always pray and hope for success and be inspired even more. Please, be sure to cling on to His knowledge wherever you can find it. Learn to appreciate inspiring books and learn all that you can from the words of wisdom that are contained in these books. Most importantly, please develop your passion to fulfill your dreams and to never give up for God blesses us everywhere!

Once you are able to open your heart and your mind, you will see that the inspiration for our growth and progress is all around us, spurring each of us to find our true joy and happiness. However, to be open to that inspiration, you need to have a loving heart that is dedicated to Him is a harmonious lifestyle, which includes serving and giving glory to the Lord. He is ever-loving and faithful as the Creator of the universe, as well as hope for all of the world's troubles Answer.

I can never say enough how grateful I am to God. His promises shall forever be fulfilled in our lives as long as we meet the conditions for those promises. As stated in one of my books, "A Daughter's Love," "His plans are the best for us." Also, according to Jeremiah 29:11, it says, "For I know the thoughts that I think toward you, said the Lord, thoughts of peace and not evil, to give you an expected end." God is relevant in our lives, and He has given us the tools that we need to work with and succeed. I am so grateful that He daily blesses us and as His large family.

Please, be sure to count all of your priceless treasures, and do not take His blessings for granted. Do not ignore His warning to love the words of inspirational wisdom, because there is power in inspiration! As you seek to know the Author of "infinite wisdom," know that He wants you to rely upon His will more than anything else. Rest assured that you will find happiness and with a loving heart filled with joy and that is right there for your greatness knowledge is of God. With love in our hearts, we can cherish the friendships that we develop amongst one another all.

This chapter, along with the rest of this book, encourages inspiration in the hearts of men, women, boys, girls, the young, and the old. It shows you that you too can be empowered to live a fulfilling, meaningful life full of love and happiness. You can make a big difference in your life as well as your family and community's lives and the lives of others throughout the world. Is live life to its fullest when we are blessedly rewarded with faith that works alongside words of love and actions wisdom, for as the wise proverb says, "Awareness adds to quality to life," fact! Remember, a quality education can open our hearts as well as our mindsets, and it can also open many doors. For us to have both formal and informal education (school of wisdom), ideally both quality education as all matters and these are my reasons, ideal to gain knowledgeable insights.

That is sure with understanding, is for a quality lifestyle there is value in wisdom both for personal and also public lives-yes, when in business and professional fields able to relate well is properly and foster good human and public relations is great for unity and progress collectively and individually. How as well about proper managerial skills? It is useful for socio-political and economic development. Above all, there is power and prospects with wisdom in soundly raising our children-that is hope right there for all of us! That is also why this work emphasizes positive encouragement to give us and our youth mostly them hope a brighter future, has every page tips.

For using unconditional love and acceptance to shape faith and today's youth that will all help to minimize with many delinquency offense, if we show them love and teach words of love and wisdom it will help with building character and enhancing academic excellence and integrity too as Much as it offer hope and inspires to motivate them. We should gladly glorify Him, for He has made it possible for us to realize our dreams and to live our lives to the fullest, God so good. He is the name above all names and this is how God redeems us at countless costs, we know His name is Jesus: Emmanuel's name is so sweet, and yes, Jesus' name is so sweet, "God is with us" (Matt. 1:23).

And is always I thank Him being the Supreme Higher Being, Lord, and God Almighty, of whose goodness is what gives us greatness in our hearts. We must take a stand in God's name is where for a good, quality education, for there is hope of a brighter future when we are educated. Ultimately, when you are giving from your heart, please give Him all the glory and honor first, it is enhance! Once we are able to share His blessings of hope, and love is He will turn all sorrows into joys. Do not give up on God's gift to you, for it blesses you and makes you established love and life of Canaan's land, more testifying to His glory and honor for what He has done for you and I what no one else could have and we definitely are blessed to possess the very special Joy!

Love that comes from above all inspiration is awesome for it medicates heart with hope. Without peace and love and joy and them, we would not be able to have a loving, giving, caring, and sharing heart. It may not be an easy road to travel, but it will all pay off, end is always joy as always when you endure. It makes it all thrilling and worthwhile journey of love and faith all is a blessing inspires during your journey. Please read Proverbs 12:24 and 14:23 to help you in your travels. I hope and pray that all of your joys be endless, that your dreams are fulfilled, and that you are able to achieve true greatness in your heart and blessings that you are searching for is all message of the power of inspiration is that all of your endeavors bring you happiness everyday.

Please, let's take time to appreciate one another and to have a kind and sensitive heart us all. Most importantly, please don't forget to be thankful, use the wisdom that you are surrounded with inspiration is like the air that we breathe and that is also the love of God given to us freely. I continue to thank God for us all and happy for The United States is blessed in that it has an open-door educational policy along with an effective, quality education system in place for everyone. Which can open many doors on the path to being successful as have been blessed with being able to take advantage of this rare of its opportunity of being able to freely go to school to become as a person more educated, and inspired by that love and ideals of huge hearts of love extended to me. I and others, and the disabled too are protected from being ridiculed as the government takes care of us.

And, I thank God for America and, is lesson to learn as blessed is a nation blessed of love by God who is compassionate and God of love and simplicity. Believe that you can be the best! And can excel in getting a quality education and you will be blessed with enlightened heart and is only transformed mind. Both scriptural and academic education, when combined, can lead to the knowledge of being able to better one's life. Your life will be blessed and enriched, and your spiritual awareness will be more in focus than ever is knowledge of God and wisdom transforms us as human and that says simply mental knowledge from formal school alone does not add up.

When it comes to wisdom, you have to taste the joy that springs from above is love that is the knowledge to help us find truth and find love and joy and prevent panicky more and traumas. Ultimately, quality love matters more than not quantity, and needless to say, wisdom is quality is love of God's mouth it is a priceless treasure of life and is far richer and healthier for the heart as well as the mind is "pills of wisdom" words of wisdom state, "Man does not live by bread alone" (Matthew 4:4)! It is with these words, along with countless others, that have been able to give me the power of inspiration to do the writing that I so love to share. You need inspiration to put the words that you believe into action it takes love of God and prayer of faith, grace and believing.

Believe Him makes miracles and inspires us to rather than boasting about what you have learned, put what you have learned from school and put to good use, mostly by "practicing what you preach!" We need to hear kindness in words and actions more than cheap chit-chat in order to have encouragement and confidence and is also in thinking good thoughts for profoundness is will be a blessing much and in giving money too also all are what creates love and to continue on in our quest for greatness in the heart, indeed, a gift of kind words matters, for us and well said is this eloquent word of wisdom, "a gift with kind words is double the gift." That is unequivocal!!

When we are able to express words of love in kindness amongst one another, creates in us confidence and love within us, is what makes us and along with a quality education, we can be assured a love is of a productive life and happiness also makes to be what God loves us all to be. However, even if you are not in a position at the moment to obtain a higher education, you can give love and still acquire words of wisdom that will inspire your heart motivates as it spurs you on to greatness, but please still you pursue that and think of also formal education when you can.

As Martin Luther King, Jr. stated, "Intelligence plus character – that is the goal of true education." By now, you have realized that this book you are now reading has been engaging us with words of love, educational, and entertaining. I highly recommend that you not only take in the wisdom you have discovered in this book, but that you absorb wisdom from all books that is you read and learn and apply the wisdom that you obtain wisely use and cultivate. By doing this, you will have the tools in place to achieve the inspiration needed to fulfill your dreams, and there is the love is inspiring the world could definitely use more inspired hearts and knowledge from. An informed mind is an educated mind, and inspiration helps us achieve our goals in life is hope.

We need to be educated so that we can realize our dreams as well as help others realize theirs. Whether we are meant to be leaders or followers, we should all be knowledgeable people and open to what the world has in store for us. We can be either charismatic leaders or patriotic citizens who follow these leaders, but what matters is that we all have the knowledge needed to give ourselves and others the hope and inspiration needed to progress as a society. This includes being knowledgeable on what is going on in the world around you, offers opportunity that helps too. In order to gain knowledge and wisdom, we must all be aware of our surroundings, whether it is the news or current events happening in our own communities and is it beneficial everyone?

By being aware of our surroundings, we are better able to cope with obstacles that we may face in attempting to fulfill our dreams. As these words of wisdom say, "The young should be taught and the old should be honored." Inspiration matters to every heart, and it blesses us to do great things in our lives. It brings beautiful memories to the forefront and enables us to look at the present with hope and the future with promise. Inspiration is my legacy, and I want you all to remember to please never give up on inspiration, for it will give you greatness in the heart all is hope for God loves to see in us soaring, gives strength and grace to endure regardless of trial.

He is there is with us daily and His presence goes with us as He offers peace in the desert. Love abides and grace is His sufficient is to have more hope and is with love and abundant grace. Faith to endure to the end of our journey and is no matter the pain is there is a cure for us so far there is also a loving God who heals and can always handle cures and, so there's hope for us and "all power belongs to Him". He gives grace to the humble and His Love endures to the end with us He abides with us, my family using His name did for them what they asked and He answered.

He answered them and opened my eyes to see and I can, testify more today on the Great God and greatness and Great Healing Power. Of everyday are more those say how much His love rescued us. Saved us from His power, love and grace because cares deeply. He is wonderful and in all He does marvelous and mightier things greatly, very merciful to me and this is another one testimony and this time is even more increases my faith with brand-new confidence and brand-new joy. It takes faith evermore, not so much the righteous things we do, though that may play.

Its role also, significantly is a noble thing for Scripturally confirms, "But the path of the just is as the shinning light, that shineth more and more into perfect day" Moreover, "The Lord gives sight to the blind, the Lord lifts up those who are bowed down, the Lord loves the righteous"

(Pro.4:18/Ps.146:17). He made me to walk this time and this is my rehabilitation. But, I know mostly the only reason am here is because of His love, grace's fervor blessed. Is hope that inspires my faith to sing along through the hour of trial and the Lord uses His words to teach me the secret of contentment and never to give up for me that is why I am more focused on Him too.

Faith in God and that can sing through days of sorrows inspired is to call upon Him, and I take my situation all to Him in prayer and continue to watch, serve and trust by faith in actions as always, you hope and will find strength and power and joy and peace of mind with Him glimpse. Of hope when you call upon the Lord and clinging to Him and I called and claimed by that name is That is how much He answers and shows up for me, that is always faith in Him matters always and in trusting He is an answering God and Savoir of the world and surely that is who makes me. To be alive and able in doing what I had lost hope, now more hope for what may have seem to be hopeless. A near death situation God reversed them and brought His Love and Majesty to me all.

My life, this child and daughter of His is alive an action God is by grace and transformed by love of God and by the Holy Spirit to finally become that love for others and that is what God has destined my life and wanted it to be a blessing. Is joy for to inspire hearts and nurture lives through creative expression of faith in Him, is inspiration and that sure meliorates the heart is of love and power of God is certainty. God loves is enduring and nothing takes Him by surprises at all! Sure, so never give up on your journey to inspiration, joy, and happiness, for your blessings will benefit not only yourself but you along with others the world over. The inspiration that we receive strengthens our hearts and minds and enables us to be active in supporting one another.

We must always cherish the gifts from God and use them to their fullest potential. As stated by the great philosopher Aristotle, "We ought to so far as it is within our power, to aspire to immortality, and do all that we can to love in conformity with the highest that is within us; for even if it is small in quantity, in power and preciousness, it far excels all the rest." That is so true. Unequivocally, remember, the past always ushers in the present, and the love in your heart can ease your pains, even those pains caused by others. If you believe in the greatness of your heart!

Trust in your gut and God's love is all ability to excel against all odds, for in the end, you will be stronger and much as a better person. Hopefully, by now your hearts are inspired and this book will guide you in the right path to lifelong success to do more than you had thought and to know you are more trust and obey inspirational words of wisdom and have faith in our Lord and Savior. Inspiration can do wonders for one's life, and I want to encourage you to aspire to grab the knowledge hold of inspiration. And, please don't give up and do not let your faith to fail you either and never let go inspiration and words of God's mouth as the best of instruction and love.

This work is a blue print and a book that summons everyone all nations and all people to rise up and serve with a heart of love is greatness for the sake of our children's future is at stake. It is time for us to take action and, Regardless of age, sex, nationality, race, tribe, and affiliation. We must rise up and strive for a quality way of life. Let's make it a priority to form an alliance that to love and to care for others. I keep believing cherishing in my heart that with faith in our Creator, we can overcome our trials and live a happy, peaceful and purposeful life with all. We must remember to train our children when they are young so that they are equipped with love the proper armor to and is to help to succeed happily in our world. Education is needed for a quality way of life, and when you come up against adversity, the hope and inspiration you have in your heart will get you through those trying times.

Conclusion, Greatness is in the Heart –A Tribute to Inspiration, and love is greatest and it is the heart's power and it is in our humility before God that our greatness is revealed to us all! But before we go, let me ask you, please, if you don't mind, do any of you recall events that have transpired in your lives and someone that deserve recognition? If so, how do you feel about that very special person much as well those events today? Do they still give you satisfaction? Do you find it being blessings and they enlighten you and enable you to use your gifts properly? Dare to think and dream big dreams, and be not slothful in passion of hope and investment, for there is of higher power Hope is inspiration helps you to realize your dreams. Good attitude and good deeds done in the past can also serve being helpful as inspiration for your future inspires.

Please, help spread the good news around the globe, for the world is in dire need of love and inspiration. We need more people of integrity and honesty than who tell lie, steal, and curse and also blames more and love to cheat and get quick fix instead of working and getting decency of life to be of hope. We must keep in mind that in order to realize all of our dreams, we need the love and wisdom that God gives to us. Remember this and take to heart that "power belongs to God." Our Greatness is in the heart, and we must trust in His hope and have faith in His inspired words of wisdom. As the Scripture states, "He is a just God, who owns everything in the world, even the king's heart is in His hand" (Proverbs 21:1).

May the love and passion in our hearts make us all that God intended for us to be, and as it pleases Him and May we as well receive the marvelous breakthroughs bestowed upon us excel. Love makes life more bearable, and ultimately enables us to have a beautiful life, and thank God. "By humility and fear of the Lord are riches, honor and life" (Proverbs 22:4). The kind of wealth that is secured by wisdom and knowledge does amazing things for our lives and takes power that is of God's grace and faith to do things that are of the heart and great strength comes from faith. Is the heart of wisdom is well-protected by the love and knowledge that we acquire from above.

Scripture teaches us that "the eyes of the Lord preserves knowledge" (Proverbs 22:12), and "every way of a man is right in his own eye; but the Lord pondereth the heart" He is Lord is all the Redeemer too (Proverbs 21:2). Dear friends, I want you all to keep in mind that we must have the right frame of mind and live by the inspired words of wisdom that are in our hearts hope is there for us and all in dire need of hope, and we need inspirational words of encouragement to satisfy both our physical and emotional needs and mostly spiritual fulfillment and reaching goals.

The soul needs the satisfaction found with inspiring words just as the body needs all of nutrients to be healthy. There is a huge difference between the happiness offered by this world and of that from above. I crave inspirational wisdom more so now than ever, and I give all of my heart with thanks to God, for His passion in humanity is never-ending love, joy and inspiration. I speak from my heart and blessed being loved passionately by Him has changed everything in my life and love changes everything and that the heart's power too is of great and deeper joy. I have definitely had a more fulfilling life since I gave my heart to Him totally surrendered and my joy.

Heart is full of joy transforming is of the emotions in my heart by the love of God, and by the Holy Spirit to gradually become that love for others and using my weakness point to become strength and problem to power and is prosperity that is Teacher and my God is awesome Power. He that coaches me gradually and gently and daily encourages my heart to see things differently and opens my heart and mind. To be of hope is of being a heart rejoices daily for His blessings. We must never give up on our faith, for without it, we have nothing and please keep hope alive. For that is all that makes glimpse that shines us on and there is no more despair, once suffering becomes a healing power that love is so never give up! I have been healed and empowered also.

And nothing beats being in love more blessed being resilient also. Hopefully, we all can begin to love God most and well appreciate the love of God and as well each other through the same power of love as joy is of inspirational reading. Ultimately, regardless of our status, race, tribe, or nationalities, remember, "rich and poor meet together, for the Lord is the maker of all" (Proverbs 22:2). Pray that God can make His way into every heart, for we are brothers and also sisters working together towards the common goal of love for everyone. The Book of Proverbs and Psalms and Chronicles 22:19 are excellent passages to read for powerful words of inspiration and in trusting in the power of God's love and believing in the miracle of faith in God's power.

If you want a successful life that is filled with social, physical, financial, and spiritual all prosperity, never give up on true happiness and truths. Remember, inspiration offers hope, faith, love, passion, joy, and much more. God's love is always there for you, and His promises of joy are all boundless and timeless. Rather than give up, always be hopeful, cheerful, and happy, and keep pursuing the knowledge that inspires us to greatness. Wisdom encourages hearts to dare to love and to pursue peace, happiness, and thankfulness and God is always with us and all we do!

As you have read, inspiration enables us to transform our hearts for the better. Whether you choose being happy and productive is a personal decision, and I am proud to say that I chose to be happy to trust in Him. Your passions can help you fulfill your dreams, and remember that the road to success is not without hard work. By examining one's attitude daily, we can make it is adjustments when needed so that we can achieve all that we imagined, for out of it comes "the well spring of life" (Proverbs 4:23). Book of Isaiah 59: 20, testifies, "The Redeemer shall come".

When we are actively pursuing our inspiration, you can be assured that once you find it, you will be filled with joy, confidence, and energy. When you tap into your inner creativity, you will be focused on the task at hand. The kind, encouraging words that you give and receive will fill your spiritual needs, and ultimately, provided you think positive, the power of inspiration will lift you in prayer is as simple as was eloquently said by Arthur Ashe, "from what we get, we can make a living; what we give, however, makes a life." That what makes for hope inspires words.

Thankful also for my daughters, that their inspirations also offers hope, as greatly as their words of encouragement what God used to keep me with more hope, and they kept me on track. Fostering my love of writing to also to publish like other moms to share my story to offer hope also, I treasure you being there for me and, wishing the best is so happy and am, so proud of you. Both being in my life; I love you as it's of joy of your inspiration what I borrowed for my hope. That is of strength as well when my hope was gone-Mom's heart is grateful and greatly for God inspires my passion writing, inspiring hearts to offer hope as your love wishes for my life and for others to live life fully. Mom is so happy and so thankful to God for you, your passion and love is thanks dear and for being my joy and friends, looking out for me and others; you both know.

Mom's love is a given is unconditional and as is always mom's is forever sweet love and always and for you. As my blessings from God and together we've come from a very tedious and a long emotional journey and, we're as well happy to endure and to work hard, struggled together and that is am thankful for God loves us. That is all your love and commitments and the bonding that is of God's grace and mercy shows upon us. Blessed to have you and your love and so proud to be your birth mother and, I'll always be thankful to God for His unfailing love has brought you to my life and also your thoughtful input is heart warming. Blessed and thanks is for your enthusiasms is of joy and love too is from start to finish one of my blessings and gifts that is loving God offers me, includes both of you is of His grace, love given is for everlasting, no more beloved than Him is for He loves, offers us life is with hope and passion that can't be substituted.

No is one like Him, Evermore is of joy for there is hope and all that struggles is paid off. I say this is worth being thankful nothing like Him, fulfilling for us that family, love of friendship is a blessing is manifesting this is the book. God Love assures us hope, this too shall pass!

Throughout this book, I have stated repeatedly that life in general is a matter of the love greatness in one's heart. Happiness, like success, takes faith, vision, courage, hard work, prayer, and wisdom. The world we live in today has too much misery in it – it is up to us to use our love hearts of wisdom to transform the world into a place of happiness and progress. We must build our lives on the foundation of God's unshakeable love. He is love and His love is unconditional, which means we can get through anything. As these wise word says, "He who walks with wise men become wise" (Proverbs 13:20). Walking with God is the best of the best of friends to keep.

On July 8th, 2012, I had the blessing of hosting the women of the Houston chapter of the Akwa Ibom Association. I had such a wonderful time with them as we interacted with each other and shared stories of joy and love. They made me so proud of them, and I am honored to have such a faithful, extended family of sisters and I have shared also what experiences of faith is and joy of inspiration from the inspired hearts both of young and old and from across borders. Nothing endures like friendship and love, and I hope that all of us will remember that God is all. Is Love is the essence of life NEVER GIVE UP! Gratitude is the memory of the heart, keep love and, a song in your heart!

Its power and inspiration its legacy also keeps that hope in you alive and you will never regret it! In closing, this is my life's dream to have been able to write *Greatness Is in the Heart-A Tribute to Inspiration*, to you, is blessing of hope. It is of great humility and passion to share with you how inspiration has brought joy to my life. I have God to thank for all of my blessings. May the glory and the honor be in His name forever more! My wish is that we all find greatness in our hearts, and I also wish each of you/us best that life has to offer and I thank God being Joy!

This is what a blessing and that is loving life of love and living and relating happily with God makes it rich for your soul and any human being kind hearted, is great character and attitude makes you even happier and healthy in heart, mind and sprit right there living a life of hope also I have seen that fountain flowing for the soul that was thirsty is now full and well is of success as well right there we can relate easily with people easily and foster love and unity with prospect. Once that love is joy, in you saturates thoughts for God more love is when you find happiness is there with all of peace and harmony deeper joy all of them is there and with those that you come across in life is all and everyone but it is all in God's hand. Is the love of God that inspires most joy what I have found and His blessings are for all of us to enjoy also worldwide with everyone in sharing!!

Ultimately, He is "Greatness is in the Heart," and Inspiration is its legacy, Gratitude is the memory and Love is the Heart's power! Friend, if you enjoy this, you will also enjoy other books by the author and thanks for your reading the volume as five series each is racy sure we are also blessed. More to read and coming soon is the Joy of Living a Dream, and, I know you will love the second series. As this and others thank you so much, for your support and God bless you, and all of us. Love, Caroline, your inspired friend at heart! And of reminder that next edition is going to be of even more interesting. Here for you to enjoy is fully of blessings, health and happiness!!

Carol Thompson is my by line and that was my first name for publishing and now again! Please, take note and any comments or input for this and subsequent work is highly appreciated.

Biography

Caroline Arit Okon Thompson (popularly known as Arit Ema/Carol Ita) is a naturalized U.S. citizen and the author of six books, including her latest, Greatness Is in the Heart: *A Tribute to Inspiration!* In December 2006, she successfully completed her requirements for the Master of Science degree in counselor education at Florida International University (FIU) in Miami, Florida. Prior to that, she graduated cum laude from Spelman College in Atlanta, Georgia where, as a work-study student, was a peer counselor to new students in the sociology department. After graduation, she worked briefly with C&S Bank and in October 1981, traveled to Nigeria, served in the National Youth Service Corps (NYSC), which is similar to the U.S. Peace Corps as a news reporter for the Nigerian Television Authority (NTA) Channel 9 in Calabar, Cross River State.

Throughout her academic career, Ms. Thompson also received numerous educational honors. In 1980–81, she was on the National Dean's List (the Thirtieth Annual Edition of which she was selected to be featured in 2007), was featured in *Who's Who in American Universities and Colleges*, received the Amy Chadwick Foundation Scholarship Award, Spelman Seniors Honors Class, and joined the Alpha Kappa Delta International Sociology Honor Society. In 1987, she was awarded the Mortar Board, the highest honor for college females.

The Cross River State Government of Nigeria sponsored her trip to the United States in recognition of her excellence. In 2005–2006, her biography was published on the Chancellor's List 11 (#25605423-3), on which only 1 percent of the students from the 3,000 U.S. colleges and universities are honored each year for their academic achievements, community leadership, and positive performance. In 2006, she was one of the three recipients of Dade County's Counseling Association Student Scholarship, based on her academic endeavors. Professionally, has been also awarded several certificates, including a certificate in

Public Information (1985) obtained from the National Institute of Public Information in Kaduna, Nigeria.

Certificate in Middle Management (Madrecon) in 1985; both programs were sponsored by the NYSC Directorate, Lagos, Nigeria (Abuja now is national headquarters); been certified in Medical Terminology Training, Vocational Rehabilitation Counselor Training, others are Sexual Harassment Liaison Training, Americans with Disability Acts Training, Basic Computer Skills Training, all sponsored by job also, achieved various certificates of recognition for community service. Ms. Thompson relocated to Miami, Florida, in December 1989 and worked as a VR counselor for the State of Florida for more than ten years. One of her most great professional accomplishments was Counselor of the Year nominee by the Miami-Dade Community College's MEED Program in 1998. One other best professional as well as memorable moments, among others, was when she was a senior VR counselor met and shook hands with then president of United States, President Clinton in October 1996 at Miami Dade Community College(North Campus), during one of his visits to South Florida.

Ms. Thompson has worked predominately in the media and public relations field, including serving as an Information Officer/Head of the Information Department Unit (NYSC) Secretariat in Calabar for seven years (from 1982 to 1989) where last posting was Port Harcourt. She has been a freelance writer for several publications and has written articles for renowned newspapers and news agencies in Nigeria, such as *Nigeria Chronicles, Pioneer, Daily Times, Guardian, Observer, Sketch,* and *Community Concord,* which have featured her work as an NYSC Public Relations Officer.

Ms. Thompson has also penned feature stories on women, youth, and religious issues for many agencies and organizations and has additionally appeared on numerous radio and television programs, both in Nigeria and, United States, and contributed to various newsletters and papers, such as *Spelman Spotlight* and the *Techtorial Newsletter* in Rock Hill, while as a student at York Technical College, in South Carolina and served as the editor/historian of the Spelman class and in upon her returning to Nigeria one of her major achievements was to successfully author, *Cross River State at a Glance,* published in 1987 under married name (Arit

Ema), which constituted a memorable piece of her professional work of her most appreciated, honored by a corps member.

A poem-ARIT EMA-ENERGETIC MADAM, dedicated by a youth corps member, Israel C. Uhuegbu (1984–85 service year), highly commended her dedicated and selfless service to the world and honored her with an inspiring poem published in the book mentioned above and poem is also featured in this book. It speaks highly of her traits and what she stands for, as attested by all her published works and personality. Other noble duties performed as an NYSC officer to her first country of Nigeria included the production of the *Cross-Corper Magazine*/ "Cross-Corper Calling" (a weekly radio program for corps members), news analysis for both state and federal.

Radio corporations and the quarterly Cross-Corper newsletters served as great tools for information guides for Youth Corps stationed in the Cross-River State of Nigeria and beyond, all during her tenure as public relations officer. Over the years Ms. Thompson has been an active member in the Nigerian American community. She has been involved in many community, civic, and Christian associations both in Nigeria and America, including serving as a board member of the City of North Miami Beach Library and Commission on the Status of Women; was a member of the Black Caucus of the American Library Association and the Rotary Club of Opa Locka, Miami. She was pioneer treasurer of the Nigerian Association of South Florida.

Also served as assistant secretary the Akwa-Ibom Association of Nigeria (Miami Branch) in a similar capacity for a two-term period was briefly the secretary during Hurricane Andrew; was an active member of the women's prayer group and choir of the Northwest Baptist Church; visited frequently with the women's prayer group of Evangel International Church under Pastor Jenkins Jennings. She was a member of the Virtuous Women Ministries group of the Beulah Pilgrim Holiness Church, was named the president of Women in Action Association of the Faith and Life Fellowship Ministries. She was a member of the Good Women's Association, as well as the associate editor of the *Calvary News,* was the secretary of the fund-raising committee.

Ms. Thompson actively as a choir member; founded the first Prayer Breakfast Ministries in Christ Apostolic Church in Miami. Thompson pursues her goals, social growth, and spiritual is progress both with focus on molding youth and family unity with a gift of compassion for others, is her passion in helping people to solve problems so wherever she goes, her mission is same too. Write, and to encourage and inspire all, mostly youths with actions as such is her passion for this and all her works, world wide ministering of love and mercy is her gifts heart's work and faith is what motivates to (young/old) with love. Worships with Apostolic Church, which is her loving maternal grandparents' faith, but birth and family church is Qua Iboe Church of Nigeria, where she has been actively involved with since youth. In 1988, she served as the first female assistant secretary with the board of Qua Iboe Church Committee (Calabar District), Nigeria.

And also the treasurer and assistant secretary of the Nka Emem (Peace Association), the Women's Fellowship, church building finance committee, more to name an associate member of the Nigerian Institute of Public Relations (NIPR). Ms. Thompson has done extensive research on issues relating to youth, women, slavery, and power of faith in God. Her work has drawn wide attention. Her first public involvement on humanitarian service in the United States dates back to the late 1970s, when she was a student in Spelman Atlanta, Georgia. She was selected, among others, to speak on a televised program as a parent at City Hall on Title One issues, specifically advocating school lunch for pre-school children.

When she questioned former UN Ambassador Donald McHenry at Spelman College on issues relating to foreign students and immigration in April 1980, this was featured on the front page of the *Atlanta Constitution* newspaper. Her first public inspirational speaking on the subject "The Power of Faith—Lord, Increase My Faith" was in 1998 at Beulah Pilgrim Holiness Church. In that same week, she was interviewed and featured on the front page of the *Miami Times* by its then-editor, Mohammed Hamaludin, now with the *Miami Herald*, who was inspired by her book, *The Joy of the Overcomes: Slavery from an African Perspective*. The interview was titled "Book written over three years is testimony of the power of faith."

In 2005, Ms. Thompson released a new book, *A Daughter's Love*, and was featured on the FIU Web page in an interview conducted by

Alejandra Serna, Contributing Writer for Flu's *Beacon* newspaper, as she presented the hard copy of the book to former Vice Provost (Biscayne Bay Campus) and Professor Raul Moncarz. It was captioned "Death inspires student's new book." Other media, including radio, featured the book as well, and the *Miami Times* show cased it in a piece by Gigi Tinsley.

Ms. Thompson is blessed with two daughters: Mrs. Comfort Usoro-Chevannes and Mrs. Patricia Asari I. Efa. She is a powerful, inspirational speaker as a mistress of ceremonies. She loves to sing (mostly gospel songs), listen to jazz, travel, and dance. She has a strong interest in reading, writing, singing, community service, and church work.

Often, Ms. Thompson's very friendly, simple, humorous, and kind characteristics—among other unique qualities—put her in a tough situation. She is sometimes misunderstood by those who do not appreciate or understand her and/or what it means to be blessed and endowed with the favor of demonstrating priceless love to others.

Her work, Priceless Love, published by I-universe (2010), was also acknowledged by president Barack and First Lady Michelle Obama in 2011; she was also recognized for her work with a grant for more publications to Nigerian children, and by Inspire Women Ministries same in 2012. She is a contributing columnist: "Word of wisdom, and volunteer for the Christian Herald Newspaper.

Ms. Thompson was a member of the United Teachers of Dade and has never relented in her selfless service as a motivational speaker, youth advocate, and counselor. She was a coach for America Scores Miami for the Boys team Writing Workshop, which enabled her opportunity to teach poetry; while also the 1st grade teacher between 2007/2008 school year at Oak Grove Elementary Community School, and was an after school tutor to 3rd grade students as well. She briefly served the position of Public Relations Officer for the Akwa Ibom State Association of Nigeria (Houston, Texas Chapter). She has worked as a radio producer, a new analyst, as a freelance writer, and now with her focus on molding youth and family unity, just completed her Leadership training at Inspire Women Institute, which is a one year certificate program designed to develop leaders to have the spiritual fortitude to define, pursue, and finish God's mission.

Completed from the Whole and Made Free Ministries, Inc. War 2 Win School of Prayer trained as an intercessor. Her passion for God and humanity is also her motivational driving force forging ahead, even in hard times, she is always happiest and laughs with passion to serve more and even committed to build a community of authentic friendships. And that inspiration is strength in turning suffering always into opportunity. She is a certified inspire women motivational speaker, mentoring as a leader, you will enjoy her as an inspired master of ceremony, now lives in Texas. She last worked 2010 with the Health and Human Service Commission, Texas Work Adviser 111 when she took ill on January that was one of her saddest moments as well in life of unexpected!!!

Praise for the Author

The following excerpts, gleaned from the little known so far about Ms. Thompson by those who appreciate her work and admire her spirit as NYSC Public Relations Officer, a VR Counselor, and a writer, speak voluminously about her dedicated spirit:

So far, keen watchers of the NYSC activities in the state agree that she (Caroline Thompson) has demonstrated her worth as a Public Relations person in the area of publicity and image-building of the scheme in the nation, particularly in Cross River State... Above all, she is dynamic, rich in ideas and possesses a sense of initiative. That she is able to combine meeting the pressures of her demanding job with the task of researching for and writing this handbook, Cross River at a Glance, provides confirmation of her spirit of hard work and sense of initiative. These attributes stand out in her wherever she goes and often earns her noble accolades.

(Nnamso Umoren, Editor,
Community Concord Newspaper, 1987)

On April 15, 1987, the Mortar Board Incorporated, a prestigious national honour society of college seniors in the United States of America invited and honoured Mrs Ema by initiating her into the Spelman Senior honour society in recognition of her high scholarship, leadership and service while in the United States.

Arit, a mother of two, has among her credentials, certificates in Public Information from the National Institute of Public Information (NIPI) Kaduna, 1985 and in Middle management course from MAD-RECON, Lagos in December, 1982.

She is very friendly, simple, and kind and has interest in reading, writing, singing, community service and church work (she is currently Assistant Secretary, Nka Idorenyin and member of Women Fellowship of Qua Iboe Church, Calabar). Arit is an active member of Nigerian Institute of Public Relations (Cross River State Branch), and has many publications in Newspapers and Magazines to her credit.

Nnamso Umoren
Editor, Community Concord Newspaper
Calabar

The author interviewing a youth corper.

From an article entitled, "Nigerian Author Explores the Struggles of Africans in Overcoming the Legacy of Slavery": She shows others how the words of God can help them make their lives more productive and happier

(The *African Sun Times*,
New York, June 14–20, 2001)

I Ier words illuminate the spiritual twilight between believers' today and their eternity. Too many people want and do claim victory as something they accomplished themselves. In an encouraging and uplifting way, the author lets the readers know that they must give God the glory... Overall, this beautifully written text will help readers overcome depression and defeat misery, instead of wallowing in it." (2005)–(late) Robert B. Ingram PhD was vice Chair, Miami-Dade School Board; Assistant to the President for Urban Affairs, Florida Memorial College University.

(Culled from *A Daughter's Love*, p. xix.)

Caroline,

A wonderful testimony of your love for your deceased father and mankind: May your life always be that blessing that God has purposely designed it to be; this book should be read prayerfully and with seriousness of heart. Receive the blessings of the Lord from reading *A Daughter's Love*."

(Ozzie Richey, Retired Administrative Officer,
FIU, Miami, Florida)

"Caroline Ita has a manifest love for her family, both biological and religious; her country of Africa, as well as her adopted country of the United States of America; and God. Her love is expressed throughout the book, and having completed [reading] the book, I'm sure that you would agree with me. *Slavery from an African Perspective* is a book that should not [only] be read by people who know Caroline, but should be used as a fact-finding resource, and placed in homes, schools, and religious institutions. Editing *Slavery from an African Perspective* was heartwarming, because I felt Caroline's love being generated throughout the book. It was very interesting because I learned so much while reading it; and finally, a blessing from God, because I got the chance to meet and become friends with a young lady whose aim is to exalt her brothers and sisters and glorify God. Caroline's aim and aspiration is to love everyone, acting just like Jesus."

(Gigi Tinsley, Religious Editor: *The Miami Times*,
Miami, Florida, 2000)

Dear Caroline:

I was delighted to finally meet you at the First Annual Spirit of Independence Award Luncheon on 2/13/98.

I am enclosing a copy of MEED Alumna Julia Walters' nomination for you to keep. Always remember that your guidance, encouragement and dedication is noticed, appreciated and regarded by those who have crossed your path.

May you continue making a meaningful difference in the lives of people with disabilities!

Best wishes,
Stephanie Layton
MEED Program Director, April 6, 1998

Although Ms. Caroline Ita became my counselor in the later half [of the program], she has followed my progress even after my completion of MEED (i.e. further education/degree-seeking). Her passion for making sure that I was okay didn't just stop at finding out about me; she even reached out to my family...She has taken an interest in my future endeavors.

(1998 – Julia Walters)

Caroline has demonstrated her drive to excel in her goals by being dedicated and working hard...*A Daughter's Love* shows the love of a daughter for her father, and [deals well with the subject of] coping with the loss of her father. Her heart-felt words encourage and help others learn how to deal with the loss of a loved one ... In sum, Caroline is a disciplined, well-rounded individual.

(2006 – Raul Moncarz, Vice Provost and Professor, FIU Biscayne Bay Campus)

I have observed and found Ms. Ita to be a valuable asset to our school system and society at large...She has written a most valuable and stimulating book, *A Daughter's Love*, that speaks to her intellect and ability as a person who loves humanity. Ms. Ita will ... be there for every child with an open mind. I have known Ms. Ita to be of a high moral and ethical character.

(2006 – Geneva Lewis, Guidance Counselor,
Crestview Elementary School)

I have known Ms. Ita for the past three years and have found her to be competent, diligent and committed to learning. Caroline is ambitious and self-motivated. These qualities, in particular, allow her to achieve her best at all times ... Ms. Ita wastes no opportunity to serve and support others, and in doing so inspires those with whom she comes in contact. She is a quick study, and approaches challenges with determination and courage."

—2006 – Dwight N. Nimblett,
Coordinator, University Learning Center –
FIU Biscayne Bay Campus

Dear Caroline,

I thank God for giving me the opportunity to meet a very beautiful and special friend like you. God is awesome. I'll keep in touch so you will know how much knowledge I gain from your wisdom. You are an outstanding writer. God bless you. It is a blessing to know you and a pleasure to work with you.

Gloria Barnes, Principal
Treasure Island Elementary School
Miami, Florida, 2005

ARIT EMA-ENERGETIC MADAM
A dedication to the author

By

ISRAEL CHINYO UHUEGBU
NYSC 1984/85 SERVICE YEAR

I

A woman among women
Like a Hercules, she swiftly runs for the rescue. Like an
Eagle, she flies high above problems, obstacles and difficulties
To have an assignment or the day's task accomplished.
Mere looking at the mind it seems to say: I have a goal to reach
And with determination, all will be done neatly and to its
Logical conclusion;
Behold a willing mind.
Behold a heart pure and sincere like the colorful Rose flower.
Behold a broad and a hospitable mind; like the prestigious
Broad Avenue of the French Presidential Palace: Champs Elysees.
Behold a genius of the very finest quality. Behold a talent.

II

Madam If I put in few lines these prophetic verses: I make and
Declare them very voluntarily and they are pure and just.
I am undertaking to honor you with my pen because silver and
Gold have I none. In honoring you, I do also remember your very
Numerous co-workers; Almost a year has elapsed for a service year.

It is a year of stocktaking. It is a period of national experiments.
See this sea of corps members from different ethnic groups—all
Converge to search for a national identity.
Soon we shall disperse to our different States, and to our different
Calls by the divine, to the nation; Keep this national spirit up.
In the words of the French President Francois Mitterand, "everything is
A struggle and everything requires patience and courage."

On this beautiful
On this prestigious
On this magnificent
Tablet, I print and decorate
Your respectable name;
On our veritable national history

Eagles have voices
Doves have voices
Diamonds speak in clear accent
Oceans and deserts are wide
Mountains and heavens are so high
But yours speak of care, concern,
Devotion to duty and commitment to the national call.

Let humanity hear
Let speech be the principles
Let talent and art reign
Your enthusiasm, dear Madam,
Your determination to display this humanism,
have encouraged the writer.

Ami Ndifreke (I will not forget)
Cross River State
Ami Ndifreke
Hard working NYSC State
Secretariat Co-workers
Ami Ndifreke
Itam Corps members,
Ami Ndifreke
Itu Paramount Ruler
Ami Ndifreke
Itam
Ami Ndifreke
Mbiatok, Obong Itam ye Ekritam

Ami Ndifreke Itam Secondary School
Ami Ndifreke
NYSC Liaison Officer Itu
1984/85. Dosunmu, J. O.
Ami Ndifreke
The people of Cross River
Ami Ndifreke *Afo (you)* Madam.

Swifter than eagles
Purer than Diamond
The daughter of Destiny
A woman of letters.

To your very children
A lesson is being given to them
these motherly footprints.
These treasures of motherhood.

To the other woman folk
They are to learn these paths to:
Selfless service, diligence,
Honesty, concern, care and commitment.

It is not a mistake to place
You on our National history
because I know of what
stuff you are made.
Your very name like the
foundation of a house is built
on the precious stones.
Your mind, your spirit
all are made of precious material.

The task before you is enormous
Your office is one that must continue to attend to the

problem of corps members:
be it when in hardship
lack, help, advise, guidance …

I keep treasuring all of you in my mind.
Keep up in your very spirit.
Hard work and after hard work
Independence, so said a poet.
In the words of the French
President M. Francois Mitterand: Everything is a
Struggle and everything requires courage and effort
May the God Almighty keep watch over you.

Bibliography

Books

Bell, Buddy. *Faithfulness Is The Crowbar of God.* Tulsa, Oklahoma: Christian Publisher Services, Inc, 1986.

Beulah Pilgrim Holiness Church Youth: *Celebrating Black History Month.* Miami, Florida,

Blaustone, J. *The Joy of Parenthood: Inspiration and Encouragement for Parents.* New York: Meadowbrook Press, 1993.

Boose, L. & F. Berry. *Daughters and Fathers.* Baltimore: The John Hopkins University Press, 1989.

Carman, A. Transforming Emotions In A Leader's Heart-Foreword by Jill Briscoe. Houston: Inspire Women Ministry publishing, 2007.

Carman, A. & R. Carman. Making Sense of Your Life: Breakthroughs to Finish the Dream. Houston: Inspire Women publishing, 2012.

Cosby, J. *Childhood.* New York: G. P. Putnam's Sons, 1991.

Dash, L. *When Children Want Children: The Urban Crisis of Teenage Childbearing.* New York: William Morrow and Co., 1989.

David, J. & H. Harrington. *Growing Up African.* New York: William Morrow and Co., 1991. Department of Information and Publicity, SWAPO of Namibia. *To be Born a Nation – The Liberation Struggle of Namibia.* London: Zed Press, 1981.

Ema, Arit. *Cross River State at a Glance.* Calabar, Nigeria: Government Printing Press, 1987.

Esen, Akpan J.A. *Ibibio Profile.* Calabar, Nigeria: Paico Press & Books Ltd., 1982.

Etuk, E. *Fatherhood Is Not for Babies.* Washington, DC: Emida International Publishers, 1997.

Gardner, R. *The Girls & Boys Book about Good & Bad Behavior.* Cresskill: Creative Therapeutics. 1990.

Helen Steiner Rice, Daily *Devotional Calendar.* Compiled and edited by Virginia J. Ruehlman. Gibson Greetings, Inc. 1996.

Hoskins, Bob. *They Still Want the Truth.* Miami, Florida: Life Publishers International, 1987

John, Apostle. God Is Love. The Holy Bible: 1 John 4: 8 and 16.

Kelly, R. *Divine Discipline: How to Develop and Maintain Self-Control.* Gretna: Pelican Publishing, 1992.

Michael, E. *The Father's Role: Cross Cultural Perspective.* Hillsdale: Lawrence Erlbaum Associates, 1987.

Oshodi, J. *Sex, Violence, Drugs and America.* Miami: The Oshodi Foundation Inc, 1994.

Richter, C. The Light In The Forest. New York: Bantam Books Publishers, 1980.

Sadiku, M. *Secrets of Successful Marriages.* Philadelphia: Covenant Publishers, 1991.

Thompson, C. A. O. *Priceless Love: A Matter of The Heart And The Gift For A Lifetime.* Lincoln: iUniverse, 2010.

Thompson, C.A.O. (Jonathan Essien; (The Christian Herald p. 32 (February 2012)

Thompson, C. A. O. *Parental Influence Matters.* Lincoln: iUniverse, 2007.

Thompson, C. A. O. *A Daughter's Love: Remembering My Father, Teacher and My Friend(s).* Lincoln: iUniverse, 2005.

Thompson, C. *The Joy of the Overcomers: Slavery from an African Perspective.* Pittsburgh: Dorrance, 2000.

The Holy Bible: Various Selected Versions & Internet research.

Woolfolk, W. *Daddy's Little Girl: The Unspoken Bargain between Fathers and Their Daughters.* Englewood Cliffs: Prentice-Hall, 1982.

Quarles, Benjamin. *The Negro in the Making of America.* New York: The Macmillan Company, 1964.

Selected Writings by Leading Inspirational Authors. Dallas, Texas: Word Publishing, 1993.

The Holy Bible. Various versions as indicated in the text.

Van Lugt, Herb and Kurt DeHann. *What Does It Take to Follow Christ? Christian Living: Obedience.* Grand Rapids, Michigan: Thomas Nelson Inc. Publishers, 1979.

Vannes, C.C. Self-Employed And Profitable: Lessons In Business. HYPERLINK "mailto:Smallbusinesstexas@gmail.com" Smallbusinesstexas@gmail.

com: Senuav Solutions, LLC, Texas: 2014. Visit http://ccvannes.com. (Amazon.com/ibook.com.
Wallis, Arthur. *Pray in the Spirit.* First United States edition. Fort Washington, Pennsylvania.
Wright, H. Norman. *Quiet Times for Couples.* Oregon: Harvest House Publisher, 1990.

Magazines and Newletters/Bulletins

Bidstrup, Scott. "Aso Rock Unsafe." *Ultimate,* August 1997, 5-7
Lesesne, Tony C. "Giving Comes From the Heart." *In Focus,* Summer 1996, 2.
Newsletter by courtesy of Rehabilitation Engineering, Inc. (at no cost to the Division of Vocational Rehabilitation)
Nigeria Today: A Newsletter of Nigeria's Positive Role in Africa and the World. "In South Africa, Nigerian Discovers the Cure for Herpes Simples." *Word Citizen,* August 1996, 8.
Olumide, Oluwale. "Fighting Over Homeland." *Ultimate,* August 1993, 6-7, *Our Daily Bread,* 1991-1999 editions.
Phiri, Isaac. Chiluba Claims Africa for Christ." *Charisma,* April 1995, 55-56
Strang, Stephen. "Easing Racial Tensions." *Charisma,* December 1995, 96
The Consulate-General of Nigeria. News Bulletin (No. 4/96 July 1999).
"U.S. Based Association Donated Computer Equipment to Poly" Letter to President on Nigeria." February 2, 1996.

Newspapers

Alexis, Alexei. "Rediscovering the Lord." *Howard University Community News* (March 14, 1996): 18
Burch, Auda D.S. "High Hopes: Road to Miss America begins in Miami." *Miami Herald* (February 7, 1998): Section G.
Elias, Marilyn. "Routine Discrimination May Be Health Hazard." *USA Today* (March 12, 1994)
Harpaz, Beth H. "Texaco Chairman Apologizes for Racist Remarks." The Associated Press, N.Y. *Miami Times* (November 14, 1996): Section C.
Ita, Eyobong. "Rodney King: The African Version." *Nigerian News Digest* (May 22, 1992): 4

"It Takes a Whole Village." *Howard University Community News* (March 13, 1996): 18

Jones, Woody. "Putting Things in Perspective: (Someone Has to Stand Up)" *South Florida Newsweek* (April 3, 1995): 6.

Joseph, Tasha C. "Folklore Village in South Dade Aims to Promote African Culture." *Miami Times* (June 20, 1996): 6D -"In the Public Eyes: Black Women on Television-Black Women on TV Cope With Work, Family Life and Racism." *Miami Times* (June 20, 1996): Section B

Josiah, Dagogo. "Nigerians Point to Positive Achievements." *Miami Times* (November 7, 1996) 6, 1-2A.

Ruane, Michael. "Waiting 50 Years for the Medal of Honor." *Miami Herald* (January 14, 1996)

Superville, Darlene, "Woman Sues Bloomingdale Over Salon's Refusal to Cut Her Hair." The Associated Press. *Miami Times* (September 5, 1996): Section C.

Just on footnote: Please, note this work is in U.S. English and, we know you don't expect it to be super perfect book either (both in British/ American English)! Again, blessings!!!

Photo Album

I would like to personally use this chance to thank God for leading and guiding me to be embraced by all the great leaders both young/old (living and dead) for all that they have taught and blessed my life and showed to me love and of while in the (journey of life). As, a student and in my profession starting from childhood and too in adulthood; thank God for the following Governors of former Cross River State of Nigeria who launched my first book. That is as featured in the section as-Testimony in Picture (insert) - Brigadier U.J. Esuene/Chief (Dr.) Clement N. Isong; and taking salute; Commander Ibim Princewill and Col. Dan P. Archibong), was also a blessing for all of us and my children. My heart and prayers also is always with them and their lovely families and that love for their people and the community and NYSC and for me can never be forgotten thank God for them is as acknowledged!

I also thank God for their administrations and those that worked alongside their regimes. My special thank to Commissioner of education in 1987 (Affiong AbasiAttai (Mrs.) was there to launch of that book and Media, is of joy to be a part of the blessings and for all my colleagues (journalists, editors, staff and managers and writers and it is for radio, television and newspaper as well Commissioner(s) for Information that as we know is representative of the State as Chairman of NYSC. At the time was also, (2015), Deputy Gov. of Akwa Ibom State (Mr. Moses Ekpo). And, I thank God for that! Thank you Mr. Godwin Ofuka for the photographs that you took for my book goodness is and works as then Senior Information officer for the State; thank you Local Government Chairman later Governor of New Cross River State, Mr. Clement Ebri, bought the book for all the local government areas for the loving dear Youth Corps members to have free copies! I thank God, and was for social studies in school also, God's all for me. Gov. (Obong) Victor Attah, Akwa Ibom State, Sir, an honor that you and your deputy and administration launched my second book, *Slavery From an Africa Perspective* and, third book along with my former boss and (NYSC)

Employer inspiring and encouraging me in the U.S, General Edet Adam Akpan. Thank you, you're advising from time to time; even today in the US is joy, to appreciate all of you!!!

That goes to show how much love is from one heart to the other and that exchange is receiving God's daily guidance! God's is love as helps me and blesses with great loving hearts worldwide. That's of the beauty Love is of that Inspiration, and is of what makes inspiration and happiness and, I also was blessed by Governor Akpabio's regime his cabinet the staff from commissioners down the line patronized my work. Especially, I also recall that as publicly my book was being acknowledged, "I also thank the woman for the book(s), all will be rewarded," when I officially donated to the Governor (2011) a copy of "Priceless Love! Just thought, is encouraging to me who knows is what I treasure encouragement that I do everyday thank God same goes for me in America! We have read from dedication chapter, down to the end and how much God has always blessed my life with the right people at right time great leaders (prominent figures) and is same everywhere of His grace miracles happens to me here America, as back home; loving to bless undertaking and what a joy and what a blessing! God is faithful and that is amazing grace that thrills my heart right there and many more reasons for my gratitude!! Governor Godswill Akpabio & Obong Victor Attah, both their efforts **developed my proud State of origin; former President Ibrahim B. Babangida (Military) regime's created it in 1987. Passion is collective memories family/friends.** Those are what I am being grateful!

Also, as love's heart's power and that greatness is in the heart and inspiration is its legacy-thanking God is this! He has blessed and makes me a testimony to His Greatness and Goodness that is why; I have my testimony in this as well —More acknowledgement/Testimony in Pictures-my life and my journey, everyday thanksgiving is also!

TESTIMONIES IN PHOTOGRAPH

The author's first book, Cross River State at a Glance, published in 1987, was launched by three Governors. The book gave a detailed account of about the history, the culture and the socio-economic features of Cross River State in a single volume of facts. Upon her return from the U.S. the local government bought the book outright as they were so impressed with her account of their history. Photos shown are the back cover and pages from the book.

The author over the years has been blessed by God to meet great leaders, including the former UN Ambassador, Donald McHenry as a foreign student in April of 1980 at Spelman College, Atlanta, GA. Others in the photographs are Rev. Norman M. Rates, Spelman College Minister, and President Elias Blake of Clark College. Also, the former Cross River State Governor, Col. Dan P. Archibong.

Author with her friend, nurse (R.N.) Offiong Ononokpono (Picture by Sotex Photos 2014).

Author in her African Attire (Taken by Photographer Tony).

Printed in the United States
By Bookmasters